# Gardening

## I can do it!

by Ivan Bulloch & Diane James

Photography by Daniel Pangbourne

Illustrations by Emily Hare

World Book

in association with

TWOCAN

First published in the United States and Canada by

World Book, Inc.

525 W. Monroe

Chicago, IL 60661

in association with Two-Can Publishing Ltd.

**Art Director** Ivan Bulloch
**Editor** Diane James
**Design Assistant** David Oh
**Editorial Assistant** Katherine Harvey
**Gardening Consultant** Sue Hook
**U.S. Editor** Karen Ingebretsen

With thanks to Jimmy and Winsome James for letting us use their garden
and also Jackie Hyde, Sue Gibbs, Nicky, Katie, George, and Sam

**For information on other World Book products,
call 1-800-255-1750, x 2238, or visit us
at our Web site at http://www.worldbook.com**

"Two-Can" is a trademark of Two-Can Publishing Ltd.

ISBN 0-7166-2601-2 (hard cover)
ISBN 0-7166-2602-0 (soft cover)
LC: 97-62334

Printed and bound in 1998 by Proost in Belgium

# contents

# watch it grow

Gardening is great fun! It also takes some work and patience, but the results are worth it. Even a beginner can grow colorful, healthy plants.

You can learn a lot about gardening just chatting with friends who garden. You can also get ideas by looking at books on gardening, exploring other gardens, and visiting garden centers. The scarecrow in this book has plenty of good advice, too!

Work, watch, and enjoy.

Once you start growing your own plants, you won't want to stop. It's a great way to enjoy the outdoors.

Have fun!

# getting started

Plants are living things. Just like people they come in lots of different shapes and sizes. Some plants can survive cold, windy conditions. Others need warmth and shelter. All plants need light, food, air, and water. They benefit by being looked after, too!

Before you begin gardening, here are some things you need to know.

flower
leaf
stem
root

**Growing up** Nearly all plants grow from either seeds or bulbs. Each seed contains enough food for a plant to start growing, but the seed also needs soil and water. When you plant a seed in soil, it grows roots that push downward. The roots anchor the plant in the soil and take in water and food from it. The seed pushes a stem and leaves above the soil. The leaves use sunlight and carbon dioxide (a gas in the air) to make food to help the plant grow.

**Now or later** You can start your garden with seeds, bulbs, or ready-made plants. Growing plants from seeds takes a little longer, but it's really fun to watch the sprouts come up! Bulbs must be planted in fall for a colorful show of flowers in spring.

These bulbs will make a colorful display when it is too cold for other plants to grow.

**Color and space** There is a huge range of plants to choose from. Think about colors, shapes, and which ones will look good together. You should also keep in mind how much space you have!

**Annuals** These are plants that "visit" the garden. They are easy to grow from seeds, but they die in the same year. You'll find lots of annuals in garden centers as ready-to-grow plants.

Brightly colored annuals look good in pots and window boxes.

Trees are the tallest plants. They provide shade and shelter for all kinds of animals. This apple tree will also provide delicious fruit that you can eat.

**Biennials** These grow from seeds into young plants one year, then flower and die the following year.

**Perennials** These flowering plants grow from seeds and come up year after year. They disappear in winter but shoot up again when the weather warms up in spring.

**Bulbs** A bulb has layers of fleshy leaves which contain food for the growing plant. Some bulbs push strong, green shoots above the soil even in cold, frosty weather.

**Shrubs** You can recognize a shrub by its woody stems and chunky shape. The plant on the right is a small shrub.

**Trees** These giants of the plant world live longer than anything else in the garden. They need a lot of space for their long, strong roots and branches to spread out.

# tips and tools

When you start gardening, you'll only need a few basic tools. You can get more equipment as your garden grows bigger! Good tools will last for years if you take care of them. Be very careful of sharp edges!

**Trowel** Use a trowel for digging in small spaces, such as pots and window boxes. A trowel can also be used to dig out the roots of stubborn weeds in the garden.

**Rake** Use this to level the soil, comb off stones, and break up the surface into fine crumbs. A rake with long, thin prongs is good for scraping leaves from the lawn.

**Watering can** This is important, especially during dry weather. Plants need a good soaking, not a sprinkle, to keep them from drooping! Watering cans have a spray attachment over the spout so that the water showers out gently. In a large garden, use a hose to water in early morning or early evening. Collect rain water in a bucket.

**Trays, pots, and labels**
Use seed trays to grow plants from seeds. Small pots are useful for seedlings or cuttings before they are planted in the garden. Use labels if you think you might forget what you have planted!

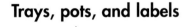

**Fork** A small fork will help with the same jobs as a trowel, especially weeding. Use it to break up the soil, too.

**Sticks** Use long wooden or bamboo sticks to keep tall plants upright. Poke one into the soil next to the plant and tie the stem of the plant to it.

**Tie it up** Support plants by tying them to sticks with soft string or garden twine.

Never eat anything from the garden without asking a grown-up first! Many plants are poisonous.

**Spade** A spade with a long handle is best for turning soil over to break up lumps. It is also useful for digging large holes to plant trees and shrubs. Clean your spade and all your garden tools before you put them away.

These berries are for animals only!

**More care, less speed** Don't rush jobs in the garden. Take your time or you may damage plants and even yourself. Try to finish one job before you start the next.

**Clothes** Gardening clothes should be comfortable and practical. Gardening gloves will help stop blisters and cuts. Always wash your hands after gardening.

9

# seed sowing

Growing your own plants from seeds is extremely satisfying! Sow seeds by scattering them over your planting area and covering them lightly with soil. If you live in a cool climate, sow seeds indoors to give them a head start. Wait until the danger of frost is past before planting the seedlings outdoors. Tender young plants won't survive the cold!

> It's best to sow seeds thinly.

> If you don't, the plants will grow much too close together.

**Seed trays** Buy plastic seed trays, or make holes in the bottom of empty food containers and egg cartons. You can put your trays on a windowsill indoors, or in a cold frame in the garden. Some trays are sold with protective covers.

**Patience!** It may be several weeks before you see the seedlings appear, although some seeds sprout very quickly. Check them daily. Make sure that the soil is moist and the trays are not in direct sunlight. Some seeds need darkness to sprout. If you have put a protective cover over the seeds, take it off when you see the first green seedlings.

**Indoors or outdoors?** Some seeds can be sown outdoors. Make sure you prepare their space first. Dig and rake the soil to get rid of lumps and stones and to make a level surface.

# how to do it

**1** Fill a seed tray almost to the top with potting soil and level the surface. Water the soil using a watering can with a spray attachment.

**2** Sprinkle the seeds on the surface. Cover them with a thin layer of soil. Use a spray to moisten the soil without disturbing the seeds.

**Growing bigger!** Keep a careful eye on your new seedlings. Don't let the soil dry out. Turn to the next page to find out what to do next.

**Soil for seeds** Use potting soil or a special seed-starting mixture, which you can buy at garden centers. These have all the food your seeds need to start them off. It's like buying special food for babies!

**3** Cover the seed tray with a clear cover or plastic wrap to protect the seeds. Put the tray in a warm, lighted place. Label the tray.

# moving on

When your seeds have pushed their way up through the soil and grown leaves, they are called seedlings. Now they need more space to grow. Moving seedlings to a new home is called pricking out. Treat them carefully and your seedlings will grow into strong, healthy plants. Give any spare seedlings to your friends.

**Time to move** Check your trays every day. The first two leaves that a seedling grows are called "seed" leaves. Don't be surprised; the next set of leaves will look quite different! When these "true" leaves appear on the seedlings, it's time to prick them out.

**1** Fill a seed tray, or pots, with potting soil. Water the tray and level the surface. Use a plastic plant label or a wooden ice-cream stick, to help separate out a small clump of seedlings from the rest. Hold the leaves of one seedling and gently pull it away from the others.

**2** Make a small hole in the soil with the plant label or stick. Put the seedling in and firm the soil around it. Give each seedling's roots plenty of room. Now water the trays and pots using a fine spray attachment.

**Weather watch!** In late spring when the weather is warm and there is no frost, you can put your pricked-out seedlings outside for a few hours during the day. This is called "hardening off" and it prepares the seedlings for being planted in the garden.

**Planting outdoors** Treat seedlings bought from a garden center in the same way as seedlings you have grown. Prepare the soil by breaking up lumps with a fork. Pull any weeds, then rake the surface to even it out. Make a hole large enough for each new plant. Support the plant with both hands, then put it into the hole. Push soil gently around the plant, then water.

Give each new plant plenty of space to grow upward and spread outward.

Don't plant your seedlings outdoors too soon. Wait until they have strong roots.

Check the packet to find out how tall your plants will grow.

Put tall plants toward the back of the flower bed.

13

# planting bulbs

One of the best known bulbs is the onion we eat! Lots of flowering plants also grow from bulbs. Favorites are the brave, colorful bulbs that push their way through frosty ground to let us know that warmer weather is on its way! You can grow bulbs in flower beds or containers. Some bulbs are happy to grow indoors.

Look for bulbs that are heavy, solid, and not badly marked or moldy.

**When to plant?** The best time to plant most bulbs is in the fall. Many bulbs don't like being out of soil for long periods, so try to buy them when you have time to plant them right away.

**Top and bottom** Sometimes it is tricky to tell which way is up when planting a bulb. Usually, the pointed end produces the growing shoot and the flat end produces the roots. With small bulbs you may not be able to tell the difference. If in doubt, plant the bulb on its side. As a general rule, plant bulbs twice as deep as their height.

It is easy to see the roots on this bulb!

Leave your bulbs in the ground and they will spread and come up year after year.

**Bulb planter** This is a special tool to help you plant bulbs, especially if you want them to push up through your lawn. Use it to remove a small, circular plug of soil and turf. Plant the bulb in the hole and replace the turf.

**Next year's food** When a bulb has finished flowering, don't cut back straggly leaves. Be patient and wait until they go brown. The bulb's leaves make food for the next year's growth.

**Where did I put it?** Label your bulbs as soon as you have planted them. That way, you won't forget and dig them up before the leaves and flowers appear above the soil.

how to do it

**1** Plant a container with bulbs to make a colorful spring display on an outdoor windowsill or patio. Put small pebbles in the bottom to help water drain.

**2** Half fill the container with a rich potting soil. Place the bulbs, root sides down, on top of the soil. Put them close together, but not touching.

**3** Cover the bulbs with more soil. Some can have their tips showing. Make sure the soil is moist but not soggy, or the bulbs will rot.

# keep at it!

After you have planted your seeds, bulbs, and new plants, there's still plenty to do to help your plants grow strong, healthy, and beautiful. Try to do one or two chores in the garden each day, so the work doesn't pile up.

Save water! Collect rain water in buckets and use it to give your thirsty plants a drink.

**Thirsty work** On hot, sunny days, the soil soon dries out and plants need a drink. Nothing is as good as a shower of rain, but you can help. Wait until early evening and give everything a good soaking. Direct the water at the bottom of plants so that you don't waste it and damage flower heads. Remember the plants in pots, too!

**Look out!** When you are doing different jobs in the garden, keep an eye out for damage caused by garden pests. Look for tell-tale holes in leaves, discolored leaves, and droopy plants. Can you see what is causing the damage? You'll find some tips to help you deal with troublemakers on pages 22 and 23.

Use a hose for large flower beds and lawns, and a watering can for small areas.

Tie plants up carefully. Very tall plants will need securing in several places.

**Stand up!** Tall plants with heavy blooms will droop if you don't give them support. Before they grow tall, poke a stick into the soil beside each plant. Tie the stem to the stick.

**Spick-and-span** General jobs include raking up dead leaves and keeping borders neat and tidy. Deadheading is also important. This means cutting off flower heads when they have finished flowering. It encourages more flowers to grow.

**Weed it out** A weed is any plant growing where you don't want it. Some plants have long, spreading roots which take food away from other plants. Some even wrap themselves around other plants, eventually strangling them. Make sure you get rid of all the roots of an unwanted weed. If you don't, before you know it, the weed will grow back again.

If you've got a big garden, share the jobs with friends who like gardening!

**All year long** There always seem to be more jobs in the summer when the garden is in full bloom. Tidying up and keeping an eye on things is important, even in winter when there is not much growing.

Dig around weeds and pull them up gently with their roots. You may have to dig deep.

# plants to eat

There is nothing more delicious than eating home-grown vegetables and fruit. You don't need a lot of space to grow plants to eat. Many will be quite happy in containers. When the weather is sunny and there is no danger of frost, try growing some tasty pole beans in a big pot.

**1** Make a teepee for your pole beans in a large pot or in the garden. Push three sticks into the soil and tie them at the top to make a pyramid. Plant a bean seed, or small plant, at the bottom of each stick.

**2** As the plants climb, wind them around each stick. After a few months, you will see red flowers which will turn into beans. When the beans are about 4 inches (10 cm) long, they are ready to be picked.

Tomatoes need lots of water, especially on sunny days. When the fruits appear, give them plant food (see page 25).

The fruits can become heavy. Support your tomato plant by tying it in different places to one or more sticks.

Pick the fruits as soon as they are ripe. Wash them and eat them right away to get the best taste!

**Ready to eat?** The parts of vegetables that you eat can grow above or below the soil. Test vegetables growing underground by digging one up. Tiny carrots taste sweet and delicious. Don't let them grow big and woody.

**A whole meal!** Vegetables are delicious and easy to grow. Think about what you like to eat in your salad. How about lettuce, tomatoes, zucchini, radishes, and carrots? Buy seed packets for your favorite veggies. Start sowing in spring for tasty and healthy treats in summer!

**Always fresh** Vegetables and fruits grow at different times of the year. Some, such as beans and tomatoes, prefer warm, sunny weather. Others, like potatoes, can brave winter frosts. Work out a timetable using the information on seed packets, and you will have something fresh every day.

Protect young vegetable plants or the birds will eat them!

Dig up root vegetables carefully so that you don't damage them. If you are left with too many vegetables, don't forget your friends and neighbors.

# herbs

Herbs are another kind of plant you can eat. They add amazing flavor to your cooking and to salads. Herbs often taste and smell quite strong, so you only need to use a few leaves at a time. For hundreds of years, people have used herbs as a cure for different illnesses – from colds and headaches to bruises and tummy aches. They are good-looking plants, too. Always ask a grown-up to tell you if an herb is safe to eat.

**Happy together** Many herbs grow well in dry, stony soil. Choose a sunny patch of ground, or a large pot, and plant a selection of herbs. Traditional herb gardens are often planted so that the herbs grow in patterns. Herbs can be planted in an area on their own, or in flower beds with other plants.

Pinch off the tops of the growing shoots.

Stop your herbs from growing straggly.

**All year long** To make sure you have fresh herbs in the winter, sow seeds in small pots toward the end of summer. Keep them on the kitchen windowsill and snip leaves off when you need them. For an even bigger supply, harvest herbs from the garden and dry them.

# how to do it

**1** Try drying herbs so you have a supply over winter. Pick bunches of your favorite herbs and rinse thoroughly. Tie them with garden twine or raffia. Remove leaves that are damaged or discolored.

**2** Hang the bunches in a dry, airy room, such as a pantry or closet, and leave them for a couple of weeks. When the herbs are completely dry, they will feel slightly crackly.

**3** Take the dry leaves off the stems and rub them into tiny pieces. Put them in clean, dry jars with screw-on tops. Label each jar. Dry herbs taste stronger than fresh ones, so you don't need to use as much of them.

**Tastes good!** Try experimenting by adding herbs to food to find out which flavors you like best. Chopping or tearing fresh herbs into small pieces releases the flavor and makes it easy to scatter them evenly.

# know your friends

Gardens are full of other living things besides plants! It's good to know which creatures to encourage to share your garden, and which ones may damage your plants. A bit of detective work will sort out the good guys from the bad ones!

**Slugs and snails** These slippery creatures love to feed on plants and can do a lot of damage. The best way to stop them is to put up barriers. You can protect young plants by surrounding them with a collar cut from a plastic bottle. Or, cover the surface of the soil around the plant with broken eggshells. Keep a special eye on young seedlings.

Grow plants that provide food for insects such as butterflies.

**Making seeds** Flowers must be pollinated before they can make new seeds, which in turn grow into new plants. Insects carry a special powder found in plants, called pollen, from one flower to another. The patterns on flower petals guide the insects to the pollen, which is in the middle of the flower. Pollen carriers are important. Look out for bees with thick powder on their legs!

> Worms are a gardener's best friend. They work day and night to enrich the soil.

**Friends** Ladybugs, hedgehogs, frogs, and toads all feed on harmful insects and will not damage your plants.

Slugs and snails hate crawling over anything prickly or sharp – like eggshells!

# how to do it

Don't forget that birds need water as well as food. They need your help most in the cold winter months when they cannot find their favorite meal of worms and insects.

**1** Pests love to hide in dark places. Keep your garden clean and tidy. Don't leave piles of leaves, bits of wood, or stacks of old flowerpots where pests can hide and multiply.

**Feathered friends** No garden is complete without the sound of birds chirping, but you may have to put up with a bit of damage! Birds like to nibble young shoots and buds. In return, they are happy to gobble up snails, as well as slugs, caterpillars, and other bugs that may damage your plants.

**Spraying** Think twice before using a chemical spray to get rid of pests. You may harm some of the creatures that your garden needs. Spray the culprits with soapy water, or pick them off the plants by hand. If you spot the problem soon enough, you can act before the bugs eat your plants.

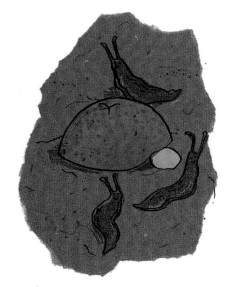

**2** Prop up an empty grapefruit half with a small stone. Slugs will shelter under it. Pick up the grapefruit with the slugs inside and put it out of harm's way!

**3** Look for caterpillars on leaves. Lift them off gently with your fingers and put them where they can't do any damage!

Give plants a soapy soaking, paying attention to the undersides of the leaves.

# planting in pots

You don't need to have a large space to enjoy growing plants! Pots and tubs come in many different shapes and sizes and will fit into all sorts of spaces.

**What to plant** Most plants – from a tiny herb to a bushy shrub – will grow in a container. Find out how tall and wide each plant will grow, and choose a big enough pot. Try growing different kinds of plants in the same pot.

**What kind of pot** The ideal pot is waterproof and will stand firmly on the ground without wobbling. It should have at least one hole in the bottom to allow water to drain through. Most plants do not like to grow in waterlogged soil.

**Looking after pots** Plants growing in pots need the same amount of care as plants growing in the garden. Make sure the soil does not dry out, and check for pests! Look out for nipped-off buds and holes in leaves.

Use a large can to make an instant container. Ask a grown-up to punch drainage holes in the bottom. Don't try to do it yourself!

Plants in pots need watering more often than those in the garden!

**Grouping** Think about the best way to display your flower pots. Try having one large central pot and surrounding it with smaller ones. What about several single flower pots in a row, perhaps on a window ledge?

**Feed me** Because potted plants grow in less soil than those in the garden, they sometimes need extra help to keep them growing. You can buy special plant food in garden centers to give your plants when you are watering. Make sure you follow the instructions on the package.

*how to do it*

**1** Put some pieces of broken flower pots, or a layer of gravel, in the bottom of the container to improve drainage. Pour in soil about halfway for large plants and higher for small ones. Place the pot on an old saucer or plant tray.

**2** Gently separate the roots of the plants and place them in position. Use a trowel to fill in the soil around the plants and gently press the soil down around the plant. Leave a small space at the top of the container. Now water your plants well.

Bold and bright arrangements are colorful and eye-catching. Pale and dark shades of one color look calm and peaceful.

Two planks of wood and a few bricks make a platform to display pots at different heights. It also saves on space!

# free plants!

You don't have to spend a lot of money to garden! Many plants can be grown from cuttings. With care, and luck, you can take a piece of an adult plant and grow a new one from it. Shrubs and trees grow much quicker from cuttings than from seed. You can also collect and grow seeds from plants that have finished flowering, or from fruit you have eaten.

Take cuttings from healthy side shoots. Plant them in soil as soon as possible.

**Hit and miss** Don't be upset if some of your cuttings don't grow. Take about twice as many cuttings as you need and you will end up with plenty of plants – and probably some to spare!

Swap seeds and cuttings with your friends.

**Hard and soft** Soft cuttings are taken in early summer from young, fleshy shoots. Hard cuttings are taken in autumn from older, woody stems. An easy method is known as a heel cutting. Choose a healthy looking side shoot – hard or soft without flowers – and pull it downward, away from the main stem. The extra bit left at the bottom looks a bit like a heel.

**Full speed ahead** You can take cuttings in early summer or in autumn. Gather your cuttings as quickly as possible and pop them in a plastic bag to protect them. Plant your cuttings right away.

**1** Fill small flowerpots nearly to the top with potting soil. Water them well. Use the end of a pencil to make a small hole for each cutting. Strip the bottom leaves off the cutting and poke it into the hole. Firm the soil around the stem.

**2** You can put more than one cutting in each pot, but make sure they have plenty of space. Tie a clear plastic bag over the pot, or use an upturned jelly jar, taking care not to touch the cuttings. This will help to keep the soil moist.

**3** Put the pot out of direct sunlight. Keep the soil damp, not soggy. After two or three weeks, take the bag off and keep an eye on your new plants. Outdoor cuttings can be planted in the garden when they have strong roots.

**Give it a try!** Some cuttings will grow from a single leaf and its stem. Choose a plant with a large, healthy leaf like the one below. Cut off a single leaf with a bit of stem. Poke the stem into a pot of potting soil. If you are lucky, after about a month you will see a new plant growing from the bottom of the leaf.

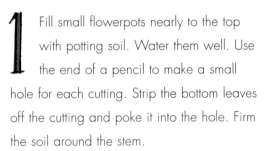

**A quick drink** Another way to try your luck is to pop a cutting into a glass of water. Keep the glass in a lighted place and watch to see if roots grow from the sides of the submerged stem. If they do, plant the cutting in a pot of soil as you did before.

**Seed bank** Another way to save money is to collect seeds from dry flower seed heads in late summer. Keep them in a labeled paper bag and sow them in spring.

# a perfect bunch

Picking flowers and leafy stems from the garden and making them into a colorful arrangement can really cheer up a room – they often smell lovely, too! A bunch of cut flowers makes a good present, especially if you have grown them yourself.

Try to keep flowers away from the hot sun when you have picked them.

**What color?** It's best to have a plan before you start picking flowers. Look around to see what is available and decide which colors you like best.

Don't pick all the flowers in the garden. Leave some so that you can enjoy them indoors *and* outdoors!

*Don't pick wild flowers in the country.*

*They are for everyone to enjoy.*

**Pick the best** Look for flowers that are about to bloom. They will last longer when you take them indoors. Use a pair of scissors to cut the flower stems close to the bottom. Try to put the cut flowers in water as soon as possible.

**The right vase** You can use any container for a flower arrangement, as long as it is waterproof. A simple jelly jar, a small bucket, or even an old teapot all work well.

**Keep still!** Here are a few tricks to keep your arrangement in place. You can buy a special type of foam from flower shops. Cut it to fit the bottom of your vase and fill the vase with water. Push the flower stems into the wet foam. Another method of keeping stems in place is to fill the bottom of the vase with marbles before poking in the flower stems.

Find a container in a color that will look good with your flower colors and you can't go wrong!

# how to do it

**1** Choose a tall vase for long stems or a small one for short stems. Put a piece of foam or some marbles in the bottom. Fill the vase with water.

**2** Start with the longest stems and push them into the middle. Then fill in around the edges with the shorter stems.

**Longer lasting** To keep your arrangement fresh for as long as possible, strip the bottom leaves off the stems before you put them in water. If you don't, they will rot and the flowers will die. Take out single stems as they die off. Change the water every day.

# indoor plants

Growing plants indoors is just as satisfying as growing them in the garden. Garden centers and supermarkets sell indoor plants. Read the instructions on the plant label to find out how to take care of your new plant. Be careful when choosing your indoor plants. Some are poisonous to pets.

When you go on vacation, give your indoor plants to a friend for safe keeping.

**Not too much!** Indoor plants need watering just like those outside, but not too much. Water them about once a week in summer and less in winter when they are not growing. Put your pots on saucers, or in a bowl slightly larger than the pot. Don't leave plants sitting in water.

**All sizes** You can buy plants to suit any space – small plants for narrow windowsills or huge ones to brighten a dark corner. Try grouping plants together to make a colorful display.

**The best place** Indoor plants like light, but not direct sunlight, which will burn their leaves and dry out the soil. Don't put your plants in a drafty place.

# how to do it

**1** Don't let your plants become dusty! Gently brush leaves with a soft brush. You can buy leaf shine wipes, which are useful for cleaning big, waxy leaves.

**2** Use a water spray to perk up your plants during hot weather. Spray a fine mist onto the leaves, but don't spray the furniture!

**Summer holiday** On hot, sunny days, most indoor plants enjoy spending time outside. Prickly cacti are especially fond of sunny days, probably because they are most at home in the desert! Handle them carefully.

# index

PRINTED IN BELGIUM BY
proost
INTERNATIONAL BOOK PRODUCTION

# Visions of the People A Pictorial History of Plains Indian Life

Evan M. Maurer

With essays by

Evan M. Maurer, Louise Lincoln, George P. Horse Capture
David W. Penney, Father Peter J. Powell

Exhibition organized by

Evan M. Maurer and Louise Lincoln

Catalogue entries by

Evan M. Maurer, Louise Lincoln
Angela Casselton, Joseph D. Horse Capture, Candace Green

The Minneapolis Institute of Arts

This catalogue was published in conjunction with the exhibition
VISIONS OF THE PEOPLE: A PICTORIAL HISTORY OF PLAINS INDIAN LIFE

The Minneapolis Institute of Arts
October 11, 1992, to January 3, 1993

The Saint Louis Art Museum
Saint Louis, Missouri
February 5 to April 18, 1993

Joslyn Art Museum
Omaha, Nebraska
May 22 to July 25, 1993


Graphic design by The Office of Eric Madsen

Editors: Elisabeth Sövik and Leslie Reindl
Typesetter: Lynne Cason
Production coordinator: DeAnn Dankowski

Distributed by the University of Washington Press
P.O. Box 50096
Seattle, Washington 98145

Library of Congress Catalog Card Number 92-85422
International Standard Book Number 0-295-97229-7


Funding has been provided by The Henry Luce Foundation, Inc.; the
National Endowment for the Arts, a federal agency; The Bush Foundation;
and the Dayton Hudson Foundation on behalf of Dayton's and Target
Stores.

Additional support has been provided by Lisa and Jud Dayton, Donna and
Cargill MacMillan, Honeywell Inc., and the American Express Minnesota
Philanthropic Program on behalf of IDS Financial Services Inc., American
Express Travel Related Services Inc., and Shearson Lehman Brothers.

Cover:
*Tipi bag* (cat. no. 270)
Minneconjou Lakota, ca. 1885
Cranbrook Institute of Science

# Contents

# Preface

V isions of the People celebrates the continuing life of the Plains tribes by bringing together a selection of objects that they created to communicate what was most important to them. These images commemorate the routines of daily living, acts of personal bravery, and that powerful spirituality and reverence for the sacred that gives comfort as well as direction and meaning to life.

Like all peoples, the Plains Indians have had a long and continuing need to document the significant events of their lives, and their art allows them to use the wisdom and power of the past as a foundation for the present and the future. For the circle of the people to remain strong, the traditions brought to them by their prophets and Holy Beings must be kept alive and passed on to the next generation. Because like other native North Americans the Plains tribes had no written language, they relied on a system of interrelated song, oral narrative, and visual arts to convey what was vital to them.

Creating symbolic or metaphorical marks and images is a basic human need. Among the Indian peoples of the Plains, abstract designs and representational images formed a visual vocabulary that, combined with their oral traditions, expressed the sanctity and interrelatedness of nature and communicated information important to individuals and communities. Being essentially nomadic, the Plains Indians put these significant images on their portable tents and clothing; on tools, weapons, and ritual paraphernalia; and on themselves through body painting and personal adornment.

Most of the literature on Plains Indian art has been limited to one particular medium (for example, painting or sculpture) or to a specific historical period or tribe. This book is intended to honor the evolving Plains traditions by constructing a general overview of their representational arts in all media and time periods. By providing a broad survey of Plains art from early precontact times (around A.D. 1300) to the present, we can chart traditions, changes, and adaptations to the historical process. Within the limitations inherent in mounting an exhibition and publishing a book, we have tried to choose objects that demonstrate the variety as well as the commonalities of Plains culture and art.

Whenever possible, we have stressed the role of the individual in the production and use of art in Plains culture. We have sought to use works with firm attributions to known men and women to honor these accomplished artists and avoid the depersonalization of Native American art and artists. Nameless, faceless "tribes" didn't create and use these objects and images, people did, and this will be stressed in the essays and entries that follow. The wide selection of works of art is also intended to celebrate those special individuals who create within a regional or tribal style.

The many contemporary Plains artists whose work is shown here represent the growing number of talented men and women creating art that, while often made of materials from our contemporary world, draws its spirituality, deep meaning, and sometimes subject matter from traditional Native American sources.

The book begins with five essays on Plains art and its cultural and historical context. Following the essays, the catalogue of the exhibition illustrates each object and provides detailed information and commentary. In writing the entries, the authors combined aesthetic evaluation with a view of the circumstances in which a piece was produced. Special efforts were made to consider the opportunities and pressures brought to bear on Plains Indian culture and individuals with the growing encroachment and ultimate political and economic domination by the Euro-American culture that established itself on this continent five hundred years ago.

The first essay, "Visions of the People," is a general overview of Plains art and art history, from ancient petroglyphs to contemporary painting. It also describes the life of a contemporary Plains village that has come together to participate in and honor an age-old community tradition of sacred ritual. This is included to acquaint readers with the cultural context, in which the objects are an integral part of a complex social and religious system.

Exhibit on cocurator Louise Lincoln's essay examines the challenges faced by Plains women and men in their swiftly changing and often hostile relationship to the Euro-American world of North America in the nineteenth and twentieth centuries. By stressing that objects are inseparable from the circumstances of their creation, the essay suggests important ways of seeing Plains art and understanding the meaning behind it.

George Horse Capture, a noted Plains Indian scholar, describes the development of his work as a distinguished curator of Plains art and culture, from his childhood growing up on the Fort Belknap Reservation in Montana to his current research in museums throughout this country and Europe. In so doing, he draws on his experience as a Gros Ventre Indian in today's world who has devoted himself to the study and nurturing of his proud cultural heritage.

David Penney, curator at the Detroit Institute of Arts, explores a specific theme in Plains art, the horse and its rapid rise to prime importance in Plains economic and social life. He addresses questions of creative cultural adaptation that demonstrate the strength and viability of the Plains peoples.

In the final essay, Father Peter J. Powell, noted historian of the Northern Cheyenne, provides a close reading of a single Lakota painting that documents the events leading up to and including the Battle of the Little Big Horn, in 1876. Using his considerable experience as a scholar, and information provided by the Cheyenne, Powell presents a narrative that approximates the tradition of Plains oratory, which was the prime means of formal communication. His attention to significant detail is the essence of Plains oral and visual systems of expression.

In a year when the world is reevaluating the social, historic, economic, and cultural effects of the interactions between Europeans and Native Americans, we offer this work as a means of understanding the complex issues at hand and as a tribute to the past, present, and future generations of Plains people from whose courage, strength, and beauty we can all learn.

Evan M. Maurer
*Director*

In preparing this exhibition the staff of the Minneapolis Institute of Arts has consulted extensively with American Indian people in communities throughout the northern Plains region. The overall direction and focus of the exhibition, as well as smaller details of installation and interpretation, have evolved throughout those discussions. In choosing to include pipes in the exhibition, we planned to follow the practice of many museums directed or curated by Native Americans which display pipes in a respectful context.

Although there is a range of opinion in the American Indian community about the appropriateness of displaying pipes in museums, it became clear in subsequent discussions that the sentiments of those opposed to such a display were particularly strong within the Native American community in the Twin Cities, where many people feel that pipes are too sacred to be used in any context other than prayer. For this reason the Institute has withdrawn pipes from the exhibition, although photographs of pipes remain in the catalogue, where they are shown in an artistic and cultural context. We hope that this decision will promote constructive dialogue between museums and those whose traditions are represented in museum collections.

# Acknowledgments

This exhibition focuses on the artistic traditions of generations of Plains men and women, and we acknowledge their heritage with gratitude and respect. In honor of the Plains people and their continuing cultural heritage, we offer the years of work that went into the preparation of this exhibition. I must also acknowledge our debt to the scholars, collectors, and observers whose work forms the base of this and future studies. I am especially mindful of the important research done by John C. Ewers, whose studies of Plains painting and sculpture are essential to our understanding of the field.

The conception, organization, and realization of a large exhibition and publication is a complicated endeavor requiring the hard work and creative abilities of hundreds of individuals. The staff at the Minneapolis Institute of Arts devoted many months to the project in support of our exhibition team. Louise Lincoln, curator of African, Oceanic, and New World art was the cocurator of the exhibition; her sure advice and experience were essential to every phase of the exhibition and publication. We were joined by Angela Casselton, research assistant, and Joseph D. Horse Capture, intern, who worked on all aspects of the project with skill, care, and patience. Their contributions, along with those of Maren Nelson, administrative assistant, were crucial to the success of the exhibition. We are grateful for the assistance of our consulting committee—David Penney, Richard Pohrt, Father Peter J. Powell, and George Horse Capture—who helped in the initial stages of planning. Candace Greene has made an important scholarly contribution in her catalogue entries on the artist Silverhorn. We would also like to thank members of our Native American Advisory Committee—Arthur Amiotte, Chris Cavender, Dale Childs, the Reverend Marlene Helgemo, George Horse Capture, Richard le Framboise, Ron Libertus, Bonnie Wallace, and Ernest Whiteman—for their months of advice and support, especially in the planning and organization of the programs that accompanied the exhibition in Minneapolis.

Beth Desnick and Thea Nelson of the exhibitions department coordinated budgeting aspects of the exhibition and its travel to other venues. Our thanks to Cathy Ricciardelli and Peggy Tolbert of the registrar's staff at the Minneapolis Institute of Arts, who planned the logistics of the exhibition; to conservator Mary Ann Butterfield; and to installation technicians Tom Jance, Jeanne Prezioso-Bragg, Scott Brennan, Charley Foster, Bill Skodje, Brian Stieler, and Steve Williams. Doug Kroeger expertly mounted numerous objects for the exhibition. A special thank you to installation designer Roxy Ballard, who understood the exhibition and made it come alive. Kate Johnson, Sharon Schroeder, and Jennifer Layton of the museum's education division have offered invaluable assistance in the preparation of didactic materials for the exhibition.

The catalogue production was made possible by the work of Elisabeth Sövik, DeAnn Dankowski, Marcia Riopelle, Kathleen Lucht, Lynne Cason, and designer Eric Madsen. Gary Mortensen and Bob Fogt photographed many of the artworks in splendid detail. The research, sorting, and publication represent years of work. We hope our efforts will be a resource for future scholarship and study as well as providing a better understanding of Plains art and life.

A project of this scope takes many resources, and on behalf of the Institute I would like to thank those who generously gave their support to make the exhibition and catalogue possible. We are especially grateful for funding received from The Henry Luce Foundation, the National Endowment for the Arts, The Bush Foundation, and the Dayton Hudson Foundation on behalf of Dayton's and Target Stores. Additional support, for educational and outreach programs related to the exhibition, has come from Lisa and Jud Dayton, Honeywell Inc., American Express Minnesota Philanthropic Program, KSTP TV, and Donna and Cargill MacMillan.

Colleagues and friends in museums across America and in Europe have been generous with their time and assistance, and many private collectors have opened their homes to us as well. We are particularly indebted to those who have lent objects to the exhibition; they are listed on page 11.

Our sincerest personal thanks to the Native American men and women who received us on their reservations and into their homes and gave us friendship, guidance, and support: Karen Artichoker, Florentine Blue Thunder, Sam Dresser, Gary and Gloria Goggles, Rita Means Halmi, George Horse Capture, Jr., Theresa Horse Capture, Warren Matte, Norman and Zona Moss, Howard Mount, Ollie Nepesni, Jimmy Oldman, E. Norbert Running, Jeannette Warrior, Joe Waterman, Albert and Marlys White Hat, and many others. AHO!

EMM

# Lenders to the Exhibition

Academy of Natural Sciences, Philadelphia

American Museum of Natural History, New York

Amon Carter Museum, Fort Worth, Texas

The Art Institute of Chicago

Bern Historical Museum, Ethnography Department, Bern, Switzerland

Buffalo Bill Historical Center, Plains Indian Museum, Cody, Wyoming

Canadian Museum of Civilization, Hull, Quebec

Cincinnati Art Museum

The Cleveland Museum of Natural History

Cranbrook Institute of Science, Bloomfield Hills, Michigan

Lisa and Jud Dayton

The Denver Art Museum

Denver Museum of Natural History

The Detroit Institute of Arts

Eastern Montana College Library, Special Collections, Billings

The Eiteljorg Museum of American Indian and Western Art, Indianapolis

Ethnographic Museum, University of Oslo

Field Museum of Natural History, Chicago

Folkens Museum-Etnografiska, Stockholm

Foundation for the Preservation of American Indian Art and Culture, Inc., Chicago

The Thomas Gilcrease Institute of American History and Art, Tulsa

Glenbow Museum, Calgary, Alberta

Hampton University Museum, Hampton, Virginia

The Heard Museum, Phoenix

P. A. Hearst Museum of Anthropology, The University of California at Berkeley

Heritage Plantation of Sandwich, Sandwich, Massachusetts

Jonathan Holstein

Adelheid Howe

Oscar Howe Art Center, Mitchell, South Dakota

Joslyn Art Museum, Omaha

The Kansas City Museum, Kansas City, Missouri

Mark Lansburgh

Logan Museum of Anthropology, Beloit College, Beloit, Wisconsin

Mandan Indian Shriners, El Zagel Temple, Fargo, North Dakota

Manoogian Collection, Taylor, Michigan

Milwaukee Public Museum

Minikahda Club, Minneapolis

The Minneapolis Institute of Arts

Missouri Historical Society, St. Louis

Montana Historical Society, Helena

Museum of Indian Art and Culture, Laboratory of Anthropology, Santa Fe

National Anthropological Archives, Smithsonian Institution, Washington, D.C.

National Museum of the American Indian, Smithsonian Institution, New York

National Museum of Natural History, Department of Anthropology, Smithsonian Institution, Washington, D.C.

Natural History Museum of Los Angeles County, Los Angeles

The Nelson-Atkins Museum of Art, Kansas City, Missouri

The Newark Museum, Newark, New Jersey

Dr. Ruth M. O'Dell

Oklahoma Historical Society, State Museum of History, Oklahoma City

Oklahoma Museum of Natural History, Norman

Peabody Museum of Archaeology and Ethnology, Harvard University, Cambridge, Massachusetts

Peabody Museum of Natural History, Yale University, New Haven, Connecticut

The Philbrook Museum of Art, Tulsa

Richard A. and Marion D. Pohrt

Royal Ontario Museum, Toronto

Seton Memorial Library, Philmont Scout Ranch, Cimarron, New Mexico

Sioux Indian Museum and Crafts Center, United States Department of the Interior, Indian Arts and Crafts Board, Rapid City, South Dakota

Société Musée du Vieil Yverdon, Yverdon, Switzerland

South Dakota Art Museum, Brookings

South Dakota State Historical Society, Pierre

Southern Plains Indian Museum and Crafts Center, United States Department of the Interior, Indian Arts and Crafts Board, Anadarko, Oklahoma

Staatliche Museen, Museum für Völkerkunde, Berlin

Stanford University, The Horace Poolaw Photography Project, Palo Alto, California

State Historical Society of North Dakota, Bismarck

Taylor Museum for Southwestern Studies, Colorado Springs Fine Arts Center, Colorado Springs

Texas Memorial Museum, The University of Texas, Austin

Gaylord Torrence

The University Art Galleries, The University of South Dakota, Vermillion

The University Museum, University of Arkansas, Fayetteville

The University Museum, University of Pennsylvania, Philadelphia

Wyoming State Museum, Cheyenne

Anonymous lenders

# Maps

### LOCATION OF PLAINS PEOPLES
about 1750

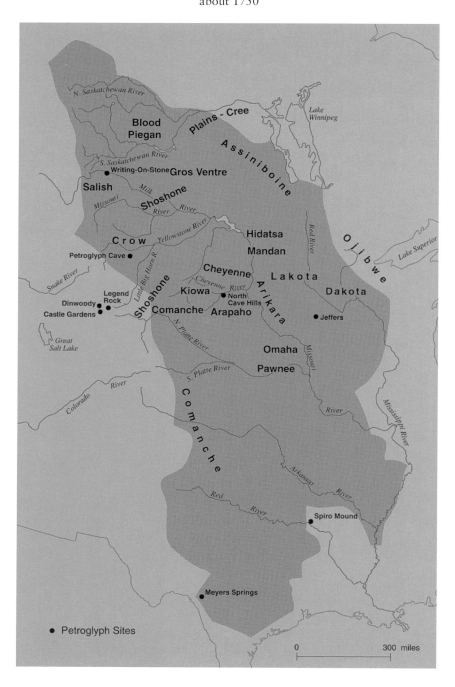

### LOCATION OF PLAINS PEOPLES
about 1850

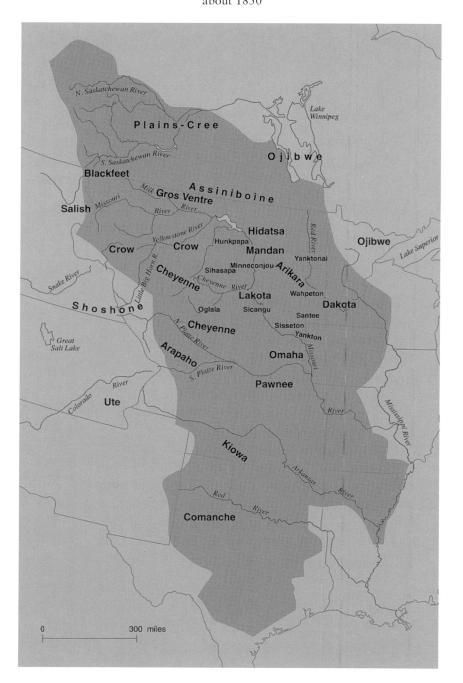

During this period the Lakota and Dakota people moved around throughout the Minnesota and Dakota territories.

# PRESENT-DAY LOCATION OF PLAINS PEOPLES

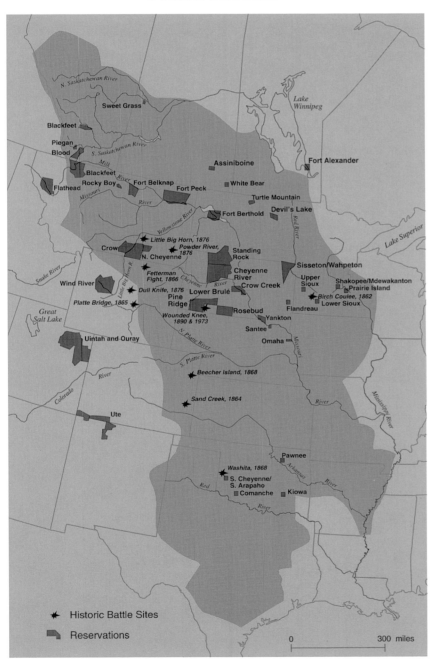

Historic Battle Sites

Reservations

0 — 300 miles

## Reservations

**Assiniboine**
Assiniboine

**Blackfeet** (Alberta and Montana)
Blackfeet

**Cheyenne River**
Lakota

**Comanche**
Comanche

**Crow**
Crow

**Crow Creek**
Lakota

**Devil's Lake**
Sisseton Dakota
Wahpeton Dakota

**Flandreau**
Santee Dakota

**Fort Belknap**
Gros Ventre
Assiniboine

**Fort Berthold**
Gros Ventre
Arikara
Mandan
Hidatsa

**Fort Peck**
Assiniboine

**Kiowa**
Kiowa

**Lower Brulé**
Sicangu Lakota

**Lower Sioux**
Mdewakanton Dakota

**Northern Cheyenne**
Northern Cheyenne

**Pawnee**
Pawnee

**Piegan**
Piegan (Blackfeet)

**Pine Ridge**
Oglala Lakota

**Prairie Island**
Mdewakanton Dakota

**Rocky Boy**
Ojibwe
Cree

**Rosebud**
Sicangu Lakota

**Santee**
Santee Dakota

**Shakopee/Mdewakanton**
Mdewakanton Dakota

**Sisseton/Wahpeton**
Sisseton Dakota
Wahpeton Dakota

**S. Cheyenne/S. Arapaho**
Southern Cheyenne
Southern Arapaho

**Standing Rock**
Teton Lakota
(South Dakota)
Yankton Nakota
(North Dakota)

**Turtle Mountain**
Ojibwe

**Uintah and Ouray**
Ute

**Upper Sioux**
Santee Dakota

**Wind River**
Arapaho
Shoshone

**Yankton**
Yankton Nakota

# Visions of the People  Evan M. Maurer

**T**he Great Plains occupy a vast central area of North America, reaching from the Mississippi in the east to the Rocky Mountains in the west and from Canada south to Texas. Although many geographic characteristics differentiate subareas of the region, all parts of the Great Plains share certain basic similarities. The climate can be harsh and demanding, ranging from intense sun and heat in the summer to snows and bitter cold in winter. When these extremes are amplified by the strong winds that sweep across the open, treeless country, the environment can present formidable challenges to all living things. But the climatic extremes are balanced by periods of fair weather and a rich, clear light that allows a wide field of vision. From a promontory one can see up to fifty miles in all directions as the rolling hills march to the horizon. A human being is physically infinitesimal in the midst of this vastness, and the living earth so muscularly expressed in the hills and mountains has a presence that is emotional and spiritual as well as physical.

The many varieties of grasses and other plants are a rich source of nutrients capable of supporting vast herds of herbivores. Chief among these in the past was the buffalo, the large, powerful bovine whose numbers reached into the millions. Early European travelers reported that one could ride for five days or more and still be surrounded by the immense herd. It was the buffalo that made life possible for the human inhabitants of the Plains from early prehistory through the third quarter of the nineteenth century. The people depended on the animal for their staple food, clothing, and shelter. The destruction of the buffalo herds as part of United States anti-Indian policy in the nineteenth century abruptly altered thousands of years of uninterrupted cultural history for the first inhabitants of this land.

Humans have lived in the Great Plains region of North America since they first arrived on the continent from Asia twenty-five thousand to forty-five thousand years ago. The earliest indications of habitation show that these people had a lithic technology: they made stone tools and weapons, as well as objects of wood, bone, and antler, for the needs of daily life. They sustained themselves by hunting buffalo, deer, elk, and antelope and by gathering the wild fruits and root vegetables growing around the isolated water sources which also attracted the animals. Specialized tools such as knives, scrapers, and awls indicate a well-developed system of creating clothing and shelter from dressed animal skins. This use of materials made sense in a nomadic culture whose everyday equipment had to be portable so groups could move easily as they followed the herds on which their lives depended (fig. 1). The introduction and proliferation of the horse in the eighteenth century had a profound effect on Plains culture. The mobility provided by the horse allowed heavier loads to be carried more quickly over greater distances. Both hunting and warfare were made more efficient by the horse's endurance and speed, and this animal soon became an indispensible part of Plains life.

In tracing the cultural sequences of Plains inhabitants, archaeologists have found that while the pattern of nomadic hunting and gathering continued for thousands of years, a horticultural life-style developed concurrently along the Mississippi and Missouri rivers. The people of these semisedentary and sedentary agricultural villages cultivated corn, beans, and squash as the staples of the Native American garden. The development of these communities was made possible by the production of a significant food surplus and the technology to preserve and store it for future use. Because of their location and stability, these communities became the natural locus of trade with the Plains groups farther to the west and with the Woodlands and Mississippian societies of the east. The evolution of these two interrelated cultures through trade, war, and political alliances determined the human history of the Plains until the Europeans arrived in the mid-sixteenth century.

As is true for all other Native Americans, the lives of the Plains tribes have changed more drastically over the past two hundred years than during the previous millennium. In the past the people had had to adapt their life-styles to new climates and the pressures of intertribal aggression and expansion. Nothing in their previous experience, however, could compare with the cultural trauma inflicted on them by the European invaders, whose appetites for territory and power were matched only by their blatant disregard for any racial group other than their own. The sacred wheel of the people is still intact only because the American Indian has had the strength to endure severe hardships and the will to survive, not only physically but culturally and, above all, spiritually. Losing the freedom to follow their age-old patterns of existence and being confined on reservations was a cultural and economic shock whose negative effects can still be clearly seen. However, over the past twenty years the tribes have renewed and nurtured their pride in being Indian and the importance of following, and in some cases reviving, the cultural and religious traditions on which their societies were founded. Native languages, arts, and religious rituals that were repressed by the government from the late nineteenth century through the 1950s are now being revitalized, and new generations of Indian children are growing up in environments where the ancient ways of their people are honored and strengthened to provide support and blessings for all.

In many Indian homes in cities, towns, and reservations across the continent, color TVs and VCRs provide the same worldwide communications available to the rest of the population. But along with these modern devices, American Indians can still claim the feather and the pipe, their traditional vehicles of cultural and spiritual expression. The car and the pickup truck may have replaced the horse as the principal means of transportation, but each summer thousands of Plains Indian families still load up tipis and camp gear and travel to ceremonies and social events that celebrate cultural, tribal, and family ties. During the summer months, they participate in festive powwows at which elaborately costumed men, women, and children perform dignified but spirited dances to the rhythm of chanting drummers. Throughout the year people may also attend giveaways in honor of a deceased relative, or the healing and prayer rituals of the sweat lodge, which still are an important aspect of the people's lives.

Among the many traditional events that mark the yearly cycle on the Plains, none is more elemental and powerful than the Sun Dance, an elaborate ritual of prayer and personal sacrifice that stresses the importance of individual as well as communal responsibility. The events related to the Sun Dance vary, and not all tribes perform this most ancient of Plains sacred celebrations. But each summer great camp circles are formed on the Plains by the Lakota, the Arapaho, the Cheyenne, the Crow, the Shoshone, and others. It is in these camps that one comes closest to experiencing traditional Plains Indian life as it was in the days of freedom.

Participation in Sun Dance ceremonies across the Plains has been increasing in recent years; among the Northern Arapaho there have been between seventy-five and ninety men in the last several Sun Dances. While the life of the camp goes on around them, all the persons gathered are conscious of the hardships and sacrifices of the men in the Sun Dance Lodge and mindful of the special nature of the event as a time of beauty and blessings for all. The men who have made the vow to perform the Sun Dance will live in the central lodge for the three days and nights of the ceremony, fasting, praying, and following the ancient rituals taught to them by their instructors.

At the hour before sunrise on the Wind River Reservation, the camp crier chants his morning message. The rich, melodious tones and rhythms of the Arapaho language rouse the sleepers in their tents. The air is chill, the light has a dim, predawn cast. The day is beginning, and the people are urged to make their way to the Sun Dance Lodge to join the dancers who honor Person Above and the sun as it makes its way over the rim of the earth. As the sunrise prayers are completed and the dancers rest, the people quietly make their way back to the family camps. These are arranged in several concentric rings over one-quarter mile in diameter around the great circular lodge of cottonwood trunks and brush that is erected for each year's

Fig. 1
Cheyenne village, Cimarron Valley, Oklahoma, 1872. At the right is an important tipi painted with large crosses symbolizing stars. Courtesy of the Oklahoma Historical Society, neg. no. 12060.

ceremony. The Sun Dance camp is a traditional Plains village, in which each family is assigned an area within the tribal circle. With its hundreds of tipis, tents, and rectilinear brush arbors used for cooking, eating, and visiting, the camp presents a glorious sight. The tall, conical tipi lodges dominate the scene, with their long, tapered lodgepole pine supports extending gracefully into the sky. Each lodge is from fourteen to twenty-two feet in diameter and incorporates enough space to comfortably house large families and their guests. But since these are the fine, bright, hot days of summer, when the tipi is used only for sleeping and dressing, both the pleasures and the work of the camp take place in the open air.

While the dancers prepare themselves for the ceremonies in the Lodge, in the surrounding camp the day's work begins. As in many traditional societies, the responsibilities of daily and ritual life among Plains people are organized by gender and age. There is much to be done, and everyone, even the children, is expected to help. The families of the dancers, of the dancers' ritual advisers or tutelary "grandfathers," and of the painters who assist them alternate the responsibility and honor of preparing a feast meal, which is blessed by the priests and then brought to the other family's camp to be shared by them and their guests. The older children make trips to the pump on the periphery of camp to bring the water needed for the morning's work, while the women begin preparing enough food for twenty to forty people, to be ready for distribution by late morning. The Plains Indian feast meal generally includes several meat dishes such as fried or roasted elk, venison, and beef, the elk and deer being shot by the men from the herds that share the open range with the people. The Indians hunt for food, not sport, and the rifleman reverently leaves an offering of tobacco to the spirit of the animal he has killed as a mark of respect and gratitude for its life-sustaining nourishment. Soups made with dried venison or antelope, wild turnips, and other vegetables are served, along with sweet fruit soups made from Juneberries or chokecherries, platters of fry bread, salads, fruits, and desserts. Large pots of water, coffee, tea, and juices round out a meal whose bounty is in keeping with the importance of the occasion.

While the women are hard at work preparing the day's main repast in the brush arbors, the men and older boys pursue a variety of tasks to support the men who are dancing and the ritual activities of the Sun Dance. Each day of the three-day ceremony, men of the dancers' families go out to search for the sacred sweet sage, which is an essential element of the costumes and rituals. The more experienced men and family leaders teach the younger ones where to look, how to identify the correct variety of sage, and the proper gestures of respect for the plant and its gifts. After the bundles of sage have been gathered, the men move to different areas to search for a particular variety of tall water reed that grows along the banks of small, isolated lakes and ponds dotting the plains. The reeds must be pulled whole from the soft, malodorous mud while the gatherers endure cuts from various sharp-edged plants and bites from insects and leeches. The large bundles of plump, moist reeds are cleaned and brought to the Sun Dance Lodge, where they are used by the dancers as daybeds after their bodies have been ritually painted, before they perform dances and prayers. Each man who participates in the Sun Dance will be painted with a special color and sacred design on each of the three days of the ceremony. The color and design are a prerogative of the tutelary grandfather. The men are first painted with a solid color from head to foot—red, yellow, white, black, or blue. The designs then painted on the body consist of symbols such as rabbit tracks and images of the moon and animals. The painting is a primal and deeply sacred act—the oldest and most traditional form of ceremonial art still practiced as a central form of Plains religious life.

By now the sun has climbed higher into the vast blue sky and is felt as a palpable force commanding gratitude and respect. The men take the food to be blessed and delivered, and then the family goes to the camps of friends and relatives to receive their hospitality. This period from the middle of the day through the evening is the most relaxed and social part of camp life, the time when local people and visitors share gifts, news and opinions, stories, problems, and joys. Although everyone is mindful of the vital importance of the occasion, the village is alive with activity, conversation, and laughter. Throughout the day groups of children run about playing games in emulation of their parents or in their own world of imagination.

By midafternoon the pledgers (who are fasting) have been ritually painted with sacred colors and designs and dressed in beautifully decorated prayer skirts, breechclouts, belts, and special ornaments of sacred sage. They are ready to begin the long cycle of prayer and dancing. The men express their prayers outwardly by blowing with each exhalation on eagle-bone whistles, which produce a clear, high-pitched tone. They bounce in place facing the center pole, which is wrapped with offerings of cloth. They are accompanied by a group of male drummers and singers and a chorus of women whose strong chanting can be heard throughout the camp. A United States flag belonging to a veteran is often raised on one of the tall cottonwood posts that flank the entrance to the Sun Dance Lodge. As the flag is raised, the veteran's military citations are read aloud, honoring his service to his country. The drumming, singing, and prayers continue steadily as night falls and the families gather for the evening meal while the men in the Lodge continue to dance. It is again a time for visiting, friendship, conversation, and storytelling. It is also a time for people to return to the Lodge to experience the ceremony and pray.

As the younger children are put to bed, their older brothers and sisters gather in small groups to socialize and stroll through the village. Campfires and lanterns add a soft glow to the tipis and brush arbors but do not detract from the extraordinary night sky over the plains, far from the interfering lights of the city. The black vault of the heavens is studded with brilliant stars of astonishing clarity and multiplicity, its center banded by the star-dusted swath of the Milky Way. Under such a sky it becomes clear why the stars and planets figure so importantly in the mythology and art of the Plains Indians, as they have in all preindustrial societies that witnessed this awe-inspiring spectacle.

The steady, pervasive rhythms of the drumming and singing and the high-pitched cadence of the dancers' prayer whistles continue through the night and into the early morning, making everyone mindful of the sanctity of the event. Family members and worshipers can always be seen around the east half of the Lodge, where they have come to pray and to support the men who are fulfilling their vows. The Sun Dance camp of a contemporary Plains tribe exhibits the salient features of their traditional culture: prayer and personal sacrifice combined with a commitment to the common good. Hard work and courage bolstered by the joys of communal and family support make the celebration, its music and visual arts, a vital expression of deeply held religious beliefs.

Like all peoples, the Plains Indians have had a long and continuing need to document the significant events of their lives, and their art allows them to use the wisdom and power of the past as a foundation for the present and the future. For the circle of the people to remain strong, the traditions brought to them by their prophets and Holy Beings must be kept alive and passed on to the next generation. Because like other Native North Americans the Plains tribes had no written language, they relied on a system of interrelated song, oral narrative, and visual arts to convey what was vital to them.

Creating symbolical or metaphorical marks and images is a basic human need. Among the Indian peoples of the Plains, abstract designs and representational images formed a visual vocabulary that combined with their oral traditions to express the sanctity and beauty of nature and to communicate information important to individual and community events. Being essentially nomadic, the Plains Indians put these significant images on their portable tents and clothing (fig. 2); on tools, weapons, and ritual paraphernalia; and on their bodies through body painting and personal adornment. Most Plains men and women engaged in some aspect of art

Fig. 2

Shoshone village, probably in Wyoming, ca. 1875. The painted tipi has images of medicine wheels and a horse. Smithsonian Institution photo no. 1668.

19

making, which they learned as children by watching their elders. Those with special skills gained a reputation for their talents and might be asked to create an object for a friend or relative. The terms "art" and "artist" do not exist in Plains languages, because art was an integral part of life and had no specialized, separate social function. The closest approximation in an Indian language is the Choctaw phrase *to*ⁿ*ksali imponna*, the first word meaning "work" and the second connoting skill, workmanship, talent, and understanding.[1]

## THE PETROGLYPH TRADITION

An overview of Plains Indian representational art must take into account the ancient pictorial traditions on which it was built. First among these are the images created on rock formations located near water sources scattered throughout the Plains. These petroglyphs range in date from about 2500 B.C. through the mid-nineteenth century. None of the sites show evidence of continuous habitation; they seem to have been visited seasonally as the people followed the great herds in the hunt for food. The extensive literature on what is popularly called "rock art" has been enriched by scholarly study over the past twenty years, most notably in the Plains region, by Robert F. Heizer, David Gebhard, and James D. Keyser. However, little is known about the function of most petroglyph images because they were created in prehistoric times. We can only infer their purpose from the visual arts and oral traditions of nineteenth- and twentieth-century Indian peoples.

Interesting exceptions have been reported by George Bird Grinnell in his study of the Cheyenne and by John Cooper in his book on the Gros Ventre people of Montana. Grinnell described a petroglyph site called Painted Rocks that was actively used by Cheyenne warriors during the middle of the nineteenth century as a place to pray and make sacrifices for success in battle and in other aspects of their lives. The Cheyenne said they did not paint these images, nor did they know who did. The site was considered especially mysterious and powerful because the images were thought to have appeared "without anyone having painted them."[2] As these drawings were therefore associated with spirit beings, they were considered *wakan* (as the Lakota would say), made viable with spiritual force.

Cooper records a Gros Ventre oral tradition that differentiates two varieties of petroglyphs.[3] One group was said to have been made by Indians; the other group was believed to have been produced by supernatural beings called *tciya :tsine :n*, which was translated as "ghost men" or "little men." These spirit beings are part of traditional Gros Ventre lore and are still reported to be in the forests and around rock formations on the Fort Belknap Reservation.[4] The rock drawings made by human beings are considered permanent, but those ascribed to the ghost men or "petroglyph people" are considered temporary and liable to change or to disappear from time to time. Cooper was told that in prereservation days petroglyph sites were regarded as special places imbued with spiritual power. War parties traveling to them made offerings to the ghost men, who might create new drawings during the night that could be interpreted to reveal the outcome of the warriors' venture.[5]

Finally, in his study of Salishan tribes of the adjoining Plateau region, James Teit documented the creation of pictographic drawings by peoples of the Columbia Plateau as part of their Vision Quests.[6] After several days of solitary fasting at a remote location, men who had successfully completed a quest honored the vision by creating images on rock formations near the place of their retreat. It is inferred that these images represent the spiritual guides or helpers who appeared to the men in their visions.

Plains petroglyphs were produced by various methods of rubbing away or cutting into the rock surface. One method was to "peck" the surface with numerous blows of a small, hand-held stone. Another was to scratch the design into the rock so as to remove the dark layer of weathered surface and reveal the lighter stone beneath. The mark produced by these techniques varied from approximately one-eighth to one-half inch in thickness and could form a curved or a straight line. Some petroglyphs were colored with earth pigments, which provided an additional ritual offering as well as giving greater visual impact. At some sites, such as Pictograph Cave, outside Billings, Montana, images were created exclusively with pigments. Because of the wear and damage caused by centuries of weather, these pictographs are rare and often extremely faded and difficult to read.

Plains rock art can be divided into four basic categories: abstract marks such as circles, crescents, dots, lines, and grids; animal tracks and human handprints and footprints; images of animals such as deer, elk, buffalo, mountain sheep, bear, eagles, and birds; and representations of humans and anthropomorphic beings. Many petroglyph sites have only a few drawings, whereas others have a variety of images that often spread over stone walls for hundreds of yards and contain many figures. In his study of Plains Indian rock art classification and stylistic development, Keyser identified ceremonial and biographical art as two major categories of style and subject matter.[7] The ceremonial art tradition has earlier roots (ca. 1300–1600) and includes both anthropomorphic figures and animals. These figures are primarily depicted as single units without reference to other images around them, and they are generally represented without much detail of form or articulation.

The Dinwoody site in Wyoming includes various ceremonial rock art images that occur within half a kilometer of each other on hillsides and rock outcroppings surrounding a lake framed by the Wind River Mountains. The most powerful and well-known drawings are located on the face of a cliff wall that can be reached only by climbing along extremely narrow ledges or irregularities in the vertical surface (fig. 3). There, hundreds of years ago, Indian men pecked images into the dark surface of the rock. The figures defined by this lighter line have anthropomorphic features but are clearly of an otherworldly nature. Like the drawings described by Teit, they seem to depict spiritual beings, encountered perhaps in a Vision Quest or some other ceremony created to access the power of the spirit world. As is the case with many petroglyph sites, it is difficult to establish a firm date for the drawings at Dinwoody. Gebhard places the large figures with elaborate interior linear decoration between about 1650 and 1800.[8] In earlier research, H. A. Cahn found that many of the drawing panels have a consistent pattern of overlapping images of similar subject and style. These enabled him to identify a sequence of seven categories, of which the large figures are the most visually impressive.[9]

A detail of the highest section of the wall shows six of these large figures (fig. 4). Their height of three to five feet makes them clearly visible from the valley below. They have frontally described, rectilinear bodies with short, outreaching arms and large hands with widely spread fingers. Legs are not drawn, but feet are indicated by means of three or more lines that fan out at the bottom corners of the body. The broad mouths crossing the bottom of the heads have a series of short vertical lines that could indicate teeth. The other consistent details on the

Fig. 3 (above)
Sacred images on the rock walls overlooking Dinwoody Lake, ca. 1600–1800. Photo by Evan M. Maurer.

Fig. 4
Anthropomorphic figures, Dinwoody Lake. Photo by Evan M. Maurer.

**Fig. 5**
Horned and winged figures,
Dinwoody Lake. Photo by
Evan M. Maurer.

heads are large, round eyes; rudimentary ears; and pairs of horns, either curved or straight. Since the addition of horns to an anthropomorphic figure in historic Plains art is a common method of portraying a spiritual being, we can infer a similar meaning in these early Plains petroglyphs (cat. nos. 108, 109).[10]

The design that covers the full length of the two largest figures' bodies is another indication of spiritual identity. The central vertical line with upward-angled lines branching off on either side can be interpreted as a reference to the spinal column and ribs—a design commonly associated with the shaman. For the native peoples of North America and in many other cultures around the world, the role of ritual healer and spiritual intermediary is filled by the shaman. Since one of the crucial prerequisites of shamanistic practice involves the ritual death and rebirth of the shamanic initiate, representations of shamans or their spirit animal helpers are often identified by the major elements of the skeleton.[11] Yet another detail suggesting that these images are spiritual in nature is the long, wavy lines emanating from the hands and eyes. In many paintings on historical Plains shields and in ledger drawings, these lines refer to the presence of spiritual power (cat. no. 7).[12] Given the conservative nature of traditional religious ritual, this historical evidence seems to provide a valid clue to the interpretation of the earlier drawings.

In an adjoining section of the cliff wall, where holes in the upper sections resulted from recent vandalism by rifle fire, anthropomorphic figures are accompanied by three similar images with outstretched wings in place of the arms. (fig. 5). Each figure has different wings and a varied design drawn over the entire body. Below these are three smaller anthropomorphic figures whose frontal, static forms are indicated only by outline; the interior of each is completely pecked to create a uniform light color with no further

articulation. These stark figures also evoke a direct and powerful spiritual presence. Like the images at most other Plains sites, the figures at Dinwoody were drawn quite close to each other, and in some instances they overlap or are drawn on top of preexisting images. Because there are no indications of a narrative relationship between the figures, it is possible that each image was made to commemorate a unique experience or event associated with a Vision Quest, a shamanistic ritual, or another spiritually meaningful activity.

The Legend Rock site in central Wyoming is larger than Dinwoody in terms of the number of images and their stylistic range. The petroglyphs are located on the side of a long ravine that is still watered by a small stream. A wide variety of anthropomorphic and animal images can be seen over more than two hundred yards of weather-stained rock walls. Many of the anthropomorphic figures are small and easily reachable from the narrow trail that runs along the base of the rock. Unlike the Dinwoody images, most of these were made to be experienced at close range and cannot be viewed clearly from a distance. Like the short figures with striped patterns on their bodies, many of the humanlike forms at this site have the pairs of curved horns that associate them with spiritual beings or sacred ritual events (fig. 6).

This site features an extraordinary set of figures drawn in a boldly attenuated style quite different from the style seen at other Plains sites (fig. 7). The tallest figure maintains the normal rectilinear body style, although its interior linear design is more random and overall than is typical. Most unusual, however, is that its horned head does not sit firmly on the trunk but floats over the body, attached only by a stringlike neck. This large figure is surrounded by six other figures, five of them depicted in an elongated linear style that in its visual freedom recalls the work

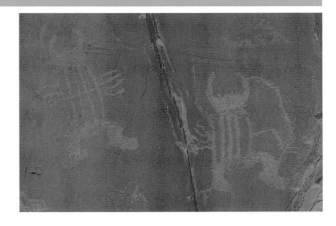

Fig. 6 (top)
Horned figures, Legend Rock, ca. 1000–1775. Photo by Evan M. Maurer.

Fig. 7
Horned figures with elongated bodies, Legend Rock. Photo by Evan M. Maurer.

**Fig. 8**
A pair of deer or elk, Legend Rock. Photo by Evan M. Maurer.

**Fig. 9** (far right)
A bull elk, Legend Rock. Photo by Evan M. Maurer.

**Fig. 10**
Warrior wearing a shirt with bear-paw designs, Castle Gardens, ca. 1625–1775. Photo by Evan M. Maurer.

**Fig. 11**
Shield-bearing warrior holding a feathered coup stick, Castle Gardens. Photo by Evan M. Maurer.

**Fig. 12** (page 25)
Shields, animals, and human figures, Castle Gardens. Photo by Evan M. Maurer.

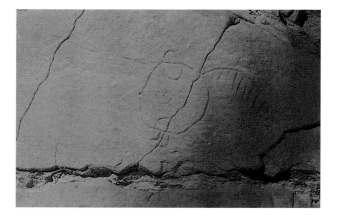

of European Surrealists like Joan Miró, who sought inspiration in American, Oceanic, and African cultures.[13]

Legend Rock also has a variety of animal images that are more directly representational and close to natural form than the drawings of the anthropomorphic figures. They range from simple pecked images of deer or elk (fig. 8) to a later style (fig. 9) that features a larger scale and a greater degree of anatomical detail achieved by a combination of pecked and incised lines. This stylistic and technical change reflects what Keyser called the transition from ceremonial rock art (ca. 1000–1700) to protohistoric rock art (1625–1775) and demonstrates that the site was in use for centuries. The presence of images of essential food animals lends weight to the theory that the images were produced as part of a hunting ritual.[14] Animal images are widely associated with rock art in many parts of the world, especially the renowned Neolithic cave art of France and northern Spain, dating from 25,000 to 15,000 B.C. Unlike the anthropomorphic figures, these representations of animals are usually drawn in profile with added detail to indicate horns or antlers, ears, tails, and sex organs. Although they must have had strong spiritual significance, these figures are very much of this world and are clear precedents for the animal imagery in historical Plains art (cat. nos. 24, 35). They seem solid and realistic, in contrast to the supernatural anthropomorphic figures, which seem to radiate spiritual power.

The protohistoric period (ca. 1625–1775) was marked by a shift from the individual, static figures of the ceremonial style to a more detailed depiction of both human and animal forms, with references to time, action, and historical events as well. Keyser called this the biographic style. Early examples can be found at the Castle Gardens site in west central Wyoming.[15] An oasis of water and vegetation in the midst of hundreds of square miles of brush and desert, Castle Gardens was for thousands of years a haven for the hunters and warriors who crossed the vast areas of the Plains by foot and later by horse. Most of the petroglyphs at Castle Gardens are from the protohistoric period and are probably of Shoshonean origin.[16]

Unlike the supernatural figures of Dinwoody or Legend Rock, the images at Castle Gardens are clearly representations of individual humans: male warriors with the kinds of garments and ritual objects that are familiar to us from the historical period. The finest example is a frontal figure of a tall man wearing a long shirt decorated with nine images of bear paws, a sign of power closely associated with Plains warfare (fig. 10) (cat. no. 147). This figure has the characteristic V-shaped neckline found on many of the human images of this period. A second important protohistoric motif is the shield-bearing warrior (fig. 11), here depicted frontally with only the feet and head protruding around the protective disk of the large hide shield. The object at the right is probably a feathered coup stick, a commonly used ritual object in Plains warrior societies (cat. no. 221). Figures of this type can be found at various northern Plains sites and in the basin area of Utah and Colorado.[17]

The shield was a vital object of protective power for the Plains warrior. One large vertical section of sandstone wall at Castle Gardens contains the largest concentration of petroglyph shield images on the northern Plains. On a space approximately fifteen by twenty feet were engraved a group of twelve decorated shields ranging from two to three and one-half feet in diameter (fig. 12). Although they are probably datable to the protohistoric period, their shape and the designs engraved on them are closely related to nineteenth-century examples (cat. nos. 9, 37). Four of the shields depict animals that could relate to visions or dreams experienced by the warrior.

**Fig. 13** (top)
A shield with a horned figure and two animals, Castle Gardens. Photo by Evan M. Maurer.

**Fig. 14**
A mountain sheep pierced by an arrow or spear, Castle Gardens. Photo by Evan M. Maurer.

The subjects of these visions were sometimes deemed appropriate to paint on a shield because their images represented powerful forces that could be called on to protect the warrior and help ensure his success in battle. In the Castle Gardens panel, three of the animal shields can be found in the second row from the top. From right to left they represent a pair of small mammals that might be otters; two birds, possibly eagles or vultures; and two buffaloes, placed one on top of the other, accompanied by a small human figure at the top left edge of the disk. Below these and to the right is a shield with six bear-paw designs set around a central circle. (The areas of white on this shield are modern patches applied to the surface in an effort to conserve the image.) The other eight shields are decorated with a combination of abstract circular and cruciform designs that might refer to celestial bodies and the sacred cardinal directions. The rock wall on which these images are located also contains a few figures of animals, animal tracks, and one human figure.

One of the most striking shield images at Castle Gardens was incised at a different area of the site. It features a large human head flanked by two small spirit animals resembling horned otters or beavers (fig. 13). This powerful head, which sits on a long, thin neck decorated with a broad necklace or collar, has ears, eyes, nose, mouth, and a pair of large, curved horns that denote its sacred role. The set of vertical lines between the horns might represent a forehead hairlock of the type favored by many historical northern Plains tribes.

This intriguing and beautifully situated site also contains scenes of hunting that convey direct narrative action, a concept not found in the earlier, ceremonial style of rock art (fig. 14). One of the most interesting of these scenes is an unusual representation of a mountain sheep shown in profile with an almost hemispherical

body; sticklike legs ending in oval bifurcated feet; a small, triangular head; and curving horns. An oversized arrow or spear shaft with oval feathers can be seen protruding from the animal's back. The presence of the weapon that has hit its mark bespeaks a whole series of actions taken in the hunt; so the basic visual elements of this image constitute a historical or biographical statement. Early images of action and time-sequenced narrative such as this are among the first examples of a genre that, by the late eighteenth century, developed into a major Plains art form (cat. no. 147). Many other examples, such as the figures of fighting men from Writing-On-Stone, in Alberta, Canada (fig. 15), establish an even more direct link between this ancient rock art tradition and the development of eighteenth- and nineteenth-century Plains art.[18]

Located in the Milk River valley in southern Alberta, just eight kilometers north of the Montana border, Writing-On-Stone is the largest petroglyph site on the northern Plains. This area has been occupied by various Plains tribes since at least the early eighteenth century, including Shoshone, Blackfeet, Cree, Assiniboine, and Gros Ventre. In his study of the site, Keyser found that there were over fifty-eight groups of nearly seven hundred images at Writing-On-Stone, created over an extended period.[19] An analysis of the petroglyphs indicates that 95 percent of them were made by scratching and incising. These methods yield a thin line capable of a greater amount of graphic detail than the techniques of pecking or abrading. Most of the more broadly conceived images are characterized as ceremonial art and date to the late prehistoric period (ca. 1300–1700), whereas the majority of images created with engraved and scratched lines are of the biographical art type from the early historic period (ca. 1750–1850). The earliest figures at Writing-On-Stone are similar to the V-necked warrior and the shield-bearing warrior from Castle Gardens, proof of the wide geographic range of this style. Either the images were made by related peoples (perhaps Shoshone) or they are evidence of a general style or visual convention of graphic representation that was common in the northern Plains from southern Wyoming to Alberta. Both of these iconic types depict single warriors viewed from the front. Since they have no direct or implied relationships to other figures or animals, they don't seem to be engaged in communicating historical or biographical events.

The most important images at Writing-On-Stone are narrative statements depicting two or more warriors in combat. Using a fine incised line, the men who produced them were able to give a good deal of visual information about the costumes and weapons used by these warriors. They also represented the horses that, along with firearms, had become a commonplace and vitally important element of Plains life by about 1750. One of these line drawings portrays combats between adversaries on foot and between a warrior on foot and one on horseback (fig. 16). They are the record of specific historical events that were honored and celebrated visually in this way just as they would have been perpetuated orally in the stories told by the victor himself and by his family for generations. The pedestrian warriors carry large, mostly undecorated shields that were used for physical defense in close combat. The mounted warriors have much smaller shields, which were easier to handle on horseback. Two of the three shields held by horsemen have symbolic "medicine" or power designs painted on them and closely resemble their nineteenth-century counterparts. One image group at the site represents 10 figures involved in one event, and the largest group describes a battle of 115 warriors with additional details such as tipis, rifle pits, horses,

travois, tracks, and weapons (fig. 17). Both of these examples are direct precedents for biographical art produced by nineteenth- and twentieth-century warrior-artists on their hide robes and shirts and later on paper and muslin, objects that will be discussed later (cat. nos. 150, 151, 181, 158). Petroglyphs provide the earliest evidence of a long Plains tradition of pictorial representation devoted both to dream or vision imagery and to historical or biographical events—the two basic categories of Plains representational art.

**Fig. 15**
A shield-bearing warrior and a V-necked figure, Writing-On-Stone, Alberta, ca. 1750–1850. Redrawn from a diagram in the Glenbow Museum, Calgary.

**Fig. 16**
Battle scenes with shield-bearing warriors and V-necked figures, Writing-On-Stone. Redrawn from a diagram in the Glenbow Museum, Calgary.

**Fig. 17** (bottom)
Battle scenes, Writing-On-Stone. This unusually large scene describes a sequence of historical events with images of flintlock rifles, bows, horses, travois, and tipis. Redrawn from a diagram in the Glenbow Museum, Calgary.

one foot

## GREAT LAKES AND SOUTHEASTERN INFLUENCES

Northern Arapaho elder I once met on the Wind River Reservation in Wyoming asked where I was from. When I replied "Minnesota," he smiled and quietly said, "We used to live there too!" Many groups now considered to be quintessential Plains tribes originated farther to the east, in the Woodlands and Great Lakes area. Military pressures from such Great Lakes people as the Ojibwe and Iroquois, both of whom were furnished with firearms by the French and English around 1650, caused them to begin seeking a safer home to the west, across the Mississippi and then the Missouri rivers. The Cheyenne, Arapaho, Gros Ventre, and Lakota, all of whom had lived for hundreds of years as agriculturalists in and around Minnesota's Red River valley, began their move west in the middle of the seventeenth century.

As the main means of sustenance changed from agriculture to hunting, the new environment on the open plains necessitated many changes in life-style and material culture. Given these peoples' long development in the Great Lakes area, however, it is understandable that certain aspects of their old myths, rituals, and ceremonial art persisted. Grinnell notes that the Cheyenne have myths concerning the Thunderbird and the Underwater Monster, two characters that are also important in Great Lakes mythology. One underwater monster in Cheyenne myth is the *mĭh'n'* described as a large lizard or serpent with one or two horns and often depicted with a series of curved lines representing hair.[20] These monsters are not necessarily dangerous, but like all spiritual entities they possess strong powers and must be treated with respect. Images of and stories about these monsters occur throughout the Plains, from the

Blackfeet to the Pawnee and the Kiowa (cat. no. 69).[21] We find versions of this horned serpent also among such Great Lakes tribes as the Ojibwe, Potawatomi, and Menominee, where they are conceived as powerful beings associated often with magic and sorcery.[22] Images of these creatures can be found at Great Lakes pictograph sites and engraved on the birchbark scrolls of the Midéwiwin Medicine Society.[23]

Another important mythological figure central to both Great Lakes and Plains cultures is the thunderbird, usually represented with outstretched wings, frontal body, and head in profile. This image can be found both in a variety of Great Lakes petroglyphs and in the decoration of objects and paraphernalia associated with dreams, medicine, and spiritual societies (cat. no. 7).[24] The same general style of thunderbird can also be seen in Plains petroglyphs at Legend Rock and Castle Gardens and in shields and other Plains ritual objects from the late nineteenth century (cat. no. 137). Moreover, in both culture areas the Underwater Monster and the Thunderbird are enemies fighting epic battles in which the powers of the sky are pitted against those of the underworld.

Mythical anthropomorphic beings are also common in the oral traditions and visual arts of both culture areas. In most cases the spiritual nature of the being is indicated by a pair of curving horns on either side of the head: this generic figure type can be found among the petroglyphs of Dinwoody, Legend Rock, and Castle Gardens. These horned male figures are some of the most common images in late prehistoric ceremonial art and are generally associated with powerful dreams and visions. Their appearance in later historical art of many categories reveals what a crucial aspect of Plains culture they signify (cat. no. 108).[25] The same type of horned man can also be found throughout the Great Lakes and Woodlands regions. The Dakota, for

example, carved wooden sculptures of these figures and associated them with forest spirits. The sculptures were kept in secret locations, hidden in the trees that also sheltered the spirits.[26]

Carved wooden bowls with rim decorations in the form of anthropomorphic or animal heads are another important object type found in both Great Lakes and Plains cultures (cat. nos. 13, 101). In the Woodlands and Great Lakes areas these bowls were commonly used at ceremonial feasts, and the sculptural representation on the rim referred to clan totems or mythological beings.[27] Most of these finely carved bowls were made from the burls of deciduous hardwoods common to the Woodlands. The density of the burl made the bowls difficult to carve, and once finished they were treasured as important social and ceremonial heirlooms.[28] The clearest historical antecedent of this kind of wooden feast bowl is a type of ceramic produced during the Mississippian period by southeastern peoples such as those of the Caddoan culture, which flourished in Arkansas and areas farther west from the twelfth through the seventeenth century. A comparison of Plains wooden bowls (cat. no. 30) and Mississippian ceramic vessels of the same basic form reveals a clear visual connection, which is reinforced by a historical pattern of cultural relations.

During the first part of this period, from about 1200 to 1400, an extraordinary cultural phenomenon developed over a broad area from Georgia to Alabama and Oklahoma. Scholars have shown that sites such as Etowah, Georgia; Moundville, Alabama; and Spiro, Oklahoma, share so many architectural, ceremonial, and iconographic forms that they must represent a widely based social and religious system. These societies were hierarchical, with an elite class of leaders, priests, and warriors who were honored in life and in elaborate mortuary rituals.[29] Male members of this elite class wearing elaborate ritual costumes were the subject of an early tradition of representative imagery. The artists used materials such as clay, shell, wood, and copper; their techniques included engraving, carving, and repoussé bas-relief. Ceremonial art associated with high-status individuals included the depiction of iconic images on shell gorgets worn around the neck. The image on an example from Spiro (cat. no. 1) honoring the sun's great life-giving power is still commonly referenced in Plains art in works such as the popular star quilt (cat. nos. 308, 309). The human hand on another gorget (cat. no. 91) is a common symbol of individuality, presence, and action, which can also be found in Plains pictographs and in later examples of Plains art (cat. nos. 224, 225).

The concentration of large numbers of images of bird-costumed dancers and warriors at Spiro is especially significant for this study because of the site's strategic location. The Spiro Ceremonial Complex is situated in the Arkansas River valley, which archaeologists have found was a major corridor of travel and trade between the rich waterways of the southeast and the broad western plains. With this trade came cultural contacts that remained a feature of life in the region through the nineteenth and twentieth centuries, and the intertribal gifts, marriages, and visits encouraged the development of new styles in many traditional art forms. Early evidence of this interrelationship can be seen when southeastern artifacts are compared with those of the Nebraska and Republican peoples who lived on the east-central Plains in the prehistoric period. Several scholars have also proven that the influence of the "Southern Cult" extended far into the Plains.[30] The most impressive examples of this interwoven cultural tradition are the copper and shell images of men wearing elaborate costumes with wings, tails, and beaks that identify them as birds of prey. Through their details of costume, jewelry, and other personal adornment, these

symbols differentiated individuals, and it is evident that the communication of this information was vital to the function of the image. The need to visually communicate specific facts of personal identity and status is also a crucial aspect of Plains biographical art.

## THE SCHOLARLY RECORD

 lthough detailed descriptions of Plains Indian ceremonial and secular arts did not appear in Euro-American accounts until the nineteenth century, many travelers who ventured out onto the plains were impressed enough by these handsomely made objects to mention them in their journals. The earliest reference was made by Castaneda, a member of Coronado's expedition of 1541. Visiting the agricultural villages that were the winter homes of the Wichita and the Pawnee, he noted that they possessed finely tanned hides with painted designs.[31] Early nineteenth-century explorers also left descriptions of Plains painted robes, but it wasn't until the 1882 publication of Garrick Mallery's "Pictographs of the North American Indians" that the subject of American Indian representational imagery was studied in a systematic fashion.

In 1876, during his stay at Fort Rice on the Upper Missouri River, Colonel Garrick Mallery obtained a copy of Lone Dog's Winter Count, the best-known Lakota calendrical history documenting the years from 1800 to 1876 (fig. 18). Mallery was fascinated by the images and published a description and interpretation of this pictorial calendar in 1877. His article attracted favorable government attention, and Mallery was transferred to the U.S. Geological and Geographical Survey to conduct research on the ethnology of the North American Indians. After five years of work, he published a preliminary paper

Fig. 18
Kills Two, a Sicangu Lakota, painting a winter count, Rosebud Reservation, South Dakota, ca. 1910. Nebraska State Historical Society.

on North American Indian pictographs in the Fourth Annual Report of the Bureau of American Ethnology for 1882–83. While that in itself was a considerable effort, Mallery continued his research another five years to produce the first compendium of Native American pictorial representation, *Picture-Writing of the American Indians*. This massive book, with its 822 pages and over 1,300 illustrations, was also the first study ever to take up an entire annual report of the Bureau of Ethnology. Fortunately, the original work has been reprinted by Dover in two paperback volumes, making it accessible to a larger contemporary audience.[32]

The first two hundred pages of the book survey North American petroglyphs in juxtaposition with examples from other continents that place the American images in a general historical context. By presenting corollary information on similar forms used by contemporary tribes, Mallery acknowledged that these petroglyphs were significant images with deep cultural importance. Throughout the book he wove these ancient witnesses of Indian culture into his review of contemporary forms of image making. Mallery proved that representational imagery created by the native peoples of this continent continued to have meaning over a long period of time. He also recognized that these signs often imply a personal rather than a tribal system of symbolic meaning and that, while comparative studies can suggest general categories of subject, we can never hope to discover a secret "code" that will allow us to "read" these images fully as if they were hieroglyphics with specific word equivalents.[33]

Mallery's study of traditional Indian imagery from petroglyphs to works on paper established a historical context for American Indian art, but Mallery also tried to place this art within a system of nineteenth-century European cultural evolution. Nineteenth-century European scholars typically viewed human social organization and arts as evolving along a linear path of development and improvement that would, in time, bring them from an early crude to a later sophisticated state. While this attitude reflects a Victorian conception of human progress that values the European industrialized model above all others, Mallery had the insight and sensitivity to acknowledge that there were deep philosophical and psychological meanings encoded in the Indian pictographic forms which played the same fundamental role in Indian cultures from the past to the present. In his introduction, he summarized his observations on American Indian pictographic art and noted:

*The old devices are substantially the same as the modern, though improved and established in the course of evolution. The ideograph and symbolism displayed in these devices present suggestive studies in psychology more interesting than the mere information or text contained in the pictures. It must also be observed that when Indians now make pictographs it is with intention and care—seldom for mere amusement. Even when the labor is undertaken merely to supply the trade demand for painted robes or engraved pipes or bark records, it is a serious manufacture.*[34]

Mallery's study concludes with remarks that express his sensitivity to and respect for the people who created the great visual legacy he had surveyed:

*The character of the drawings and the mode of their execution tell something of their makers. If they do not tell who those authors were, they at least suggest what kind of people they were as regards art, customs, and sometimes religion. But there is a broader mode of estimating the quality of known pictographs. Musicians are eloquent in lauding the great composers of songs without words. The ideography, which is the prominent feature of picture-writing, displays both primordially and practically the higher and purer concept of thoughts without sound.*[35]

The generation of Plains scholars following Mallery were active field researchers who spent many seasons living with the tribes to learn more about their lives and their cultural past. Men such as Clark Wissler, George Bird Grinnell, James Mooney, Robert Lowie, and George Dorsey spent years among the tribes interviewing the elders: men and women who were born at the middle of nineteenth century and who had participated in the old, free life-style before Europeans had changed the land and the lives of the native peoples. The work of these scholars forms an essential foundation for any student of Plains Indian culture, for in addition to recording social and historical data, they transcribed myths, stories, songs of honor, parables, and elaborate religious rituals. These valuable documents reveal cultures that are rich in heroes and heroines and in wisdom and knowledge that are both practical and esoteric.

That Plains Indian art had an international appeal is evident from the fact that the next significant survey to be published was by the German scholar Ernst Vatter in Frankfurt am Main in 1927.[36] This study of early painted hide shirts and robes classifies their iconography of heraldry and warrior exploits, and Vatter proposes a grouping of the major examples by graphic style and tribal attribution. Vatter also offers an interesting examination of basic visual conventions in the depiction of such categories as human heads, figures, and weapons. Twelve years later, in 1939, John C. Ewers, who had studied with Clark Wissler at Yale, published a version of his master's thesis on Plains painting.[37] This brief but careful survey was the first among Ewers's many important contributions in this field.

Complementing his later work on general aspects of Plains cultures, and his more detailed studies of the Blackfeet with whom he lived for many years, Ewers's book on Plains painting is an invaluable reference for the study of the painted hide robes that were the most common large garment worn by Plains Indians of both sexes before the advent of the European blanket. The first chapter provides a review of the materials and techniques used by Plains men and women in painting on leather, information that is essential for understanding the nature of the medium and its capacity for representation. A brief history of Plains hide painting follows, and then a survey of other object types painted by Plains artists. The study ends with a comparative summary of hide painting by native artists in other areas of North and South America. In his conclusion, Ewers recognized the cultural conservatism inherent in limiting the geometric painting on hide robes to only five basic designs and in not pursuing artistic innovation and variation. There is much evidence, however, to indicate that this visual conservatism is not a flaw of impoverishment, but instead an affirmation of tradition that honors deep cultural and spiritual values.

Ewers's early study was followed by a gradual increase in publications dealing with Native American art and Plains Indian representational imagery in particular. Historians, anthropologists, art historians, collectors, and amateur scholars have added a wide range of material to the exploration of this important area of American art, two examples of which are J. J. Brody's *Indian Painters and White Patrons* and Dorothy Dunn's 1968 study *American Indian Painting of the Southwest and Plains Areas*.[38] While the majority of Dunn's work is devoted to a historical survey of southwestern painting, she also presents a well-documented review of the history of Plains painting and its stylistic development from the late eighteenth century through the 1960s. Dorothy Dunn was closely involved with American

Indian art because of her important role as director of the Santa Fe Indian School from 1932 to 1937 and her strong influence as a teacher who encouraged members of the Kiowa group of painters and many others, including the influential Lakota artist Oscar Howe. Dunn and Brody have contributed to Native American studies by recognizing the continuity of the Plains pictorial tradition and emphasizing its aesthetic and cultural values. More recently these efforts have been continued through a growing number of publications and exhibitions that have been redefining contemporary Native American art by recognizing its ties to the traditional models as well as its innovative and powerful expressions of the Indian experience in the modern world.

Previous studies of Plains art have established its categories of subject matter and have broadly defined the sequence of stylistic development in Plains painting. However, little attempt has been made to view painting in its true context as simply one of the most visible means of communicating important aspects of ritual and history within a larger symbolic system. Frequently used images embellished many object types and were created in a variety of media. For example, body painting was traditionally an integral part of the ritual ensemble, and warrior societies had identifiable styles of face and body painting that still persist. Participants in the Sun Dance have their bodies covered with ritually prepared paint and sacred designs that reproduce many of the representational and abstract images found in the other pictorial arts. By examining the ways in which visual expression relates to its broader spiritual context, we can acquire a better understanding of both the role and the efficacy of ceremonial and biographical art. The following illustrations are offered as a brief survey of the range of Plains Indian art. A more thorough and detailed examination of the

historical, cultural, and aesthetic basis of Plains art is contained in the other essays and in the catalogue entries.

## IMAGES OF CEREMONIAL ART

The petroglyph images already discussed have many direct relationships to nineteenth-century paintings on shields, shirts, and other ceremonial objects used by the Plains tribes. The surfaces of objects as large as tipis or as small as a child's amulet carried sacred images with strong visual ties to the older petroglyphs (fig. 19 and cat no. 22). We must assume that the tradition of making images on the hide surfaces of special ritual paraphernalia is also an ancient one; the men who made the earliest petroglyphs must also have created their sacred designs on portable and fragile objects, which have not survived as the rock art has. Like the petroglyphs at Dinwoody or Legend Rock, the ceremonial arts of the historical period were created to be icons of power: abstract or representational symbols of a spiritual concept that must be honored through specific rituals. Most ceremonial art is limited in subject to a single primary image accompanied by at most a few supporting ones. The forms were depicted for maximum visual impact to convey the power and efficacy of a spiritual presence whose assistance was granted to a chosen few.

Consider as an example the shield used by the Plains warrior. Its thick rawhide certainly made it an effective defensive object in hand-to-hand combat, but its real value lay in its being the locus of a spiritual power that could protect or aid its proper owner as long as he performed the rituals necessary to its use. The images painted on personal rather than societal or clan shields were dictated by dreams or visions received by their original owners. While these

shields could be transferred, duplicated, or even sold, their central image remained unchanged because it was the source of power. As we can see in the example of a Crow shield painted with a buffalo (cat. no. 35), the animal is shown in profile to communicate its identity clearly and create the strongest sense of its presence. The representation was meant to portray not a particular buffalo but Buffalo in general, the affective and eternal essence of Buffalo-ness.

The subjects of most ceremonial art range from metaphorical references associated with color and abstract design to natural phenomena, animals, and anthropomorphic figures. That these elements were used in the decoration of all types of ceremonial objects allowed the Plains artist to create ritually and socially affective images in a variety of media and sizes. For example, pipe containers such as the fine Cheyenne "stripe"-style bag (cat. no. 229) were an important part of men's personal paraphernalia. Because the tobacco container and pipe are used for prayer and ritual, these bags and their decoration convey strong spiritual meanings. The main panel of this example has four centrally placed horizontal bars flanked on each side by four stripes, and four triangular forms in its corners. Sets of four are often used in Plains art as an honorific reference to the powers of the four cardinal directions, which were also identified with specific colors. While these color associations can vary from one group to another or even from individual to individual, the basic pigments red, blue, yellow, white, and black are commonly used to signify and show reverence for the directions as manifestations of the all-encompassing unity of creation. The number four also emerges in repeated gestures of respect during ritual activity. The pipe and its sacred smoke are offered to the four directions, and even the structure of prayers and vows often reflects this spiritually meaningful number. The

number four in its myriad uses and references to the totality of the world denotes a fundamental idea and attitude in Plains Indian culture.

While abstract forms clearly carry symbolic meaning in Plains Indian art, the interpretation of symbols is most often a personal system and not one shared by the culture as a whole. The most extensive studies of meaning in abstract Plains art were done by Alfred Kroeber, who worked with the Arapaho around the turn of the century to compile a lexicon of symbols used to represent objects in nature and objects of the camp. Kroeber carefully pointed out the individuality of interpretation and provided a firm base for the understanding of abstract designs as part of a larger system of social and artistic communication.[39]

The world of nature is expressed on a variety of objects by images such as the sun, moon, and stars. The crosses and circles painted around the uppermost sections of many tipis refer to stars, which play an important role in tribal mythology and religion (cat. no. 3). Stars are used as decorations on objects as diverse as Lakota baby bonnets[40] and a Comanche shield cover with an intensely charged image of sun and stars (cat. no. 2). The zigzag lines coming from the left side of the sun represent emanations of power, symbolizing not only the physical manifestation of lightning and thunder, but also, as noted in the discussion of the Dinwoody petroglyphs, the presence of affective spiritual energy.

The ultimate pictorial use of stars in Plains art was in the elaborately painted Ghost Dance costumes made by the Arapaho, Lakota, and others (fig. 20 and cat. nos. 127, 129). The Ghost Dance was an important cultural and spiritual revivalist movement that spread across the Plains in the 1880s. The leaders prophesied a world of peace, where the ancestors and the buffalo returned and the land was rid of the white men and the changes they had imposed on the

Indian way of life. The rituals were celebrated with communal dances in which men and women sang and danced wearing costumes painted with an elaborate iconography of stars, birds, animals, trees, and human figures prominent in the songs and stories of the Ghost Dance. These star-covered shirts and dresses clothed the dancers in a cosmic image that placed them securely within the universe at large. They were dressed in the manner of priests, wrapped in holy ceremonial vestments in which art is used in the service of a religious and cultural revival.

The most frequently depicted subjects in Plains Indian art are the animals, which are also most prevalent in the oral traditions of myth, song, and story. These multiple references indicate that particular animals are central to Plains religious and social systems and therefore serve as the principal metaphorical expressions of nature's material and spiritual forces. In the ceremonial arts, the images of these animals were considered to be special because they were associated with sacred rituals. The anthropologist Clark Wissler understood that the deeply religious imagery of Plains cultures "seems to be a symbolical appeal to the source or concrete manifestation of a protective power," and that Plains ceremonial art has an active character that makes the image an integral part of an animated process.[41]

Images of animals occur both in body painting and on all types of ceremonial and utilitarian objects from tipis to clothing, and their making crossed gender lines. They are central to women's quill- and beadwork (cat. no. 44) as well as to men's carving and painting, and among the Cheyenne Nation the creation of animal sculpture for ceremonial purposes was even shared with the children. At important medicine dances the priests directed children to make two-to-three-inch-high mud sculptures of animals such as buffalo, elk, deer, antelope, and birds. Pairs of

Fig. 20
Chief Hail wearing a Ghost Dance shirt, Arapaho, ca. 1890. Hickox Collection, courtesy of the Oklahoma Historical Society, neg. no. 9563.

these small sculpted effigies were brought into the medicine lodge, where they were placed around the central altar to honor the animals who, as the quarry of the hunters, share their bodies with the people and sustain them.[42]

Because of their ability to fly, birds of many types are important subjects in Plains art. Cranes were associated with courting; their carved heads decorated flutes and whistles used by men to serenade their ladies and play at ritual events. These elegant birds also decorated feast spoons and dance batons, elongated forms that accentuated the bird's long neck and beak (cat. nos. 19, 20). For images of power, birds of prey were a more appropriate symbol. Of all the great raptors, the eagle is most important in the Plains ceremonial system. It is closely associated with the Great Creator, and its body is essential to the culture and rituals of the Plains tribes. Eagles are found on objects from clothing to food bowls. On one finely carved bowl that was used in sacred feasts (cat. no. 14), the bird's strong head and sharp beak are punctuated by the visionary glare of its brass-tack eyes, while its body is more abstractly represented by the oval bowl and the geometric forms extending from the rim. The bowl's function as a container for food at a sacred feast was perceived as an extension of the eagle's role as a source of spiritual power. For similar reasons of association, the preserved bodies of birds of prey were often included in sacred war bundles to epitomize and inculcate the exceptional powers of these fierce hunters, and their feathers were used by warriors as amulets of protection and as signs of valor and military achievement. Eagle-wing fans are still treasured parts of a man's personal bundle that must be earned by devotion and self-sacrifice, and eagle feathers are integral to rituals of prayer and blessing. In the words of the Lakota holy man Lame Deer: "We are an eagle nation, that is good, something to be proud of because the eagle is the wisest of birds. He is the Great Spirit's messenger; he is a great warrior. That is why we always wore the eagle plume, and still wear it. We are a great nation."[43]

The eagle is also associated with the Thunderbird, one of the principal characters in Plains mythology and art. Conceived as a symbol for the powerful forces that invest the skies, the Thunderbird was especially associated with storms, thunder, and lightning. The most extraordinary visual image of this mighty spiritual presence is the Pawnee Ghost Dance drum in the Field Museum of Natural History in Chicago (cat. no. 134). The great mythic bird is centered on the drumhead as it brings down the dark storm clouds, and the lightning crackling from its eyes and wings causes the split-tail swallows to wheel and dive under its force. The Thunderbird's massive, darkly colored body becomes an even more effective icon of immutable power through its contrast to the small swallows. This combination of forms resembles the visionary experience of Plains spiritual leaders like Black Elk, the famous Lakota holy man, who described the sky in one of his visions this way: "The thunder cloud was coming on with lightning on its front and many voices in it, and the split tail swallows swooped above us in a swarm."[44]

One of the two most important and powerful mammals in Plains art is the bear, which was associated with magical abilities and is found in many myths and dream visions as a source of protective medicine. Bear-paw designs decorated a warrior shirt and shield in the early historic petroglyphs at Castle Gardens, and images of bears were carved on wooden feast dishes and on pipe bowls used in various rituals (cat. no. 30). A black-stone pipe with lead inlays and the single figure of a bear was collected by the artist George Catlin around 1832 (cat. no. 28). When its stem was attached and it was being smoked in prayer, the bear would be aligned with the smoker's face and would look directly at him, a position that emphasizes its vital role in the prayer ceremony. Bear imagery is also often found on visionary dream shields such as a famous example painted by a Crow warrior around 1875 (cat. no. 23). The six designs on the right represent grizzly-bear paws with long, curving claws—a motif symbolizing a set of tracks with implied movement in a specific direction. The bear itself is represented by the front part of its body charging unharmed into a hail of bullets; it is surrounded by an upper red area said to signify the sky and a lower green section referring to the earth. Because the bear was closely associated with healing, shaman doctors who possessed the power of the bear were held in great esteem. The following medicine song, which was sung the sacred four times, was the property of Eagle Shield, a well-known nineteenth-century Lakota Bear Healer. It is called "an appeal to the Bear," who is referred to in the song as "Father."

*Father send a voice*
*Father send a voice*
*A hard task I am having*
*Father send a voice*
*A hard task I am having*[45]

The principal mammal in Plains culture was the buffalo. Because it was the main source of sustenance, clothing, and shelter, the buffalo had a primary place in the oral and visual traditions of both the ceremonial and the secular worlds. An early protohistoric work that captures both the look and the power of the buffalo is a compact stone sculpture found in Alberta, Canada. It was probably carved in the late Mississippian period around 1400 to 1650, before the introduction of the horse (cat. no. 31). With extreme economy of means, the sculptor captured the fundamental physical qualities that epitomize the animal, an ability often associated with artists from hunting cultures, who know intimately the animals they depend on for their sustenance. There are many Plains stories about

people who possessed the special ability to find or call buffalo to feed the people.[46] It is likely that buffalo sculptures similar to this one were associated with the buffalo-calling ceremonies that were a crucial aspect of Plains life.

Like many other Plains ethnic groups, the Mandan and Hidatsa of the Upper Missouri had important male and female societies that honored the buffalo. The Bulls Society (*ki'rup i'ke'*) was one of the highest warrior societies. The women's group was called the White Buffalo Cow Society (*ptī' take ō'xat'e*) and was ranked as the highest woman's group in the tribe.[47] In their dances, Buffalo Society members wore horned masks and robes of buffalo hide and imitated the animal's movements. These performances had meaning on many levels, but their chief significance was to ensure that herds would be found to feed the people. Plains cultures had many special societies whose members had received sacred visions from an animal. When these Buffalo Dreamers or Elk Dreamers performed society dances, they were often dressed in masks and hides of their tutelary animal. By taking on the shape and features of the animal, the dancer experienced a process of transformation in which he was physically and spiritually united with the spirit of the animal whose skin he wore and reanimated (cat. no. 46).

Buffalo were also used to decorate shields like one which probably represents the dream medicine of a Crow warrior (cat. no. 36). The artist transformed an element from the warrior's vision into an iconic symbol of the spirit buffalo that had revealed itself and its affective power to the dreamer. Using natural pigments and a continuous, curving line to draw the buffalo's muscular body, the artist created a strong profile that conveys a direct and immediate sense of the animal's presence. Signs of the bull buffalo's strength and energy are minimally but sufficiently repre-

sented by the few added details of the curving horns, protruding tongue, shaggy mane, and genitals. This image and others like it are very similar to the pictographs drawn by European Neolithic hunters on cave walls in France and Spain. The great bulls on the ceiling of the first main chamber at Lascaux are much larger in scale than this small shield yet are closely related to it in vision and spirit. Because the buffalo have returned from near extinction like the Plains tribes themselves, the animals have come to symbolize cultural as well as physical survival. The buffalo has therefore been revived as an important symbolic image in contemporary Plains art, from the paintings of the Kiowa school to quillwork and sculpture (cat. nos. 33, 43).

Other mammals found in traditional Plains ceremonial art include the wolf, which is associated with hunting and war (cat. no. 103); the bull elk, which is identified with male power (cat. no. 50); and the horse, a newly introduced animal that quickly became an essential part of Plains life (cat. no. 76). These animals make up the largest group of living creatures in sacred representation, and from the extensive oral tradition it is clear that the people felt a strong spiritual kinship to them as fellow inhabitants of a shared world. In myths and stories this identification was expressed by the ability of animals and humans to speak to each other in a common language. In daily life this mythic structure was reflected in the special relationships humans established with animals and communicated through their clan and society affiliations and their personal dreams and visions. It was by the favor of the animal that a human was endowed with knowledge, insight, and power, and it was only through their relationships with animals that humans could thrive and prosper.

The turtle is one of the water animals that appears most often in myths and stories.

Many peoples of the Great Lakes and Plains have origin myths in which the turtle plays an essential generative role as the creature on whose back the dry land was formed.[48] With the Lakota, the turtle was especially important to women and was associated with their healing and protection. The birth amulet of a female child was made in the shape of a turtle and often decorated with a beadwork design that represents the pattern of its shell (cat. no. 60). The U-shaped abstract design in the middle of the breast of a traditional Lakota woman's dress symbolizes the sacred turtle that is vital to the wearer's well-being (cat. no. 201). This simple, significant form on the yoke of beaded hide dresses has been the most common design used by Lakota women for over 150 years. That it is still in use today testifies to the continuing validity of such images for a people whose traditional values remain strong.

Plains culture embraces all manifestations of nature, including the insects and other small creatures that live around us. In the oral tradition one of the most popular and frequently mentioned of these is the spider, a creature central in Lakota traditions, where it is personified by a powerful and mischievous character called Iktomi.[49] Because the dragonfly was observed to be a swift and agile hunter, darting quickly about to dodge and attack, it was associated with warriors and its image is often found in sacred arts associated with military activity. It was painted as war medicine on shields (cat. no. 71) and on the flanks of favorite war ponies[50] and was also represented on amulets attached to a warrior's hair. A striking example of Crow dragonfly medicine is cut from rawhide and painted in vivid green (cat. no. 70). Its attached feathers and trailing plumes approximate the shimmering motion of the dragonfly's brightly colored and often iridescent body and wings.

Anthropomorphic figures are also found in Plains ceremonial art, in most cases represent-

ing spiritual beings and not ordinary humans. The most commonly occurring anthropomorphic image is the type of stylized male figure with a set of curved horns attached to its head that appears in so many Plains petroglyphs. Comparing the image on a rattle (cat. no. 108) with similar forms in ancient rock art, we see yet another example of the long tradition of sacred visual representation. The figure that combines human and animal attributes is an image of transformation, a rich metaphor expressing the Indian's perception of the underlying spirit that animates and unifies all forms in nature. It symbolizes a world of shared powers and responsibilities in which the respect inherent in ritual, as well as ecological balance, is needed for all to survive in harmony.

A painting on muslin by the Cheyenne warrior-artist Red Cloud (cat. no. 143) is an unusual work that combines animal and human images and serves as a bridge between the themes of ceremonial and biographical art. The lower section, a consummate example of ceremonial art, represents a vision of Buffalo Man and three similar buffalo tipis. The bases of the tipis have friezes of running buffalo around their perimeters; the midsections depict the dark night sky with large images of the sun, moon, and lightning; and the top sections are decorated with a pattern of small stars and a large eagle or hawk sitting on the ends of the tall lodgepoles. These medicine tipis are a metaphor for the universe, where the buffalo inhabit the earth and the skies are the domain of birds and celestial phenomena. The circular form of the tipi is a reference to the sacred wheel of life, the ultimate symbol of the Plains Indian understanding of the law of eternal continuity that governs the cosmos. A large bull buffalo is painted between the two tipis on the right, its head tilted upward and alert, its vibrant breath pulsating from mouth and nostrils. This is not an ordinary buffalo: on its side are a sun,

moon, and star, and it floats above the groundline, an indication of its supernatural significance. A line drawn from the animal's mouth to its heart is a pictorial device for showing the physical and spiritual vitality of living things, a convention that came from the Great Lakes region, which was previously the home of many Plains tribes, among them the Cheyenne.[51]

Red Cloud's vision included an anthropomorphic figure on the other side of the central tipi. This is the spirit buffalo transformed into Buffalo Man, and the forms reveal many parallels. Buffalo Man strides in the same direction, and he too moves just above the groundline. His body has human features except for the buffalo tail and feet; like the spirit buffalo, his breath or speech is graphically rendered to express vital energy. The four circular shapes around him are probably references to the sun or to different stages of the moon. Again, like the spirit buffalo, the body of Buffalo Man is decorated with images of the sun, the moon, and a star, which link him with the universe and also with the three buffalo tipis. In addition to the shared astral imagery, the fact that tipis were originally made of tanned buffalo hides deepens the metaphorical relationship that binds all these entities into a spiritual synthesis. The pipe held by Buffalo Man is significant because for Plains people it is the essential ceremonial tool of human prayer, the vehicle by which breath ascends to the heavens, and therefore a direct spiritual conduit between man and the spiritual beings visualized in the painting. In all areas of the Plains the pipe is still in daily use as a sacred instrument of prayer. Each year, in summer's full heat, men of the Plains participating in the Sun Dance still have their bodies painted with the images of sun, moon, stars, and anthropomorphic figures as part of their vow. These boldly drawn iconic images remain at the heart of Plains Indian religious life, a strong expression of the continuity and renewal of ceremonial culture.

## THE BIOGRAPHICAL ART TRADITION

The upper section of Red Cloud's muslin presents detailed depictions of three battles in which Red Cloud fought against the Cheyenne's traditional enemies, the Crow. These are biographical images, accounts of historical narrative, which describe the world in a very different way than the conventions of ceremonial art. The visual narrative form of biographical art was created by Plains men to represent important events in their lives as warriors. This tradition is hundreds of years old, as evidenced both by petroglyphs such as those at Writing-On-Stone and by the references to painted robes in the accounts of mid-sixteenth-century European travelers.[52] The earliest extant examples of Plains figurative painting on hide date only from the eighteenth century, but from these examples and from their petroglyph counterparts we can identify the characteristics of this early style, perceive how it relates to ceremonial art, and trace its subsequent changes over time to its expressions in contemporary Plains art.

As already observed, Plains ceremonial art depicts a variety of natural and composite forms directly related to the Indian's spiritual world view and religious rituals. For the most part these images are iconic and singular, with one central image providing a symbolic focus of devotion. Images of ceremonial art are also limited in detail and therefore in the amount of visual information they convey. Especially in its earliest phases, biographical art has many characteristics in common with ceremonial art. However, while ceremonial images have remained much the same over time, biographical ones have changed with social and historical circumstances, resulting in new objectives and methods of pictorial representation. Pre-1850

examples of biographical painting on hide garments, such as a rare warrior's shirt (cat. no. 144), reveal the close stylistic relationship between this genre and ceremonial art. Painted on the front of the shirt are two columns of abstract human figures, each a repetition of the same simplified outline drawing of an hourglass shape topped by a circle. This common Plains symbolic design is a visual metaphor whose roots lie in the relationship between the abstract hourglass form and the vertebra, a skeletal part that, like the skull, is associated with the essential structure of humans and animals and is therefore used to symbolize it.[53] Variations of this form are still used to honor the great Creator Spirit in the Man Above symbol of Cheyenne and Arapaho Sun Dance body painting.[54]

As in ceremonial art, the figures on this shirt are simply drawn and positioned frontally and centrally for maximum visual impact. Details are reduced to a few essential characteristics, and there are no articulated limbs or faces. The major pictorial difference between these early examples of biographical art and ceremonial art is that the images are organized in a serial order that implies a narrative sequence of historical events—the actions of the accomplished warrior who wore the shirt. Each hourglass figure represents an enemy warrior honorably encountered or killed in close combat, and the few details added to each figure provide information about the person's identity or the manner in which he was touched or killed. In the right-hand column of figures, for example, the second figure from the top wears a military society sash that indicates a man of high rank and valor. The second figure from the bottom in this row wears a buffalo-horn headdress, which is another specialized piece of military society gear that indicates personal achievement and status. The angled forms pointing to the chests of these figures are spears, wrapped in fur and decorated

with feathers. These were the weapons used to inflict the fatal wounds indicated by the red blood. The U-shaped marks to the left of the figures are conventional symbols for horse tracks. The mounted warrior next to the column of figures on the left represents the hero of this narrative, whose active relationship to the figures is shown by the dotted line that extends from his horse to the top of the shirt.

This visual symbolism is directly related to the oral narrative tradition that provided the fundamental means of religious, social, and historical communication. In his study of the Cheyenne, Grinnell noted that the Plains people conveyed information orally through conversation, storytelling, and speechmaking.[55] Warriors celebrated their own victories and those of their fellow tribesmen. Communicated in all three forms, their recitations became part of the people's social fabric. Credit and status were given to men who acted bravely, because the entire tribe depended on the protection these men provided in a hostile environment. Acts of bravery also established positive examples that helped prepare the younger men and boys for the defense of the people. Images of war honors were an integral part of this system of social communication. As a warrior described his particular achievements he would illustrate his story by pointing out the images painted on his special clothing or his tipi (fig. 21). In this way the visual and oral aspects of the narrative worked in tandem to make the events more dramatic and memorable to others. The visual notations of warrior biographical art were also used as a means of communication, such as messages concerning the movement of a camp or war party that were drawn on bone or wood and left at a site to be found and read by others, or bride price negotiations in which images of goods to be paid for a marriage were exchanged between the suitor and the bride's family.[56]

Fig. 21
Comanche and Kiowa Indians painting a buffalo robe, Oklahoma, ca. 1875. Photo by Jack Hiller, C. W. Kirk Collection, courtesy of the Oklahoma Historical Society, neg. no. 8820.

**Fig. 22**
Ute warrior and boy, Uintah Valley, Utah, 1871. The man wears an elaborate coiffure and has decorated his body and face with painted designs. The boy carries a large beaded bag over his shoulder. National Anthropological Archives, Smithsonian Institution.

Because the warrior depended on spiritual power and protection, any account of military exploits was by extension also a celebration of the validity and efficacy of those powers. Warrior biographical art therefore reflects the unity of the traditional cultural system in which the most significant activities of secular life are wholly integrated with the peoples' spiritual beliefs and ceremonial rituals.

Warfare was a fundamental aspect of Plains Indian life, and the warriors were also the hunters who provided the animals from which the women prepared the food, shelter, clothing, and other material needs of the family. War was also the principal way by which men increased their material wealth and status. Successful raids on the enemy were deeds of valor that proved a warrior's ability, but they were also one of the only means of acquiring the horses that had become crucial to the newly expanded life-style of the Plains tribes (fig. 22). Within a few generations of acquiring the horse, the Plains warriors earned the reputation of being the best light cavalry in the world. They were riders of extraordinary skill, renowned for their agility and endurance. By capturing horses a warrior obtained a vital commodity not only for himself but for the other members of the family and tribe, with whom such possessions were customarily shared. Because there existed a fundamental social imperative to share one's belongings, the more successful a man was as a hunter or warrior the more status he could achieve by supporting less fortunate members of the community.

The character of the Plains warrior combined physical attributes of strength, endurance, and agility with moral qualities of dependability and courage. To be fully successful, a Plains warrior also needed to have received a vision or a gift of some sort of war medicine—a ceremonial element of power, such as a shield or an amulet to aid him in battle. Although there were some set battles between large bodies of opposing warriors, most Plains warfare consisted of small-scale raids into enemy territory by small groups of men.[57] The usual strategy was to come upon the enemy unseen so that the riders could attack by surprise or capture the horses and escape. It was the solemn responsibility of the war-group leader to take care of the men who had joined his venture, and casualties were avoided whenever possible. Personal valor was the essence of this system of warfare, and each individual was eager to perform acts of bravery that would increase his status and reputation as a warrior. Each tribe had its own system for ranking the war honors, called "coups" after the French word meaning "hits" or "strikes."[58] More value was placed on the act of touching an enemy with an object or the bare hand than was placed on killing him. A warrior who came close enough to touch a rival and yet get away performed a deed more dangerous and skillful than killing from a distance.

Each Plains tribe had associations or societies to which most of the warriors belonged. Their purpose was to provide structural organization and a unifying spiritual focus to the warrior groups responsible for policing the camp and the hunt and for protecting the people in war. Although each tribe had its own ceremonies associated with each society, some societies, such as the Kit Fox and the Crazy Dogs, could be found in many tribes.[59]

The traditional military societies waned during the reservation period, especially with the passing of the last generation of men who had fought in the wars of the nineteenth century. However, Peter J. Powell shows us that the military society has remained an active force among the Northern Cheyenne. They still have traditional associations that perform rituals for soldiers who have returned from battle and also carry out other ceremonial responsibilities within the tribe. Among the Kiowa people of Oklahoma, the need for a tribal military association for veterans of World War II and Korea was answered by the organization of the Black Leggings Warrior Society, which performs annual tribal ceremonies as well as private ones. Their lodge is a version of the historic Little Bluff Tipi that has honored Kiowa warriors since the 1840s (cat. no. 208).

The shirt with the columns of hourglass figures is an example of an early style of pictorial representation. Another warrior's shirt exemplifies the next stage in an evolving stylistic development (cat. no. 145). The long body of the earlier shirt extended to the wearer's knees in a style associated with the first decades of the nineteenth century and before, whereas the later shirt is of a shorter and less tailored style that can be generally dated to the period between 1830 and the 1850s. The mode of figural representation has also been modified in the later garment. The hourglass symbol of the human figure is now a long, tapering rectangle with a head and articulated arms and legs. This increase in anatomical detail is reinforced by a more exact rendering of hairstyles, clothing, military society paraphernalia, and weapons to provide more information about the individual figures. The later shirt has twenty-one figures painted on the front and fourteen on the back. None of them seems to represent the victorious warrior, only the enemies he has killed or counted coup on in personal combat. Each figure stands for a specific action even though the action is not described. Since war deeds were publicly celebrated by the entire community, the accomplishments of each warrior were well known. The people would therefore have understood the references of the mnemonic devices painted on the warrior's garments, without needing full articulation of the action's sequential details. In later nineteenth-century biographical art, the painter often added a small image just above a drawing of an individual and often connected to him by a line. This was a rudimentary form of picture writing that represented the name of that man and provided positive identification.

The earliest known biographical hide robe is a famous example collected among the Mandan by Lewis and Clark in 1805 (cat. no. 147). This extraordinary work of art was painted by two or three Mandan warrior-artists to record "a battle of the Sioux and Ricaras against the Minetares and Mandans."[61] These artists had a figural style very similar to that on the shirt just discussed, but instead of standing alone, these figures describe engagements between two or more combatants. This large, finely tanned buffalo robe is divided horizontally by a thin strip of white, black, and orange porcupine quill embroidery. The quilled strip was a common type of decoration that often covered a center seam if the robe had been cut in half for easier handling during the tanning process. The strip also acts as a dividing line that creates two equal zones. A total of sixty-three figures are painted on the robe: thirty-three in the top half and thirty in the bottom. Though a definitive identification of the battle scenes is difficult without the accompanying oral narrative, relationships of scale and interaction enable us to differentiate the figures into possible combinations of twenty-two separate actions.

In some instances, such as in the upper right corner, a specific act or narrative relationship is expressed by a dotted line connecting a group of figures. Even more frequently we find one figure striking another with a weapon or some other object, a clear example of which can be observed above the dotted line in the upper right corner. The victorious warrior on the right sports a spiky coiffure, a single feather standing in the middle of his head, and a red and black

military society sash decorated with feathers that runs over his shoulder and across his chest. These sashes, worn only by the highest ranks of warriors, were testaments to the individual's proven abilities and reminders of his grave responsibility in battle.[62] The fact that this war leader also had strong spiritual powers is indicated by the imagery of his shield. He is depicted standing next to a long-haired warrior carrying a bow and arrows, and the barrel of the flintlock rifle the sash-wearer holds in his right hand is placed against his opponent's side as an indication that the latter has been touched or killed in personal combat.

Although Plains figure drawing became more naturalistic and detailed during the middle years of the nineteenth century, this basic style of pictorial narrative remained constant, a lasting visual convention that is still used in traditional forms of Plains Indian hide painting (cat. no. 206). Like all biographical Plains art until the later nineteenth century, these images of figures in action are represented without indications of groundline, horizon, or other elements of the specific setting. This allows the figures to float in a timeless world of indeterminate space, where past events are honored by present actions. As exemplars of a social and personal ideal, the images have almost reached the realm of the mythic as they are repeated and celebrated in the stories told by continuing generations. This Mandan pictorial robe not only is the earliest piece of its type, it is also one of the few examples of documented pre-1850s Plains art of any kind. Given that for over two hundred years there were many thousands of adult male warriors who could have produced or owned a painted shirt or robe, it is surprising that only a few dozen have survived to serve as examples of their type.

The role of the individual must be recognized in studies of American Indian and other non-European art traditions. Native American

art has too often been presented as anonymous, the product of a generic culture. This has been caused as much by a general lack of respect for the Indian as a person as by the paucity of documentation in museums and private collections. It is unfortunate that early amateur and professional collectors didn't think it important to ask who had made the objects they were taking away. This project addresses that problem by using works made by or owned by known individuals whenever possible.

We do know of a great Mandan warrior chief named Mato Tope (Four Bears), a man of many accomplishments and a gifted draftsman, who was an acknowledged leader of the Mandan tribe living around the Upper Missouri River in what is now North Dakota. In the early 1830s his village of large earth lodges was visited by two white artists trained in the European tradition. Their work effected a significant change in Mato Tope's own style and altered the production of later Plains art in general. George Catlin was an American painter whose years of travel among the Indian peoples of the Great Lakes, Prairie, and Plains provided extensive visual and written descriptions of their lives.[63] Karl Bodmer was a Swiss artist who accompanied Prince Maximilian zu Wied on a lengthy journey to the Upper Missouri to document more accurately the land, flora, fauna, and native peoples of this vast area.[64] Both artists knew Mato Tope, drew his portrait, and took a keen interest in the Mandan's own style of pictorial representation (cat. no. 149, fig. a). Both also gave the chief some of their working materials and in effect provided him with informal drawing lessons in their own more naturalistic style.[65]

Their impact can be clearly seen in one of the painted hide robes that Mato Tope produced for these non-Indian friends (cat. no. 148). A comparison of this painting and other work by Plains men of the same period reveals a new,

European-influenced attitude toward realism and detail. Whereas most Plains figurative painting of this time used simple, flat, faceless figures, Mato Tope has represented his warriors more fully, endowing them with facial features, rounded body forms, and a greater amount of graphic detail. Mato Tope also employed more narrative action to describe his war exploits, shifting from forms that simply imply some preceding event to its actual depiction. In the two sets of figures at the bottom of the robe, for example, Mato Tope can be seen on the left locked in mortal combat with a rival Cheyenne chief.[66]

This stylistic change became widespread as more examples of European art and graphic representation became available to Plains artists through trade and other types of contact. At the same time, nonbiographical robe designs, such as the feather circle pattern in the center of Mato Tope's robe, continued to remain fairly constant. The feather circle and the box and border design were more closely related to ceremonial images, and their iconic forms were maintained because they represented general cultural ideas rather than specific historical events. These designs, which were usually painted by women, can still be seen today in contemporary Plains hide painting and in the star quilt that replaced the buffalo robe as the Plains garment most closely associated with Indian cultural identity (cat. no. 309).

Expansion by the United States government over the course of the nineteenth century brought about the end of the free life of the Plains tribes. The "manifest destiny" of the United States called for the destruction of the Indian's power and freedom of movement over the land. The process of the Indians' genocidal extermination or removal to the confinement and dependency of the reservation, which began in the east in the seventeenth century, quickly moved westward over the prairie to the plains,

and by the late 1870s many bands had retired to reservation life.[67] The drastic economic and political pressures of the reservation brought not only hardship but severe problems of social and cultural continuity in Plains Indian life.

The fundamental changes in life-style necessitated by the reservation system also affected artists, who had to respond creatively to the loss of certain traditional subject matter as well as to new materials and new commercial markets for their work. By the 1860s Plains warrior-artists had begun to draw their exploits on the pages of ledger and roster books obtained from the whites by trade or war. The new small-scale rectilinear formats these provided brought about changes in representation, as did the influx of new media. Because the drawing surface was now small, a single exploit was shown on a page and the figures were allowed to fill the available space (fig. 23). Ink, pencils, watercolors, and paper were much easier to draw with than the stick and bone brushes used to paint on hide, and the result is a smoother, more easily controlled line that facilitated the creation of representational images and enabled artists to develop a more complicated and detailed graphic style. The availability of different materials coincided with a newly evolving function for biographical art. As the traditional culture of the Plains was curtailed and eventually forbidden, biographical art became a principal means of recalling and confirming cultural values and identity. Images were made by the men to document and celebrate the way things used to be, not so much as a nostalgic recollection of the past but as a crucial method of reaffirming the ancient and essential values of their society. The pictorial means of biographical art were also used to document the past in calendrical histories known as winter counts, in which one image recalling a particular event was used to signify

an entire year in the history of the tribe. Most of these historical calendars were kept by the Lakota, who used them to document events gong back over hundreds of years (cat. nos. 285, 286).

Today the tradition of representational art that celebrated the achievements of warriors is used to honor athletics and other areas of cultural pride and awareness. Sports, especially running and basketball, have become areas of achievement identified with tribal, family, and personal pride. Tournaments and running events are organized to honor programs that support Indian cultural pride and health. Participating in and winning these contests is regarded as an honor and is often celebrated by a new expression of biographical art—the T-shirt. During a visit with friends on the Wind River Reservation, one of the daughters of the family was wearing a T-shirt bearing a traditional representational image of a dancer and a buffalo along with the name and date of the event. When I admired the shirt and asked if I could get one, she replied proudly that you could not buy this shirt, you had to earn it.

## THE MODERN TRADITIONS OF PLAINS ART

The reservation separated the Indians from their traditional means of life support and replaced it with a system of public assistance that quickly and deliberately made the Plains tribes dependent on the government for food, clothing, and other life necessities. This economic situation necessitated developing new sources of income. The production of traditional Indian arts for sale to whites not only filled an economic need, it also stimulated the creation of many new types of Plains representational images in media ranging from drawings to beadwork (fig. 24). In pre-

**Fig. 23**
Richard Wooden Leg drawing in a ledger book, Cheyenne, Montana, ca. 1928. Photo by Thomas Marquis.

reservation times, biographical art was limited to representations of the two most important aspects of a warrior's life: personal combat and the capturing of enemy horses. The changing environment of the early reservation period from the late 1870s through the early years of the twentieth century called for a pictorial system capable of depicting the full range of traditional Plains Indian existence. Scenes of war honors were still the most popular category of images (cat. nos. 171–176), but to these were now added visual descriptions of the entire life of the camp. These included vital activities such as the hunting and preparation of animals, especially the buffalo that had all but disappeared from the Plains by the late 1870s (cat. no. 236), and ceremonies such as the Hot Dance (fig. 25) and the Sun Dance (cat. no. 115). Plains male artists also now drew images of children at play (cat. no. 258), couples courting, and women cooking (cat. no. 239).

This expansion of subject matter was accompanied by a further change in traditional artistic representation. By the mid-1870s, Kiowa artists such as Wohaw had absorbed enough of the European pictorial method to incorporate elements of landscape and perspective that placed figures within a naturalistic context (cat. nos. 237–239). People and animals now moved in an approximation of real space and time instead of floating in the featureless environment of a timeless world where they could be brought to life only by the revivifying descriptions of oral narrative. These new images were made for a new, foreign audience that lacked the cultural information needed to appreciate and understand themes depicted in the old ways.

The new commercial market and the vicissitudes of social change also led to an expansion of the variety of media and the pool of artists. Warriors who had been captured and sent east to prison and "reeducation" were encouraged to

Fig. 24
A display of Lakota beadwork and quilts produced for sale, Fort Yates, North Dakota, ca. 1915. Among the items are commercial bags covered in pictorial beadwork depicting scenes that vary from traditional courtship to cowboys, from George Washington to Custer's Last Stand. Photo by B. Fiske. State Historical Society of North Dakota.

Fig. 25
Crow men participating in a Hot Dance, Crow Reservation, Montana, 1898. The dancers wear a variety of headdresses, bustles, and ornaments and carry military society insignia and other objects, including a horse effigy baton in the right foreground. Montana Historical Society, Helena.

draw as a rehabilitation activity that also provided them with some extra income. When some of them went on to study at the Hampton Institute, their work was soon extended from drawings on paper representing their new environment to images painted on souvenir objects such as ceramics and even fans (cat. nos. 243, 266). Plains women who had previously created decorated buffalo hides for intertribal trade[68] now contributed to the reservation economy with an increased production of beadwork. Because the market offered higher prices for work with recognizable images, women of many Plains tribes, especially the Lakota, began to produce pictorial beadwork representing the most popular themes of male art— images of mounted warriors wearing feather headdresses. Some pieces of pictorial beadwork, however, such as dresses with scenes of combat (cat. no. 201) were made and worn by Indian women in a tradition of honoring husbands and other male family members who had distinguished themselves in battle. But objects like the pictorial tobacco bags and vests made by Lakota women from the turn of the century to the 1920s were primarily for the Euro-American market, where they were sought after as souvenirs of trips west or as nostalgic mementos of a clichéd, bygone age.

Plains Indian art has continued to change as Plains people become more integrated into the larger cultural environment of the United States. Since the 1920s, many Plains men and women have attended art schools that provided them with even more varied ways of expressing their traditional values. Artists of the Kiowa school that developed in Oklahoma during the 1940s used a very stylized system of drawing to portray a romanticized vision of the past.[69] From these roots have come modern Plains artists with unique personal styles that set an example for creative freedom in succeeding generations. The best known of these innovators is the Lakota artist Oscar Howe, whose artistic achievements

have been honored by both the Indian and the non-Indian communities for their power, sincerity, and beauty. In paintings such as *Calling on Wakan Tanka* of 1967 (cat. no. 142), Howe pays homage to the traditional spiritual foundation of Plains Indian life with an image of prayer that binds the figures into the world around them. By linking people and nature through form and color, Howe expresses the sense of spiritual unity that has always been the fundamental cohesive power of Plains culture.

Today most reservations suffer from an 80 to 85 percent unemployment rate because jobs are not available in or near these isolated locations. As Oscar Howe observed in 1946, "I see so much of the mismanagement and treatment of my people. It makes me cry inside to look at these poor people. My father died there about three years ago in a little shack, my two brothers are still living there in shacks, never enough to eat, never enough clothing, treated as second class citizens. This is one of the reasons I have tried to keep the fine ways and culture of my forefathers alive. But one could easily turn to become a social protest painter. I only hope the Art World will not be one more contributor to holding us in chains."[70]

Sales of art have been an important source of income for Plains Indian men and women since the beginning of the reservation period in the late nineteenth century. Contemporary Plains Indian art has been supported by a number of museums and galleries that provide opportunities for exhibition and sale. Continuing efforts such as the annual exhibition organized by Brother Simon at the Red Cloud Center on the Pine Ridge Reservation and the valuable series of exhibitions and publications presented by the Indian Arts and Crafts Board at the Sioux Indian Museum and Craft Center in Rapid City, South Dakota, offer an excellent forum for display and education. Many Plains artists also show their work at exhibitions organized in con-

junction with powwows held throughout the West in the spring and summer. And in cities throughout the country Indian art expositions have become popular events; hundreds of artists rent booths for exhibiting and selling their work.

Contemporary Plains artists represented in this exhibition and catalogue continue to find new means to depict the history, social pressures, and proud traditions of the Plains Indian people. In the painting *Nightshield*, Robert Penn, who studied with Oscar Howe, uses modern media to express traditional forms and values, of both ceremonial and biographical art, in the form of the shield and the images of warriors riding in the background (cat. no. 4). "As a Native American living in modern society," writes Penn, "I have attempted with my paintings to use contemporary forms to express cultural themes. As an artist it is my goal to expand and explore new ways of expressing the duality of the world through my art. . . . Abstraction of symbols and themes can reinterpret and integrate the modern world as seen from an Indian viewpoint without strict adherence to traditional artforms, and can transcend both worlds to become contemporary art as well as cultural statement."[71]

This attitude of respectfully using past traditions as an artistic theme as well as a cultural statement is fundamental in contemporary Plains art of all types, from beadwork and star quilts to paintings and sculpture (cat. nos. 33, 276, 302, 308). The Plains men and women who work as artists today continue an ancient and honored tradition that celebrates the history and spiritual values of their people.

1. Cyrus Byington, *A Dictionary of the Choctaw Language*, Smithsonian Institution, Bureau of American Ethnology Bulletin 46 (Washington, D.C., 1915), p. 355.

2. G. B. Grinnell, *The Cheyenne Indians* (New Haven, Conn.: Yale University Press, 1923), 2:148.

3. J. M. Cooper, *The Gros Ventres of Montana* (Washington, D.C.: Catholic University of America Press, 1953), pp. 20–21.

4. Personal communication, G. Horse Capture, Jr., Fort Belknap Reservation, October 1991.

5. Cooper, *Gros Ventres*, pp. 418–19.

6. J. Teit, "The Salishan Tribes of the Western Plateaus," Smithsonian Institution, 45th Annual Report of the Bureau of American Ethnology (Washington, D.C., 1930), pp. 23–396.

7. J. D. Keyser, "A Lexicon for Historic Plains Indian Rock Art: Increasing Interpretive Potential," *Plains Anthropologist* 32, no. 115 (1987): 43–71.

8. D. Gebhard, *The Rock Art of Dinwoody Wyoming* (Santa Barbara: University of California Art Galleries, 1969), p. 22.

9. Ibid., pp. 11–12.

10. P. J. Powell, *People of the Sacred Mountain: A History of the Northern Cheyenne Chiefs and Warrior Societies, 1830–1879* (New York: Harper and Row, 1981), p. 120.

11. E. M. Maurer, *The Native American Heritage: A Survey of North American Indian Art* (Chicago: Art Institute of Chicago, 1977), nos. 125, 155, 440.

12. Powell, *People of the Sacred Mountain*, p. 148.

13. E. M. Maurer, "Dada and Surrealism," in *Primitivism and Twentieth Century Art*, ed. William Rubin (New York: Museum of Modern Art, 1984), pp. 535–93.

14. J. D. Keyser, *The Central Montana Rock Abstract Art Style*, British Columbia Provincial Museum, Heritage Record no. 8 (Vancouver, 1979), p. 10.

15. Ibid., pp. 10–12.

16. J. D. Keyser, "A Shoshonean Origin for the Plains Shield Bearing Warrior," *Plains Anthropologist* 20, no. 69 (1975): 207–15.

17. Ibid., pp. 211–13.

18. J. D. Keyser, "Writing-On-Stone: Rock Art on the Northwestern Plains," *Canadian Journal of Archaeology*, no. 1 (1977): 55–58.

19. Ibid., pp. 19–23.

20. Grinnell, *Cheyenne Indians* 2:96–97.

21. Ibid., p. 97.

22. V. Barnouw, *Wisconsin Chippewa Myths and Tales* (Madison: University of Wisconsin Press, 1977), pp. 134–37.

23. S. H. Dewdney and K. E. Kidd, *Indian Rock Paintings of the Great Lakes* (Toronto: University of Toronto Press, 1967), pp. 36, 83.

24. Ibid., pp. 113, 118, 119, 125. See also Maurer, *Native American Heritage*, no. 122.

25. N. Feder, *Two Hundred Years of North American Indian Art* (New York: Praeger Publishers in association with the Whitney Museum of American Art, 1971), nos. 81, 87, 100, VI.

26. J. C. Ewers, *Plains Indian Sculpture: A Traditional Art from America's Heartland* (Washington, D.C.: Smithsonian Institution Press, 1986), pp. 126–28.

27. E. M. Maurer, *Representational and Symbolic Forms in Great Lakes–Area Wooden Sculpture* (Detroit: Detroit Institute of Arts, 1986).

28. Grinnell, *Cheyenne Indians* 1:171.

29. D. S. Brose, *Ancient Art of the American Woodland Indians* (New York: Harry N. Abrams, 1985).

30. D. Dunn, *American Indian Painting of the Southwest and Plains Area* (Albuquerque: University of New Mexico Press, 1968), pp. 124–31.

31. Ibid., p. 128.

32. G. Mallery, *Picture-Writing of the American Indians* (1893; reprint, New York: Dover Books, 1972).

33. Ibid., pp. 768–75.

34. Ibid., p. 2a.

35. Ibid., p. 774.

36. E. Vatter, *Historienmalerei und heraldische Bilderschrift der Nordamerikanischen Präriestamme* (Frankfurt am Main: Ipek, 1927).

37. J. C. Ewers, *Plains Indian Painting: A Description of an Aboriginal American Art* (Palo Alto, Calif.: Stanford University Press, 1939).

38. Dunn, *American Indian Painting*; J. J. Brody, *Indian Painters and White Patrons* (Albuquerque: University of New Mexico Press, 1971).

39. A. L. Kroeber, "The Arapaho," *Bulletin of the American Museum of Natural History* 18, pt. 1 (1902).

40. Maurer, *Native American Heritage*, no. 191.

41. C. Wissler, "Some Protective Designs of the Dakota" (1907), *Anthropological Papers of the American Museum of Natural History* 1, pt. 2, intro.

42. G. A. Dorsey, *The Cheyenne*, Field Museum Anthropological Series, vol. 9 (Chicago, 1905), p. 49.

43. R. Erdoes and A. Ortiz, *American Indian Myths and Legends* (New York: Pantheon Books, 1984), pp. 93–95.

44. J. G. Neihardt, ed., *Black Elk Speaks* (New York: William Morrow and Co., 1932), p. 143.

45. F. Densmore, *Teton Sioux Music*, Smithsonian Institution, Bureau of American Ethnology Bulletin 61 (Washington, D.C., 1918), no. 87.

46. Grinnell, *Cheyenne Indians* 1:264, 266, 267.

47. R. H. Lowie, "Societies of the Hidatsa and Mandan Indians" (1913), *Anthropological Papers of the Merican Museum of Natural History* 11, pt. 1:291–93 346–47.

48. J. Mooney, *The Ghost-Dance Religion and the Sioux Outbreak of 1890* (1896; reprint, Chicago: University of Chicago Press, 1965), pp. 205, 225.

49. M. W. Beckwith, "Mythology of the Oglala Dakota," *Journal of American Folklore* 43, no. 170 (1930): 429.

50. Maurer, *Native American Heritage*, no. 200c.

51. Ibid., nos. 69, 77, 122, 141.

52. Dunn, *American Indian Painting*, p. 145.

53. The metaphorical and visual relationships between the hourglass figure and a vertebra were confirmed by an Oglala woman who grew up on Pine Ridge Agency, in an interview in 1991. This reference is also made in the parfleche painting.

54. A. L. Kroeber, *The Arapaho Sun Dance* (New York: American Museum of Natural History, 1907), p. 164.

55. G. B. Grinnell, *By Cheyenne Campfires* (New Haven, Conn.: Yale University Press, 1926), p. xxiii.

56. K. D. Petersen, *Plains Indian Art from Fort Marion* (Norman: University of Oklahoma Press, 1971), p. 27.

57. Grinnell, *Cheyenne Indians* 2:29–36; C. Taylor, *The Warriors of the Plains* (New York: Arco Publishing Co., 1975); F. R. Secoy, *Changing Military Patterns on the Great Plains* (Seattle: University of Washington Press, 1953).

58. B. Mishkin, *Rank and Warfare among the Plains Indians* (Seattle: University of Washington Press, 1940).

59. C. Wissler, ed., *Societies of the Plains Indians*, Anthropological Papers of the American Museum of Natural History 11 (1916): 14–23, 155–62, 191–95, 253–58, 280–82, 296–301, 306–8.

60. Powell, *People of the Sacred Mountain*, p. 1285.

61. R. G. Thwaites, ed., *Original Journals of the Lewis and Clark Expedition, 1804–1806* (Cleveland, 1904), p. 281.

62. Lowie, *Hidatsa*, pp. 195–97.

63. G. Catlin, *Letters and Notes on the Manners, Customs, and Conditions of North American Indians* (London, 1844).

64. D. Thomas and K. Ronnefeldt, *People of the First Man* (New York: E. P. Dutton and Co., 1976).

65. J. C. Ewers, *Early White Influence upon Plains Indian Painting: George Catlin and Carl Bodmer among the Mandan, 1832–34* (Washington, D.C.: Smithsonian Institution, 1957).

66. Thomas and Ronnefeldt, *People*, pp. 220–21.

67. G. Hyde, *Red Cloud's Folk: A History of the Oglala Sioux Indians* (Norman: University of Oklahoma Press, 1975).

68. J. Jablow, *The Cheyenne in Plains Indian Trade Relations* (Seattle: University of Washington Press, 1954), pp. 41–46.

69. Dunn, *American Indian Painting*, p. 145.

70. F. Dockstader, *Oscar Howe* (Tulsa, Okla.: Thomas Gilcrease Museum Association, 1982), p. 19.

71. Correspondence with author, 1992.

# The Social Construction of Plains Art, 1875-1915 Louise Lincoln

The great majority of the objects in this exhibition and book were made during the period between the 1870s, when many Plains Indian peoples were initially confined to reservations, and World War I. In this the project is not unique; the same pattern can be seen in most collections of Plains material, both public and private. There are many reasons for this chronological distribution, the most obvious being the intensive collecting activities of turn-of-the-century white scholars and amateurs who believed that traditional ways of life were being eradicated and felt a zealous obligation to preserve material culture. Yet because this temporal emphasis is so common, it is easy to take the part for the whole, easy to forget that these objects do not represent Plains culture in toto but belong to and speak about a very specific period of history.

Without question, the central issue and greatest problem in the lives of Plains peoples of the time was to sort out what their proper relation to the Euro-American world should be. This was a time of social turbulence and severe economic stress—the era of the Battle of the Little Big Horn and the Wounded Knee massacre; of treaties made and abrogated; of forcible incarceration in boarding schools and prisons; of territorial loss and the imposition of what amounted to colonial rule.[1] Indian peoples' identity, even their existence, was challenged on every front. Missionaries and United States government agents worked together to suppress the practice of traditional religion and to eradicate traditional culture, language, and ways of thought, while Indian people struggled to survive, to resist further encroachment, and to maintain what they could of the past. One has only to look at period photographs of people, showing the uneasy mix of indigenous and imported dress, hairstyle, and deportment, to understand that this struggle over identity permeated every aspect of their lives, from the spiritual to the banal (fig. 1).

Within a rather short period in the middle of the nineteenth century, a trickle of white traders, missionaries, and adventurers in the Plains region had become a flood of settlers from the east. In the early period of the fur trade whites had found it necessary to maintain good relationships with Native Americans, whose assistance was essential to their success.[2] Indian men hunted and trapped the fur-bearing animals whose pelts were in such high demand in Europe; Indian women tanned the hides. Together they functioned as intermediaries or middlemen for the traders, converting a natural resource into an exchange commodity. The next wave of settlers from the east, however, expected to make their living directly from the land,

following the European-derived model of isolated farmsteads managed by relatively small family units, producing crops, fodder, and livestock. There was no role for Indian people here, and their use of land for their own sustenance constituted an obstacle to white expansion. A succession of treaties restricted Plains peoples to ever-smaller territories, eroding older patterns of subsistence as land tenure was exchanged for payments of annuity goods (rationed textiles, clothing, staple foods, and fresh meat provided by the United States government) (fig 2). As struggles over access to land increased, a spectrum of opinion developed among whites, from the few who championed Indian people's rights to those who openly advocated genocide.[3] The United States government pursued a mixed course, interspersing military campaigns with notably unsuccessful attempts to remake Plains people into farmers.

Similarly, Native Americans held a broad range of views that evolved with time and circumstance. In the early period, contact with whites presented attractive opportunities to acquire goods and technology and to contract economic and military alliances.[4] The relationship became less advantageous and more problematic over time. Indian people became more dependent on white-produced goods, abandoning their own means of production and becoming vulnerable to the considerable fluctuations in quality and quantity of annuities.

Perhaps the most profound change came in the nature of their relationship to the land. The transition from hunting for subsistence to hunting in order to accumulate goods for trade certainly modified Indian peoples' attitude toward the land and toward animals,[5] but in treaty negotiations land ultimately became something to be given up in exchange for money and goods, an exchange they rightly perceived as not only economically disadvanta-

geous, but also culturally destructive. The territory that whites designated as reservations was often the least exploitable and thus proved frustrating for those families who at the government's urging attempted farming or herding. It was—and is—extremely difficult for people on reservations to make a living independent of annuity payments and other forms of assistance.

In social terms, the change wrought by the shift from hunting to reservation life was no less drastic. The traditional spiritual and emotional ties to the land were severed. A pattern of living on separate land allotments in isolated family units replaced the community life of tipi or earth lodge villages (figs. 3 and 4). Traditional gender relations were also disrupted. In earlier times men and women had worked in separate and complementary spheres. Men specialized in the high-risk pursuits of hunting and warfare, while women directed domestic life, producing and controlling the distribution of most kinds of material goods. In the reservation period men's warfare was abolished and their hunting curtailed, while more and more goods were obtained from the outside. Thus social roles and relations were in flux, as men and women individually and collectively sought to find new and appropriate ways of interacting.

As their land and supply of game animals vanished, Plains people deployed a variety of strategies to cope with rapid change, from passive resistance and selective adoption of Euro-American cultural forms to armed warfare. Goods—including the kinds of objects in this exhibition and catalogue—came to be used in, and in some instances to represent, many of those strategies. These objects were not mute tokens of human transactions. Many of them can be seen to comment on the nature of Indian-white relations: they bear a readable social meaning. A shield or a drawing or a pair of moccasins was not simply an object of practical utility. It also found use as a gift, as an indicator of reciprocal obligation, as a means of participating in the external economy—that is, it had an aspect (often overlooked) of social or relational utility. It may also have carried, as do the objects in this exhibition, a more literal kind of iconographic representation. At the nexus of social utility, economic function, and iconographic content, one may discern the social meaning of a given object. And when objects are examined in this light, the external context seems pervasive, influencing not only objects made for external consumption, but objects made for use within Plains society as well.

Among the most explicit comments on the difficulty of coping with Euro-American–imposed change is an iconic drawing produced by a Kiowa artist known as Wohaw in a notebook of drawings he made while incarcerated at Fort Marion, Florida, around 1875–78. One of the best-known examples of the genre, Wohaw's picture (cat. no. 141) shows a man, wearing a traditional dance skirt, his hair unbound, flanked by a buffalo and a bull. His arms extend a pipe to each animal, and they in turn blow clouds signifying power toward him. Beside the buffalo is a small tipi; beside the bull is a frame building, perhaps a church, set by a plowed field. Widely interpreted as a commentary on the situation of Indian peoples between two worlds,[6] this drawing has been minutely dissected by white art historians seeking to resolve its intended meaning. Does the turn of the figure's head toward the bull signify an acceptance of new ways in the future? Or does the position of the bison at his right hand suggest a preferred status? Is there meaning in the different colors of the two pipes and power clouds? In the astral images? In his clothing?

Wohaw may have intended his drawing to be autobiographical. "Wohaw," the name by which he was known at Fort Marion, is pen-

Fig. 1
Children at Little White River Indian School, 1888. Nebraska State Historical Society, John Anderson Collection.

Fig. 2
Sioux Indians receiving their beef rations, Rosebud Reservation, South Dakota, 1893. Nebraska State Historical Society, John Anderson Collection.

Fig. 3
Earth lodge village, 1871.
Photo by William Henry
Jackson. National
Anthropological Archives,
Smithsonian Institution.

Fig. 4
Red Cloud's house, Pine
Ridge, South Dakota.
Nebraska State Historical
Society.

ciled over the head of the central figure,[7] and his own situation when the drawing was made was certainly that of a person between two worlds. Arrested and jailed for involvement in the murder of several settlers in the Oklahoma territory, Wohaw was transported to a Florida prison fort along with seventy-one other Kiowa, Cheyenne, Arapaho, and Comanche men to serve a three-year sentence. The commandant, Captain Richard Pratt, subjected the prisoners to rigorous military discipline and an aggressive campaign of assimilation, from haircuts and military uniforms to English classes and religious training. Yet in his zeal to "convert" his charges, he allowed them unusual latitude in their contacts with white St. Augustine residents and encouraged the men to produce drawings and other objects that they could sell to tourists to earn spending money. Two albums by Wohaw, now in the Missouri Historical Society, were brought back from Florida by a St. Louis couple after their honeymoon.[8]

Thus Wohaw clearly knew who his intended audience was: Captain Pratt, and beyond him a wider audience of whites in St. Augustine who were interested, perhaps even sympathetic. Presumably Wohaw, like other Fort Marion prisoners, had frequent contact with visitors to the fort and with residents and tourists in town (fig. 5). He doubtless perceived both their confident assumption of superiority and their simultaneous fascination with the exotic. It is hard to imagine, reading Captain Pratt's accounts of the time at Fort Marion, that Wohaw did not also know the outcome that Pratt and others desired: total assimilation ("In order to save the man we must kill the Indian," Pratt wrote).[9] Yet the drawing neither endorses this idea nor rejects it. All analysis to the contrary, the artist's view remains elusive, and the central figure remains impassive, stretched between two worlds.

I want to suggest that this represents neither a failure of expression nor a failure of nerve on Wohaw's part, but rather is a strategic exercise in directing certain messages to known audiences. The ambiguity of the image is deliberate. It claims a parallelism and equality between the two worlds that Pratt would surely have denied,[10] yet does so in terms that are calculated to evoke both respect and sympathy. His use of the pipe image and traditional dress roots the picture in a Kiowa context, while the solitary figure emphasizes the difficult situation of an individual in Wohaw's position. Wohaw does not avoid the issue: he lays out the white way, symbolized by the bull, church, and tilled field, clearly. But perhaps because of personal integrity, and perhaps because fellow prisoners at Fort Marion constituted a secondary audience whose good opinion he valued, Wohaw does not capitulate. In its deliberate and strategic ambiguity, the drawing allows varying interpretations of multiple messages.

As this example suggests, the making of any object engenders dialogues, however silent or unconscious, between the maker and the intended audiences. Anticipated reactions and interpretations shape the process of creation itself and are answered through negotiation and modification of the product. This is true whether the audience is cohesive or diffuse, although the dialogue is more complicated when it involves multiple audiences. Adopting a form he knows will be acceptable to his consumers, Wohaw shapes the content of this drawing, and of the book as a whole, to conform to the expectations of whites, without losing the opportunity to inject, through a bit of Victorian pathos, an insistence on respect.

Another example we know to have been made for an outside audience may have grown out of a more straightforward attempt to meet the expectations of an outside audience. Here the strategy is not one of ambiguity but rather an acknowledgement of both market demand and the limited knowledge of consumers. An elk-hide painting by a Wind River Shoshone man named Cadzi Cody, now in the Minneapolis Institute of Arts, is one of several dozen known by the same hand and of similar subject matter (cat. no. 248). Cody apparently produced many such images to sell or give to whites; all of them are characterized by buffaloes, horses, and human figures scattered evenly over the surface. (The scale of the figures is also remarkably uniform, so much so that the artist appears to have used a stencil to produce the buffalo torsos.) A number of them, including the Minneapolis example, represent successive stages of the Sun Dance. On the periphery the ceremonial buffalo hunt takes place, followed by careful butchering of the carcass. At the center dancers surround the Sacred Tree, the buffalo head secured in its forked branches.

But here we find an anomaly. Rather than wearing traditional Sun Dance skirts, the men are dressed as Wolf Dancers—in other words, as participants in a less sacred performance. Present-day Wind River Shoshone noted but did not interpret the discrepancy.[11] The United States government had banned the Sun Dance during the time Cadzi Cody likely made these paintings in the late 1880s or 1890s, yet he surely would have seen earlier performances or even secret performances, so it is unlikely to be a mistake of ignorance. Did he recostume his figures in the more flamboyant dress of Wolf Dancers to satisfy white stereotypes of Indian life? Is he camouflaging the real (and forbidden) subject matter from white authorities? Did he deliberately alter this (and other) details to preserve the sacredness of the event for Shoshone people? In fact, he seems to have arrived at his preferred iconography in a completely different way. As Joseph Horse Capture's research has

Fig. 5
Fort Marion prisoners dancing for tourists, 1875–77. From *A Cheyenne Sketchbook*, by Cohoe. Copyright © 1964 by the University of Oklahoma Press.

shown, Cadzi Cody's early paintings were rather generic representations of buffalo hunt scenes and Wolf Dance performances, but the banning of the Sun Dance stimulated whites' awareness and curiosity to such a degree that the painter found it advantageous to replace the central flagpole with a Sacred Tree, leaving other elements unchanged. Incorporating a recognizable symbol of an event so "dangerous" it had to be outlawed, Cadzi Cody also acknowledged that strict accuracy was less important than images that emphasized otherness.

Men were not the only producers of goods for outside consumption. In the buffalo days women had been the processors of pelts and hides for trade; in reservation days as well it was primarily the fruits of their labor that provided access to the outside economy. Women's needlework, chiefly beading and quilling, constituted the majority of "export" goods made in the reservation period.[12] To satisfy external demand, much of it was pictorial, a change from earlier patterns of artistic production in which representational imagery was largely made by men, and women produced geometric abstractions. A beaded vest from a private collection (cat. no. 203) provides an excellent example of women's reservation-period work. The image of the mounted warrior derives from the conventions of men's narrative style, here translated into the difficult (and tedious) medium of beads. As David Penney demonstrates elsewhere in this catalogue, this representation of horse and rider became in the reservation period a generalized image of Indian identity.

The three examples discussed above are modified forms, produced to reach an outside audience. The vest is an item of Euro-American men's clothing, literally transformed by its decorative component, and worn by Indians and whites alike. The elk hide—scraped, tanned, and painted with a nonspecific event of the past—

was not intended to be worn, as were its antecedents that advertised specific heroic episodes of an individual man's life. It was made to be sold or traded to a white person, who would in all probability have nailed it to a wall. Similarly, books of drawings applied a traditional style of men's graphic art to a new form. While there is evidence for use of drawing books among Plains peoples,[13] most, including the Fort Marion examples, were made for the outside market, where they functioned mainly as curios.

Whites sought out works that were representational (perhaps precisely because their meaning seemed transparent!) and in which the representation corresponded to their own conscious or unconscious assumptions about Indians. They also sought out media that corresponded in some way to categories for images in Euro-American material life of the late nineteenth century: things that could be hung on the wall or displayed as an album in the parlor. From the maker's point of view, however, such objects were not "paintings" or "drawings" or items of clothing but primarily a means of entering the external economy. They were a response to perceived market demand, a strategic economic product. But because they had iconographic content, they also became a means of addressing a white audience, of conveying both direct and subtle messages, and of affecting the nature of the relation.[14] They were, in short, social in their use and meaning.

If the most pressing and controversial problem for Indian people of the early reservation period was indeed the nature of their relation to whites, as I have suggested, it is easy enough to see how objects exchanged between the two groups might both reflect and shape that social tension. But does the issue manifest itself as well in objects made for use within Plains society? A Lakota cradle cover with elab-

orate beadwork decoration (cat. no. 287) offers a particularly interesting example.

Cradleboards were a standard item of traditional Plains household equipment, unlike the introduced or modified objects discussed above. Usually they were made and decorated by relatives of a pregnant woman, often her sister, and their giving represented family bonds of affection and responsibility. They were thus unlikely to be made for an outside market, although they might be sold or disposed of after use. A beaded cradleboard now in the American Museum of Natural History shows indeterminate signs of use and highly unusual iconography. At the top of the hood two figures in Euro-American dress are joined in a handclasp. Large inscriptions identify one as "Red Cloud" and the other as "Genl. Smith." Smith is further distinguished by his short yellow hair, heeled boots, and the addition of epaulets and a stripe on his pants, while Red Cloud has longer hair and wears colorful moccasins. In his left hand each man holds an American flag and the lead rope of a spotted horse. Behind Red Cloud's horse and filling the side panel of the cover are figures of two men bearing flags, one in Euro-American dress and moccasins, the second in shirt, leggings, and a full-length feather bonnet. On the other side General Smith's followers are dressed similarly, except that the first wears heeled boots.

This scene is remarkable both for the parallel construction of its imagery and for its use of minute but significant distinctions. Red Cloud and General Smith are dressed similarly, their retinues are nearly identical, and American flags abound. Yet through details of dress, the artist has been at pains to distinguish whites and Indians. And by identifying the principal figures by name, she has further emphasized the particular nature of this encounter between two military men.

**Fig. 7**
Portrait of John E. Smith.
National Archives photo
no. 111-BA-886.

Red Cloud, an Oglala leader and by far the more significant of the two, is a complex figure (fig. 6). A formidable warrior, he counted eighty coups in military action against Pawnees, Crows, and other neighboring enemies. In the 1860s he played a prominent role in the resistance to white settlement. Yet Red Cloud was a signatory to the controversial treaty of 1868, by which the United States government understood the Lakota to accept confinement to reservation lands. Lakota groups, including those of Red Cloud and the Sicangu leader Spotted Tail, refused to move thereafter, provoking the army to sporadic military action. In 1870 Red Cloud and Spotted Tail were invited to Washington, D.C., to confer with the president and other government officials. Red Cloud and his delegation were escorted on the journey by Colonel John E. Smith of the United States Army (fig. 7),[15] who was under instructions to attend to their needs and wishes with care and respect and to ensure their safe passage through the western regions where hatred of Indians was so rampant that lynching was a real possibility.

In Washington, discussions were not fruitful. Red Cloud stunned the government negotiators by declaring that the 1868 treaty had never been fully explained to him before he touched the pen, and was therefore meaningless. Ultimately both sides struck a compromise by which the bands of Red Cloud and Spotted Tail would each be settled in new, unspecified reservation land. Red Cloud's greater victory was one of public relations, however. The press covered his visit closely and for the most part sympathetically, and on a side trip to New York he made a spectacular public speech to a vast, cheering crowd of humanitarian reformers.

On his return home, by contrast, his position among Oglala people was in decline. Red Cloud had always been somewhat controversial as a leader, and in the years following,

the more militant factions, now led by Sitting Bull, overshadowed him. After their disastrous loss at the Battle of the Little Big Horn in 1876, the government forced nontreaty Indians onto reservation land. Red Cloud's band was disarmed and their horses, more than seven hundred, were taken away, a humiliation Red Cloud felt strongly.[16]

Curiously, horses had formed a sort of subtheme during Red Cloud's trip east. In Washington, Spotted Tail's delegation, which had arrived earlier, was mounted on horses presented as gifts by the government; Red Cloud's delegation by contrast was transported in carriages, which they deemed an insult.[17] Contemporary sources make it clear that the failure to treat the two delegations equally, particularly with regard to horses, remained a sore point. At his final meeting with the secretary of the interior, Red Cloud's parting shot was a reminder of this slight: "I want good horses, the same as you gave to Spotted Tail. I am not mad with you. I have got a better heart. I am going home. If you will not give me horses, very well."[18]

Red Cloud asked for seventeen horses, one for each of the men in his party, but the secretary refused to commit himself, instead speaking vaguely of "gifts." Fearing that the peace agreement would founder on the government's tactlessness, a group of humanitarian citizens intervened and offered to buy the horses privately. After prolonged discussions the secretary capitulated and instructed Colonel Smith to outfit the party with horses and equipment on their way home, and they made the last leg of their journey home in proper style.

The narrative scene on the cradle cover likely represents the moment of presentation, a triumph of sorts for Red Cloud. Horses were not merely a preferred means of transportation for Plains people. As the use of this story as a subject for beadwork suggests, horses and horse

exchange carried enormous symbolic significance; David Penney's essay elsewhere in this book elucidates their importance as wealth and as representations of male power. Gifts of horses were a means of forging political and social alliances; they were used as bridewealth, as wergild, and as honor gifts within families. Capturing horses from an enemy was a supreme assertion of honor and power. At the moment of presentation, Colonel Smith tried to assert that the horses were "merely a token of good will" and "not in consideration of any treaty made, or hereafter to be made."[19] But Red Cloud certainly saw the matter differently: as honor gift, as restitution for killing, as partial compensation for numerous affronts. The horses were a concession, won with difficulty through hard negotiation, and symbolic as well of his (compromise) victory with regard to territory.

At first glance this incident of personal history is perhaps a surprising subject for baby cradle decoration.[20] The motif of horses appears on other Lakota cradleboards, most often as a repeating decorative pattern (see cat. no. 84). In such uses horses seem to be a straightforward representation of wealth, perhaps in the form of a wish for the future well-being of the infant. The Red Cloud episode may build on that allusion. Yet it surely has other implications as well.

If the cradleboard was indeed made, as seems most probable, for traditional consumption—that is, made to be given as a gift within a Lakota family group—then this single object carries a host of symbolic meanings. The primary image of the form itself is one of nurture and protection of infants and, by implication, care for generations yet to come. In its production and exchange, it represents kinship ties—the family relations of mutual support, assistance, and affection.

The parallel treatment of Indians and whites and the handshake as gesture of friend-

**Fig. 8**
Woman quilling moccasin tops, Rosebud Reservation, South Dakota, ca. 1893. Nebraska State Historical Society, John Anderson Collection.

ship seem intended as an allegory of peace, and the appearance of this scene on a baby's cradle can only be read as a hope that future generations will experience harmonious relations with whites. Given the tumultuous history of the time, however, the dating of the cradle is essential for a clear interpretation. If it was made shortly after Red Cloud's return from Washington it can be seen as a hopeful view of future relations. If, on the other hand, it postdates Red Cloud's humiliating confinement and the loss of his horses, it may be a bitter commentary on promises unfulfilled, but this is hard to reconcile with the vehicle of a baby cradle. The style and extent of the beading, however, point to a date somewhat later, perhaps around the turn of the century. Lacking clear information about the history of the piece, one might even speculate that it was made around the time of Red Cloud's death in 1904 for use within his family, and in that context is among other things a remembrance of a significant episode in his life.

Unlike the Wohaw drawing and the painted elk hide discussed above, however, here the artist is not trying to address multiple audiences simultaneously and thus does not need to rely on ambiguity or covert imagery. To the degree that such things can be read in a different time and place, the iconographic content seems to be a straightforward message directed to a Lakota audience and emphasizing the desirability of conciliation and peace. Yet because Red Cloud's leadership was challenged over time, and his role in representing those opposed to assimilation was becoming less clear, the image may also be a defense of his past actions and of his position. Ironically, what seems to be a commentary on relations with whites is simultaneously a commentary on factionalism among Lakota people themselves. In strategic terms, the cradleboard attempts to unite Oglalas behind

Red Cloud, implying that the best hope for future generations lies in negotiation and accommodation rather than through resistance.

It is easy enough to assert the importance of historical context in objects like this cradleboard which, although made for internal use, comment on "outside" events. But are things made for internal use and decorated with traditional iconographic forms similarly inflected by the social conflicts of the time? A pair of moccasins is perhaps the quintessential item of internal exchange. Made by a woman for a specific member of her family, a beautifully decorated pair of moccasins was a declaration of the maker's skill and of the family's social position (fig. 8). Perhaps more important, it was also a material representation of the bond of kinship between maker and recipient. Although moccasins made by Plains women most commonly bear quillwork or beadwork in geometric patterns, a number of examples have representational imagery.

A pair of Mandan moccasins now in the collection of the American Museum of Natural History provides a classic example of the form (cat. no. 86). Liberally decorated with quillwork, these display a pattern of multiple hoofprints, an iconic device representing success in horse raiding. The motif probably refers to actions of the wearer; the moccasins are of a size appropriate to an adult man. Thus the maker is calling attention to the exploits of a man in her family, to the family's wealth, and to her own relationship to him. Another Mandan example (cat. no. 307) bears quilled representations of feather bonnets and scattered eagle feathers, a motif that alludes more indirectly to honorable exploits of the wearer; George Horse Capture examines this system of interlocking symbolism elsewhere in this catalogue. A third pair of moccasins bears a pattern of small quilled horses, probably suggesting the association

**Fig. 9**
Interior of a girl's initiation
lodge, showing moccasin tops
hanging in the background,
Rosebud Reservation, South
Dakota, ca. 1892. Nebraska
State Historical Society, John
Anderson Collection.

between horse ownership and wealth. In each of these the artist situates the wearer (and herself as maker) in a traditional social context, emphasizing family prestige, male economic success, and female diligence.

What did it mean to make and wear moccasins in the reservation period? Production of moccasins, like that of other items of clothing in hide, was labor-intensive, and the factory-made shoes sometimes included in shipments of annuity goods might seem as attractive as the readily adopted iron cooking pots or woolen blankets. Yet photographic and other evidence indicates that many people, both men and women, continued to wear moccasins even when much of their other clothing was manufactured goods. Comfort and habit may have been important factors here, yet there may have been a more powerful impetus. On the Lakota baby carrier discussed above, and in numerous drawings, moccasins are one of the signs used to distinguish figures of Indians from those of whites, suggesting that they are an important indication of Plains identity.

Among Sicangu Lakota women, construction and decoration of moccasins was an important activity during the White Buffalo Ceremony, which initiated girls to adulthood (fig. 9), a demonstration of industry, productiveness, and social worth.[21] It is interesting that such an equation of needlework and moral virtue found a strong parallel in the thought of white missionaries and social reformers, who were profoundly troubled by what they saw as the inappropriate social role of women. Traveler and missionary accounts of the nineteenth century are filled with critical observations of the heavy labor performed by women in contrast to the "idleness" of men.[22] Attempting to impose a view of women's lives derived from middle- and upper-class Euro-American models and failing to understand the gender spheres of Plains people, they encouraged needlework—that is, passive, highly controlled handwork usually performed indoors—and tried to discourage the active physical labor women performed daily.[23]

By making and wearing moccasins, reservation-period Plains peoples were adhering to tradition and asserting group solidarity among themselves. With reference to the outside world, however, the persistent use of moccasins can be seen as an act of resistance, a refusal to remake personal identity in accordance with assimilationist policies of the church and government, an external indication of the continuity of other traditional ideas and practices. If the creation of goods for an outside market represented an economic and communicative strategy employed in a time of social and economic upheaval, the continuing production of goods for an internal market unmistakably represented a cultural and social resilience, a tenacious retention of identity against extraordinary pressures for change.

In examining how the theme of relations with whites affected Plains art of the late nineteenth century I do not mean to revive the rightly discarded view that a "pristine" means of expression was adulterated through contact with the Euro-American world, that later objects are somehow less authentic and less representative of culture than those that pre-date contact. I want to suggest, rather, that objects are never separable from the circumstances of their creation; that the circumstances under which much of the material shown here was made were extraordinary indeed; and that these objects were made with an acute consciousness of their social context, both within Plains societies and in the Euro-American sphere. Finally, such objects can reveal much about their makers and their time: the intellectual and emotional struggles of coping with assaultive change, the often-effective strategies Plains peoples put to use, and the ways in which they preserved, sometimes covertly, the traditional grounding of their lives.

1. Although not often thought of in such terms, the situation of American Indian people corresponds to that of colonized peoples elsewhere in terms of control through military force and exploitation of land and natural resources. Absent, for better or worse, is the more usual practice of systematic extraction of labor.

2. Many traders married into Indian families, establishing bonds of support that were mutually advantageous; see Gary Anderson, *Kinsmen of Another Kind* (Lincoln: University of Nebraska Press, 1984), pp. 58–76ff.

3. It is tempting to view the systematic eradication of the buffalo, which was accomplished in the mid-1870s, not just as a means of controlling Indian mobility, but also as a metaphoric fulfillment of genocide.

4. Raymond DeMallie, "Pine Ridge Economy: Cultural and Historical Perspectives," in *American Indian Economic Development*, ed. Sam Stanley (The Hague: Mouton Publishers, 1978), pp. 240–41.

5. See among others the provocative work of Calvin Martin, *Keepers of the Game: Indian-Animal Relationships and the Fur Trade* (Berkeley: University of California Press, 1978).

6. See Karen Daniels Petersen, *Plains Indian Art from Fort Marion, Florida* (Norman: University of Oklahoma Press, 1971), pp. 90–91, 209; Janet Catherine Berlo, "Wohaw's Notebooks: Nineteenth Century Kiowa Indian Drawings in the Collections of the Missouri Historical Society," in *Gateway Heritage 3* (Fall 1982): 2–13; Moira Harris, *Between Two Cultures: Kiowa Art from Fort Marion* (St. Paul, Minn: Pogo Press, 1989), pp. 128–29; Larry Barness, *The Bison in Art* (Flagstaff, Ariz.: Northland Press, 1977), pp. 92–93. The Wohaw ledger at the Missouri Historical Society contains several drawings on similar themes of cultural juxtaposition and contrast, which is unusual among ledgers. The scene of uniformed prisoners attending class taught by a white woman, watched by a blanketed Indian man, is exceptional; see also note 10 below.

7. See the discussion of the artist's name below, cat. no. 141.

8. Berlo, "Wohaw's Notebooks," p. 3.

9. Ibid., p. 8.

10. In this regard it is interesting to note another of Wohaw's drawings (cat. no. 296) that pairs a double portrait of Kiowa warriors with a double portrait of American military men. Here the structure of the drawing, as two framed images of similar size, scale, and pose, again suggests parallelism. The dress and accoutrements of the Kiowas, however, are rendered in far greater detail.

11. Personal communication to Joseph Horse Capture, April 1991.

12. In an unusual early economic development scheme, missionary women taught and promoted lacemaking on the Minnesota reservations in the 1880s, selling the products at a shop in New York; see Kate C. Duncan, "American Indian Lace Making," *American Indian Art Magazine* 5, no. 3 (Summer 1980): 28–35.

13. Berlo, "Wohaw's Notebooks," p. 4.

14. The overwhelming preponderance of military encounters as subject matter in drawing books and other media made for the outside market surely echoes earlier male artistic conventions and was probably received by an internal audience as an exercise in nostalgia for glory, but addressed to an external audience it must also have been intended as a reminder of military prowess and potential aggression. Still, it is notable that few Plains works on paper represent conflict between Indians and whites, which was perhaps too threatening as a subject.

15. Colonel Smith had attained the rank of brevet major general during the Civil War. In 1870, breveted veteran officers were restored to their normal rank but in common usage often retained their former grade; see James C. Olson, *Red Cloud and the Sioux Problem* (Lincoln: University of Nebraska Press, 1965), p. viii.

16. George E. Hyde, *Red Cloud's Folk: A History of the Oglala Sioux Indians* (Norman: University of Oklahoma Press, 1937), pp. 175–76.

17. Olson, *Red Cloud*, p. 233.

18. Ibid., p.110.

19. Ibid., p. 116.

20. Representational decoration itself is relatively rare on Lakota cradleboards. The vast majority of the beaded covers use geometric motifs alone.

21. Hamilton and Hamilton, *The Sioux of the Rosebud*, pp. 151–53.

22. Katherine Weist, "Beasts of Burden and Menial Slaves: Nineteenth-Century Observations of Northern Plains Indian Women," in *The Hidden Half: Studies of Plains Indian Women*, ed. Patricia Albers and Beatrice Medicine (Washington D.C.: University Press of America, 1983), pp. 29–33.

23. Samuel Pond drew a particularly strong contrast between the menial and artistic work of Santee women: "Those who have seen the ornamental work of Dakota women will admit that much of it is tastefully designed and executed. They would admire it if they knew the disadvantages which the artists had to labor under, working in their dark tents, with hands that were most of the time employed in the rudest labor, which laid down the ax and hoe to take up the needle." Samuel Pond, *The Dakota or Sioux in Minnesota As They Were in 1834* (St. Paul: Minnesota Historical Society Press, 1986), p. 42.

# The Warbonnet: A Symbol of Honor  George P. Horse Capture

**A**s youngsters being raised by our grandmother on the Fort Belknap Indian Reservation in the 1940s, our world seemed full. The summers were especially fun. We would wake up when we wanted to, run barefooted outside, play down in the ditch or river, and spend many hours on our rope tire swing: we enjoyed life to the fullest. We may have been hungry at times or even cold, and the mosquitoes were fierce, but we figured all of these things were normal for that normal world of ours.  I remember that whenever we traveled great distances, like the four miles to Harlem, Montana, my Uncle Charlie would get up early in the morning to catch the horses in the field, lead them to the corral, harness them with big leather contraptions that required endless adjustments—pulling and yanking on the straps—and finally attach them somehow or other to the wagon. We would then start loading essential items into the wagon box: bundles, blankets, food, and water. Stepping on the spokes of the wooden wheels, my grandmother would climb aboard and end up perched atop the driver's seat alongside Charlie, and with a slap of the reins on the horses' rumps we would be off.

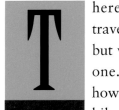

There was very little comfort in traveling in a wagon in those days, but where we lived everybody had one. Once we got into Harlem, however, there were only automobiles, and we felt like intruders. After seeing the town citizens we suddenly became aware of our hair being shaggy, our feet being bare, and our lack of money. The town folk frowned upon us, so we were always uncomfortable and tense. We relaxed again only after we jumped from the wagon in front of my grandmother's house back on the reservation.

My grandmother Clementine had a few head of horses and a small plot of land that we farmed. It wasn't much, but we tended it as a family. Periodically, we would all be involved in other family activities, such as the digging of a new toilet hole for our outhouse. The soil where we lived was cool and sandy beneath the weeds because of the annual spring flooding, so digging with hand shovels was relatively easy and even fun. The sheer walls of the finished excavation, its coolness and depth, were wondrous, and the high pile of dirt was nice to play in as well.

More frequently than not we had to haul in drinking water. (The local river and ditch were probably contaminated for consumption, but not for swimming). So we rode the wagon out to the campground area and spent most of the day filling buckets with water from the hand pump, passing them up to the wagon and filling the barrels. To reduce spillage, a tarp was wrapped over the barrel top and lashed down the sides with rope. This would be our drinking water, and it was good.

Our nights were filled with the sounds of the humming mosquitoes or, on special occasions, by mysterious stories about the early reservation told by visitors or my great-grandmother Coming Daylight. Charlie would wake us in the morning singing Indian songs. These activities filled our time and we were happy—we fit into our happy and free world.

Then one day my grandmother told me that I had to go to school, and the carefree innocent days ended. There were a lot of kids in my grandmother's house, and we had little money; this situation became painfully evident in school. Our classmates never allowed us to forget that we were poor people. Most likely repeating the words of their parents, they told us how Indians are always on welfare, are poor, lazy, and not much good for anything.

This was my first taste of the outside world. We weren't accepted as part of the world; we were Indian, and the town folk we lived among believed Indian people were different and bad. Sadly, many of us believed them, and our inferiority complexes were born, growing like monsters in the following years. No longer carefree and normal, we tried to contend with our new life as best we could. We knew we had to survive, but it was hard to believe anything else for we had no reservation public schools, no libraries, no theaters—nothing. Consequently we embarked upon life shaped by racial prejudice, our feelings of inferiority and sense of displacement causing us to wander mentally and physically for years.

A long time later, as I sought the comfort of stability, my searching led me back toward my Indian beginnings. I have pursued that course ever since. This journey of awareness that I had to travel comprised many steps and was long and torturous. But each step produced a measure of self-confidence. All people must have self-confidence and must build their confidence on a securely laid foundation. To be strong enough to withstand all assaults, self-confidence must be built of solid, irrefutable facts that have purpose and direction, that are based on something credible and honorable. Thus, as I began my journey, I searched for something secure to build upon, some solid, inarguable, positive facts about the Indian race. I needed proof that the town folk were wrong about us. And I realized I would have to travel alone and make the discoveries myself.

Being the first in my family to go to college, I began with a pragmatic, focused purpose: I would center my studies on tribal research. Anthropology provided the skills that would address tribal structures and other elements, and the other wonderful opportunities offered by the academic setting seemed limitless. I crossed many informational thresholds during these initial years as I earned a bachelor's degree in anthropology at the University of California at Berkeley.

Old photographs revealed the faces of our traditional leaders long thought lost. Other research uncovered traditional arts and ethnographical materials around the world, also thought lost. These were unquestionably strong and beautiful. As the factual pieces grew in number, so did my confidence.

I found that all peoples love art but their individual artistic expressions differ. Some carve trees, some weave, some make pottery or jewelry, some do beadwork or quillwork. The Plains people incorporated their life-style and life views into their art style. Their early artwork shows the incredible ingenuity and creativity that these Indian people possessed and how much beauty flowed from their hands, minds, and hearts under the most difficult of life's situations.

On the Plains, the artwork media ranged in size from the large painted tipis to the tiny, incised bone awls. Most items were decorated in some way—everything was fair game for artistic experimentation. The diversity and creativity of the Indian people in disciplines that were important to them are truly amazing.

Over the years since my initial discoveries, I have studied many ethnographic objects that leave no doubt in my mind about the capabilities of these early Indian artists. If their life-style had been different they would have been equally talented in other areas. Therefore I am comfortably convinced that their brainpower, and mine as I am their blood descendant, equaled or exceeded most other people's. Indian mental ability and creativity are rarely acknowledged by others because Indian people are still stereotyped as the descendants of warriors and hunters who did not develop technical capabilities and "only" lived close to the environment and the religious world. Interestingly, that limited view has led to new respect for Indian life. Today, seeing that technology may have gone too far, some technicians, scientists, and others are looking for guidance elsewhere, lest they destroy our world. Perhaps the Indian people have walked the proper philosophical, environmentally sensitive path all along. But our people have Ph.D.s and work computers as well.

Once my discoveries formed a solid foundation of confidence, the remainder of the structure was easy. Today I continue to add new blocks of information as they become available, but I no longer seek proof that the Indian people have been and are as good as any other people. Finally I am beyond insecurity; now I desire only knowledge. My college studies ended with a master's degree in history from Montana State University, but that was a secondary reward for my own journey of discovery.

Indian people have a wonderful history beginning tens of thousands of years ago and extending to this very day. No one part of this history should be extracted and separated from the rest: that would be an injustice to all of the culture. Some would consider it ideal if the styles and quality of our classical 1890 period of traditional art and life-style were to continue. But these have changed, as all things do, and that is the

way it is. However, by studying the past we can understand more of our present.

I remember as a child lying in my grandmother's featherbed covered with a large, brightly colored, soft, warm quilt. When the bed was made up, the smoothed quilt revealed a multipointed circular star pattern composed of small elongated diamond-shaped pieces of colored cloth sewn together (cat. no. 309). I often wondered if that pattern represented something. The sun? The moon? Early settlers? Hutterites? Or was it an Indian design telling a story? The answer seemed important because there were few Indian symbols or designs known or displayed during this poverty-stricken and culturally impoverished period. But there was no answer.

Later in life, as a museum curator at the Buffalo Bill Historical Center in Cody, Wyoming, I enjoyed the special patterns on the painted buffalo hides in our collection, one of which in particular reminded me of the quilt at my grandmother's house. These paintings are beautiful. One, called a box and border (cat. no. 306), is an important part of a Lakota girl's puberty ceremony. Others recount important battles; some have parallel lines that are beaded, painted, or quilled. The motifs most interesting to me were the so-called sunburst or star designs. Triangles or elongated diamonds, made up of at least two colors, radiate outward from the center of the hide in equally spaced concentric circles, forming a design that appears to be a shining sun with rays streaming out in full circles (cat. no. 305).

The elongated diamonds or triangles show many variations, but they are usually all transversely divided in the center, either by a line or by a different color on each half. The edges and the outlines of the colors are often painted with a transparent paint. Later, as the hide darkens from use, the original color of the hide is preserved by the transparent coat and adds a new color to the aging mural.

When this circular pattern of diamonds is used on moccasins, the beadwork is usually in black and white, appearing as stylized eagle feathers (cat. no. 307). The feathers probably represent the eagle, which is the most spiritual animal in the Indian world. It is revered for its beauty, strength, and ability to fly into the heavens, perhaps carrying messages to God. If the diamonds on moccasins do represent eagle feathers, then perhaps the same motif and meaning are used on other Indian objects as well. In considering the sunburst pattern it is difficult to imagine a circle of feathers revolving or oriented around the sun. Although a manifestation of the Plains Indian belief system is the Sun Dance, the actual sun is only a point on which to focus prayers and has this religious role only during the four-day dance. Indian prayers are always directed to the One Above. The only circular orientation of feathers in the Indian world is the warbonnet.

The circular arrangement of diamonds highlighting a central element is a powerful design. The pattern is so attractive that, while teaching at the College of Great Falls, I designed a T-shirt with the diamond rays highlighting the name of the college. It looked classic, neat, and Indian. Still, the traditional Indian interpretation and/or connection to this design element remained elusive to me, and life went on.

Some scholars of Indian art assume that traditional Indian artists incorporated important elements of their world into their artwork, often in an abstract manner, whereas others believe their designs were merely aesthetic. Usually there is no way to confirm or dispute these beliefs, but a substantiated interpretation of some traditional motifs would reveal aspects of the Indian value system.

Over the years, I have had occasion to travel and see the world, and at most sites I have visited the local museum and viewed its Indian materials. Although there are a finite number of classical Indian materials in the world, many of them are yet to be discovered and others are unknown to most students of Indian art. Searching for these Indian art pieces is much like prowling garage sales: you never really know what treasure you will find in the storage vaults of the next museum. The more one studies, the more one learns.

Surprisingly, a massive amount of Plains Indian material is located in Europe. When Indian people were under siege by the Euro-Americans, Europeans collected Indian ethnographic and artistic materials and took them back to Europe, where they still exist in spite of the turbulent history of that area. Europeans generally have a romantic perspective on American Indian people. To them, Indians represent a free people, unsoiled by civilization—clean, close to the earth, and deeply religious. Long viewed as curiosities of a noble but vanishing race, the art of the American Indian people has been recognized and appreciated as artwork only within the last twenty years.

One of the most famous European collecting expeditions was that of Prince Maximilian zu Wied, who along with the famous Swiss artist Karl Bodmer recorded aspects of the Plains Indian culture of the Missouri River in the early 1830s. There were many other collecting expeditions as well. Now some of the earliest, finest, and largest collections of American Indian materials in the world are stored in the museums of Europe, far from their place of creation and seldom displayed. The largest European collection from the northern Plains region is in the Museum für Völkerkunde, in Berlin.

These early materials consist of robes, moccasins, shirts, leggings, parfleches, bags, containers, and other eye-catching items. Conceived and constructed during a period relatively free from non-Indian influences, they potentially contain the purest essence of American Indian philosophy and creativity available.

Opportunity once carried me to the European continent for a brief period. On this journey of discovery I visited the Musée de l'Homme amid the towers and sparkling fountains in Paris. The people in the museum, helpful and courteous in spite of a language barrier, allowed me to study their older Plains Indian materials. Although the collection is small, the materials are very impressive because many were created before 1850, an early time for Plains Indian material. Two components of this relatively unpublished collection are spectacular and unique.

The first extraordinary item is a pair of moccasins, but what a pair! They are made from the back feet of a bear with the hair and claws still intact. Not only are they beautiful, but they also have power. The physical and spiritual power of the bear was retained in the moccasins and transferred to the wearer, rendering him extraordinary as well. For who but a spiritual person could conceive of such a thing, and then have the courage to wear the bear's feet as footwear? Viewing these moccasins always gives me a special feeling.

The other remarkable part of this collection is the selection of decorated buffalo robes. Overall the grouping is the earliest that I have ever seen. The curator, Ms. Anne Vitart, is in the process of publishing a catalogue that will tell their story and show their beauty for all to enjoy.

On a recent trip to the museum I delighted in a lengthy and close-up inspection of these robes. Ms. Vitart carefully laid out robe after robe, each more beautiful than the last. In the presence of such early and lovely pieces, I began to babble, reciting many things I had learned about painted buffalo robes over the years—the robe is worn with the head skin on the left side, the Indian artists usually retained the holes that were used to stake down the hide instead of trimming them off, and so on.

The more interesting robes originated in the central and northern Plains. Some are similar in style to known tribal types, but others are not. It is fun to study them to see what in these early styles is recognizable today and what they might reveal. The evolution of some designs can be mentally traced, whereas others are almost unrecognizable. The quality of the robes is excellent. Most of the hides are clean and supple (considering their age) and the colors vivid. Because of this the tiniest details are preserved in their original clarity.

In addition to early renditions of the box and border, the sunburst, and other patterns, there are a number of pictograph exploit robes showing figures in action. These pre-1850 robes are rare and highly prized murals. Painted by the men, they present exploits, particularly in battle, by which the men achieved honor, such as defeating an enemy, counting a coup, or stealing horses—all admirable deeds that ultimately allowed the tribe to survive.

By studying the styles of the artists one can roughly determine the age of the robes. The artists presented their perceptions in a symbolic manner. Creating realistic, recognizable images was not as important as truthfully telling the story of the action. For example, the riders of horses are usually in profile and almost indistinguishable from each other except for the different tribal hairstyles. The subjects lack three dimensions, and the outline of the horse can be seen through the rider. The horses are wonderful—strong, classic, many in color (blue, green, black, etc.). Action is paramount, though without actually hearing the story one can only speculate about the events.

There is one great robe, massive in size and weight, filled with painted warriors and horses engaged in action across a battlefield (fig. 1). Its beauty is dazzling. The classic Plains art patterns and styles divide the mural into several smaller vignettes that center on a single

**Fig. 1**
Painted hide. Musée
de l'Homme, Paris.

**Fig. 2**
Detail of painted hide. Musée
de l'Homme, Paris.

fray, later contributing to the whole. Feathered lances, tribal hairstyles, britch cloths, hair skirts, muskets, bows and arrows, knives, horses and their equipment, bead and quill designs, and many other things are pictured. Studying these details is much like studying a photograph of long ago: the visuals are tiny time capsules from the past.

Although this robe told a story, I couldn't hear it all. But I scrutinized the vignettes one after another, as if looking through a window to a better time. Near the bottom of the robe, mounted on a strong and graceful steed, a proud chief looked straight at me (fig. 2). I felt a shock of surprise at his power. My heart leapt when I saw what he wore on his head. It was a warbonnet, presented in an extraordinary way—a nearly complete circle of triangles or elongated diamonds, a duplicate of the sunburst motif! Suddenly it was clear to me that at that early, formative time this pattern was meant to represent a warbonnet, and the motif has continued across the ages.

The incorrect terminology used by non-Indians often creates problems of identification. For example, the United States Postal Service recently printed stamps showing warbonnets, but the accompanying literature calls them "headdresses." As curator at the Plains Indian museum in Cody, I assisted the artist in selecting, from our collections, the models for the stamps. I repeatedly stressed that they were warbonnets, not headdresses, but apparently to no avail. Warbonnets are constructed of eagle feathers, while the main elements of the headdress are long porcupine guard hairs bordered by deer tail hair. The two items look completely different and are worn for different purposes.

Warbonnets have two key segments: a skullcap and feathers. The cap is sized to fit snugly and can be made of leather pieces or felt material. Feathers of the pheasant, grouse, turkey, and bald or golden eagles are the most acceptable. The preferred feathers are from the tail of the golden eagle, the spotted and black-tipped ones, with the prized symmetrical middle feather assuming the middle position on the crown. The bottom shafts of the feathers are fashioned into hinges, which in turn are laced to the crown all around its edge. A lace is threaded midway through the feathers and tied together in back, pulling the feathers into the familiar circular inverted crown "flower" shape. The structure allows much flexibility and fluid, graceful movement. A brow decoration of quill-work or beadwork highlights the bottom front, and rosettes or flowing pennants added near the temple balance the head decoration. Occasionally long trailers, either a single one or a pair, lavishly decorated with feathers cascade down the back, almost to the ground (cat. no. 214).

Stories state that the warbonnet is the compilation of years of great deeds accomplished by its wearer, for each worthy deed earns one feather. This is a nice story, but I don't believe it for a moment. If such a process were observed by all tribes in strict compliance with one set of requirements (which is impossible), there would naturally be conflicting interpretation of what constitutes "great deeds." More important, no man became an instant "chief," accomplishing the scores of deeds needed for a warbonnet at one "sitting." Honors and a reputation for helping one's people are earned over a long period of time, during which a warrior gradually develops into a chief. If the "honor warbonnet" story were true, then there should be "half warbonnets" to acknowledge the deeds to date: of course, there are no such things. I believe the feathered warbonnet is an entity unto itself: it is one complete unit.

Traditionally, only men of honor and accomplishments could wear such magnificent "crowns"; this privilege was a society standard. Due to the spectacular and symbolic image of the warbonnet its use spread among the tribes of the Plains and, in recent years, far beyond.

Today most Indian groups at one time or another use the warbonnet, because they all have great Indian men.

A non-Indian might suppose that the most attractive symbolic feathers for use in such a prestigious item would be from the bald eagle. This is hardly ever the case. Some time back, when a friend of mine gave me a set of bald eagle tail feathers, I felt honored but I didn't like them. They were plain white, resembling turkey feathers. Indian people prefer the fancier feathers of the golden eagle, which have either banded colors or black tips contrasting with the white. The only feathers that surpass these in beauty are feathers from an immature bald eagle. The dark tail feathers of the young bald eagle turn white as the bird matures, and halfway through this metamorphosis the feathers are a mixture of white and flecks of dark color. This speckled "chocolate chip" feather is the most attractive and special of them all.

In spite of the tremendously destructive forces applied against them since 1492, Indian people and many of their cultural traits have somehow survived. As we look around us we can see and feel the ancient pulse of our music, and we still dance in the attire and style of our forefathers; we pray and fast on the buttes and in the Sun Dances as did our ancestors. These cultural elements provide us with hope for the future, and they remind us of our heritage.

Warbonnets still play a vital role in this continuity. I was struck by them in the venerable painted robe of the past, and now I know I enjoyed comfort in their symbolic representation upon my grandmother's bed. Locating and recognizing surviving elements of our culture around us is a delight. Star quilts hang on walls of our offices and homes everywhere in Indian country and are special items at our ceremonial giveaways. I still find much pleasure in seeing star quilts, knowing that long ago this pattern

designated that proud symbol of the warbonnet and the Indian people and still does today.

As I have said, my confidence is high and built on a sturdy base, and I'm also getting older. Both of these circumstances create a sense of well-being. I no longer have to reaffirm to myself what I should have known all along: the American Indian race is a good one. My years spent studying Indian art convinced me of this. Indian art is wonderful. As star quilts cover our beds, warm us in the car, shelter us in the Sun Dance, and color our walls, they are in reality our warbonnets from our enduring culture; they cover the normal and special Indian world with honor, prestige, beauty, and our proud traditions.

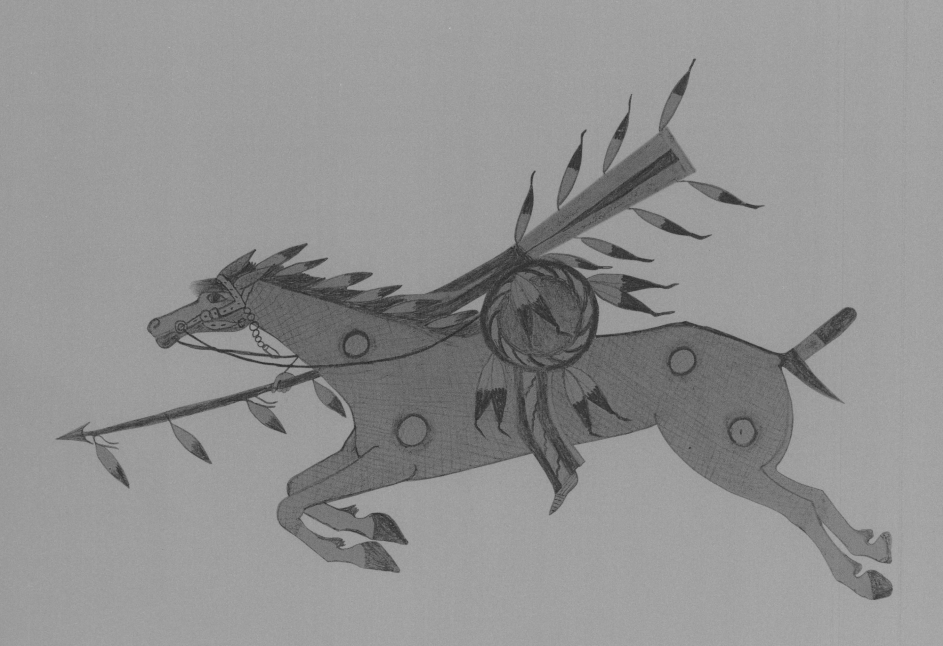

# The Horse as Symbol: Equine Representations in Plains Pictographic Art  David W. Penney

**T**he image of the horse plays a prominent role in Plains Indian pictographic art, as did the horse itself in the lives of Plains Indians. An important point to remember, however, is that the horse was a newcomer to the Americas, just like the European American who brought it as a domesticated animal. Its introduction initiated sweeping changes in demographic geography, economy, and overall style of life among America's indigenous peoples. Hence, the idea of the horse as it became absorbed within cultural thought was rife with symbolic potential. The symbolism of the horse is clearly perceived in the arena of visual expression, more specifically in the medium of pictographic art, a flexible and adaptable pictorial language. The horse was drawn, painted, inscribed, and sculpted, at first customarily by men. Late in the nineteenth century, embroidered images were produced by women. These images of horses are worthy of our attention because they make visible how symbolic thought, as manifested in pictorial language, interacted with the broad events of Plains Indian social history after the contact era.

The act of drawing, painting, sculpting, or embroidering images of horses may seem, on the surface, to have been a cultural practice motivated by aesthetic concerns. There is no question that aesthetic considerations led to the production of horse images in various media that today can be admired as great artistic accomplishments. To overemphasize these acts of individual creativity, however, may obscure an understanding of the broader social contexts in which such works were produced. This essay refers not so much to the creative act of making art as to the purposes to which art is put.

Plains Indian artists created images of horses prior to the modern era for three basic purposes: (1) as part of a prayer for blessings, which included ownership of horses; (2) as part of a rendition of personal history in which horses (as prizes of battle or as mounts) played a role; and, later in nineteenth-century American history, (3) as part of a constellation of symbols applied to dress and other media to convey and assert a distinctive American Indian identity. The traditions involved in creating horse images for these various purposes built one upon the other. But shifts in the purposes were contingent on significant historical events. Hence the language of Plains Indian pictorial art can be demonstrated to have had a reflexive character as it addressed new cultural concerns and deployed innovative ideas in response.

This characterization of "traditional" American Indian art may not be in keeping with some popularly held notions about the conservative nature of this art. A customary way to think about innovation and change in American Indian art is as a process of steady erosion of traditional practices with replacement by acculturated ones. A study of horse images, however, shows a much more complex and certainly more interesting historical process

in which a European cultural institution (horses and horse technology) was absorbed and subverted in relation to its acculturative implications into a potent symbol of Plains Indian solidarity and separateness. The proactive potential of art to create symbols by which people and cultures define themselves, or to undermine symbolically their domination by others, is the larger theme of this brief analysis of horse imagery in Plains Indian pictorial arts.

## METAPHORS OF POWER

The first Europeans to enter the New World and confront its indigenous peoples well understood the potential of the horse to serve as a symbol of intimidating power. Early during the conquest of Mexico, Hernando Cortes plotted to frighten emissaries of Moctezuma, who had never seen a horse, with the sudden appearance of an excited mare. Knowing that the Mexicans were unsure whether horses were mortal, Cortes buried the corpses of his slain mounts at night during his march to Tenochtitlán.[1] Mounted cavalry clearly offered military advantage in battle, but Cortes was also aware that, symbolically, horses conveyed the notion of an almost supernatural superiority.

New World Indians learned quickly, however, that horses were mortal. They also learned through armed conflict the military advantages of European steel, horses, and guns. Their experiences perhaps contributed to their view of the horse as a metaphor of power. When the Tewa Pueblos of the Rio Grande valley rose up against the Spanish army of occupation under Coronado, they herded all the Spanish horses inside their palisaded villages and "chased [them] as in a bullfight and shot [them] with arrows."[2] Although Coronado's army easily besieged the pueblos and ruthlessly punished the

Tewa, this event reveals how close the Tewa considered the relationship between Spanish horses and Spanish power—one was the expression of the other.

As a metaphor, the image of a horse joins a constellation of other symbols with related equivalence. The appropriation of the horse, and even symbols of Christianity, into a lexicon of power symbols is apparent among the pictographs at the Meyers Springs Rock Shelter, located close to the Big Bend region of southwest Texas, just north of the Rio Grande and west of the Pecos River. There, hundreds of painted images range across the smooth limestone wall at the rear of a rock shelter at the base of a formidable cliff. The site had served as a haven for traveling parties since the Paleo-Indian period. Three episodes of painting are visible, the earliest perhaps more than two thousand years old. The most recent paintings were produced either by the Mescalero Apache, who had inhabited the region since the seventeenth century, or by parties of Kiowa or Comanche, who frequently passed through on their way south across the Mexican border to raid in the nineteenth century.[3]

The relationship between Europeans and their horses is noted among the paintings by an image of an equestrian Spanish priest, identified by his bell-shaped robe and a cross above his cap (fig. 1). Instead of being astride the horse, the crudely drawn figure stands above it. In addition to the cross above the priest's hat, crosses are scattered elsewhere among the rock shelter paintings, and there are also images of churches. All of these images occur among representations of thunderbirds, handprints, sacred circles, and other symbols of power. These many separate acts of painting by visitors to the site can be understood as analogous to prayers for power. The white priest and his horse join other, more traditional symbols and references of the sacred because of the priest's otherworldliness, his access to wealth, and his self-professed spirituality. Missionaries among the neighboring Pueblos stressed "veneration of the cross, respect for the clergy, [and] instruction concerning the sacraments" in their proselytizing, emphasizing the material symbols of the sacred over liturgical narrative.[4] In the Meyers Springs paintings, Christian crosses, the person of the priest himself, and the horse merge with indigenous symbols as painted prayers for wealth and well-being. This does not necessarily represent an instance of Christian syncretism; it is simply an appropriation of symbols as references to power.

## PICTOGRAPHIC ART ON THE PLAINS

s knowledge and ownership of horses moved northward during the seventeenth and eighteenth centuries, the patterns of Plains "buffalo culture," as it was known in the nineteenth century, began to emerge. Bands with mounts enjoyed better and more sustained access to the buffalo herds and greater offensive mobility when contesting hunting territories with intransigent neighbors. Horses were truly the key to power, especially when combined with guns traded south from Canada.

Pictographic prayers for horses dating to the earliest episodes of horse diffusion have been located at several rock art sites in the northern Plains and eastern Rockies. At many of the North Cave Hills sites in northwest South Dakota, images of horses' hoofprints combine with buffalo heads and animal figures in the "hunting magic" style of the protohistoric period.[5] Images of horses along with those of handprints, mountain sheep, and buffalo left by the early historic Ute in northern Utah may have had the same purpose.[6]

**Fig. 1**
Pictographs at Meyers Springs Rock Shelter, Big Bend region, west Texas. Copied July 24, 1935, by Forrest Kirkland. Courtesy of the Texas Memorial Museum, acc. no. 2261-71.

The rock art sites of the northern Plains also document a major paradigmatic shift in the kinds of messages that images of horses were intended to convey. James Keyser called attention to this when he differentiated between an earlier "ceremonial" style and later "biographic art" at a number of sites he studied in North Dakota, Wyoming, Montana, and Alberta.[7] The ceremonial style includes images of figures with shields, animals, and additional enigmatic symbols arranged without any implication of narrative relationship or sequence, like horses' hooves and buffalo heads. Functionally, these would correspond to the prayers for power just discussed. In contrast, biographic art stresses action in narratives of hunting and combat. Keyser estimated that the transition from ceremonial to biographic art at his rock art sites occurred sometime between A.D. 1625 and A.D. 1750, which corresponds to the period when the resident Shoshone had been pressured westward by migrations of Siouan and Algonkian-speaking people from the east who were responding to the promise of equestrian buffalo culture.[8]

The biographic art Keyser found in the northwest Plains corresponds to the kinds of pictorial language employed by Siouan and Algonkian people farther east, although pictographs by the latter were often executed in more ephemeral media. Joseph Nicollet, who traveled extensively among the Dakota and Ojibwe of Minnesota during the 1830s, noted that

*they use this figurative language strictly for their needs as they travel or hunt or wage war in order to make known their whereabouts and the events they witnessed, to show where they came from, where they are heading, and what they saw, etc. They mark all these things at the confluences of rivers, on lake shores, on portage trails, always in the most conspicuous places.*[9]

When the Algonkian-speaking Blackfeet, Cheyenne, Arapaho, and Gros Ventre migrated westward from territories located most likely north or northwest of Lake Superior, they brought with them the tradition of narrative and pictorial biographic art. The Siouan speakers did likewise during their era of expansion from Minnesota across the Dakotas and into eastern Wyoming and Montana during the later eighteenth and nineteenth centuries. During this dynamic historic episode in which tribal peoples competed for advantage in a new economy that included horses, guns, and trade with whites, scenes of combat dominate early biographic representations on the Plains.

Since the primary purpose of pictographic narratives at rock art sites was to convey information, it was customary for the creators to employ a kind of reductive shorthand. These same kinds of representations were painted on clothing, such as buffalo robes and deerskin shirts, as expressions of personal accomplishment. Few of these "personal biographies" before 1800 have been preserved. The historical development of Plains pictographic art from the reductive stick figures of the early nineteenth century to the highly detailed and embellished "ledger book art" of the 1860s, 1870s, and 1880s has been discussed in great detail by John C. Ewers.[10] It is important to note, however, that as long as the purpose of the art remained focused on personal military accomplishments, the structure of these representations remained constant throughout their history of artistic elaboration and transfer to additional media.

Plains pictographic art is a highly codified system employing representations of figures, equestrian or on foot, engaged in various episodes of personal combat. The combatants are identified by means of singular details of dress: a distinctive feather bonnet, hairstyle, or garment.

The emphasis of weaponry specifies the occasion and the degree of risk, and hence honor, involved. And always, the event is portrayed from an individual point of view: the coups counted, enemies slain, or wounds received. Pictographic art almost invariably represents the heroic act tied to a specific historical event in the life of the artist or those he witnessed.

## HORSES IN PICTOGRAPHIC NARRATIVE

orses play two roles in pictographic narratives. They are portrayed either as the prizes of successful military actions or as the mounts of participants. Within the context of the perennial border skirmishing that characterized life on the nineteenth-century Plains, horse-stealing raids provided young men with the chance to test their skills. When the raids were successful, the wealth gained and the record of military accomplishment contributed to social recognition.

An armed party might have the opportunity to run off a herd of horses during the pitch of battle, and those who touched individual horses could claim them. Far more dangerous and very brave was to sneak into an enemy village at night and steal horses by cutting their picket lines. The Minneconjou warrior White Bull told Stanley Vestal (Walter S. Campbell) about one such adventure during his youth.[11] He had joined a war party of some forty men during the summer of 1872, and they discovered a large Crow camp on the upper Yellowstone River.

*After dark they swam the Yellowstone [and] got near to that great camp of enemies. . . . They came to a big tipi. In it they could see the silhouettes of many enemies cast by the firelight upon the sides of the taper tent. Then all but two turned back; only White Bull and Low Dog went into the camp. . . . They found a number of fine horses picketed in the middle of the camp circle.*

**Fig. 2**
His Fight capturing horses.
Drawings from the ledger book
of His Fight, Hunkpapa
Lakota, Standing Rock Reser-
vation. From DeCost Smith,
*Indian Experiences*, The
Caxton Printers, Ltd., Caldwell,
Idaho. Used by permission.

**Fig. 3**
Detail of a pictographic tipi illustrating a group of Lakota running off horses while fighting Crows. Unknown artist, South Dakota. National Museum of the American Indian, 20/7873.

*White Bull selected a handsome pinto; Low Dog selected a bay.*

*They cut the lariats. . . . [and] the two of them walked quietly out of the camp, leading the horses.*

White Bull's accomplishment became a coup, a brave and heroic act that contributed to his reputation and esteem. No doubt White Bull had told this story, and others about similar notable deeds, on numerous occasions in the presence of witnesses who sanctioned the truthfulness of the account. Such an event might also have been recorded using the media and language of pictographic representation.

A page in the ledger book of His Fight, a Hunkpapa warrior and holy man, records a similar coup in His Fight's Life. The facts are described in two scenes, one arranged above the other (fig. 2). Above, His Fight approaches a pair of horses picketed outside a tipi. In the tipi two Crow men are visible, one smoking a pipe. Below, His Fight drives a herd of thirteen horses, the fruits of his daring. He has a lariat in his hand.

In his drawings His Fight emphasizes those details that are meaningful to his claiming the coup. His dress and accoutrements are clearly indicated, to specify his identity and the occasion. He wears a capote, a hooded coat made from a Hudson's Bay blanket. The stripes of the blanket are visible on the hood and its pendant. He also wears a wolf or coyote skin over one shoulder. His Fight had seen a vision of coyote in a cloud during the nine-day fast in which he had received his sacred power;[12] the coyote skin thus may have been part of his war medicine. He holds a rifle and a lariat in his hands. In the lower picture, His Fight wears in addition a "crow belt" or feather bustle behind his waist. Something like a crow belt had been an ornament of warriors early in the nineteenth century, as Joseph Nicollet observed in the 1830s: "a tail composed of ribbons, bird feath-

ers, and pieces of furry animal skins [that] dangles from a belt behind."[13] Later in the nineteenth century the crow belt was worn almost exclusively during the Grass Dance, a social celebration of warriors' virtues and accomplishments. In His Fight's drawing, the crow belt might allude to his identity as an accomplished warrior.

His Fight's drawings employ synecdoche as abbreviated notations referring to important elements of the narrative. Only the heads of the enemies are shown, their greased and upright forelocks specifying their ethnic identity as Crow. One smokes a pipe, indicating that they were awake when His Fight crept up on their tipi. While the two horses are outlined in entirety in the upper drawing, perhaps to portray the attractiveness of the prize, the thirteen below are drawn only from the neck up and arranged in a dense grouping of repetitive forms. In this scene the number of horses captured receives emphasis, although the variations in coloring and markings seem to indicate that each horse was regarded individually.

Many similar drawings are preserved in museum collections, each recording a specific occasion. Many of the more accomplished artists lavished a great deal of attention on the sinuous outlines of their horse trophies. An elaborate rendition of a successful horse raid is painted on a muslin Lakota tipi cover in the collection of the National Museum of the American Indian (fig. 3). The unknown artist outlined the forms of the running horses in pencil and india ink and then painted their colors and markings in browns, yellow, orange, and red. Their tightly clustered heads are arranged in diagonal rows, their arched necks angling downward to meet the next row of heads. The aesthetic attention to these representations of horses stems from the cultural values that valorized horses as symbols of wealth, prestige, manly courage, and adventure.

HENOPA WANICA

**Fig. 4**
Detail of a tipi painted by
No Two Horns, Hunkpapa
Lakota (cat. no. 169). Mandan
Indian Shriners, El Zagel Tem-
ple, Fargo, North Dakota.

Although successful men often owned many horses, the horses trained for war and buffalo hunting were especially prized. White Bull's father, Makes Room, gave his son a proven war-horse named Swift Hawk for his first war expedition. Makes Room also procured a special protective charm for the horse, purchased for the price of a bay pony from his half-brother, the holy man Horse Tail.[14]

*The medicine was in a small leather pouch decorated with an eagle feather. Horse Tail hung it on a thong around "Swift Hawk's" neck. He then painted the animal with a red wavy line from the hoof to the backbone on all four legs, and encircled its jaws just above the bridle-bit with a red line. . . . "Nephew," he said, "this medicine will make your horse strong and long-winded."*

Proven horses were honored. Later, when White Bull had grown into a mature warrior, he would tie an eagle feather to the forelock of his war-horse and fasten an imitation scalp made of woman's hair to the bridle bit. "Only horses which had been used to ride down an enemy could wear such decoration."[15]

A unique and special recognition of his horse's accomplishment in battle was prepared by No Two Horns (He Nupa Wanica), a Hunkpapa of Sitting Bull's band who had fled to Canada with him after the Battle of the Little Big Horn.[16] During a fight with some Crows, No Two Horns's war-horse was wounded seven times. The event is recorded on a tipi cover painted by the warrior (fig. 4). No Two Horns himself was apparently wounded twice in the legs. In the painting, he sits with his thunderbird shield at his shoulder and a repeating rifle leveled at his enemies. His wounded horse, contorted with pain, lies nearby, blood streaming from its mouth and from seven wounds extending from its neck to its withers. The horse has undulating medicine stripes extending down

each leg, resembling those described by White Bull. The painted tipi records several more of No Two Horns's combat adventures astride this same horse with its medicine stripes. Later, when a resident of the Standing Rock Reservation in North Dakota, No Two Horns honored this horse and commemorated its courage on that occasion by performing in the Grass Dance with a dance stick carved in its likeness and seven bullet wounds represented along its length.[17]

## SYMBOLS OF ETHNIC IDENTITY

The years following 1880 marked great changes in Lakota life, indeed in the lives of all the tribes of the Plains who had hunted the buffalo. The last buffalo herd dwindled in central Montana between the Missouri and the Yellowstone. The Cree, Blackfeet, Métis, Gros Ventre, Assiniboine, and the remaining free Lakota convened there during the summers of 1881 and 1882 until the buffalo could no longer sustain them. Thereafter they had no choice but to accept the harsh reality of dependency on the Indian agencies established by the governments of the United States and Canada.

Thus ended the time of action, and the time of remembering began. Reservation life offered little opportunity for men to distinguish themselves in battle. The reputations of those who had participated in the volatile events of the preceding decades grew almost legendary. For the first time women began to represent the coups in the beadwork that they produced for men.[18] Several beaded articles, for example, show the Minneconjou warrior White Swan's participation in the famous Lakota raid on the Crow Agency in Montana during July of 1875.[19] All told, Lakota war parties made off with over three hundred horses that summer. On two of the objects, a pipe bag and a tipi bag (cat. no.

271), a seated figure is identified as White Swan by a name glyph (the image of a white swan) that floats over its head; on another bag White Swan's name is embroidered on the sleeve. Done in the style of pictographic painting, the embroidered design illustrates stolen horses being driven through a tipi village or past the Crow Agency building. Dennis Lessard thinks that the objects may have been produced on the death of White Swan in 1900 for distribution to his family or friends.[20] When owned by White Swan's descendants and displayed as part of a formal dress ensemble worn during social events, these objects gave testimony to the great accomplishments of that earlier generation whose memory was thus kept alive.

Pictographic drawings produced by those too young to have participated as adults in pre-reservation life possess a similar viewpoint of reminiscence and nostalgia. The Oglala Amos Badheart Bull was seven years old at the time of the Custer fight, but he heard a great deal about the years of hard fighting with whites, the Crows, and the Shoshones from his father and uncles, who had been accomplished warriors.[21] He was twenty-one or twenty-two years old when he began to draw pictographs representing his elders' experiences in a ledger book purchased from a clothing vendor in Crawford, Nebraska. He drew vivid renderings of the Custer fight and documented many episodes of bravery and acts of killing based on the recollections of those who had participated. There are also pictures of notable events from long ago, such as the death of Yellow Robe and his son at the hands of the Hunkpapa Black Wolf, which took place in 1858.[22] Moreover, in a series of very descriptive drawings, Amos Badheart Bull illustrated not so much the specific events of any personal biography but the collective history of his people's past, with generalized images of the manner in which the Lakota had moved camp and conducted the

Sun Dance, the customary varieties of dress worn for different occasions, and the way they used to hunt buffalo.[23]

Those of Amos Badheart Bull's generation had developed a new sense of self-consciousness as Lakota and as American Indians. During this generation's experience of enforced assimilation by means of government schools and government policy, they may have come to realize that they were the bearers of an ethnic culture besieged by the values of "progress" and white modernity. Amos and other artists sought out symbols that defined the Lakota as a unique culture, as distinctive people among many. They thereby established a sense of solidarity and difference in relation to others. The equestrian warrior of the prereservation past became one such symbol toward the close of the nineteenth century.

During the reservation period, pictographic representations of warrior combat often lost their references to specific events. The images instead were intended to convey the notion of Lakota bravery in general. For example, in the ledger book produced by Joseph of the Rosebud Reservation (his full name is as yet unknown), there is a drawing of a warrior charging the enemy on his horse (fig. 5). The drawing is rendered in classic pictographic style, with the forward movement of the horse vividly portrayed and the rider clinging to one side for protection against enemy fire. The warrior is not identified, nor is the enemy represented. Instead of an actual event, Joseph represented the *manner* in which Lakota warriors customarily charged the enemy—the way it had been done in the past.

Even more ideographic were the pictographic representations of equestrian warriors in the beaded designs of men's vests, men's shirts, and women's dresses after the 1890s. Like the florid geometric patterning of dress ornament at this time, these designs asserted a Lakota visual identity rather than signifying any particular or individual history. They referenced a legacy of men's accomplishments as warriors with which all Lakota could identify.

Vests heavily decorated with pictographic beadwork were produced in large numbers on Lakota and Yankton reservations during the late 1880s and the 1890s. Such garments were perhaps influenced less by the European-American waistcoat than by the innovative alterations conducted by earlier generations on government-issue, ready-made clothing. Captain DeWitt Clinton Poole, the agent of the Whetstone Agency in 1869, noted that after the distribution of garments at an annuity issue "some of the young bucks . . . appear[ed] in the dress coats, with the skirts and sleeves cut off, thus making a sleeveless jacket, the military buttons being replaced by buttons procured from the trader and fastened on the improvised garment in all directions."[24]

Vests made later on the reservations were cut from cowhide and often completely covered with carefully arranged rows of parallel-stitch bead embroidery or, more rarely, quillwork. Many of these vests include symmetrically opposed images of equestrian warriors with long, trailing feather-headdresses (cat. no. 202). Alternatively, horses may appear without riders. These designs still distinguish between the two customary roles of horses in biographic art—mounts for warriors and prizes of battle. They signify the traditional cultural virtues of men, without biographic reference. They join other symbols on men's vests with similar cultural resonance: thunderbirds, eagles, elk, and distinctively Lakota geometric motifs.

In many cases the riders of horses illustrated on vests carry American flags, or flags are otherwise included in the decoration of the vests. The appearance of flags on formal garments derives in part from the occasions when the gar-

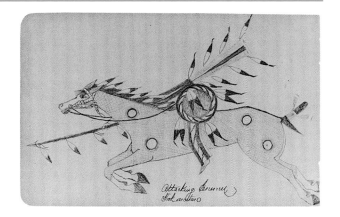

Fig. 5
"Attacking Enemy." Drawing from a Lakota ledger book, Rosebud Reservation, South Dakota. Detroit Institute of Arts, Founders Society Purchase.

ments were worn. In their effort to assimilate Native Americans, government agents repressed many traditional religious and social practices while at the same time promoting patriotic American celebrations such as Independence Day. As a result, July 4 became one of the major occasions of the year for reservation social events during the turn-of-the-century era. Its festive traditions in American life translated on the reservations into wearing formal dress, dancing, staging sham battles, and organizing feasts and giveaways. In short, the Fourth of July became a time for celebrating American Indian traditions— all accompanied by the ubiquitous display of the holiday's most prominent symbol, the American flag. Vests, along with other types of heavily decorated garments, were created to be worn on such occasions. Images of the American flag thus joined those of horses, equestrian warriors, and other symbols as updated, visual expressions of Lakota tradition.

## SYMBOLS: APPROPRIATION, SUBVERSION, AND INNOVATION

The way in which the Lakota subverted the symbol of the American flag from its presumably assimilationist intent (a symbol of melting-pot America) into a symbol of ethnic celebration and solidarity illustrates how the meaning of a symbol can be negotiated instead of fixed. If pictorial art can be regarded as a language, we can evoke a discursive framework that subjects the meanings of pictorial images to acts of appropriation, subversion, and innovation. The image of the horse in Plains pictographic art was engaged in such a discursive process—its meaning was adjusted to contemporary usage throughout the last five hundred years of white and Indian history.

When first brought to America, the horse represented a technological, even moral,

superiority over American Indians in the minds of the European owners. The power inherent in horses was successfully appropriated and subverted by American Indians, however, through simple transfer of possession: American Indians acquired horses for themselves. Harnessing the power of horses led to a thorough transformation of American Indian life on the Plains. This was true both economically and symbolically, particularly in the definition of male values.[25] Among the eighteenth-century tribes of the Plains, a large part of who a man was socially revolved around the possession of horses: horses as wealth; horses as the vehicle, literally, for self-promotion as a warrior and hunter.

The pictographic records of male biographies illustrate the degree to which horses participated in the definition of male identities. Horses became so thoroughly integrated into a male sense of self that when men could no longer engage in the kinds of hunting and combat in which horses played a role, the horse persisted as a symbol of self-definition. The innovative medium of pictographic beadwork sustained the symbolic potency of horse images by employing them as broader expressions of cultural vitality.

By the close of the nineteenth century, the process of transfiguration was complete. What had been exploited by Cortes as a symbol of European power had been transformed into one of the predominant visual symbols of pan-Indian identity. The several twentieth-century objects that employ images of horses illustrated in this catalogue testify to the strength of horse imagery as a symbol of American Indian ethnicity. The adaptability of the horse image as a symbol throughout its five-hundred-year history in American Indian visual expression highlights an alternative view of what may be understood as "traditional" in American Indian art history. The introduction of foreign ideas and technologies did not always result in cultural erosion and loss;

instead, symbolic thought, through processes that may include appropriation, subversion, and innovation, often built on these novelties to regenerate traditions for the present and future.

1. Tzvetan Todorov, *The Conquest of America*, trans. Richard Hunt (New York: Harper and Row, 1984), pp. 111, 115.

2. George Parker Winship, ed., *The Journey of Coronado*, by Pedro Castaneda (New York: Allerton Books, 1922), p. 50.

3. Forrest Kirkland and W. W. Newcomb, Jr., *The Rock Art of Texas Indians* (Austin and London: University of Texas Press, 1967), pp. 111–23.

4. Marc Simmons, "History of Pueblo-Spanish Relations to 1821," in *Handbook of the North American Indians: Southwest*, vol. 9, ed. Alfonso Ortiz (Washington, D.C.: Smithsonian Institution Press, 1979), p. 182.

5. James D. Keyser, "North Cave Hills," in *Rock Art of Western South Dakota*, ed. L. Adrien Hannus, Special Publication of the South Dakota Archaeological Society, no. 9 (Rapid City, 1984), p. 28.

6. Kenneth B. Castleton, *Petroglyphs and Pictographs of Utah*, 2 vols. (Salt Lake City: Utah Museum of Natural History, 1978), pp. 61–62, 75, 142, 173ff.

7. James D. Keyser, "A Lexicon for Historic Plains Indian Rock Art: Increasing Interpretive Potential," *Plains Anthropologist* 32, no. 115 (1987): 43–71.

8. Ibid., p. 45.

9. Martha Coleman Bray, ed., *The Journals of Joseph N. Nicollet: A Scientist on the Mississippi Headwaters with Notes on Indian Life* (St. Paul: Minnesota Historical Society, 1970), p. 266.

10. John C. Ewers, *Plains Indian Painting: A Description of an Aboriginal Art* (Palo Alto, Calif.: Stanford University Press, 1939).

11. Stanley Vestal, *Warpath: The True Story of the Fighting Sioux Told in a Biography of Chief White Bull* (Boston: Houghton Mifflin, 1934), pp. 145–46.

12. DeCost Smith, *Indian Experiences* (Caldwell, Idaho: Caxton, 1943), p. 134.

13. Bray, *The Journals*, p. 162.

14. Vestal, *Warpath*, p. 40.

15. Ibid., p. 187.

16. Ian M. West, "Plains Indian Horse Sticks," *American Indian Art Magazine* 3, no. 2 (1978): 65.

17. Ibid., no. 3.

18. Marsha C. Bol, "Lakota Women's Artistic Strategies in Support of the Social System," *American Indian Culture and Research Journal* 9, no. 1 (1985): 46.

19. F. Dennis Lessard, "Pictographic Art in Beadwork from the Cheyenne River Sioux," *American Indian Art Magazine* 16, no. 1 (1990): 57–60.

20. Ibid., p. 60.

21. Helen H. Blish, *A Pictographic History of the Oglala Sioux* (Lincoln: University of Nebraska Press, 1967), p. 7.

22. Ibid., p. 120.

23. Ibid., pp. 87–101.

24. DeWitt Clinton Poole, *Among the Sioux of Dakota: Eighteen Months' Experience as an Indian Agent, 1869–70* (D. Van Nostrand, 1881; reissued St. Paul: Minnesota Historical Society, 1988), p. 66.

25. David W. Penney and Janet Stouffer, "Horse Imagery in Native American Arts," *The Detroit Institute of Arts Bulletin* 62, no. 1 (1986): 18–25. Reprinted in *Great Lakes Indian Art*, ed. David W. Penney (Detroit: Wayne State University Press, 1989), pp. 40–50.

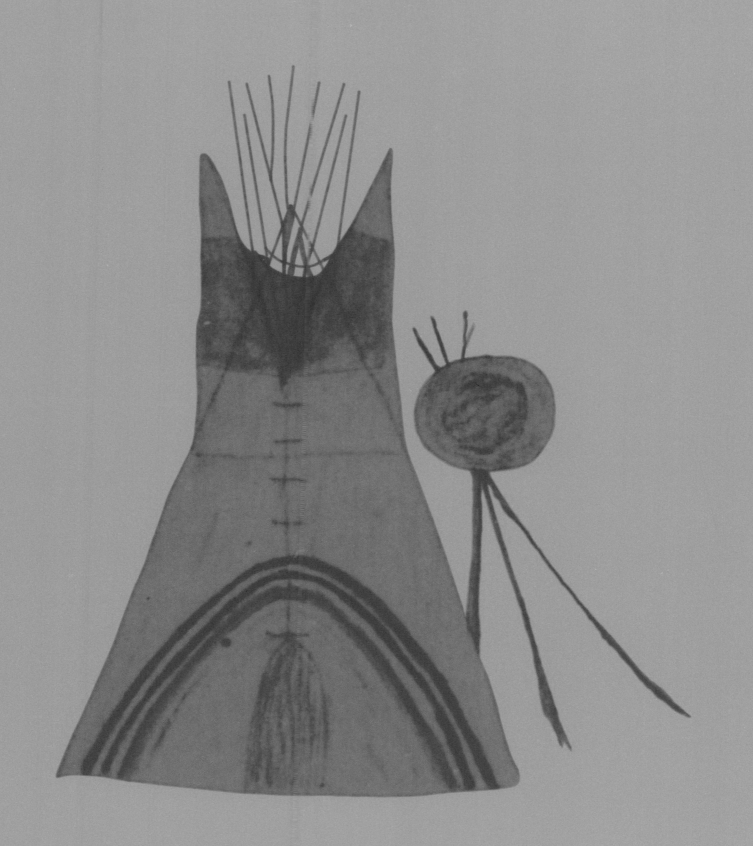

# Sacrifice Transformed into Victory: Standing Bear Portrays Sitting Bull's Sun Dance and the Final Summer of Lakota Freedom
## Father Peter J. Powell

The final summer of Lakota freedom was that of 1876, when Sitting Bull, Crazy Horse, and the free Lakotas who followed them, with their Northern Cheyenne allies, roamed the rich game lands of their own country, only to be attacked by soldiers. That summer the Lakota and Cheyenne warriors won their greatest victories over the white troopers, throwing back Three Star Crook's command at the Rosebud River, and eight days later wiping out Long Hair Custer and his men, after those soldiers struck the villages peacefully camped along the Little Big Horn. The great events of that summer are recaptured here by the Minneconjou Lakota artist Standing Bear (Mato Najin), using watercolors on muslin (fig. 1, cat. no. 155). This is one of three muslins I believe to be his art. All portray the Lakota-Cheyenne victory at the Little Big Horn. Only in this one, however, does Standing Bear portray two important spiritual events which preceded that triumph: the Animal Dreamers' Dance on the Rosebud, and Sitting Bull's Sun Dance on the same stream, where he beheld his vision of victory.[1]

B orn on Tongue River the Winter When the Children Died of Coughing (1859), Standing Bear with his family was among those Lakotas who followed Sitting Bull and Crazy Horse in the last days of Sioux freedom. Although Minneconjou, the family was affiliated with Crazy Horse's Oglalas. Sixteen winters old the summer of 1876, Standing Bear witnessed Sitting Bull's Sun Dance and himself took part in the fighting at the Little Big Horn.[2] Since he was with Crazy Horse's Oglalas, surely he beheld the Animal Dreamers' Dance in the Oglala village on the Rosebud, immediately preceding Sitting Bull's Sun Dance. Later, in accordance with Lakota and Cheyenne warrior-artist tradition, Standing Bear would paint these events, assisted by the guidance and recollections of other warriors who also saw and participated in them. Thus what he has painted here records his own experiences, verified and expanded by the eyewitness accounts of others who were also present.

Concerning the life of Standing Bear (later baptized Stephen Standing Bear), we long to know more. He was among the closest friends of Black Elk (Nicholas Black Elk), the Oglala holy man whose biography ranks among the greatest of spiritual classics. They were young men together and remained close throughout their lives. About the winter of 1879–80, at the age of nineteen, Standing Bear carried the pipe against the Crows. That was young to lead a war party, but five men followed him. They left when the snow was melting, and the journey took some three to four weeks. They were successful, capturing about thirty horses. The journey back was a hard one, however, for on the way they had nothing to eat for four days and nights. But they reached home safely, driving the Crow horses in triumph.[3]

The free days were all but ended by that time, and although he was a Minneconjou, Standing Bear chose to settle among Crazy Horse's Oglalas on Pine Ridge Reservation. Doubtless his friendship for Black Elk influenced that decision. It is recalled that Standing Bear married a woman named Red Elk and they had a daughter named Yellow Calf, born about 1883. In 1889 Standing Bear was among the Lakotas who signed on to appear in Buffalo Bill Cody's Wild West Show, and he traveled to Europe at least once as a performer. While there he became friends with the Austrian family of a retired military officer living in Vienna, and stayed with them after an injury forced him to leave the Wild West Show.

He returned to America in 1890, to find Lakota devotion to the Ghost Dance at its height. That winter saw the terrible massacre at Wounded Knee. Now Standing Bear suffered the grief of losing his wife and possibly his daughter, cut down by the soldier bullets there.

From that time of sorrow a new life for Standing Bear began. Louise Renick, the oldest daughter of the family he knew in Austria, came to America and traveled to Pine Ridge to work as a nurse, arriving sometime in late 1890 or early 1891. Standing Bear asked her to marry him and she accepted, moving into what would become the town of Manderson, in Wounded Knee District. Three children would be born to them [4]

At this time Standing Bear turned to farming and cattle raising to support his family and community, and he is recalled as being a generous man, in the tradition of the Lakota leaders from the buffalo days. During this period he would exercise his greatest power as an artist. By about 1900 Standing Bear was in his early forties, with his reputation as an artist well-established among his people. It was

apparently between 1889 and 1903 that Standing Bear created this painted muslin, and possibly the two other muslins, all portraying the Battle of the Little Big Horn. At this time the Illinois artist Elbridge Ayer Burbank was visiting the Oglala and Sicangu Lakotas, painting portraits of some. In 1899, while on Pine Ridge Reservation, Burbank commissioned a number of paintings by Lakota warrior-artists. This painted muslin was evidently one of them, for it was among the Burbank paintings and memorabilia in the home of his in-laws in Rockford, Illinois, when that home was torn down in 1956 and the Burbank paintings, with the American Indian art accompanying them, were auctioned off.[5]

At the age of sixty-nine, in about 1928, Standing Bear created an important series of drawings, all on paper. Though small in comparison to the great painted muslins, they are nevertheless invaluable, beautifully executed portrayals of Lakota life. Originally there were thirty-two drawings, including portraits of Sitting Bull, Crazy Horse, and Black Elk; scenes from the Vision Quest, the Sun Dance, and other sacred ceremonies; portraits of the Animal Dreamers; and drawings of the regalia worn by the Lakota Chiefs and warrior societies. Thirty-one are preserved in the Buechel Memorial Lakota Museum at St. Francis, South Dakota. Regrettably, the Crazy Horse portrait is missing at this writing.[6]

Glorious as the painted muslins are, Standing Bear's best-known art was created during his last years. In the spring of 1931, when Standing Bear was some seventy-two winters old, Black Elk, now a venerable holy man, chose him to illustrate his biography *Black Elk Speaks*. Standing Bear was present when Black Elk recounted his life, much of which Standing Bear himself had shared, to John G. Neihardt; and Standing Bear's recollections are mingled

Fig. 1
Muslin painted by Standing
Bear, Minneconjou Lakota
(cat. no. 155). Foundation for
the Preservation of American
Indian Art and Culture, Inc.,
Chicago, gift of Dorothy C.
and L. S. Raisch. Photo by
F. Peter Weil.

83

with those of his friend in the book itself. Their respective accounts appear in the original transcribed form in *The Sixth Grandfather: Black Elk's Teaching Given to John G. Niehardt*, edited by Raymond J. DeMallie.[7]

Standing Bear's illustrations in *Black Elk Speaks* reflect his own profound insight into the power, beauty, and sanctity of Black Elk's Great Vision. In that volume he also illustrates events that he and his friend shared: the Battle of the Little Big Horn, the Ghost Dance and other sacred ceremonies, and finally the massacre at Wounded Knee. In his portrayal of Wounded Knee, Standing Bear depicts the Lakota women and children, among whom were his own wife and possibly their daughter, fleeing from the line of soldier rifles, only to be cut down by the death-bringing stream of soldier bullets.

Standing Bear died in 1934. Black Elk lived on until 1950. Together, these two lifelong friends, the Minneconjou warrior-artist and the Oglala holy man, left the world a wondrous legacy of sacrifice transformed into blessing, of beauty mingled with holiness—the essence of the Lakota way of life.

## THE ANIMAL DREAMERS' DANCE ON THE ROSEBUD

mong the Lakotas there were, and are, a few men and women to whom a "spirit animal" or "vision animal" has appeared in a dream or vision, instructing that individual and sharing supernatural power with him or her. Among the most powerful spirit animals are the elk, the black-tailed deer, the buffalo, the wolf, and the bear. Traditionally, a person who dreamed of any of these became a member of that society whose membership shared the same dream animal's power. These persons are known collectively as Animal Dreamers, and they are respected as holy men and holy women.[8]

Each spirit animal possesses special power. Among the Lakotas the elk is closely associated with the Dakota concept of love and sexual passion. Supernatural power lies behind manifestations of sexual desire, and of those spirit animals controlling such power the bull elk is the most important. For the bull elk possesses special powers over the females of his kind. Thus the Elk Dreamers' Society possessed the greatest power for winning women's hearts. In dancing, the men wore triangular masks made of young buffalo skins, with a pair of branches trimmed to represent elk antlers. These were wrapped with otter fur, representing the horns "in velvet," as the immature horns of the elk are described. The Elk Dreamers also possessed powers for overcoming those who opposed them. Thus as they danced they carried a hoop with two cross cords, supporting a mirror at the center. These dancers were, and are, believed to possess supernatural powers, so that they can throw or shoot their influence into all whom they oppose. Therefore, as they danced about the camp circle, they stamped a foot and flashed sunlight from the mirror at persons in sight. This is believed to put those people under the power of the Elk Dreamers' Society.[9]

Unlike the Elk Dreamers, the Black-tailed Deer Dreamers were young men only. When dancing they wore a mask similar to that of the Elk Dreamers, but with horns and ears like those of a black-tailed deer. The black-tailed deer is very *wakan* (possessing power to kill a man simply by looking at him).[10] This power was shared with the Black-tailed Deer Dreamers, so that some Lakotas believed them to be the most powerful of the Animal Dreamers. In their ceremony, when one Black-tailed Deer Dreamer looked around, the others fell down as if dead. Like the Elk Dreamers, the Black-tailed Deer Dreamers were believed capable of killing people with a glance or by capturing their reflections in a mirror or by sighting

them through a sacred hoop. In dancing they thus carried a sacred hoop with an imitation spiderweb in the center.[11] Spiders possess great wisdom, great cunning; and thus possess special power over women. Thus the Black-tailed Deer Dreamers also possessed power to win the affection of women.[12]

A man who dreamed of a bear was considered very wakan, as bears possess great power for healing, especially men who are badly wounded. Thus Bear Dreamers were held in very high regard. No women were among them. "Many men were wounded by bullets or the like; the Bear Doctors make all of them well. . . . The Bear Dreamer society is the only one the people find very astonishing (wowinihanyan)," one who knew their power well recalled.[13]

Wolf Dreamers were also wakan. They possessed great power to heal the sick and to remove arrows, but they never treated wounds. They were noted as makers of war medicines, especially wakan shields. No women were among them.[14] They had other powers as well. "In the beginning a man who dreamed of wolves always went toward the enemies' tipis like a wolf, it is said. He was, therefore, very inconspicuous, hence nobody was able to see him. When there were many buffalo somewhere, a wolf came to tell the Wolf Dreamer, it is said. Therefore the man as well as the wolf is believed to be very wakan." The man who dreamed of a wolf was not very much on guard, but would haughtily close his eyes; yet he was very much on his guard, one who knew the Wolf Dreamers recalled.[15]

The Buffalo Dreamers were mostly men, with occasionally a few women. When they held their dances, a priest (shaman) appeared dressed in the head and skin of a buffalo. As he ran about the camp, a naked young man stalked him, while the other Buffalo Dreamers followed singing. At the proper time the hunter shot an

arrow deeply into a spot marked on the buffalo skin. The shaman staggered, vomited blood, and spit up the arrow point. Later another shaman would use medicine (*pejuta*) on the bleeding Buffalo Dreamer. Then he pulled the arrow out, and immediately the wound was healed.[16]

All Animal Dreamers, then, were endowed with special powers from those spirit animals who instructed them. The power was to be both used and displayed. Thus at times a dream animal would appear in a vision to the man or woman he instructed, telling that person to test the power he had given him or her. Following so powerful a vision, the person must offer a public display of his or her vision animal's supernatural power. Whenever an individual Animal Dreamer offered such a ceremony, the various Animal Dreamers came together in one celebration, making a public display of the powers bestowed upon them by their respective animal guardians. This was called a Medicine Day, and it was an important occasion, long recalled by those who witnessed the display of supernatural power then.

One who did not forget was He Dog, the Oglala Shirtwearer, Crazy Horse's brother-friend. Thus fifty winters later he recalled "that before the fight on the Rosebud some of the Lakotas performed a ceremony, which he saw, imitating the black-tailed deer, long-tailed deer, elk, and bear." This Medicine Day was held immediately before the battle with Crook's soldiers on June 17, 1876.[17]

Events of that Medicine Day on the Rosebud are pictured here (fig. 2). Two Elk Dreamers and two Black-tailed Deer Dreamers are the central dancers, led by the virgins of the Elk Dreamers' Society, their pipes extended in supplication.

The Elk Dreamers appear at the far right, wearing the horned masks and the yellow and black paint of their society. Their forearms and the lower part of their legs are painted black because elks are that way. Their masks bear figures of a star and clouds. (Black and dark blue are interchangeable in Lakota art; thus dark blue is used in place of black here.) They carry sage in their left hands. Each bears a sacred hoop formed by twining together fresh twigs and leaves of the willow. At the center of one hoop is a small mirror, held by four rawhide cords arranged at right angles, symbolizing the four directions of the universe. The sacred hoop is of great sanctity to the Lakotas because it forms the holy circle, the embodiment of all the sacred power in the universe. This is the hoop and looking glass used "to catch the eye of a girl and bring back her heart." Also, sunlight can be flashed from this mirror, placing any person that sunlight touches under the power of the Elk Dreamers' Society.[18]

Two Black-tailed Deer Dreamers move before the Elk Dreamers. Eagle feathers form their ears. Their masks are similar to those worn by the Elks but with variations given by the vision deer who appeared to each man. The dancers are painted red, with their lower arms and legs painted black. Each carries the tail of a black-tailed deer in his right hand, and a sacred hoop is in his left hand.[19]

Two virgins lead the way. These are the holy women of the Elk Dreamer Society, and they are both feared and respected by the people for the spiritual power they possess. Dressed in fine dresses, their hair hanging loose, each virgin carries a sacred medicine pipe. Now, with these pipes extended in supplication to Wakan Tanka the Great Mysterious, they lead and the others follow, going inside the camp circle and moving all around it, forming the sacred circle.[20]

Crouched behind the Elk Dreamers, with arm outstretched, is the man who has come to test their power, trying to disprove it. He is the "magic shooter," a medicine man who represents the evil-spirit element in the performance, testing the powers bestowed upon the dancers by their vision animal protectors, trying to overcome them. He it is who officially attempts to injure the Animal Dreamers by shooting at them: small stones, claws, grasshoppers, fingernails, even arrows, and on one occasion at least, a bullet. They attempt to dodge whatever he fires at them; but if their medicine is truly potent no injury will result. They will be able to evade the missiles or, if struck, will be able to throw them off or cough them up, proceeding unscathed.[21] For great is the power their dream animals have bestowed upon them.

The Elk Dreamer nearest the magic shooter wheels to ward off his attack directly. The Elk Dreamers' mirrors possess power to detect and to track ill-feeling, especially when an evil spirit is attempting to test and harass that supernatural power bestowed by their spirit elk guardian.[22] Now, turning the mirror at the center of his sacred hoop toward the magic shooter, the Elk Dreamer deflects whatever the magic shooter is firing, turning this evil aside, proving the superior power of his spirit elk guardian.

Crouching before the two virgins, held back by the power flowing from their sacred pipes, stands a mysterious figure. Possibly he is the priest of this ceremony. That is unlikely, however, for in Amos Bad Heart Bull's drawings of the Animal Dreamer dances the priest appears as a person of dignity, handsomely dressed. This man is strangely dressed. He holds a mirror in his left hand, with what appears to be the sacred circle reflected in its glass. Perhaps he is deflecting any evil power thrown at the dancers by the power of the sacred circle; or possibly he, like the magic shooter, is attempting to shine power on them. His role remains a mystery.

A Wolf Dreamer dances above the Elk and Black-tailed Deer dancers. He is dressed in the skin of a wolf, his face covered with a

**Fig. 2**
Animal Dreamers' Dance
(detail of painted muslin).

rawhide mask with holes for his eyes and one for his mouth, through which protrudes the eagle-wing-bone whistle he is blowing to summon the spirits. The mouth of the mask is painted with red earth. Symbols of the star, the moon, and the clouds are painted on the mask. Crow wing feathers are at its top. His legs and arms are painted red, his body white. He carries an imitation rattlesnake or bull snake from which he shoots wakan influence.[23]

A Bear Dreamer dances behind the Wolf Dreamer, displaying his power alone. A bear mask covers his own head, displaying his oneness with his vision guardian. He is painted red and yellow, sacred colors.

Finally, moving in from above, a Heyoka Dreamer appears. White-painted, his hair half shaved, he wears a mask of old pieces of tipi cover or tent cloth painted with vision symbols. He carries a toy bow and arrow. A string of dew claws hangs over his shoulder. He is wearing moccasins of hide from an old buffalo robe, to which weeds are attached. He is dragging a piece of old torn tipi cover or tent cloth.

Dancing in the opposite direction from the others, the Heyoka Dreamer is set apart from them. The Heyokas are the supernatural clowns of the Lakota ceremonies, their actions consistently contrary to nature, so that they speak and act backward. These are the men who in a vision beheld the Thunderbird, Lightning, or other of the Thunder Beings, those awesome and fearsome spirits of the sky. Immediately after so terrible a vision the dreamer must go through a public performance displaying the power given to him. If he does not, he will be killed by lightning,[24] for Heyoka power is terrible to bear. Thus, concerning Heyokas, some Lakotas still ask, "Who can say what they are?"

The Elk Dreamers and the Heyokas are rivals. Whenever the Elk Dreamers dance the Heyokas come near, attempting to make medicine to harm the Elk Dreamers and their followers; but normally they are unable to do so. And the Heyokas are also rivals of the Black-tailed Deer Dreamers, with whom they hold magical trials of powers.[25] Thus the Heyoka Dreamer dances alone here, throwing his power against the Elk and Black-tailed Deer Dreamers, but unable to stop them.

The Animal Dreamers' activities covered the entire camp circle, making Medicine Day an occasion of merriment. Much laughter was aroused by the dancers' antics, as they competed with one another in displaying their respective powers.

Standing Bear captures that festive aspect. Two courting couples appear above and below the dancers, wrapped in the red and blue courting blankets favored by Lakota young men. Other blanket-wrapped suitors appear nearby, waiting their turns to visit with the same young women, who are clearly popular. Standing between two painted lodges, wearing a Navajo blanket, a woman gazes at the dancers, watching their display of supernatural power.[26] At the lower right, two women friends, mounted on the same horse, head toward the Rosebud. Their horse is dressed for this special occasion, wearing a German silver bridle, with eagle feathers fastened to its mane and tail. Behind them, at the lower left, a woman boils meat while an older woman looks on. The rawhide rope stretched between forked poles before them sags beneath the weight of meat drying in the sun. For the hunting was good along the Rosebud, called Elk River by the Lakotas and the Cheyennes because of the teeming herds of elk there. And rising around them is the crescent moon circle of painted tipis, each blessed by the wakan person or wakan animal who gave the design to the lodge owner or his ancestors. Sacred bundles hang suspended from poles behind two of the lodges, with a sacred shield and a society lance hanging behind two other lodges. All are exposed to the Sun, to be blessed and renewed by his life-giving power.

However, far more important than the festive aspect of Medicine Day is the deeply supernatural nature of that which is taking place. For here beside the Rosebud, in the sight of human beings, the spirit animals themselves are displaying their own supernatural powers, through this dance of the Animal Dreamers, those men and women whose special guardians they are.

## Sitting Bull's Sun Dance

Shortly after the Animal Dreamers' Dance, the Lakotas and Cheyennes crossed Rosebud River to the west side. Here their villages were pitched in the beautiful valley lying a short distance north of the present Northern Cheyenne reservation. There, not far from the sacred Deer Rocks, where the ancient carvings appear, the Lakotas prepared to offer the Sun Dance.

All the people, Lakota and Cheyenne, camped in one great circle for this holiest of Lakota ceremonies. Now Sitting Bull, who was leader of this Sun Dance, the pledger, prepared to fulfill the vow he made the previous autumn. It had come about in this way:[27]

The summer before, that of 1875, White Dog, a chief of the Hohe, the Assiniboine, had carried a pipe to the Lakota chiefs, seeking peace after the years (winters) of warfare between the two tribes.[28] The Lakotas were camped at the mouth of Powder River, and here the chiefs accepted the Assiniboine pipe. Sitting Bull was especially pleased to smoke it. Nearly twenty winters before, in winter 1857–58, during an attack on the Hohe, he rescued from death at the hands of his comrades a brave young Assiniboine, only eleven winters old. Impressed by the boy's valor, he adopted him as his younger brother. The boy was a grown and respected warrior now, bearing the name of Jumping Bull or Little Hohe.[29] He and Sitting Bull were as close as natural brothers. Thus when White Dog had come bearing a pipe, Sitting Bull gladly smoked with him, and afterward presented him with many gifts.

Peace made with the Hohe, Sitting Bull decided to take advantage of it and pass through the country of these new allies on a horse-stealing expedition. It appeared to be a good time to capture horses from the Slota, the Canadian Mixed-Bloods, who were known to possess much fine stock.

Because the warpath led through now friendly territory, Sitting Bull decided to lead only a small party. He invited his younger nephew, One Bull, to go with him, giving him his own repeating rifle as a gift. With them went Iron Hoof (Iron Claw or Horseshoe) and One Bull's wife, White Buffalo Woman. It was early autumn when they started off on horseback, heading for the boundary of Canada, the Grandmother's Land.[30]

After several days' riding they reached the Missouri River below Fort Peck, crossed it, and pushed up Little River (as they called the stream then) to a point north of the present Assiniboine (Stoney) reserve in Canada.

There they found a camp of strangers they believed to be Slota. It was night, and across the stream they could barely make out the white blur of massed tents and the dim forms of the horses grazing about. Sitting Bull told Iron Hoof and White Buffalo Woman to stay concealed in the timber while he and One Bull went after the horses.

Sitting Bull stood on the bank of the little stream, gazing at that camp of sleeping ene-

mies. He was afoot and lame, crippled by the bullet of a Crow chief he fought and killed in autumn 1856. The Crow shot him in the left foot, before Sitting Bull's own bullet brought him down, mortally wounded. Then Sitting Bull finished him off with his own long-bladed knife. It was one of his greatest deeds, and after that the Midnight Strong Hearts, the bravest men of the Hunkpapa Strong Heart Society, had made him their leader. But because of it, Sitting Bull always walked with a limp.[31]

Now if these enemies were awakened it would be hard to escape. There were many dogs too, ready to give the alarm. And the Slota were well-supplied with guns and ammunition. Seldom had Sitting Bull attempted a more delicate and daring raid.

So standing there on the stream bank, Sitting Bull raised his open palms to the night sky and vowed to make a Sun Dance if he were successful. He prayed: "Wakan Tanka take pity on me, blameless as I am. Give me some horses to take home with me, and I shall give You a scarlet blanket and a filled pipe next summer." By a "scarlet blanket" Sitting Bull meant his own blood.

He and One Bull were successful, capturing ten good horses, and herding them back to the timber, where Iron Hoof and White Buffalo Woman greeted them happily. Then they started home, traveling fast, herding the captured horses before them. Along the way they ran into trouble in the form of twenty Assiniboines who treacherously attacked them, violating the peace. Sitting Bull and One Bull held them off until the Hohe chief Red Stone arrived, ordering his tribesmen to withdraw, accompanying Sitting Bull and his party for a time to see that no further trouble occurred.

Sitting Bull and his companions found the Lakota camp on Beaver Lake, a branch of the Little Missouri River. Snow was beginning

to fall as they reached home, charging victoriously into the village, driving the captured Slota horses before them.[32]

Now, here on the Rosebud, Sitting Bull prepared to fulfill his vow of the previous autumn. As pledger of the Sun Dance he was the leader, the chief of the dancers. The aged Black Moon, who was both a chief of the Hunkpapa and a Sun Dance priest, was the intercessor, the spokesman to the gods. Together, they were the men who must bring the Sun Dance ceremonies to a perfect conclusion if the Lakotas and their world were to be renewed with Wakan Tanka's own blessing and life.

That Sun Dance, called "Sitting Bull's Sun Dance" to this day, is the heart of this painting (fig. 3).

## The Sun Lodge

The time is the holy four days of midsummer, when it is proper to offer those ceremonies that pertain to Wakan Tanka the Great Mysterious, the One Who Is Yet Many, the Sixteen Gods Who Are One. For at this season Maka the Earth, the All-Mother, has caused the ground to bring forth abundant grass to fatten the buffalo, and fruits for the benefit of mankind, and all things that grow from the ground. Wakinyun the Winged God has caused these things to grow and ripen. Skan the Sky, the Great Spirit, with Tate the Father of the Four Winds, and Okaga the South Wind, pervade all above the world. And Wi the Sun, the Chief of the Gods, smiles upon all. Therefore the Lakota rejoice and show their joy by offering ceremonies in honor of the gods. Now they were offering the Sun Dance, the greatest of those seven sacred ceremonies brought by Wohpe the Beautiful One, the Gracious One, when she appeared on earth as the White Buffalo Woman.[33]

The Sun Lodge appears as a circular bower sided and covered with green branches, reflecting that abundant life filling the trees and

**Fig. 3**
Sitting Bull's Sun Dance (detail
of painted muslin).

vegetation that spring from Grandmother Earth. Its entrance is toward the Sun at midday, when he is at the height of his power.

The day is the bright blue day Sitting Bull had earlier prayed for as leader of the Sun Dance: a day with blue sky, unmarred by clouds; a warm, calm day without heat. On this day, Sitting Bull would meet all the supernatural beings face to face, as he offered the sacrifice of his own blood for his people and their world. And he would do so praying to the Wakan Tanka, the Sixteen Gods Who Are One, through their chief, Wi the Sun.[34]

Rising at the center of the Sun Lodge, the holy spot, is the Sun Pole, the Sacred Pole. Formed from a living cottonwood tree, felled in a sacred manner, it is painted red to show its holiness. At the top is a bunch of leaves left when the tree was cut down, so that the living spirit of the tree might be appeased and lend itself to the purpose of the Sun Pole, the blessing of the Lakota people.[35] (They are badly faded in this painting.)

A red cloth banner flies near the top, the sacred color of Wi the Sun. This is the banner of the holy men, the priests of the Sun Dance, and it shows the willingness of the people to give allegiance to Sun's will.[36]

In the fork is tied the fetish of the Sun Dance, composed of four times four wands of chokecherry wood, with a wisp of sage, one of sweetgrass, a tuft of shed buffalo hair, and offerings from the people enclosed in these branches. (It too is faded in the painting.) This bundle is extremely sacred, and it was earlier blessed by Black Moon the Intercessor, assisted by other holy men, who imparted to it the power of Tatanka the Buffalo God. Tatanka is the great patron of generosity, sexual relations, fecundity, industry, and other ceremonies. He is the comrade of Sun, and in ceremonies pertaining to Sun, his power prevails. Tatanka is also the spe-

cial guardian of the Lakota people. Now with his sacred fetish elevated on the Sun Pole, the great and gracious power of the Buffalo God prevails in the Sun Dance camp.[37]

The images of a man and a buffalo hang suspended from the forks of the Sacred Pole. Earlier, these were made with ceremony and painted black, imparting to the image of a man the potency of Iya, the patron god of libertinism, and to the buffalo image the potency of Gnaski, the Crazy Buffalo, the patron god of licentiousness. This ceremony also gave these images the receptivity of an enemy man and of the Crazy Buffalo, so that whatever was done to the images would be done to the enemy and the demon buffalo.[38]

After the raising of the sacred Sun Pole bearing these two figures, a brief period of license had reigned in the Sun Dance camp. Some Lakotas shouted the names of Iya and Gnaski, protesting that these gods prevailed in the village; and the spirits of the two obscene gods briefly possessed some people, with men and women commingling and jesting of sexual things. Soon, however, Black Moon the Intercessor sent a crier through the village, summoning the escort of brave men who earlier bore the Sun Pole into camp, with all the warriors of the Lakotas, to come and dance the war dance to drive the demon gods from the village. Then men alone, dressed in their finest clothing, carrying shields, lances, standards, and rifles, came running in single file. They circled the Sun Lodge before entering it. Then, inside, if they carried guns, they fired repeatedly at the images of the enemy man and the Crazy Buffalo, riddling them, destroying the power of the god of libertinism and the god of licentiousness. Then the warriors danced the victory dance and the women cried their approval, making screech-owl calls for joy over this defeat of the obscene gods.[39]

The shooting at the obscene gods ended, and their power broken, Black Moon the Intercessor made an incense of buffalo chips on the buffalo-skull altar rising at the place of honor in the lodge. (This altar does not appear in the painting.) This incense was to appease Tatanka the Buffalo God, whose sacred fetish hung above on the Sun Pole. Other ceremonies followed, making clear and effective the power of Tatanka to prevail in the Sun Dance camp. Now all the people would be blessed and protected by their most gracious and generous benefactor on earth, the Buffalo God, the comrade of Sun.[40]

Sitting Bull's sacrifice was offered on the fourth day of the Sun Dance, that holiest of days, for it is the midyear day. It was made during the final dance, the Sun-Gazing Dance, when the bravest of men underwent the torture. Sitting Bull knew both the sanctity and the suffering of this sacrifice. He had danced the Sun-Gazing Dance before, and his body bore scars from the piercing and tearing of his body in previous Sun Dances. He knew that self-sacrifice was at the heart of the Lakota way of life, for it was involved in the very creation of life as his people knew it. For the creation of the world occurred when Inyan the Rock, the All-Father, gave his own blood to create Earth and Sky. That first creation was accomplished through self-sacrifice and the shedding of the Rock's own life force. Now Sitting Bull and those other men who had vowed the torture in the Sun-Gazing Dance were about to participate in the very renewal of life. For as Inyan created the world by shedding his blood, so Sitting Bull and those suffering the torture with him would be sacrificing their flesh and shedding their blood to re-create the world and renew life on earth, both for the Lakotas and for all living things.[41]

Sitting Bull had vowed the offering of one hundred pieces of flesh—skin—from his arms. Jumping Bull, Little Hohe, his adopted brother, the man whose life he had saved, had agreed to do the cutting.[42] Now, during the Sun-Gazing Dance, Sitting Bull moved forward to the Sacred Tree, the holy center pole rising at the heart of the Sun Lodge. He was naked to the waist. Jumping Bull came forward too, bringing a sharp steel awl and a knife ground to a thin narrow blade, very sharp.

Sitting Bull sat down, his back resting against the Sacred Tree, to be blessed by the holy power flowing from this tree of life. His legs were outstretched straight out on the earth before him, his arms relaxed and resting on his thighs.

Jumping Bull knelt beside him. Then, beginning at the bottom of Sitting Bull's right arm, near the wrist, he stuck the awl into the skin of the arm. He lifted the skin clear of the flesh, then using the knife he cut away a small bit of skin, "the size of a large louse" in Sun Dance terminology.[43] Then letting the skin fall again, he withdrew the awl, only to pierce the skin a short instance above. And so he continued upward, thrusting, lifting, then cutting. Soon Sitting Bull's arm was covered with blood.

When Jumping Bull reached the top of the right arm, having cut fifty pieces of skin from it, he rose and crossed to Sitting Bull's left side. There he cut in the same manner, beginning at the wrist and working toward the shoulder. As he cut away each piece of skin he offered it above, to Wi the Sun, the Chief of the Gods. Then he placed each sacrifice of flesh on the bosom of Maka the Earth, the All-Mother.

Throughout this ordeal Sitting Bull remained perfectly calm, never wincing, but wailing continually, not because of the pain but to beg Wakan Tanka's pity upon him and his people.

For half an hour this painful, cruel, seemingly endless piercing, lifting, cutting, and offering of skin continued. One Bull, Sitting Bull's younger nephew, who was present when he made the vow, was dancing with him in this Sun Dance, looking on as he was being cut. Sitting White Buffalo was pierced in this Sun Dance, and so was another man. The entire camp was watching.

Finally, Sitting Bull's sacrifice was completed: one hundred pieces of skin, the "scarlet blanket" he vowed in the darkness outside the Slota camp.

His offering of flesh made, Sitting Bull still had to complete the four periods of the Sun-Gazing Dance. He rose to his feet stiffly, and with blood flowing down his arms and fingers, slowly congealing in the heat, he took his place facing the Sacred Tree. There as the holy songs rose from the singers' voices, he began to dance, gazing at the sun, bobbing up and down, his eyes fastened on Sun's blazing brightness. All day long he danced, then all night on into the morning of the new day.

As noon of this second day drew near the watching crowd saw Sitting Bull falter. He appeared faint, barely able to stand. He did not drop, still holding on; but they knew something was wrong. Black Moon the Intercessor and other men moved in, and laying him down they put water on him. He spoke, saying he had seen, right below the sun where he looked, a vision. Then he asked Black Moon to announce what he had seen to the people. Black Moon walked to the entrance to the Sun Dance enclosure. There he cried:

*He (Sitting Bull) hears a voice from above saying "These have no ears." So Sitting Bull looked up and saw men coming down like grasshoppers, their heads and hats falling off. "These are to die but you are not supposed to take their spoils."*[44]

The Sun Dance was brought to a swift end after that. The final song of the Sun-Gazing Dance, the song of victory, was sung in loud and joyous tones by the singers, their buffalo-tail sticks pounding vigorously on the dried buffalo hide before them. Outside, the air was filled with the victory cries of the men, the shrill tones of the women's screech-owl calls of praise rising above them.[45] It was a great outpouring of joy at this Sun Dance that brought both new life to the people and their world, and the promise of victory over their enemies.

## The Sun Dance Participants

**Sitting Bull**   The movement in Lakota and Cheyenne warrior drawing normally begins at the right, with the artist drawing the principal figure first and at the right, facing left. The artist would continue drawing from right to left, symbolically following Sun's movement across the sky. Thus he received Sun's blessing as he worked.

The most prominent figure in the Sun Dance scene is the man wearing a split-horn, single-tail warbonnet. He stands farthest right, closest to the place of honor at the west side of the lodge, the leader's position. This man is stripped to the waist, and he carries a crooked lance as he dances gazing at the sun. A white horse stands beside him, head lowered.

This is Sitting Bull, we believe. For Sitting Bull is known to have worn a warbonnet of this type.[46] He was entitled to carry a crooked lance, for before being chosen head chief of the free Lakotas surrounding him here, he was chief of the Hunkpapa Midnight Strong Heart Society, whose two bravest men carried such lances.[47] Finally, the Lakota chiefs rode white horses.[48]

Sitting Bull's body is painted yellow, and he is wearing a dress breechclout of strips of red trade cloth, worn over his ordinary breechclout. These were called "tails" because they are long and hang down.[49] Evidently he has not yet offered his sacrifice of flesh, for no blood appears on his arms.

Standing beside Sitting Bull is his horse, head drooping in exhaustion. He is dressed in his finest, as if for battle, his tail tied with red trade cloth, a bridle of German silver covering his head, with eagle feathers tied to his forelock and tail. A red-painted scalp dangles from his bit. Only a horse who has ridden down an enemy in battle could wear such a decoration.[50] Hanging below his neck is a strip of red trade cloth bearing the symbol of Hanwi the Moon. Created by Sun himself to be his companion, Hanwi is one of the Associate Gods; thus she possesses great power to bless.

Throughout the heat of this entire day Sitting Bull's horse will share his sacrifice, drinking no water and eating no food, "standing against Sun" with his master. Thus he is said to be dancing with Sitting Bull. At sundown he will be taken from the Sun Dance Lodge and led away to water and food, his sacrifice complete.[51]

**The Two Pierced Men** Two men are offering the highest form of the Sun-Gazing Dance, the fourth form. One dances on the north (right) side of the lodge with Sitting Bull, the other on the south (left) side. They are undergoing the torture, their chests pierced through both skin and muscles, with sharpened sticks thrust through the wounds. These pointed sticks are bound by two braided rawhide ropes, securely fastened to the sacred Sun Pole.

The holy men who are their mentors, their instructors, who taught them the correct behavior to be observed in the Sun Dance ceremonies, also informed them about the tortures inflicted as part of the sacred rites. In doing so, they addressed them in words such as these:
*Such torture should cause the blood to flow, for when the blood flows as a token, it is the surest guarantee of sincerity, and without such a guar-antee the people or the Sun may doubt the professed purposes of the dancer. They [the tortures] should cause pain, for to endure pain willingly for the accomplishment of a purpose proves fortitude, the greatest virtue that he must manifest when in the presence of the people he appears before the Sun. The first great virtue, bravery, is made most manifest by enduring the greatest flow of blood and the most suffering that the rites of the Sun Dance demand.*
Then the mentors would have added:
*A Dancer should endure the torture of gazing at the Sun while dancing, so that no one can say that he did not dare to look into the face of the Sun when making a request of Him. One who endures the torture to the uttermost of the demands of the rites of the ceremony performs his part in a manner acceptable to the Gods and can expect a communication from them.[52]*

The two men who vowed the torture now fulfill their vows, throwing themselves back, pulling hard on the wounds that penetrate both flesh and muscles, attempting to pull themselves free. If that does not work they will dance from side to side, pulling away backward with a mighty effort, hoping thus to tear themselves loose, thereby completing their sacrifice.[53]

Both pierced dancers are warbonnet men. The man on the south side carries a crooked lance, apparently identical to the lance borne by Sitting Bull; thus possibly he is a Strong Heart Society member. However, this style of lance was also carried by the bravest men of the Wiciska, Sotka Yuha, and Iroka societies; so he may have been a member of any of these. Possibly, also, he is Sitting White Buffalo, who was pierced at the Sun Dance vowed by Sitting Bull.

Outside their relatives stand looking on, suffering at the sight of their loved ones undergoing this great agony. And if either pierced man is unmarried, his young woman stands by weeping in great sorrow.[54]

**The Two Dancers with Sitting Bull** Both men dancing in a line with Sitting Bull wear variations of the traditional Sun Dance sacred regalia. The dancer directly before him holds a sacrifice banner of cloth tied to a forked pole, with offerings of tobacco fastened to the forks in red cloth pouches. The dancer in front, described earlier, offers the highest form of the Sun-Gazing Dance, the piercing while fastened to the sacred Sun Pole.

The traditional, time-honored way of painting and dressing a candidate for the Sun Dance was performed by the holy man who was the man's priest-instructor.

First the entire face of the candidate was given a base of vermilion or brownish red paint. This is Sun's own color, the color of holiness. Then blue paint, symbolizing Taku Skanskan, the Blue Sky, was added. A blue line the width of a man's finger was made completely around the face. A straight blue line of the same width was made down the center of the forehead, ending at the bridge of the nose. A similar blue line ran down each cheek, and also one down the chin, from the center of the lower lip to the bottom of the chin.

The man's entire body was given a red base, with his feet painted red too. And down the shoulders and the outer arm, down to the hand, a blue line was made. The line divided down the back of the hand and extended along each finger, but the palm was left unpainted, untouched. All these lines were made with bluestone.

Then the priest painted on his candidate's body the design he devised to be the man's totem. After that he fastened around the candidate's loins a red-painted skirt, formed from two soft-tanned deerskins, cleaned of hair. "A skirt of red worn by a man is an emblem of holiness," a venerated Sun Dance priest recalled.[55]

Next he placed around the candidate's shoulders a cape of otter skin, the emblem of power over land and water. Four hair ornaments, sticks decorated with braided porcupine quillwork in bright colors, with dyed horsehair clusters attached, were pinned into the base of the scalp lock, at the crown of the head.

Fastened around the candidate's wrists and ankles were strips from a jackrabbit skin, or bands made of shed buffalo hair or by twisting hair that comes off a buffalo robe in tanning. (Some holy men declared that the armlets were made of buffalo wool, while the anklets were of jackrabbit skin.) An armlet of jackrabbit skin is an emblem of fleetness and of endurance on long journeys or during marches. In the buffalo hair bands abides the power of Taktanka the Buffalo God, the patron of the chase and of the Sun Dance. They are emblems of strength, of love, and of cunning in the chase.

Then the priest-instructor placed on each candidate such insignia as the man was entitled to wear. Traditionally this was a pendant of rawhide cut in the form of a disk and notched around the rim. This was painted blue, and a single tail feather from the spotted eagle was attached to the center. The pendant hung directly in front of the dancer, over his heart. This disk, forming the sacred circle, is a symbol of the world and time, and therefore of all things. The eagle feather is a symbol of bravery and fortitude.

Finally, the holy man placed on each candidate's head a wreath of sage, for sage is the favorite herb of Sun and is offensive to all evil beings.

Each candidate wore a special Sun Dance whistle, made from the largest bone in an eagle's wing. Sage was tied around the mouthpiece, and a single eagle breath feather was tied to the other end in such a way that it could not dangle. The dancers blew these continually, their eyes fixed upon the Sun, follow-ing his path across the Blue Sky. For the eagle is the bird who flies closest to the Sun.

All who danced wore their hair loose and hanging, for this is a sign of supplication.[56]

**The Elk Dancers and Their Companions**   In this final ceremony of the Sun-Gazing ritual some of the dancers portray those supernatural animals who appeared to their respective priest-instructors in a dream or vision, sharing their power with these holy men.

Two Elk Dancers appear on the north (right) side, wearing the antlers and the yellow paint associated with the Elk Dreamers. Sage wreaths encircle their heads. Both wear modified forms of the holy pendant in the form of the sacred circle, symbol of the world and of time, and therefore of all things, resting against their hearts. Both carry sacred hoops in their left hands. The first Elk Dancer carries a sacrifice banner of red and white striped cloth, tied to a sapling thrust into the earth, in his right hand. Red cloth pouches of tobacco are tied to the forks (leaves?) of the sapling, offerings to the Wakan Ones.

Two warbonnet men dance behind the Elk Dancers. The first, a long-tail warbonnet covering his head, wears a wreath of white sage (or perhaps willow) across his shoulder. His body is painted yellow. His wristlets of buffalo hair and anklets of rabbit skin, worn by all the Sun Dancers, are clearly visible. The second warbonnet man, his body painted blue, carries a sacrifice banner in his right hand while holding the reins of his roan war-horse in his left hand. The horse's head droops in exhaustion as he too offers his sacrifice, "standing against Sun" with his master.

**The Black-tailed Deer Dancers and Their Companion**   Two Black-tailed Deer Dancers and a warbonnet man (south side, lower left) face the Elk Dancers across the Lodge. The warbonnet man carries a sacrifice banner with yellow and blue cloth streamers in his left hand. Suspended from his neck, resting against his heart, is "a hoop covered with otterskin ceremoniously, a symbol of the Sun and of the years. For the years are a circle."[57] The Black-tailed Deer Dancers dance with him, the two upright eagle feathers on either side of their heads representing the great ears of that deer whose power is so strong. They are wearing the traditional Sun Dance regalia.[58]

**The Men Dancing with the Buffalo-Head Carrier** On the south side (upper left) is a dancer wearing much of the traditional Sun Dance sacred regalia. Instead of his body being red-painted, however, his upper body is yellow, evidently a variation used by the holy man who instructed him. His "tails" are of black or dark blue trade cloth. Black and dark blue are interchangeable colors in Lakota sacred regalia. Thus it is possible that he wears the color of Taku Skanskan the Blue Sky, indicating that he is engaged in a holy undertaking.[59]

Beside him the pierced warbonnet man, perhaps Sitting White Buffalo, throws himself back, attempting to tear himself free. A warbonnet man dances beside him, a sacrifice banner of striped cloth, tied to a sapling thrust into the earth, held in his left hand.

**The Buffalo-Head Carrier**   Holding fast to the Sun Pole, strengthened by the holy power flowing from it, a Buffalo-Head Carrier dances bowed beneath the weight of four buffalo skulls, one unseen.

His upper body is painted yellow, and suspended from his neck, resting against his heart, is a sacred pendant in the form of a six-pointed star, a mirror at the center in the form of the sacred circle, with two eagle feathers attached. Evidently this is part of the special vision regalia given by the Wakan Ones to the holy men who are the priest-instructors of the dancers in this upper line, as all four men wear variations of it. Over the red-painted deerskin skirt worn by all the Sun

Dancers, the Buffalo-Head Carrier wears "tails" of dark blue trade cloth. Blue is the color, the emblem, of Taku Skanskan the Blue Sky, and may indicate that he is engaged in a sacred undertaking, seeking power to be a holy man.

The Buffalo-Head Carrier offers the second form of the Sun-Gazing sacrifice. The flesh in his shoulders is pierced in four places, two on each side of his spine. Pointed sticks are thrust through these wounds, and the buffalo skulls are bound with strong thongs to these wooden pins. He will dance until the weight of the skulls tears the pointed sticks from his wounds, fulfilling his sacrifice.[60]

**The Holy Men**   Seated along the south (left) side are those men and women who make their own offering in the Sun Dance by guiding or assisting the dancers—the holy men, the musicians or singers, and the four brave men and four virgins.

Seated closest to the honor place, on the west side of the Sun Lodge, are the holy men, the priests. They are from the Gentle Speech Society, whose membership includes the chiefs. "There are many holy men, but only some are qualified to dance in the Sun Dance," Sword, who was himself a holy man and a Sun Dance instructor, declared.[61]

The intercessor, the chief instructor who guides the leader, must be a holy man "who knows all the customs of the people. He must know all the secret things of the shamans. He is the chief and wakiconze (magistrate) of the ceremonial camp. Other shamans help him as his council. He appoints the akitcita (marshalls) of the ceremonial camp."[62]

Black Moon, who was both a chief of the Hunkpapa and a venerated Sun Dance priest, was the intercessor of this Sun Dance vowed by Sitting Bull. He is probably the priest seated at the head of the line, closest to the place of honor on the west side. He is hold-ing an eagle-wing fan, a symbol of his chieftainship. He sits there in holiness and dignity, interceding for Sitting Bull, using his supernatural powers to bless him and those dancing with him.

Three other holy men sit below the intercessor, making the sacred number four. The three priests next to Black Moon probably each hold a bundle of white sage, that favorite herb of Sun, whose fragrance brings blessing and refreshment to the men offering their sacrifice to Sun. (The drawing of the sage is faded in the painting.)

All four holy men are interceding for the dancers, sharing the sacred power bestowed upon them with the dancers in their ordeal, ready to come to the aid of any who falter.

**The Musicians or Singers**   Seated below the holy men are the musicians. These are skilled singers from the *akitcita* societies, the marshalls of the Sun Dance camp. Appointed by the intercessor, they sing day and night, rotating from time to time, making this the akitcita sharing in the Sun Dance sacrifice.

They are drumming on a dried buffalo hide stretched taut upon the earth and staked. Each man carries a long slender wand with a dried buffalo tail tied to the smaller end, to do the drumming as they sing the ceremonial songs.[63]

The intensity of their singing is greatest now, as the men undergoing the torture struggle, throw themselves back and forth, attempting to tear loose, thereby fulfilling their vows and bringing the Sun-Gazing Dance to an end. From the singers' lips flow the sacred and majestic songs of the Sun-Gazing Dance. And rising above their deep voices, the shrill, piercing crying of the dancers' eagle-wing-bone whistles summon Wi the Sun to look down upon the dancers and take pity on them, blessing them in their sacrifice to renew the Lakotas and their world.

**The Four Brave Men and the Four Virgins**
Seated below the singers are the four brave men who counted coup on the living cottonwood tree chosen to be the Sacred Pole.[64] Behind them, closest to the entrance, are the four virgins who chopped the Sacred Tree.

Traditionally each virgin wears four eagle plumes erect at the scalp lock, the sage wreath, and the necklace with the dry hide disk—all worn by the Sun Dancers—but with no eagle quill attached to the disk. (Here, only three of the virgins wear sage wreaths. The fourth wears an eagle breath feather in her hair.) The virgins also wear anklets of shed buffalo hair. They are permitted to sit in the dedicated space in the Sacred Lodge and to take such part in the ceremony as they may be requested to do, usually to minister to the comfort of the dancers.[65]

As the men who vowed the torture were being pierced, the virgins stood beside them, encouraging them to bear the pain without flinching and to smile and sing a song of defiance. And it is they who wipe away with sweetgrass the blood that flows from the wounds, for the incense made of sweetgrass with such blood on it is potent to ensure constancy and reciprocity in love.[66]

During the four or more intermissions of the final day, the virgins, with the priest-instructors, give the dancers such refreshment as the rites will permit. If the dancers perspire, these attendants wipe away the perspiration with wisps of sage. And if one dances far into the night, a woman who loves him may chew a little bark of the cottonwood tree and mingle it with water, surreptitiously giving him this to drink.[67]

Here the virgins appear carrying shoots of sweetgrass (white sage?) in their hands, ready for use in wiping away the blood of the pierced ones, that offering of blood necessary to renew the Lakotas and their world. (The colors of three of the shoots are faded. Only the fourth branch is clearly visible.)

## The Final Dancing

The Sun-Gazing Dance continues all day until all the "captives," the pierced ones, have escaped, or until the next day has dawned. Then, if they have not escaped, they will be freed from their bonds and the sticks removed from their wounds, and it will be considered that they have been rescued, which is as meritorious as an escape.

As each pierced dancer breaks loose, his freedom is celebrated by the people of his band accompanying him from the Sun Lodge, the holy man who is his attendant and one of the virgins supporting him as he leaves, his vow fulfilled, his sacrifice completed.[68] As each pierced man breaks free, his relatives "throw away" three or four horses, honoring the man and displaying their generosity.[69]

That moment approaches in the painting. Relatives of the pierced ones move toward the Sun Dance Lodge, leading horses to be given away the moment their relatives tear themselves loose. Women carry kettles of food, gifts for the singers and their akitcita brothers.

Standing at the Sun Lodge entrance are three women bearing painted parfleches upon their backs. These contain dried meat, or possibly clothing, gifts for the holy men or the singers. Two of these women hold slender poles with scalps dangling from them—scalp staffs. Elsewhere, two other women come forward, carrying scalp staffs in one hand, buckets of food in the other. One (left) follows a mounted woman dressed in her finest. Her face is painted, her husband's warbonnet is on her head, and a scalp dangles from her horse's bridle. All these women are coming to take part in the woman's portion of the Scalp-Staff Dance. This will be held during the fourth intermission of the Sun-Gazing Dance, the last intermission before the final dancing, now fast approaching.[70]

This is a day of great rejoicing and celebration, with holiness and new life flowing from the Sun Dance Lodge. People are dressed in their finest, honoring the Sun, the Sky, the Buffalo, and all the Wakan Ones.

Courting couples appear outside the Sun Lodge, on both the south and the north sides, the men wearing their red and dark blue courting blankets in which they envelope women of their choice. At the southwest direction (upper left), a handsomely dressed man, carrying an eagle-wing fan with fox-skin guard—evidently a prominent man in one of the akitcita—rides beside a woman richly clothed in an elk-tooth dress. The man's horse has the notched ears of a racehorse or buffalo horse. They appear to be leaving camp, so possibly they are eloping, for elopements were frequent at Sun Dance time. At the northeast (lower right), two finely dressed young men, faces painted, come riding on a horse handsomely dressed as well, wearing a German silver bridle, with an eagle feather tied to his tail.

Watching before the entrance to the Sun Lodge is a prominent man, his single upright eagle feather, symbolic of a first coup, his long-stemmed pipe, and beaded, long-fringed pipe bag proclaiming the dignity of his position. His wife stands wrapped in a richly colored Navajo blanket. She carries a bucket that probably contains water for one of the pierced dancers, to be given him after he tears loose. For these are relatives of one undergoing the torture. Their little son or grandson watches beside, seated on a fine horse with a German silver bridle, his tail tied up for war, his master's war honors painted upon him. This horse will be given away to honor the escape, the tearing free, of a man who stood against Sun and prevailed, winning Sun's pity and blessing.

When at last all the pierced men had torn free, Sitting Bull, as leader of the Sun Dance, stood at the entrance of the Sun Lodge and announced that the Sun Dance was finished. The red-painted herald proclaimed his announcement throughout the camp, and immediately all those within the Sun Dance Lodge came out, the organization of the ceremonial camp ended, and the ordinary organization of the camps revived.[71]

In the painting, some people have evidently anticipated that announcement. For at the far south (left) side, distant from the Sun Lodge, two women are already on the move, horses loaded, with a little boy following, riding a child's travois. A dog brings up the rear, pulling his own tiny travois. And off to the side, attempting to keep up, an aged woman, bowed with years, hobbles along supported by her staff.

In the Sun Dance camp, great joy will fill all hearts, with the spirit of Tatanka the Buffalo God, the great patron of generosity, sexual relations, fecundity, and industry prevailing in the lives of those present. And because Sitting Bull and those with him endured the torture, because they shed their blood, the world and all living creatures were now re-created, life on earth again was renewed, not only for the Lakotas, but for all creation.

## THE FIGHTING AT THE ROSEBUD

Two days after Sitting Bull's Sun Dance ended, wolves (scouts) came riding into the camps, reporting that the valley of the Rosebud was black with soldiers.[72] Two large warrior parties, Lakota and Cheyenne, rode out to meet them. They traveled all night, and shortly after sunrise the next day the Lakotas reached the soldier camp. This was General George Crook's command, with Crow, Shoshone, and Arikara scouts, all bitter enemies of the Lakotas and Cheyennes. The date was June 17, 1876.[73]

The fighting continued all day, the action shifting back and forth, with great bravery displayed on both sides. When it ended the soldiers buried their dead. Then with their Indian scouts, they moved back toward the south, following the trail they had taken when entering the Rosebud country.

The Lakota and Cheyenne warriors rode home pleased with the coups they had counted, the soldiers turned back from their villages. Yet this was not the fulfillment of what Sitting Bull saw and heard at the Sun Dance Lodge. This was not the fulfillment of his vision of victory.[74]

And so they waited.

## The Fight with Long Hair

After this fighting on the Rosebud the chiefs ordered camp broken. Then with the chiefs leading the way, their long-stemmed pipes across their arms, the Lakotas and the Cheyennes rode on to the flat, broad, grassy valley of the Little Big Horn River. Soon the tipis were up and the valley west of the river was covered with six great tribal circles, the Hunkpapas at one end, the Cheyennes at the other.[75]

Here, eight days after the Rosebud fighting, soldiers suddenly struck, charging into Sitting Bull's Hunkpapa village, firing into the lodges. Among the first to die were the two wives and three children of the Hunkpapa warrior Gall, all five of them cut down by the soldier bullets.[76] These were the troopers of Major Marcus Reno's command, with their Crow and Arikara scouts, enemies all. The date was June 25, 1876.

The Lakota warriors quickly rallied, driving the soldiers out of the Hunkpapa village and into the nearby timber. For a time the soldiers, with their Crow and Arikara scouts, remained there. Then suddenly they came charging out, headed for the river. The Lakotas, with some

Cheyennes, swept in, striking the soldiers with quirts, war clubs, or lances to count coup, then knocking them off their horses. Warriors were yanking troopers from their horses with bare hands, not wasting a bullet or arrow on them, leaving them to be trampled under foot by the horses of the warriors charging in behind them. "It was like chasing buffalo, a grand chase," American Horse, the Northern Cheyenne chief who took part in this fighting, recalled later.[77]

Then a cry "More soldiers coming!" was heard, and some of the warriors looked up to see a column of troopers slowly advancing along the distant hill on the east side of the river. This was Long Hair Custer and his command, although the warriors had no idea who it was they were fighting.

Four brave Cheyenne fighting men rode out to meet these soldiers, halting their advance, giving the other warriors time to rally. Then the warriors moved in quickly, some on foot, others charging in on horseback, scattering the troopers, killing them, until finally only ten remained on a hill above the Little Big Horn, the last ones alive. Then warriors rushed them, cutting them down, wiping out these enemies who came attacking the Lakotas and Cheyennes on their own land.[78]

Sitting Bull's vision of victory had come true.

Standing Bear captures the final fighting (figs. 4 and 5). The remnants of Lieutenant James Calhoun's and Captain M. W. Keogh's troops had joined the soldiers around Custer on the hill, near where the monument now stands. The day was hot and windless, the air filled with mingled dust and powder smoke. Here and there a wounded trooper had been unhorsed and left behind. The warriors came moving in, killing them one by one.[79]

Then the troopers on the hill let their horses go. Bays, sorrels, and grays raced off in all directions. Many warriors stopped shooting

and chased the loose horses. The firing was hot, so that horses as well as men were going down. Some of the mounted warriors had dismounted. It was hand-to-hand fighting by that time. White Bull, Sitting Bull's older nephew, recalled the scene:

*Then for a time all the soldiers stood together on the hill where the monument is now, ringed in by the Sioux, dying bravely one by one as the Indians poured a hail of lead and arrows into their dwindling strength. They lay or knelt on the bare ridge, firing across the bodies of dead horses or taking cover behind the shallow shelter of a fallen comrade, selling their lives dearly. Only a few remained alive.*[80]

Lame White Man, the Cheyenne Elkhorn Scraper Society chief, charged these soldiers. He rushed in among them and was killed there, so that his body lay in the midst of the soldiers. By this time many warriors had armed themselves with rifles and pistols taken from dead troopers, filling their belts with cartridges found in the saddlebags of captured horses. The power of their fire continually increased now, while the soldiers' shooting grew weaker.

White Bull, Sitting Bull's nephew, lay in a ravine pumping bullets into the soldiers on the hill. He was one of those who shot down the group in which Long Hair Custer made his last stand. All this time he was between the river and those soldiers on the hill. Then *the few remaining troopers seemed to despair of holding their position on the hilltop. Ten of them jumped up and came down the ravine toward White Bull, shooting all the time. Two soldiers were in the lead, one of them wounded and bleeding from the mouth. White Bull and a Cheyenne waited for them. When they came near, he shot one; the Cheyenne shot the other. . . . The eight remaining soldiers kept on coming, forcing White Bull out of the ravine onto the ridge.*[81]

**Fig. 4**
Battle of the Little Big Horn
(detail of painted muslin).
Photo by F. Peter Weil.

White Bull snatched up the dead soldier's gun and started up the hill. Suddenly he stumbled and fell; his leg was numb with no feeling in it. Then he saw that his ankle was swelling, the skin bruised. He had been hit by a spent ball. He found a shallow ditch, crawled into it, and lay there until all the soldiers were killed. At the time he stopped fighting, only ten soldiers were on their feet. These were the last ones alive.[82]

Standing Bear pictures those ten soldiers, making their stand on the ridge above the Little Big Horn. Dead and dying troopers lie before them, with a handful of soldiers fleeing on horseback. Warriors move in, striking the soldiers, counting coup on them, then killing them.

At the upper center, below the line of still-living soldiers, a warbonnet man wrenches a guidon from the trooper struggling to keep it, holding on to it with both hands. Henry Little Coyote, Frank Waters, and John Stands in Timber, the sons and grandson of Cheyenne warriors who fought at the Little Big Horn, identified this warrior as Yellow Nose, who captured the Custer guidon. Captured from the Utes as a child by Chief Starving Bear, and raised to be "all Cheyenne," Yellow Nose is respected by both Lakotas and Cheyennes as being among the bravest men in this fighting.[83]

At his right, a warrior wrenches a rifle from the hand of a badly wounded soldier, an arrow protruding from his forehead. The warrior fights stripped to the breechclout, his hair knotted over his forehead, an old-time warriors' style among both Lakotas and Cheyennes.

Behind him, a shield owner counts the first coup on a fallen soldier, one of the ten on the hill, struck down by a warrior bullet now. The shield owner is a seasoned warrior wearing two upright eagle feathers, symbolizing two first coups. His lance is of a style favored by some Cheyenne fighting men, patterned after the lances borne by the Mexican lancers the Cheyennes fought in the far South Country.[84]

Directly behind the shield owner, the mounted warbonnet man whose bullet brought down this soldier, appears firing at him. Meanwhile, at the far right, four cavalrymen attempt to escape, while warriors come charging in after them. Following in hot pursuit is a warbonnet man who wears a split-horn warbonnet. He is a very brave man, for he carries the crooked lance of the style borne by the bravest men of both the Cheyenne Elkhorn Scrapers or the Lakota (Oglala) Strong Heart, Wiciska, Sotka Yuha, and Iroka societies. Thus he is either Cheyenne or Lakota.[85]

Now he displays his valor again, reaching out to touch the closest soldier with his bare hand, to count the bravest of coups. Turning in his saddle, the soldier fires at him point blank, missing him. Meanwhile the trooper next to him wavers in his saddle, an arrow protruding from his body. At the same moment his two soldier companions twist about in their saddles, firing at the crooked lance bearer. The soldiers' horses are suffering with their masters, the third trooper's mount wounded by an arrow in the back, the fourth soldier's horse bearing a broken arrow embedded in his lower forehead.

Racing in to head off these four fleeing cavalrymen come four mounted warriors. Three are warbonnet men; the fourth wears a war cape painted with sacred vision symbols.

The leading warbonnet man carries a notched quirt with a fox-hide guard. He is a headman of either the Oglala Iroka Society or the Cheyenne Kit Fox Society. His horse's ears are split, as are the ears of the horse following him. For these are not only war-horses, but also racehorses or buffalo horses.

The warrior behind him wears a warbonnet with the feathers colored red and white alternately. Among the Lakotas it is said that these red feathers commemorated wounds received in battle. A man who wore such red feathers did not dare to tell a lie or he might be wounded in battle. Such a warbonnet possessed no protective power. It was worn for its beauty alone.[86] The man wears leggings with broad beaded strips, "tails" of red trade cloth, a cloth shirt, German silver arm bands, and a breastplate of hairpipes. He carries an ordinary lance. His horse wears a scalp tied to his bridle of German silver, the mark of a horse that has ridden down an enemy.

Both this warrior and the warbonnet man below him wear leggings with broad beaded strips. The beadwork designs are typical Lakota designs of this 1876 era. However, by the time Standing Bear painted this scene (the late 1890s to early 1900s) the Cheyennes were also using these designs. It is possible, therefore, that Standing Bear "read back" these later Cheyenne designs into his portrayal of Cheyennes who fought Custer in 1876. Thus an exact tribal identification is impossible.[87]

The war-cape wearer has his hair bound in front, two eagle feathers thrust through it—again an old-time Lakota and Cheyenne warrior style. His cape bears symbols of the moon, the rainbow, the stars, and (probably) the lightning, providing him with great power for protection and blessing.

The lower warrior wears a split-horn warbonnet, probably with a single trail of eagle feathers beginning at the crown of his head and extending down his back. He too wears a cloth shirt, German silver arm bands, and "tails" of red trade cloth. He is armed with a bow and arrows.

All four horses these warriors ride are dressed for battle. Two have German silver bridles—prized possession—and their tails are tied with red stroud. One horse's tail is notched, the other's bobbed—forms of battle dress for horses among both the Lakotas and the Cheyennes.

Elsewhere at bottom center, a warrior who is a double-sash wearer, a very brave man, fires an arrow at the soldiers. His sashes resemble those worn by the bravest members of the Oglala Miwatani Society, who were vowed never to retreat. However, he does not wear the Miwatani headdress, nor is his body painted red, as were the bodies of the Miwatani sash wearers. Nor are his sashes those of the bravest of the Cheyenne Dog Soldiers. Thus his identification remains a mystery.[88] His hair is knotted in front with a single feather thrust through it, again in the old-time warrior style used by both Lakotas and Cheyennes. And apparently he is painted with a vision design, one revealed to him by a Sacred Being.

Fighting close to the double-sash wearer are three warbonnet men.

At the left, a warbonnet man carrying a banner lance, his horse rearing, fires his pistol at a soldier who falls backward. This warrior's eagle-feather banner lance resembles those borne by brave men of the Strong Heart Society. However, similar lances were carried by the brave men of the Northern Cheyenne Crazy Dog Society or by their Southern Cheyenne counterparts, the Bowstrings. Thus his exact identification remains unknown.[89]

This warrior seems to be wearing a blue soldier coat or perhaps a blue cloth shirt. His leggings are apparently cut from a white blanket, with yellow stripes added. His "tails," like those of many of the warriors around him, are of red trade cloth with a white selvage. His braids are wrapped with otter skin, and he wears arm bands of German silver.

The middle warbonnet man falls from his horse, struck by a soldier bullet. His otter-skin-wrapped straight lance, with four eagle feathers, is of a style carried by either the Cheyenne Elkhorn Scrapers or the Lakota (Oglala) Strong Heart, Wiciska, Sotka Yuha, or Iroka societies.[90]

The third warbonnet man, wearing a double-tail warbonnet and carrying a crooked lance, charges in from the right. His horse is painted and dressed for battle, with eagle feathers in his mane and his tail tied. A scalp painted half red, half black (or covered with cloth of the same colors) hangs from the mouthpiece of his German silver bridle. Again, both the Cheyennes and the Lakotas used such a decoration to honor a horse ridden when a scalp was taken in battle.

Below these three warbonnet men, to their left, are the soldiers who fled from the hill, racing to the ravine below, as White Bull described. A warbonnet man appears in their midst, perhaps White Bull himself, for he was in the ravine when the soldiers made their break for it and was forced out when the survivors arrived there. Two of the soldiers, one looking back in fear, carry guns in their hands. Possibly they are troopers whose guns jammed, the cartridges stuck in the barrels in the heat and constant firing of this sun-scorched day. Two other soldiers are shot down as they flee.

Charging in upon them, saber in hand, comes a mounted scalp-shirt wearer. His shirt is painted in the sacred colors used in decorating a Cheyenne scalp shirt, black at the top and yellow at the bottom. On most Cheyenne scalp shirts of this time, the strips were beaded in a black (or dark blue) and white block design, a sacred design. This shirt, however, has beaded strips with a Lakota design of this 1876 era. Thus the man's identity is a mystery. Two upright eagle feathers are in his scalp lock, and his legs are painted yellow, Sun's own color in Cheyenne holy painting. Clearly he is both a brave man and an important one. Perhaps he is Lame White Man, the Cheyenne Elkhorn

Scraper Society chief, who died charging into the midst of the soldiers on the hill, showing no fear of them.[91]

Above the action around the soldiers in the ravine, other soldiers flee on foot, dead soldiers and a dead soldier horse lying behind them, as they too are cut down. A Lakota Omaha Society man charges in among them, riding down a trooper, his horse trampling the soldier underfoot. The roach and the crow belt identify the warrior's society.[92]

Chaos reigns, with the horses released by the troopers on the hill fleeing in fear. Four mounted warriors race after the stampeding soldier mounts (upper left).

The uppermost warrior, a warbonnet man carrying a crooked lance, reaches out and grasps the bridle of a soldier horse, turning his head toward him.

The next warrior below is a brave man also, for he carries the otter-skin-wrapped straight lance borne by the bravest men of his society. (Both the Cheyenne Elkhorn Scrapers and the Lakota [Oglala] Strong Heart, Wiciska, Sotka Yuha, and Iroka societies carried these.) He has been fighting stripped to the breechclout. Now he reaches out and catches the bridle of a soldier horse, turning him in his direction, capturing him.

The third warrior, a shield carrier, also stripped to the breechclout, captures a soldier horse too. A strip of red cloth wrapped around his forehead holds his hair in place for battle. A single upright feather, symbol of a first coup counted, rises from his scalp lock. His warhorse bears the symbol of the moon on both withers and flanks, assuring him of Moon's blessing and protection.

The lower warbonnet man has already captured one soldier mount, which he is leading with his right hand. Now he catches a second. His war-horse is beautifully trained, running

Fig. 5
Battle of the Little Big Horn
(detail of painted muslin).
Photo by F. Peter Weil.

with reins loose, as the man uses his free left hand to catch this second soldier mount. The captured horse's reins, hanging in two pieces, evidently snapped when he broke loose from the picket pin, frightened by the noise of the battle.

This warbonnet man wears a war cape of red stroud. Lightning marks and hail marks are painted on his body, blessing him with a share in Thunder's awesome power. His legs are painted yellow, his blue blanket folded and held in place about his waist by his cartridge belt.

His war-horse is a beloved horse indeed. His split ears indicate that he is also a racehorse or a buffalo horse. The five red stripes and three horse tracks painted on his left flank mean his master had struck enemies five times on that side of him and captured three horses while riding him.[93] On his left wither is a red-dripping disk, signifying that either he or his master had been wounded by a bullet in battle.[94] Four eagle feathers—the sacred number—are fastened to the horse's mane. His tail is tied for war, and a red and black painted scalp (or a red and black cloth-covered scalp) hangs from his German silver bridle, symbolizing that he had been used to run down an enemy.[95]

Across the Little Big Horn River, the great activity in the camps is portrayed in abbreviated form by Standing Bear.

Only three of the six tribal circles pitched at the Little Big Horn are shown. In the midst of two of them a warbonnet man races to catch his horse, to join the fighting. A warrior carrying a rifle chases his horse, among those frightened by the noise of battle across the river. Two women head for the horse herd, each carrying a rope. One appears distracted, looking backward toward the camps. At the lower edge women are leaving on foot, two bearing babies on their backs. They seem unafraid, so perhaps they are going to join those women watching the fighting from the bluffs, sounding the screech-owl call to urge the warriors on. A white-painted Heyoka races along with them, toy bow and arrow in hand. Ahead of him a lightning-painted horse, reins dangling, gallops off. Apparently he has broken loose, frightened by the sounds of battle.

In the midst of this chaos and death, one figure of serenity appears. Larger than any man in the fighting, set apart from it, he comes riding majestically forward.

He is dressed in the dark blue and yellow painted scalp shirt of the Shirtwearers, the grand councilors and executives of each of the Lakota tribes, the "owners of the tribe."[96] His leggings are painted yellow—the color of Sun himself when used on war clothing—the flaps painted blue and fringed with hairlocks. These are a chief's leggings. Beautiful quill-embroidered moccasins cover his feet. Two eagle feathers rise erect in his scalp lock, the emblems of a Lakota chief. The vein of one is painted red, possibly to symbolize blood shed in battle. Both eagle feathers are tipped with red-dyed horsehair.

His horse is painted *wakanyan* (sacredly) as for battle or some other great occasion. The sun appears painted in yellow on the horse's chest and right flank, a most holy and powerful blessing. From the bridle of German silver hangs a black (dark blue) and red painted (or cloth-covered) scalp. The horse's tail is tied with red cloth, as if for war. However, he does not charge into battle now but with his owner looks on serenely.

This is a great chief, a brave man who radiates power and dominates the entire scene. Clearly Standing Bear considers him the leading figure in this fighting at the Little Big Horn. Possibly he is Sitting Bull or Crazy Horse. But he is not dressed and painted like Sitting Bull in Standing Bear's drawing of him from about 1928. Nor is he dressed and painted like Crazy Horse and Sitting Bull in Amos Bad Heart Bull's portraits of them in the Little Big Horn Fighting.[97] Whoever he is, this chief beheld the greatest of Lakota-Cheyenne victories over the soldiers. He witnessed the fulfillment of Sitting Bull's vision of victory.

First I would honor the memories of Father Vine Deloria, that deeply loved and venerated Sioux priest, and Ella C. Deloria, the distinguished Sioux anthropologist and linguist, brother and sister. Together they taught me, with so many others, the beauty, holiness, and wisdom of the Dakota People. I would also honor Dr. Vine Deloria, Jr., their own distinguished son and nephew, and with him Elva One Feather and Gerald One Feather of Oglala, South Dakota, mother and son. All, in words and lives, continually manifest the traditional Lakota commitment to sanctity, generosity, bravery, and wisdom. And I would express gratitude to Dr. Bea Medicine, Dr. JoAllyn Archambault, Arthur Amiotte, and Rhonda Holy Bear, who in their scholarship and art display the old-time Lakota devotion to beauty blessed by holiness.

Profound gratitude to Dr. Raymond J. DeMallie, Director of the American Indian Studies Research Institute, Indiana University, Bloomington, who great-heartedly shared not only his transcription of the One Bull–White Bull interviews in the Walter Campbell papers at the University of Oklahoma, but also his colored slides of the Standing Bear drawings in the Buechel Memorial Lakota Museum, St. Francis, South Dakota. Those slides were taken by Steve Valandra of Rosebud, South Dakota, and Harvey Markowitz, Acting Assistant Director, D'Arcy McNickle Center for the History of the American Indian, The Newberry Library, Chicago. My thanks to both.

Warm thanks also to Alice Marriott, distinguished author and ethnologist, who in 1959 loaned me the Standing Bear painted muslin, then in her custody, and encouraged me to carry it to the Cheyenne elders. Without Alice Marriott's kindness I would have known nothing about this painted muslin. J. Joe Bauxar, Archivist of Northern Illinois University, De Kalb, retired, owner of the painted muslin when I carried it to the Cheyenne elders, graciously permitted me to do so; and he also shared his knowledge of E. A. Burbank's relationship to it. Dr. Andrew H. Whiteford, Professor Emeritus of anthropology, Beloit College, Beloit, Wisconsin, generously shared the notes he prepared at the time the muslin was on display at the Logan Museum of Anthropology, Beloit.

Dr. JoAllyn Archambault, Director, American Indian Program, Smithsonian Institution, Washington, D.C., and Arthur Amiotte, the distinguished Lakota artist, shared their knowledge concerning Stephen Standing Bear's first marriage, his Austrian sojourn, and his marriage to Louise Renick. Arthur Amiotte is Standing Bear's great-great-grandson, and he and Dr. Archambault are at work on a biography of Standing Bear.

As always I owe a debt of profound gratitude to the staff of the Newberry Library, Chicago, for countless courtesies, endless assistance, and delightful friendships. Special thanks to the staffs of the Department of Special Collections, Robert Karrow, Special Collections Librarian; the Department of Technical Services, Margaret Taylor Brenneman, Technical Services Librarian; John Aubrey, Edward E. Ayer Collection Reference Librarian; and the D'Arcy McNickle Center for the History of the American Indian, Dr. Fred Hoxie, Director.

Deepest gratitude of all to my immediate family, whose infinite love, generosity, and good nature bless and strengthen me always; and with them my spiritual family, the director and staff of St. Augustine's Indian Center, whose love enables me to carry out the dual vocation of priest and scholar.

1. This Stephen Standing Bear–Lakota identification is based on a comparison of this painted muslin with illustrations by Standing Bear in John G. Neihardt, *Black Elk Speaks* (New York: William Morrow and Company, 1932) and the thirty-one Standing Bear drawings in the Buechel Memorial Lakota Museum, St. Francis, South Dakota. Color slides of the drawings were graciously provided by Dr. Raymond J. DeMallie, with a "List of Standing Bear drawings in handwriting of Eugene Buechel, S.J.; transcribed with comments by Raymond DeMallie, November 1991."

The two other painted muslins that I believe to be the art of Stephen Standing Bear: The first, which I have personally examined, was formerly in the collection of the late L. Drew Bax. I am informed that it is now in a museum in Japan or Europe but have been unable to verify this. The second was formerly in a private collection, at which time it was pictured in James B. Byrnes, *The Artist as Collector: Selections from Four California Collections of the Arts of Africa, Oceania, the Amerindians and the Santeros of New Mexico* (Newport Harbor, Calif.: Newport Harbor Art Museum, 1975), pp. 84–85. It is now in the Philbrook Museum of Art, Tulsa, Oklahoma, identified as Cheyenne. It is pictured in "Muslin Painting: A Gift of Mrs. John Steele Zink," *Philbrook Members' Bulletin* (March–April 1982): 6. It also appears, again identified as Cheyenne, in Edwin L. Wade and Rennard Strickland, *Magic Images: Contemporary Native American Art* (Norman, Okla.: Philbrook Art Center and University of Oklahoma Press, 1981), p. 109. I have studied only photographs of this painted muslin.

A Lakota tribal identification for these three painted muslins is supported by my study of Lakota (and Cheyenne) drawings and paintings in the National Anthropological Archives, Washington, D.C.; the American Museum of Natural History, New York; the Field Museum of Natural History, Chicago; the Denver Art Museum; the Southwest Museum, Los Angeles; the Newberry Library, Chicago; and elsewhere.

Major evidence supporting a Lakota identification also came from those Cheyenne elders who were my mentors in the 1950s. Seven of these elders examined this muslin in July and August 1959. Among the Northern Cheyenne elders were Henry Little Coyote, Keeper of the Sacred Buffalo Hat (born 1875), and Weasel Woman, the Sacred Hat Woman, his wife. Also, Frank Waters, the Sweet Medicine Chief of the Northern Cheyennes (born 1875); John Stands in Timber, the tribal historian and a headman of the Kit Fox Society (born 1884); and Rufus Wallowing, a respected elder (born ca. 1887). The fathers of all, except John Stands in Timber, were present at the Battle of the Little Big Horn. John Stands in Timber's grandfather, Lame White Man, was the only Cheyenne chief to be killed in that fighting. Among the Southern Cheyenne elders were Ben Woods, a respected priest of the Sacred Arrow Lodge (born ca. 1879), and Ralph Whitetail, a respected Sacred Arrow and Sun Dance priest (born ca. 1884). Rufus Wallowing declared the artist of the painted muslin to be a Lakota. Henry Little Coyote, Frank Waters, and Ben Woods identified the Sun Dance portrayed as Lakota, not Cheyenne. All of the elders identified individuals in the Sun Dance and Little Big Horn Battle scenes as being Cheyenne or Lakota, as was true in the actual events, when both tribes were present.

2. Standing Bear's accounts appear in Raymond J. DeMallie, ed., *The Sixth Grandfather: Black Elk's Teachings Given to John G. Neihardt* (Lincoln: University of Nebraska Press, 1984), pp. 101, 173–74, 184–90. Cf. John G. Neihardt, *Black Elk Speaks* (New York: William Morrow and Company, 1932), pp. 115–21. See also Standing Bear's account of the Battle of the Little Big Horn in Kenneth Hammer, ed., *Custer in '76: Walter Camp's Notes on the Custer Fight* (Provo, Utah: Brigham Young University Press, 1976), pp. 214–15. Also, Richard G. Hardorff, ed., *Lakota Recollections of the Custer Fight* (Spokane, Wash.: Arthur H. Clark Co., 1991), pp. 56–60.

3. Standing Bear's account of this war party, which accompanies a drawing of himself with three of the members, is no. 32 in "List of Standing Bear drawings in handwriting of Eugene Buechel, S.J.; transcribed with comments by Raymond DeMallie, November 1991." The original drawings and descriptions are in the Buechel Memorial Lakota Museum, St. Francis, South Dakota.

4. I am grateful to Dr. JoAllyn Archambault for this information concerning Stephen Standing Bear's first marriage, his Austrian sojourn, and his marriage to Louise Renick.

5. Elbridge Ayer Burbank Letters to Edward E. Ayer, 1897–1909 and June–July 1914. In the Edward E. Ayer Collection, Department of Special Collections, Newberry Library, Chicago. These letters are item 120 in Ruth Lapham Butler, compiler, *A Check List of Manuscripts in the Edward E. Ayer Collection, The Newberry Library, Chicago* (1937), p. 14. See especially the letters dated May 1, 1899; May 15, 1899; June 4, 1899; July 19, 1899; and July 16, 1899. The letters Burbank wrote while he was painting portraits of the Northern and Southern Cheyennes make no mention of his commissioning or purchasing any paintings by Cheyenne artists. This would strengthen a Lakota provenance for the painted muslin described in this article. Information concerning purchase of this muslin from the estate of Burbank's in-laws is contained in a letter from J. Joe Bauxar, the purchaser, to Father Peter J. Powell, September 28, 1959; also in documents prepared while the painted muslin was on exhibit at the Logan Museum of Anthropology, Beloit College, Beloit, Wisconsin, about 1960. These are in the archives of the Foundation for the Preservation of American Indian Art and Culture, Inc., Chicago.

6. Accompanying the drawings is a list of the Standing Bear drawings, in Lakota and English, in the handwriting of Father Eugene Buechel, S.J. Dr. Raymond J. DeMallie has added comments and additional information to this list. I am grateful to Dr. DeMallie for both.

7. For Standing Bear's role as illustrator of *Black Elk Speaks* see DeMallie, *The Sixth Grandfather*, pp. 29–30, 95, 99, 180n.

Standing Bear's interviews with John G. Neihardt during the 1931 interviews in preparation for *Black Elk Speaks* are on pp. 413–17. See also the other listings under Standing Bear's name in the index, p. 448.

8. Primary sources for this section are the following: Amos Bad Heart Bull and Helen H. Blish, *A Pictographic History of the Oglala Sioux* (Lincoln: University of Nebraska Press, 1967), pp. 38–39, 198–201, 273–74, 277–78. Frances Densmore, *Teton Sioux Music,* Smithsonian Institution, Bureau of American Ethnology Bulletin 61 (Washington, D.C., 1918), pp. 176–79. See also Alice Fletcher, "Indian Ceremonies" in *Report of the Peabody Museum of American Archaeology and Ethnology* 16 (Salem, Mass.: Salem Press, 1884), pp. 260–333. James R. Walker, *Lakota Belief and Ritual,* ed. Raymond J. DeMallie and Elaine A. Jahner (Lincoln: University of Nebraska Press, 1980), p. 135 ("Elk Dreamers"), p. 160 ("Wolves Are Wakan"), p. 167 ("The White-tailed Deer Is Wakan"), p. 167 ("The Black-tailed Deer Is Wakan"), p. 170 ("The Spider Is Wakan"). Clark Wissler, "Societies and Ceremonial Associations in the Oglala Division of the Teton-Dakota" (1912), *Anthropological Papers of the American Museum of Natural History* 11, pt. 1:81–92; idem, "Some Protective Designs of the Dakota" (1907), *Anthropological Papers of the American Museum of Natural History* 11 pt. 2:40–43; idem, "The Whirlwind and the Elk in the Mythology of the Dakota," *Journal of American Folklore* 13, no. 71 (October–December 1905): 261–68.

9. Bad Heart Bull and Blish, *A Pictographic History,* p. 199. Wissler, "Societies and Ceremonial Associations," pp. 85–87.

10. For the meaning of the term *wakan* see especially "Wakan," by George Sword, trans. Burt Means, in J. R. Walker, "The Sun Dance and Other Ceremonies of the Oglala Division of the Teton Dakota," *Anthropological Papers of the American Museum of Natural History* 16, pt. 2 (1917): 152–53. Also "Wakan. Little Wound," in J. R. Walker, *Lakota Belief and Ritual,* pp. 68–70. Also Raymond J. DeMallie, Jr., and Robert H. Lavenda, "Wakan: Plains Indian Concepts of Power" and "Teton Dakota" in *The Anthropology of Power,* ed. Raymond D. Fogelson and Richard N. Adams (New York: Academic Press, 1977), pp. 154–59.

11. Wissler, "Societies and Ceremonial Associations," p. 90. Cf. Bad Heart Bull and Blish, *A Pictographic History,* pp. 200–201; Walker, *Lakota Belief and Ritual,* "The Black-tailed Deer Is Wakan," p. 167.

12. Bad Heart Bull and Blish, *A Pictographic History,* p. 199.

13. Walker, *Lakota Belief and Ritual,* "Bears Are Wakan," p. 157, also pp. 158–59. Cf. Wissler, "Societies and Ceremonial Associations," pp. 88–90. Densmore, *Teton Sioux Music,* pp. 195–97.

Standing Bear's drawing of a Bear Dreamer is no. 16, "Mato Kage ['Bear Making']," Buechel Memorial Lakota Museum, "List of Standing Bear drawings in handwriting of Eugene Buechel, S.J.; transcribed with comments by Raymond J. DeMallie, November 1991." Amos Bad Heart Bull's drawing of the Bear Dreamers appears in Bad Heart Bull and Blish, *A Pictographic History,* p. 273.

14. Wissler, "Societies and Ceremonial Associations," p. 90.

15. Walker, *Lakota Belief and Ritual,* "Wolves Are Wakan," p. 160.

Standing Bear's drawing of a Wolf Dreamer is no. 15, "Sunkmanitu kage ['Wolf making']," "List of Standing Bear drawings," Buechel Memorial Lakota Museum. Amos Bad Heart Bull's drawing of the Wolf Dreamers appears in Bad Heart Bull and Blish, *A Pictographic History*, p. 277.

16. Wissler, "Societies and Ceremonial Associations," p. 91. Standing Bear's drawings of Buffalo Dreamers are no. 11, "Tatank kage ['Buffalo bull making']," and no. 12, "Tatank kage ['Buffalo bull making']," "List of Standing Bear drawings," Buechel Memorial Lakota Museum. Amos Bad Heart Bull's drawings of the Buffalo Dreamers and their dance appear in Bad Heart Bull and Blish, *A Pictographic History*, pp. 272, 277–78.

17. Bad Heart Bull and Blish, *A Pictographic History*, p. 200, also p. 39.

18. Standing Bear's drawing of an Elk Dreamer is no. 14, "Hehaka kage ['Elk making']," "List of Standing Bear drawings," Buechel Memorial Lakota Museum. See also Wissler, "Societies and Ceremonial Associations," pp. 87–88.

19. The identity of these two front dancers is uncertain. I identify them as Black-tailed Deer Dancers because of their masks, similar to those of the Elk Dreamers, a Black-tailed Deer characteristic according to Wissler's Lakota authorities.

See Standing Bear's drawing of a Black-tailed Deer Dreamer, no. 13, "Sintesapela kage ['Blacktailed deer making']," in "List of Standing Bear drawings," Buechel Memorial Lakota Museum. See also Wissler, "Societies and Ceremonial Associations," p. 90. But note they are hornless. Compare the Black-tailed Deer Dancers in Amos Bad Heart Bull's drawing, Bad Heart Bull and Blish, *A Pictographic History,* p. 97.

Also, the figures here are *not* painted blue and black as are the two Black-tailed Deer Dancers in Bad Heart Bull and Blish, *A Pictographic History,* pp. 200 and 274. Rather, they are painted red and black. Possibly, then, they are the long-tailed Deer Dancers mentioned by He Dog as being present at the Animal Dreamers Dance on the Rosebud. But note also that they do not resemble the Black-tailed Deer Dancers pictured by Amos Bad Heart Bull on pages 200 and 274 of Bad Heart Bull and Blish.

Cf. Wissler, "Societies and Ceremonial Associations," pp. 86–87; idem, "Some Protective Designs," p. 42; and Walker, *Lakota Belief and Ritual,* "Elk Dreamers, " p. 135.

20. Bad Heart Bull and Blish, *A Pictographic History,* p. 200; Wissler, "Societies and Ceremonial Associations," p. 88.

21. Bad Heart Bull and Blish, *A Pictographic History,* pp. 39, 200–201.

22. Ibid., p. 201.

23. Wissler, "Societies and Ceremonial Associations," p. 90. Cf. Standing Bear's drawing, no. 15, "Sunkmanitu kage ['Wolf making'],"  "List of Standing Bear drawings," Buechel Memorial Lakota Museum.

24. Wissler, "Societies and Ceremonial Associations," pp. 82–83. Also, Standing Bear's drawing no. 31, "Heyok'a—Dream Cult," "List of Standing Bear drawings," Buechel Memorial Lakota Museum. Also, Bad Heart Bull and Blish, *A Pictographic History*, pp. 277–78.

25. Wissler, "Societies and Ceremonial Associations," pp. 88, 90. Cf. pp. 82–85. See also the references to Heyoka in Walker, *Lakota Belief and Ritual,* "The Wakinyan Are Wakan," esp. pp. 155–57. Also the painting, "War Insignia no. 8. A Heyoka Warrior. By Thunder Bear. 1912," following p. 226 and the description on pp. 277–78. Also, "War Insignia no. 12. A Heyoka Warrior. By Thunder Bear. 1912," with description pp. 279–80.

26. According to White Bull's Winter Count, Navajo blankets were introduced among the Lakotas in 1853–54. There it is noted that "'Jar' (Jordan?) brought Navaho blankets over the mountains." James H. Howard, *The Warrior Who Killed Custer: The Personal Narrative of Chief Joseph White Bull* (Lincoln: University of Nebraska Press, 1968), pp. 18–19. See also Garrick Mallery, *Picture-Writing of the American Indians,* in Tenth Annual Report of the Bureau of American Ethnology, Smithsonian Institution (Washington, D.C., 1893), p. 283. Also, Kathleen Whitaker, "The Navajo Chief Blanket: A Trade Item among Non-Navajo Groups," *American Indian Art Magazine* 7, no. 1 (Winter 1981): 62–69.

27. This account of Sitting Bull's vow is from the account, largely from a Lakota source or sources, in Stanley Vestal, *Sitting Bull: Champion of the Sioux* (Boston and New York: Houghton-Mifflin Company, 1932), pp. 149–51.

28. White Dog's peace visit is the principal event for the "winter" of 1875–76 in the High Dog, Swift Dog, Jaw and Jaw Variant Lakota winter counts. See James H. Howard, "Dakota Winter Counts as a Source of Plains Indian History," in *Anthropological Papers Numbers 57–62,* Smithsonian Institution, Bureau of American Ethnology Bulletin 173 (Washington, D.C., 1960), p. 396. A Hunkpapa winter count indicating the same appears in Stanley Vestal, *New Sources of Indian History, 1850–91* (Norman: University of Oklahoma Press, 1934), p. 350. This peace with the Assiniboines lasted until 1879, when Silas Adam and other Assiniboine men served as scouts for Nelson A. Miles against Sitting Bull. Vestal, *Sitting Bull,* p. 135.

29. Sitting Bull's drawings of his counting coup on Little Hohe, the lad he saved and adopted as his brother, appear in M. W. Stirling, *Three Pictographic Autobiographies of Sitting Bull,* Smithsonian Miscellaneous Collections, vol. 97, no. 5 (Washington, D.C., 1938), pp. 11 (no. 8), 44 (no. 13), 54 (no. 9).

30. Here I follow the account in Vestal, *Sitting Bull,* pp. 135–39. Evidently One Bull, Sitting Bull's younger nephew, is the source. Cf. the brief account of White Bull, Sitting Bull's older nephew, to Walter S. Campbell (Stanley Vestal). In Walter Campbell Papers, Western History Collection, University of Oklahoma, Notebook 8, pp. 53–54, "Interview with White Bull, June 1930." I am grateful to Dr. Raymond J. DeMallie for bringing this to my attention.

31. Sitting Bull's drawings of this victory over the Crow chief appear in Stirling, *Three Pictographic Autobiographies*, pp. 10

(no. 6), 4 (no. 12), 55 (no. 11). Also in Alexis A. Praus, *A New Pictographic Autobiography of Sitting Bull*, Smithsonian Miscellaneous Collections, vol. 123, no. 6 (Washington, D.C., 1955), pl. 3, no. 5. The account of the victory appears in Vestal, *Sitting Bull*, p. 31.

32. Vestal, *Sitting Bull*, pp. 136–39. One Bull told Walter Campbell (Stanley Vestal) that they thought they stole horses from the Slota. But Big Darkness, a Hohe on the Assiniboine reserve in Canada, stated that Sitting Bull raided a camp of Crees instead. Ibid., p. 139.

33. Lakota holy men to J. R. Walker, in Walker, "The Sun Dance and Other Ceremonies," p. 100.

34. See the leader's prayer in Ella Deloria, "The Sun Dance of the Oglala Sioux," *Journal of American Folklore* 42, no. 166 (October–December 1929): 389–90. Also Walker, "The Sun Dance and Other Ceremonies," p. 101.

35. Walker, *Lakota Belief and Ritual*, "The Sun Dance Pole," p. 183, and "Short Bull's Painting of the Third Day of the Sun Dance," p. 190. Standing Bear's drawing of the Sacred Pole with its related holy objects, including the man and the buffalo figures, is drawing no. 8, "Wiwanyank Wacipi ['Sun Dance']," "List of Standing Bear drawings," Buechel Memorial Lakota Museum. See related drawings 9 and 10 as well.

36. Lakota holy men to J. R. Walker, in Walker, "The Sun Dance and Other Ceremonies," p. 109. Here it is called "the banner of the Shamans." Also Walker, *Lakota Belief and Ritual*, "Short Bull's Painting," p. 190.

37. Walker, "The Sun Dance and Other Ceremonies," pp. 84, 109. In Walker, *Lakota Belief and Ritual*, "Short Bull's Paintings," pp. 189–90, it is stated: "In the fork is tied a sacred bundle of a number of trunks of the chokecherry bush around a parfleche and digger. The parfleche contains such articles as are acceptable as offerings to the Gods and the bundle is consecrated by appropriate ceremony before it is tied in place." See also Deloria, "The Sun Dance of the Oglala," p. 398.

38. Lakota holy men to J. R. Walker, in Walker, "The Sun Dance and Other Ceremonies," p. 108; Cf. Walker, *Lakota Belief and Ritual*, "Short Bull's Painting," p. 189, where Crazy Buffalo is called the Demon Buffalo (Tatanka Gnaskinyan).

39. The Lakota holy men give differing versions of the shooting at the figures of Iya and Gnaski. See George Sword's statement in Deloria, "The Sun Dance of the Oglala," p. 399; also the statement of the Lakota holy men in Walker, "The Sun Dance and Other Ceremonies," p. 110.

40. For the remaining ceremonies on this day, see the account of the Lakota holy men to J. R. Walker, in Walker, "The Sun Dance and Other Ceremonies," pp. 110–11; also Walker, *Lakota Belief and Ritual*, pp. 36–37.

Note: This painting by Standing Bear does not portray the perspective of the Lakota Sun Dance camp, where all the lodges encircle the Sun Lodge, their doorways opening to it. The tipis depicted here face east, the direction of the sunrise, as tipis ordinarily face. Cf. Short Bull's paintings of the Sun Dance in Walker, *Lakota Belief and Ritual*, following page 226. These are

entitled "The Third Day of the Sun Dance" and "The Fourth Day of the Sun Dance." See also the notes on pages 183–91.

41. See "Creation of the Universe," in James R. Walker, *Lakota Myth*, ed. Elaine A. Jahner (Lincoln: University of Nebraska Press, 1983), pp. 206–7. A sensitive interpretation of the role of sacrifice in Lakota theology and life appears in Ronald Goodman, *Lakota Star Knowledge: Studies in Lakota Stellar Theology* (Rosebud, S. Dak.: Sinte Gleska College, 1990), pp. 25–28. Cf. also Joseph Epes Brown, "Sun Dance," *Parabola* 8, no. 4 (1978): 12, 15.

42. The account of Sitting Bull's sacrifice follows that in Vestal, *Sitting Bull*, pp. 151–52. This is from Lakota sources.

43. Deloria, "The Sun Dance of the Oglala," pp. 389, 407.

44. One Bull, nephew of Sitting Bull, to Walter Campbell (Stanley Vestal), in Walter Campbell Papers, Western History Collection, University of Oklahoma, Notebook 19, on a loose page inserted at page 76, "Interview with One Bull, July 1926."

I am deeply grateful to Dr. Raymond J. DeMallie for this eyewitness description from One Bull. This is the translation of the original Lakota as recorded in Walter Campbell's notes. However, it is not a literal translation. Dr. DeMallie's translation of One Bull's Lakota account is as follows:

"Sitting Bull instructed old man Black Moon to relate the following. He heard a voice from above so he looked there he said. 'These have no ears,' he said, so he looked beneath the sun; like many grasshoppers head downward they came, so 'I am coming,' he said. 'These, they will die, but their clothing none of you will take from them,' he said."

Further details are contained in the following sources, all in the Walter Campbell Papers, Western History Collection, University of Oklahoma: Walter Campbell's interview with White Bull, June 1930, in Notebook 8, pp. 53–54; Interview with One Bull, July 1926, Notebook 19, p. 47; Extract from a statement by One Bull regarding Sitting Bull, undated, handwriting not identified, but possibly Cecelia One Bull, Box 104; "Prophesy of Sitting Bull of complete annihilation of Custer and his soldiers as told to One Bull," Box 110, MS. 25. All of this information was generously provided by Dr. Raymond J. DeMallie.

45. "Screech owl call of praise," the Lakota description of the women's tremolo. Deloria, "The Sun Dance of the Oglala," p. 395. "It is the honoring cry, praising the warrior mentioned."

46. Stirling, *Three Pictographic Autobiographies*, p. 38, drawing O. Here, Sitting Bull, wearing a warbonnet of this type, captures an Assiniboine chief. He kept him prisoner for a while, then gave him the horse he (Sitting Bull) rode and the warbonnet he (Sitting Bull) wore in the fight and sent him back to his people with a good heart.

Clearly that is not the same warbonnet shown here, though similar in style. However, it establishes that Sitting Bull wore this type of warbonnet, which under normal circumstances would be re-created by Sitting Bull throughout his lifetime.

Also, in 1877 or 1878, while refugees from Chief Joseph's Nez Percés were with Sitting Bull in Canada, Sitting Bull presented a warbonnet of this type to Peopeo Tholekt, Bird Alighting, a brave Nez Percé who remained in Canada until about

June 1878. This warbonnet is now in the Paul Dyck Foundation collection, Rimrock, Arizona. I am grateful to Dr. Dyck for sharing this information with me.

For information concerning Sitting Bull, Peopeo Tholekt, and the Nez Percés in Canada, see L. V. McWhorter, *Hear Me, My Chiefs!* (Caldwell, Idaho: Caxton Printers, 1952), pp. 507–24, esp. 513–18.

Standing Bear's portrait of Sitting Bull shows him dressed for battle, painted with a sacred vision design, stripped to the breechclout, two upright eagle feathers in his scalp lock. His horse is painted in a sacred fashion also. See drawing 5 in "List of Standing Bear drawings," Buechel Memorial Lakota Museum.

47. However, crooked lances were also carried by the bravest men of the Oglala Wiciska, Sotka Yuha, and Iroka societies. See Bad Heart Bull and Blish, *A Pictographic History*, pp. 104, 105, 108, 109; Clark Wissler, "Societies and Ceremonial Associations," pp. 25, 31–32, 35, 57–58, 67; also Walker, *Lakota Belief and Ritual*, two of the color plates following page 226: "War Insignia. no. 13. Lance Bearer of the Brave Society" and "War Insignia. no. 14. Leader of the Sotka Society." They are described on pp. 280–81.

48. Wissler, "Societies and Ceremonial Associations," p. 41, "Ska Yuha."

49. White Bull to Stanley Vestal (Walter Campbell). In Stanley Vestal, *Warpath: The True Story of the Fighting Sioux* (1934; reprint, Lincoln: University of Nebraska Press, 1984), p. 149.

50. White Bull. In Vestal, *Warpath*, p. 187.

51. Deloria, "The Sun Dance of the Oglala," pp. 387, 407. Cf. Walker, "Horses Are Wakan," in *Lakota Belief and Ritual*, pp. 167–68.

52. Walker, "The Sun Dance of the Oglala and Other Ceremonies," p. 93.

53. Deloria, "The Sun Dance of the Oglala," pp. 404–5; Walker, "The Sun Dance and Other Ceremonies," pp. 116–17. See also Bad Heart Bull and Blish, *A Pictographic History*, p. 96.

54. Deloria, "The Sun Dance of the Oglala," p. 405.

55. Walker, *Lakota Belief and Ritual*, "Sun Dance Symbols," p. 183.

56. Ibid., "Short Bull's Painting," pp. 187–88; ibid., "Sun Dance Symbols," pp. 182–83; Deloria, "The Sun Dance of the Oglala," pp. 391, 402; Walker, "The Sun Dance and Other Ceremonies," pp. 92, 112; Bad Heart Bull and Blish, *A Pictographic History*, p. 94.

57. Walker, *Lakota Belief and Ritual*, "Sun Dance Symbols," p. 182.

58. Bad Heart Bull and Blish, *A Pictographic History*, p. 97.

59. Walker, *Lakota Belief and Ritual*, "Sun Dance Symbols," p. 183.

60. Deloria, "The Sun Dance of the Oglala," pp. 407, 412; Walker, "The Sun Dance and Other Ceremonies," p. 116; J. R. Walker, *Lakota Society*, ed. Raymond DeMallie (Lincoln: University of Nebraska Press, 1982), "The Sun Dance. High Bear," p. 99. Cf. Walker, *Lakota Belief and Ritual*, "Short Bull's Painting of the Third Day of the Sun Dance," p. 190; also Bad Heart Bull

and Blish, *A Pictographic History*, p. 95.

61. Deloria, "The Sun Dance of the Oglala," p. 390.

62. Walker, *Lakota Belief and Ritual*, "The Holy Men Tell of the Sun Dance," p. 181.

63. Ibid., "Short Bull's Painting," p. 189; Bad Heart Bull and Blish, *A Pictographic History*, p. 95.

64. See Walker, "The Sun Dance and Other Ceremonies," pp. 98–100; Deloria, "The Sun Dance of the Oglala," pp. 371–73, 395–400.

65. Walker, "The Sun Dance and Other Ceremonies," pp. 98–100; Deloria, "The Sun Dance of the Oglala," pp. 397–99.

66. Walker, "The Sun Dance and Other Ceremonies," p. 117.

67. Ibid., p. 118.

68. Ibid., pp. 119–20.

69. Deloria, "The Sun Dance of the Oglala," p. 405.

70. Walker, "The Sun Dance and Other Ceremonies," pp. 119–20.

71. Ibid., p. 120.

72. "Interview with White Bull, June 1930," in Walter Campbell Papers, Notebook 8, pp. 53–54. Also Vestal, *Sitting Bull*, p. 156.

73. Sources for the Battle of the Rosebud:

The best Lakota eyewitness account is that of White Bull in Vestal, *Warpath*, pp. 185–90; also in Howard, *The Warrior Who Killed Custer*, pp. 48–50, 60–67. Amos Bad Heart Bull's drawings and description of the battle are in Bad Heart Bull and Blish, *A Pictographic History*, pp. 188–96. Iron Hawk's and Standing Bear's accounts appear in DeMallie, *The Sixth Grandfather*, pp. 174–80.

The fullest account from a Cheyenne perspective is in Father Peter J. Powell, *People of the Sacred Mountain: A History of the Northern Cheyenne Chiefs and Warrior Societies, 1830–1879, with an Epilogue, 1969–1974* (New York and San Francisco: Harper and Row, 1981), pp. 954–1002.

A bibliography of Indian and White accounts appears in Powell, *People of the Sacred Mountain*, pp. 1363–64. For a fine overview see John S. Gray, *Centennial Campaign: The Sioux War of 1876* (Fort Collins, Colo.: The Old Army Press, 1976), pp. 110–24. Also J. W. Vaughn, *With Crook at the Rosebud* (Harrisburg, Pa.: Stackpole, 1956). The latest account from a white perspective is Neil C. Mangum, *Battle of the Rosebud: Prelude to the Little Big Horn* (El Segundo, Calif.: Upton and Sons, 1987).

74. Vestal, *Sitting Bull*, p. 156; Powell, *People of the Sacred Mountain*, pp. 947–53.

75. DeMallie, *The Sixth Grandfather*, p. 180n.

76. A Northern Cheyenne ledger painting of these deaths appears in Powell, *People of the Sacred Mountain*, p. 969. Other Cheyenne paintings and drawings of the victory at the Little Big Horn appear on succeeding pages.

77. Ibid., p. 1014.

78. Sources for the Battle of the Little Big Horn:

For Lakota eyewitness accounts see Standing Bear's and Black Elk's accounts in DeMallie, *The Sixth Grandfather*, pp. 180–95; Red Horse's account in Mallery, *Picture-Writing of the American Indians*, pp. 563–66, 39–48; White Bull in Vestal, *Warpath*, pp. 191–205, and in Howard, *The Warrior Who Killed Custer*, pp. 51–62 and 69–70; Bad Heart Bull in *Sioux Indian Painting*, with introduction and notes by Hartley Burr Alexander (Nice, France: C. Szwedzicki, 1938), pt. 2; Richard G. Hardorff, ed., *Lakota Recollections of the Custer Fight* (Spokane, Wash.: A. H. Clark Co., 1991); W. A. Graham, *The Custer Myth: A Source Book of Custeriana* (Harrisburg, Pa. Stackpole, 1953), pp. 45–100; Hammer, *Custer in '76*, pp. 195–215.

The Cheyenne accounts appear in Powell, *People of the Sacred Mountain*, pp. 1003–30, as does a summary of accounts from Indian perspectives, p. 1368. Two splendid overviews are John S. Gray's *Centennial Campaign* and *Custer's Last Campaign: Mitch Boyer and the Little Big Horn Reconstructed* (Lincoln: University of Nebraska Press, 1991).

79. This section derived from White Bull's account in Vestal, *Warpath*, pp. 197–201.

80. Ibid., p. 199.

81. Ibid., p. 200.

82. Ibid.

83. However, note the difference between this man's clothing and the clothing worn by Yellow Nose in his own drawings and account of this fighting at the Little Big Horn. See Powell, *People of the Sacred Mountain*, pp. 972–75, 1023–24, 1028.

84. Southern Cheyenne field notes, James Mooney; Little Man and Left Hand Bull, to James Mooney, March 7, 1906; James Mooney, "Cheyenne Notebook (Oklahoma), 1903–1906." National Anthropological Archives, Bureau of American Ethnology, MS. 2531, vol. 5, Cheyenne.

85. For Cheyenne drawings of the Elkhorn Scrapers Society crooked lances see Powell, *People of the Sacred Mountain*, pp. 126–29. Also, George A. Dorsey, *The Cheyenne*, I, *Ceremonial Organization*, Field Columbian Museum, Publication 99, Anthropological Series, vol. 9, no. 1 (Chicago, 1905), following p. 16, pl. 8, no. 2, "Hoof-Rattle Warrior."

For the Oglala versions of the crooked lances see: Standing Bear's drawings 24 ['Wolf hide staffs'], 25 ['White Strap Society'], 27 ['Sotka Boys Society'], 28 ['Badger Society'], "List of Standing Bear drawings," Buechel Memorial Lakota Museum. Bad Heart Bull and Blish, *A Pictographic History*, p. 104 [Strong Heart], p. 105 [Wiciska], p. 108 [Sotka Yuha], and p. 109 [Iroka]. See also Clark Wissler, "Societies and Ceremonial Associations," pp. 25–36.

86. White Bull, in Vestal, *Warpath*, p. 186.

87. Also, Lakota and Cheyenne men exchanged leggings as gifts. So it is possible for a man of one tribe to be wearing leggings made and decorated by a woman of the other tribe.

88. For the Lakota Miwatani Society regalia see: Standing Bear drawing 22 ['Mandan Society'], "List of Standing Bear drawings," Buechel Memorial Lakota Museum; Bad Heart Bull and Blish, *A Pictographic History*, pp. 106–7; Wissler, "Societies and Ceremonial Associations," pp. 41–45, 69.

The Dog Rope and the headdress of the Cheyenne Dog Men resembled the sash and the headdress of the Lakota Miwatani Society. For the Dog Soldier regalia see the Cheyenne drawings in Dorsey, *The Cheyenne*, following p. 20, pl. 9, fig. 2, "Dog-Men Warrior." Also pp. 20–24. Also, Powell, *People of the Sacred Mountain*, pp. 132–33. Compare also the photograph of the Cheyenne Dog Soldier sash in Richard Conn, *Circles of the World: Traditional Art of the Plains Indians* (Denver: Denver Art Museum, 1982), pl. 103, p. 146.

89. The Oglala Strong Heart Society banner lance closely resembles the banner lances carried by the bravest men of the Northern Cheyenne Crazy Dog Society and the Southern Cheyenne Bowstring (Wolf) Society.

See Standing Bear drawing 20 ['Strong Heart Society'], "List of Standing Bear drawings," Buechel Memorial Lakota Museum. Also Bad Heart Bull and Blish, *A Pictographic History*, pp. 104, 295, 321, 324. Also Wissler, "Societies and Ceremonial Associations," p. 26. There, as in *A Pictographic History*, the Strong Heart banner lance is described as having a row of black feathers alternating with a row of white feathers, mounted at short spaces along the red flannel sheath encasing the lance shaft. But compare also Thunder Bear's drawing of the *Cante tinza* (Strong Heart) banner lance in Wissler, "Societies and Ceremonial Associations," p. 68. There the lance is trimmed with eagle feathers alone, not alternating black and white feathers. Thus it resembles the lance portrayed here on the painted muslin.

The Northern Cheyenne Crazy Dog version appears in Powell, *People of the Sacred Mountain*, pp. 140–43. The Crazy Dogs took an active part in the fighting at the Little Big Horn. Only a few Southern Cheyenne warriors were present. However, some were Bowstrings and the banner lances carried by the Southern Cheyenne Bowstring (Wolf) Society resembled those borne by the Northern Cheyenne Crazy Dogs. See Dorsey, *The Cheyenne*, following p. 28, pl. 11, fig. 2, "Wolf Warrior," and also the description of that society on pp. 26–30.

Bowstring Society regalia is pictured often in Southern Cheyenne warrior art. For example see Cohoe, *A Cheyenne Sketchbook*, with commentary by E. Adamson Hoebel and Karen Daniels Petersen (Norman: University of Oklahoma Press, 1964), p. 47, pl. 6, "Wolf Soldiers." Also, Karen Daniels Petersen, *Plains Indian Art from Fort Marion* (Norman: University of Oklahoma Press, 1971), esp. pp. 32–33, pl. 16, "A Dance," and p. 77, color pl. 1, "On the Warpath," and p. 287, "Bowstring (Wolf) Soldier (Cheyenne)."

90. Regarding the otter-skin-wrapped straight lances with four feathers: For the Oglala versions see Wissler, "Societies and Ceremonial Associations," pp. 25–36; also Bad Heart Bull and Blish, *A Pictographic History*, pp. 104, 105, 108, 109. The Northern Cheyenne version, carried by the Elkhorn Scrapers, is pictured in Powell, *People of the Sacred Mountain*, pp. 130–31.

91. In 1959 Rufus Wallowing, the Northern Cheyenne elder, identified this man as Lame White Man, the Cheyenne Elkhorn Scraper Society chief who was killed at the Little Big Horn, charging into the midst of the soldiers on the hill. However John Stands in Timber, Lame White Man's grandson, stated that his grandfather

fought stripped to the breechclout, having ridden into battle straight from the sweat bath. See John Stands in Timber and Margot Liberty, *Cheyenne Memories* (New Haven, Conn.: Yale University Press, 1967), pp. 191–205, esp. 203–5. Also Powell, *People of the Sacred Mountain*, pp. 1019, 1020, 1025, 1028, 1033, 1074. In this case the artist may be using the scalp shirt to identify Lame White Man, who was a scalp-shirt wearer, rather than to literally portray what he wore at the Little Big Horn.

92. Bad Heart Bull and Blish, *A Pictographic History*, p. 116. Wissler, "Societies and Ceremonial Associations," pp. 48–49.

93. White Bull, in Vestal, *Warpath,* p. 24. Dark orange, occasionally used for red in Lakota warrior art, is used here.

94. Ibid.

95. Ibid., pp. 24–25.

96. Wissler, "Societies and Ceremonial Associations," pp. 7–8, 36–41, esp. 39–41. See Standing Bear's drawing of two chiefs, drawing 19 "Wicasayatapika ['chiefs']," "List of Standing Bear drawings," Buechel Memorial Lakota Museum. Cf. Chief Brave Heart's fringed blue scalp shirt and hair ornament of two upright eagle feathers in Bad Heart Bull and Blish, *A Pictographic History*, p. 324.

97. Standing Bear drawing 5, "Tatanka iyotake—Sitting Bull, also dressed for battle," "List of Standing Bear drawings," Buechel Memorial Lakota Museum; Bad Heart Bull and Blish, *A Pictographic History*, following p. 10, color pls. 128, 130, 146; also pp. 214, 216, 232, 269.

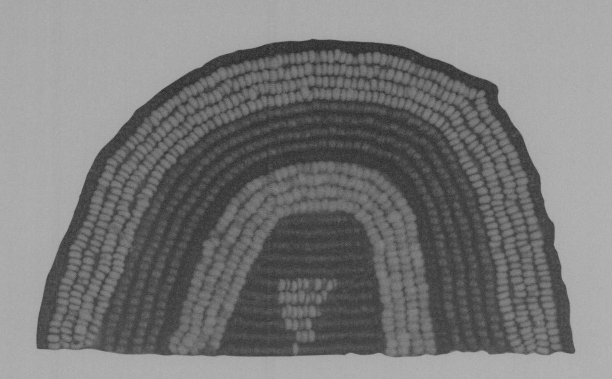

# Catalogue of the Exhibition

 *isions of the People* celebrates the continuing life of

the Plains tribes by bringing together a selection of objects that they created to communicate what was most important to them.

These images commemorate the routines of daily living, acts of personal bravery, and that powerful spirituality and reverence for

the sacred that gives comfort as well as direction and meaning to life.

**Gorget**
Spiro phase, Caddoan
culture, A.D. 1200–1350
Shell
4 in (diam)
The Minneapolis Institute
of Arts, the William Hood
Dunwoody Fund, 91.37.1
Provenance: Collected by
Judge Claude Stone at
Temple Mound, Spiro site,
Oklahoma
References: Fundaburk and
Foreman 1957, fig. 84

This shell pendant or gorget was worn around the
neck by a high-ranking
man in the hierarchy of
Spiro society. The sun is a
universal symbol of generative power and has always
been a vital element of
American Indian religion,
from the ancient mound
cities of the Southeast to
the Plains, where it appears
in many forms of ceremonial art.
EMM

**Shield cover and shield**
Comanche (Niuam),
ca. 1875
Native-tanned leather;
eagle and flicker feathers;
horsehair; sinew; brass
bells; wool cloth; felt; yellow, green, blue, and red
pigments
49 x 42 in
The Heard Museum,
Phoenix, Arizona, 258 CI-
A,B
Provenance: Fred Harvey
Fine Arts Collection
References: Maurer 1977,
p. 195, fig. 261

Stars and the sun are the
principal motifs on the inner
cover of this shield. The
powerful rays of the sun are
indicated by the zigzag and
angled lines that emanate
from the center. Like many
Plains shields, this one has
two hide covers placed over
the thick rawhide disk of the
shield itself. The covers are
painted and decorated to
represent and honor the
powers revealed to the warrior in a dream or vision.
The feathers, cloth, and
other objects are part of this
symbolic system. The

Comanche are a Shoshonean
language group of the
southern Plains closely related to the Shoshone in the
Wind River area of Wy-
oming. This tribe was one
of the first to use horses,
which they obtained from
raids on Spanish settlements
in Mexico. They maintained
an important position as
horse traders with other
tribes from the eighteenth
through the nineteenth
century. They were buffalo
hunters and courageous
warriors with a reputation
of being the finest horsemen
on the Plains.
EMM

2

1

## 3

**Tipi model**

Cheyenne (Tsistsistas),
1904
Hide, feathers, paint, wood
30⅛ x 33½ in
Field Museum of Natural
History, Chicago, 96899
Provenance: Commissioned
by James Mooney,
Darlington, Oklahoma,
1904

Stars are frequently found
as a symbolic motif in
Plains art and are often
painted on tipis to represent the heavens and the
universe at large. This tipi
design was the property of
a Cheyenne man named
Mad Bull. It was repro-
duced on a model as part of
a project to record traditional Cheyenne tipis and
shield designs. The work
was done by several
Cheyenne men in 1904 at
the encouragement of
anthropologist James
Mooney. The original tipis
and shields had long since
been destroyed in war or
lost, but their images were
still strong in the memories
of the men and women
who had lived in the days
before Indians were forced
onto reservations. Through
this project we have a vivid
record of an important
Plains tradition.

EMM

Robert Lee Penn (Wicahpe)
(b. 1946)

**Nightshield**

Sicangu Lakota–Omaha,
1990
Acrylic paint, canvas
25½ x 36 in
The Minneapolis Institute
of Arts, the John R. Van
Derlip Fund, 91.4

Robert Penn has had a
long and distinguished
artistic career, beginning as
a student of Oscar Howe
at the University of South
Dakota. In the moon,
stars, and other images of
his painting *Nightshield*,
Penn combines ceremonial
and biographical art to
recall the ancient heritage
of his people. In his words:
"The wrapped crow repre-
sents a personal medicine
spirit, and the sweetgrass
braid would also have
been used as a prayer
offering. The pictographic
riders in the background
portray warriors in battle.
The entire piece symbolizes
the spiritual strength of
those who fought to pro-
tect their people"(letter to
Evan Maurer, 1992).

Robert Penn typifies the
multiple role of an Indian
artist working in today's
modern world. "As a Native
American living in modern
society I have a dual role
as artist and interpreter.

Abstraction of symbols and
themes can re-inter-pret and
integrate the modern world
as seen from an Indian
viewpoint with strict adherence to traditional art
forms, and can transcend
both worlds to become contemporary art as well as a
cultural statement."

EMM

3

4

6

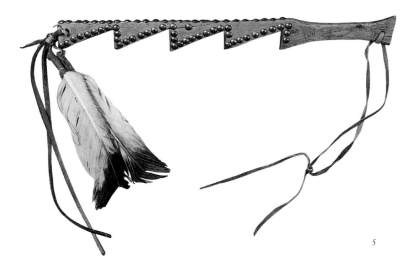

5

Bob Tailed Bull
**Quirt**
Hunkpapa Lakota,
ca. 1885
Wood, brass tacks, leather,
feathers, red wool cloth,
blue and yellow pigment
20 in
State Historical Society of
North Dakota, 86.234.74
Provenance: Collected by
Usher L. Burdick, Standing
Rock Reservation, North
Dakota, 1890

Bob Tailed Bull was a
Hunkpapa warrior who
fought in many engage-
ments, including the Battle
of the Little Big Horn, in
July of 1876. Like many
Plains equestrian warriors,
he used a short horsewhip,
or quirt, that also was carried in dances and was a
badge of office in certain
military societies. This quirt
is carved and decorated in
the zigzag line that was a
Plains symbol for lightning
and spiritual power. Quirts
with this form are illustrated in many Plains warrior
drawings (cat. no. 179).
EMM

**Shield cover and shield**
Crow (Absaroke), ca. 1870
Rawhide; native-tanned
leather; hawk feathers;
sinew; cotton fabric; stuffed
hawk; brown, red, and
green pigments
20 in (diam)
Peabody Museum of
Archaeology and Ethnology,
Harvard University, 05-7-
10/64948
Provenance: Gift of Lewis
Farlow, 1905; collected
by Coffen-Schitzer
Company; belonged to
Buffalo Calf (Berha-
Nakuse)
References: Minneapolis
Institute of Arts and
Walker Art Center 1972,
p. 114

This shield belonged to
Buffalo Calf (Berha-
Nakuse) and records his
vision of a stormy sky and
a hawk. The sky is indicated by the black, three-lobed
storm clouds on opposite
sides of the shield. The area
between them is energized
by green zigzag lines and
black straight lines that
stand for lightning and
rain. These symbols are
joined by the preserved
head and feathers of a
hawk, a fierce raptor closely associated with Plains
warriors. A miniature
shield portraying a bird is
attached to the edge. It was
often carried in place of the
full-scale shield.
EMM

No Two Horns (He Nupa Wanica) (1852–1942)
**Shield**
Hunkpapa Lakota,
ca. 1900
Muslin, wood, feathers, red and black pigment
21½ in (diam)
State Historical Society of North Dakota, 1076
Provenance: Collected by J. D. Allen, Standing Rock Reservation, North Dakota

The Hunkpapa warrior No Two Horns received a powerful dream vision that he used as a medicine shield design to protect himself in battle (cat. no. 172). His original shield of native-tanned leather and rawhide is now in the collection of the Denver Art Museum. Sometime during the early 1900s, No Two Horns made at least two versions of his shield on muslin, with the same design and colors as the original.

The central image is the thunderbird, which dominates the shield with its large body and outstretched wings. The wavy lines radiating from the top of the wings are a conventional representation of spiritual power and may also refer to thunder and lightning, natural forces prominent in Plains warrior iconography.
EMM

**Pouch**
Great Lakes, ca. 1750
Native-tanned hide, porcupine quills, metal cones, dyed deer hair
10⅝ x 11⅜ in
Société Musée du Vieil Yverdon, 00.01.10

Small leather pouches decorated with embroidered porcupine quills were used by many peoples of the Eastern Woodlands, Great Lakes, and Prairie as containers for objects associated with healing, power, and ritual societies. Until the early nineteenth century these bags were often made of finely dressed dark leather treated with a dye made from the bark of the black walnut tree and other vegetable pigments. The black hide makes an effective background that emphasizes the colorful designs and figures worked onto the pouch in several techniques of quill embroidery.

This pouch features images of the two most important and powerful of the Great Lakes spirit entities, the Thunderbird and the Underwater Panther. These *manitos*, or spiritual forces, represent the powers of the sky and the countervalent powers of the underworld; they are forever locked in a struggle that is a metaphor for the universal conflicts inherent in the natural world.

These images are found on a wide variety of objects that clearly demonstrate the importance of representational sacred images in the life of the Great Lakes peoples. They are also a precedent for the development of sacred imagery among Plains tribes who had their origins in the Northeast.
EMM

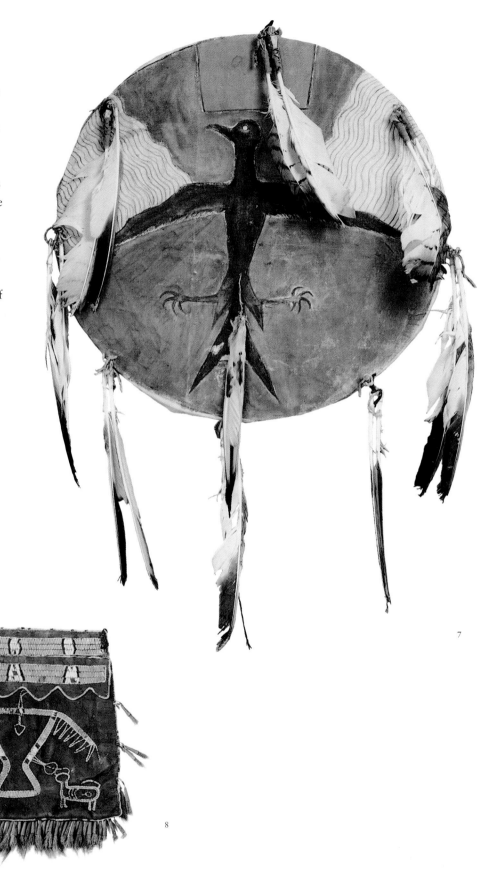

7

8

## 9

**Shield cover and shield**

Crow (Absaroke)? ca. 1860
Semi-tanned leather,
rawhide, pigment, human
hair, glass beads, wool
fabric, sinew
20¼ in (diam)
Peabody Museum of
Archaeology and Ethnology,
Harvard University,
05-7-10/64947
Provenance: Gift of Lewis
Farlow, 1905; collected by
Coffen-Schniter Company
from Jack-Cover-Up, son
of Wolf Lies Down (Chais
Cappis), a Crow medicine
man

The large black raptor
painted on this shield is
probably a reference to the
mythical thunderbird. A
scalp hangs from the shield
by a beaded, circular piece
of red wool, in the center of
which are four spokes of
white beadwork, signifying
the four sacred directions.

The image of an eagle
representing the mythical
thunderbird appears consistently in vision-inspired art.
Here the thunderbird is
emerging from the dark,
presenting himself to the
viewer. Power radiates
from the thunderbird,
shown by the wavy lines
coming from his eyes. In
most visions, the thunderbird swoops down from
above, bringing thunder
and lightning as metaphors
of spiritual energy.

JDHC

Swift Dog (Ta-sunka-duza)
(1834–1925)

**Shield**

Yankton Nakota, ca. 1865
Rawhide, native-tanned
leather, feather, red wool
cloth, pigments
19½ in (diam)
Minikahda Club,
Minneapolis
Provenance: Collected by
Major George H.
Bingenheimer, U.S. Indian
agent, North Dakota, 1911

Swift Dog was a name used
by many Northern Plains
peoples. The Swift Dog
who owned this shield was
born in 1834 to a family
known for its chiefs and
warriors. He was active in
battle and also made several trips to Washington,
D.C., to negotiate treaty
rights for his people. He
died in 1925 at the age of
ninety-one.

A large four-pointed
form is the central image of
this object of spiritual protection. Because of its equal
arms it may represent the
morning star, which is frequently found in ceremonial painting. It may

also represent the web of
Iktomi, the spider-trickster
of Lakota lore, who figures
prominently in sacred
images and stories. A thunderbird with bolts of lightning ending in three claws
emanating from the ends of
its wings rises above. Like
most representational
images in ceremonial art,
the body of the mythical
bird is shown frontally and
its head and characteristic
raptor's beak are shown in
profile. The thunderbird is
one of the principal sacred
animals of the Plains and is
closely associated with the
power of nature to affect
our lives.

EMM

9

10

## 11

**Little Rock**
**Shield**
Cheyenne (Tsistsistas),
ca. 1860
Buffalo rawhide; native-
tanned leather; feathers;
brass bells; corn husks; red,
white, black-brown, and
blue-green pigments
19½ in (diam)
The Detroit Institute of
Arts, gift of Detroit
Scientific Association,
76.144
Provenance: Collected by
Brevet Major General
George Armstrong Custer at
the Battle of the Washita,
November 27, 1868
References: Maurer 1977,
cat. no. 206; Kan and
Wierzbowski 1979, p. 124,
fig. 1

This elaborately painted
vision shield is a fine example of early Cheyenne ceremonial art. The images of
five thunderbirds are
shown against a dark night
sky, with a crescent moon
above and five white circles
below that represent the
Pleiades, a constellation
that figures prominently in
Cheyenne mythology.

This shield was owned
by Little Rock, a Northern
Cheyenne chief who was
second to the leader Black
Kettle in the Northern
Cheyenne's efforts to medi-
ate with the army. In its
westward expansion the
United States government
had ordered General
William Tecumseh Sherman
to remove any possible
threat posed by the Indians.
On November 20, 1868,
Black Kettle, Little Rock,
and other Cheyenne chiefs
met with army representa-
tives to secure a peaceful
and safe retreat for their
families. Despite these
efforts, Black Kettle's civilian encampment of about
180 lodges was attacked at
dawn on November 27 by
a force of eight hundred
men of the Seventh Cavalry
under the command of
Major General George A.
Custer. At the end of this
massacre the Cheyenne had
suffered grievous losses of
seventy-five warriors and
twenty-eight women and
children killed and fifty-
three taken prisoner. An
observer recorded that
Little Rock was killed while
covering the retreat of a
group of women and chil-
dren. Custer and his men
then proceeded to destroy
the camp and scalp the
dead. Little Rock's scalp
and shield were among the
trophies taken by the army
that day. The shield was
sent by Custer as a gift to
the Audubon Club of
Detroit in May of 1869. In
presenting the gift he wrote:
"A great deal of ceremony,
or as the Indians term it
'Medecisn' is considered
necessary to be observed
before the shield is considered as dedicated to war.
The shield I send you was
captured during the past
winter from the Cheyennes
the most war-like and trou-
blesome tribe on the plains
as well as the most powerful" (Kan and Wierzbowski
1979, p. 132 n. 4). (See
Maurer 1977, p. 170.)

EMM

**Shield cover**
Crow (Absaroke), ca. 1850
Native-tanned leather,
brown and red pigments
19¾ in (diam)
Staatliche Museen zu
Berlin, Museum für
Völkerkunde, IV B 7801
Provenance: Acquired from
the Fred Harvey Company,
1905
References: Hartmann 1973
(1979), p. 339, fig. 84

A pair of eagles or thunderbirds is the focus of this
early Crow shield. The
birds are joined at the base
of their tails and are alike
except for the wings and
details of the head, almost
as if the drawing represented a bird sitting on a
branch, reflected in the
water. A series of red lines
is painted above the birds,
and representations of iron-
bladed lances and flintlock
rifles are ranged along the
bottom. These indicate
military achievements such
as individual combats or
raids in which the warrior
participated.
EMM

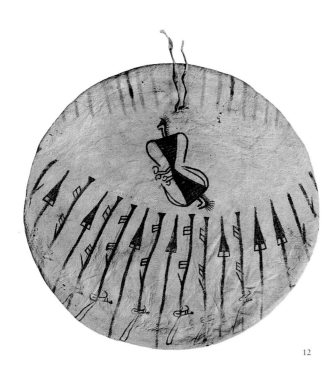

11

12

**Feast bowl**

Lakota? (catalogued as Comanche), ca. 1860
Wood, paint, brass washer, iron nails
18 x 17½ x 6¾ in
American Museum of Natural History, 1/2601
Provenance: Collected by J. H. Pell, 1869

This bowl with eagle imagery is unique in having an image of the bird's body engraved on the inner surface, manifesting the allusion to the eagle's head on the rim. The bowl is attributed to the Comanche, but since they did not have a tradition of finely carved feast bowls it is more probable that it was carved by a northern Plains man.

EMM

**Feast bowl**

Lakota, ca. 1860
Wood, brass tacks, lead
16 x 13 x 6½ in (diam)
Peabody Museum of Archaeology and Ethnology, Harvard University, 28-16-10/98291
Provenance: Collected by Colonel Sibley, U.S. Army, in 1865
References: Ewers 1986, p. 171, pl. 25

Carved in the form of an eagle, this sacred feast bowl features the round head and powerful hooked beak of the raptor. Its great staring eyes are made of brass tacks, and four tacks are also used to punctuate the shoulder and tail sections of the rim. Carved wooden bowls were precious sacred objects; their animal decorations refer to clan and society affiliations and important mythological characters. The tradition of the zoomorphic bowl can be traced to the Great Lakes area and even to the ancient Woodlands and Southeast (cat. no. 30). That this object was treasured by its owners can be seen in the two repairs made to it, one an inserted piece of wood holding together a side crack and the other a lead inlay in a diamond pattern that repairs a long break across the tail.

The bowl was captured by Colonel Sibley after an attack on a Blackfeet Lakota village. The sure carving and fine finish are typical of the Lakota and Dakota tradition of figural bowls and spoons (Ewers 1986, p. 171).

EMM

**Moccasins**

Assiniboine, ca. 1900
Tanned hide, glass beads, cotton cloth
4¼ x 10¾ x 4 in
American Museum of Natural History, 50/1969a,b
Provenance: Collected by A. L. Kroeber at Fort Belknap, Montana, 1901–28
References: Brasser 1988, p. 117; Lowie 1909, p. 22

The thunderbirds beaded on these moccasins probably derived from a vision experienced by the owner. The heart line, connecting the mouth of the animal to its heart, indicates that the animal has great power. The thunderbird is surrounded by crosses, which represent stars. The stars beaded on the border of the moccasins are emitting angled lines, which symbolize lightning and spiritual energy. Although the owner's vision is not documented, it could have referred to a thunderbird that flew out of a starry night, shooting lightning across the sky.

JDHC

15

13

14

**Woman's boots**
Dakota? ca. 1875
Native-tanned deerhide,
calico cloth, rawhide,
porcupine quills
14½ in
Cincinnati Art Museum,
1940.1227, 1228
References: Maurer 1977,
cat. no. 171

These boots are an excellent
example of the women's art
of quill embroidery. Here
the design is the typical
floral motif, with the addition of stars and eagles,
ceremonial symbols that
are unusual on women's
garments. The six different
colors the quills are dyed
add to the decorative variety of the design.

EMM

Jhon Goes in Center
(b. 1949)

**Warrior's cross**
Oglala Lakota, 1991
German silver
9⅜ x 6 in
The Minneapolis Institute
of Arts, the Christina N.
and Swan J. Turnblad
Memorial Fund, 91.94
Provenance: Purchased at
the Northern Plains Tribal
Arts exhibition, Sioux Falls,
South Dakota, 1991

Large crosses of German
(nickel) silver were fre-
quently worn as chest
ornaments by men of the
southern and central Plains.
Their reference is not the
Christian cross but rather
the star symbol traditionally used in Plains art. In this
contemporary example of
the metalsmith's art, a

finely engraved eagle is the
central symbol, flanked
by four sets of geometric
designs, heart-shaped
cutouts, and circular
pendants.

In describing his work the
artist has written: "The
ancient art of engraving still
provides a medium for the
future. As a Native American
Indian I have experienced the
beauty of my culture as a participant, observer and as a
researcher . . . ultimately I
learned a most important
concept of preservation of my
culture's attributes through
new expressions in my art. . . .
By sharing my culture, I
hope to enhance understanding and communication."

EMM

17

16

**Courting whistle**

Hunkpapa Lakota,
ca. 1875
Wood; brass tacks; yellow,
red, and black pigment
29 x 4⅝ x ½ in
National Museum of the
American Indian,
Smithsonian Institution,
23/2952
Provenance: Collected by
Margaret R. Elliot at
Standing Rock Reservation,
Cannon Ball, North
Dakota, 1880–1950

Whistles and multiholed
flutes were used in the
courting ceremonies of
many Plains people. This
single-note whistle represents a long-billed water
bird such as a crane or a
snipe. The thin body of the
whistle is textured by an
overall pattern of hot file
marks, a decorative tech-
nique commonly used in
Plains Indian sculpture. The
head is carved separately;
the long, elegant curves of
its yellow beak are emphasized by the open red
mouth. These whistles had
a soft, attractive note.
Henry Black Tail described
how these instruments were
used by the Assiniboine.
"The young man took a
wooden whistle to the girl's
tipi, stood outside and blew
on the whistle. This whistle
generally was made with
the head of an open-
mouthed bird on the front
of it. On hearing the whistle
the girl was supposed to
come out to the young
man" (Ewers 1986, pp.
160–63).
snipe. According to Densmore,
these whistles were known
by several names, which
emphasizes the multiple
identities invested in many
ceremonial objects. They
are called "elk whistles"
(*cheka'ka si' yotanka*) by
some in reference to their
role in courting (cat. no. 48);
"large pith" (*co'yotanka*)
by the Santee and Yank-
tonai because a branch of
wood with a large pith was
used to make the long,
hollow stems; and "large
prairie chicken" (*si'yotanka*)
by other Teton Lakota
because the male prairie
chicken was known for its
aggressiveness in the mating
ritual. These bird-headed
whistles were also carried
by men in the Grass Dance.
(See Densmore 1918, pp.
470–71.)

EMM

**Hot Dance Society stick**

Crow (Absaroke), ca. 1900
Wood, rawhide, dyed por-
cupine quills, feathers, tin,
brass tacks
24¾ x 6 in
American Museum of
Natural History, 50/6827
Provenance: Collected by
Robert H. Lowie, Crow
Reservation, Montana,
1907
References: Lowie 1935,
fig. 13c

Lowie documented these
crane-headed sticks as being
the insignia of the four men
who were the third highest
group of officers of the
Crow Hot Dance Society
(*batawe'disu'a*). The Hot
Dance was analogous to the
Grass Dance and was introduced to the Crow by the
Hidatsa in 1875. (See Lowie
1935, pp. 206–13).

EMM

**Spoon**

Lakota, ca. 1875
Cow horn, glass beads
14 x 5¾ x 3½ in
The Minneapolis Institute
of Arts, anonymous gift,
92.10

The Lakota were expert in
the carving, steaming, and
shaping of buffalo and
cow horn to make feast
spoons and ladles. These
were often decorated with
animal images. In this
large, finely made example
the handle accentuates the
long, graceful neck of the
crane. The round head and
extended beak are
enlivened by the subtle
addition of a glass bead set
on end to represent the
staring eyes of this stalking
hunter.

EMM

**Pipe stem**

Lakota? ca. 1860
Wood, brass tacks
24½ x 1¾ x 1¼ in
Peabody Museum of
Archaeology and Ethnology,
Harvard University,
74-18-10/7678
Provenance: Collected by
William A. Turner, Upper
Missouri River, 1873

This beautifully propor-
tioned and finished pipe
stem exemplifies the highest
level of Plains wood sculpture. The stem is the conduit of the sacred smoke as
it travels from the pipe
bowl to the man who
smokes in prayer. The crane
or crow that faces the
smoker is therefore a direct
reference to a spiritual entity associated with the
owner of the pipe and its
special ritual. The stepped
designs carved into the end
of the stem represent zigzag
lines of power in reference
to the spiritual effectiveness
of the smoking ceremony.

EMM

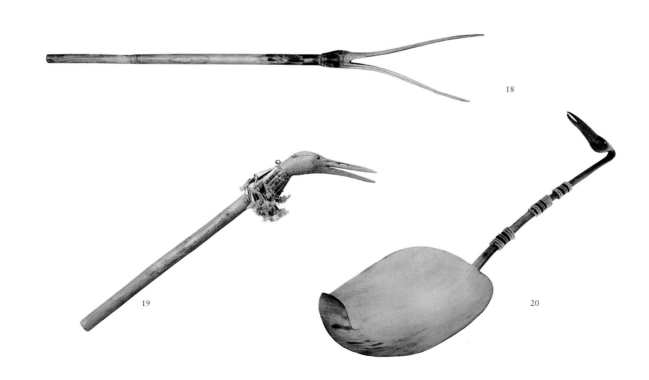

18

21

19

20

George Kicking Woman
(Three Guns) (b. 1913)
**Black Crow tipi**
Blackfeet (Siksika), 1992
Canvas, paint
18 ft (diam)
The Minneapolis Institute
of Arts
Provenance: Commissioned
for the exhibition

A painted tipi in a Blackfeet camp gives distinction and respect to its owner. Traditionally, a painted tipi was an announcement that a sacred prayer bundle rested within. The tipi owner possessed the rites and rituals of that bundle. Bundles and their particular tipi designs were passed from family to family, generation to generation. Today, the exchanging of bundles is uncommon, but tipi designs are bought and sold for ceremonial and exhibition use. This tipi design belongs to George Kicking Woman, a highly respected Blackfeet elder from Montana. He inherited it from his grandfather, who inherited it from his father.

Like many painted tipis, this one has designs that represent the basic elements of the universe. The red triangles around the bottom stand for mountains, and the white circles within are the rocks from which the mountains are made. Above the mountains, black crows walk along a horizontal line. The significance of the crows is no longer known. A red line above them signifies a rainbow. The heavens encompass the entire top third of the tipi. Stars appear as white circles on the smoke flaps in two constellations, the Big Dipper and the Little Dipper. The morning star is represented at the back of the tipi in the shape of the Maltese cross.
JDHC

22

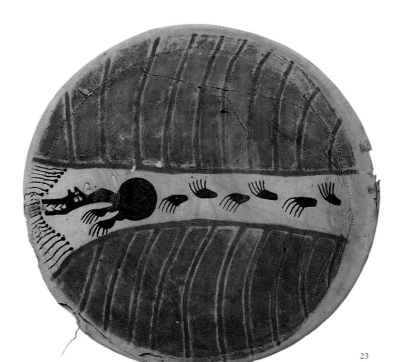

23

24

Big Bear
**Shield cover**
Crow (Absaroke), ca. 1875
Buffalo rawhide; native-
tanned leather; red, green,
and brown pigments
23 in (diam)
Field Museum of Natural
History, Chicago, 71832.2
Provenance: Collected by
S. C. Simms, Museum
Expedition, Crow Reserva-
tion, Montana, 1902

A Crow warrior named Big
Bear received a vision from
which he then painted this
medicine shield. This spiritually and visually affective
design has a green top section that refers to the sky
and a red bottom area that
represents the earth. In the
narrow area between, the

warrior-artist painted the
image of a running bear,
whose rapid forward move-
ment is indicated by the
series of six bear paws. The
bear (probably a grizzly) is
shown as a dark disk with
two forepaws, a long neck,
and an open mouth, charg-
ing into a curtain of bullets
whose speed is indicated by
the waving tails streaming
behind them.

Crow men made as
many as four versions of
some shields; one other
with this design is in the
collection of the Plains
Indian Museum in Cody,
Wyoming. A similar shield
was also collected among
the Kiowa in Oklahoma.
(National Museum of
Natural History, Washing-
ton, D.C., 229889). (For
more information on
Plains bear imagery see
Rockwell 1991.)

EMM

## 24

Bull Snake
**Shield**
Crow (Absaroke), ca. 1875
Buffalo rawhide; native-
tanned leather; horse-hair;
feathers; crane's head;
bear's ear; green, red,
black, and brown pigments
21 in (diam)
Field Museum of Natural
History, Chicago, 71828.1
Provenance: Collected by
S. C. Simms, Museum
Expedition, Crow
Reservation, Montana,
1902

Bull Snake's shield com-
bines many elements of
power centered on the red
grizzly bear cutout with
long, curving claws
attached to the upper section. A similar red bear
cutout with white wavy
lines on its body, attributed
to the Hidatsa, is in the
collection of the Plains
Indian Museum, Cody,
Wyoming. The black, scal-
lop-edged top section represents a storm cloud with

nine red zigzag lines of lightning. The red and green lines around the lower edge represent the rainbow, from which emerge sixteen black bullets that fly up toward the bear. The two white spots on either side of the animal symbolize bear holes. A bear's ear and a crane's head, which were part of the warrior's vision, are attached to the upper part of the shield. The bear was an important figure in Crow mythology concerning the creation and was associated with healing as well as war (Lowie 1935, pp. 122–25).

Wildschut reported that Crow warriors usually left their shields at home when going on a war raid because their weight and size made them cumbersome on long trips. A piece of shield medicine—the painted cover or a miniature replica—was often carried by the warrior to embody the spiritual power of the shield itself (Wildschut 1975, pp. 65–67).

EMM

## 25

**Shield cover**

Upper Missouri, ca. 1820
Native-tanned leather; red, brown, and black pigments
23½ in (diam)
National Museum of Natural History, Department of Anthropology, Smithsonian Institution, 2671

The image of the bear paw was often used to symbolize the physical and spiritual power of the bear, an animal believed to share many characteristics with humans and thus to be one of the animals most closely associated with healing and protective power. This large shield has as its central image a red bear's leg and a paw with five sharp, curving claws, which represent the animal's awesome power. Two sets of smaller, differently decorated paws extend from one edge of the shield, and a pattern of short black lines that might represent flying bullets fills the other side.

Bear paw imagery can be found on many other Plains shields, including examples from the Mandan (National Museum of the American Indian, 21/4017) and the Cheyenne (Nelson-Atkins Museum, Kansas City, 40.616). (See also Ewers 1982, pp. 36–45.)

EMM

## 26

**Medicine container**

Arapaho (Inuna-ina), ca. 1860
Buffalo rawhide; native-tanned leather; red, green, and dark brown pigments
11½ x 13⅜ x 2½ in
Peabody Museum of Archaeology and Ethnology, Harvard University, 99-12-10/53004
Provenance: Gift of the heirs of David Kimball, 1899; collected in the mid-1800s or earlier
References: Feder 1971a, fig. 34

This buffalo rawhide bag was probably made to hold materials associated with healing or other aspects of the Bear Dreamers' Society. The front of the bag is divided into three main sections. The center panel shows three green bear paws with red hourglass shapes and five sharp claws. On either side of the central panel are two large hourglass designs against a red and green background with four white circles to honor the sacred directions, a reference also made by the four red and green stars painted across the middle of the hourglass shapes. The back of the bag is divided into four triangles, each of which has a star cross as a reference to the elemental directions.

EMM

25

26

27

**Bear cutout**
Mandan-Hidatsa
(Minitari)? ca. 1860
Copper
2 x 3¼ in
State Historical Society of
North Dakota, 1876
Provenance: Collected by
Charles W. Hoffman, Van
Hook, Fort Berthold
Reservation, Montana,
1895

This small bear was cut
from a piece of sheet copper for use as an amulet
associated with the bear
cult. The choice of the
"red" metal was deliberate,
as many pieces of bear
medicine were painted red.
In its original context it
was most likely attached to
a garment, shield, or ceremonial object or was kept
as a separate amulet of
power. Charles Hoffman,
the collector, was half
Arikara and was trained in
Indian schools on the reservation. In 1895 he and his
family moved to Fort
Berthold to establish a
school among the Hidatsa.
Hoffman was superinten-
dent of the agency from
1908 to 1933. This piece
was probably collected during his early years among
the Hidatsa.
EMM

**Pipe bowl**
Lakota? ca. 1820
Slate, lead
2⅝ x 1⁷⁄₁₆ x 5⅛₁₆ in
The University Museum,
University of Pennsylvania,
Philadelphia, 38377
Provenance: Gift of John
Wannamaker, 1901;
collected by George Catlin,
ca. 1832
References: Catlin [1844]
1973, pl. 98

Pipes with bear images
were associated with men
who had received bear
dreams and belonged to the
bear cults that were found
in many Plains tribes.
Members of bear cults of
northern Plains tribes such
as the Assiniboine were
active as warriors and heal-
ers and had distinctive costumes, hairstyles, paraphernalia, and even tipis (Ewers
1967, pp. 131–45).
  Catlin collected this pipe
during his eight years of
visiting the Indian tribes.
He illustrated it, along with
other pipes, in his book
*Letters and Notes on the
Manners, Customs, and
Conditions of North
American Indians* ([1844]
1973, pl. 98). The bear is
carved as an integral element of the pipe shank and
is positioned to face the
smoker. The pipe carver
expressed the solid, round
forms of the animal's body
and its characteristic
anatomical details.
EMM

28

**Feast bowl**
Dakota, ca. 1850
Wood, brass tacks
20⅜ x 10 x 4½ in
American Museum of
Natural History, 1/2603
Provenance: Collected by
J. H. Pell, 1869

The Dakota, or Eastern
Sioux, were accomplished
wood-carvers who pro-
duced sculptured animal-
figure bowls for their
sacred Medicine Dance, in
which all initiated members
carried their own carved
wooden spoon and bowl.
In his study of Plains sculpture, Ewers found that
many Plains figurative
bowls were probably made
by the Santee, one of the
Dakota ethnic groups. The
animal crests are meant to
represent voraciousness and
the spirit of E-ya, the glutton god. It was the duty of
each participant to con-
sume all the food that was
placed in his bowl at one of
these feasts (Ewers 1986,
pp. 166–73).
EMM

**Feast bowl**
Pawnee (Chahiksichahiks),
ca. 1850
Wood
6⁵⁄₁₆ x 12¾ x 12¼ in
The Minneapolis Institute
of Arts, the Ethel Morrison
Van Derlip Fund and gift of
Carol Ann Mackay, 89.92

The Pawnee continued
many older southeastern
Caddoan customs, includ-
ing the production of
wooden animal-figure
bowls that followed the tradition of the older ceramic
models. As in many
Mississippian ceramic
bowls, this animal faces
outward and the bowl is
relatively round. Pawnee
bowls are less finely finished than those made by
the Dakota and Lakota but
have a visual power that
derives from their direct
carving style. (See Ewers
1986, p. 173.)
EMM

30

29

**Buffalo figure**
Northern Plains,
ca. 1400–1650
Green quartzite
6½ x 9 in
Glenbow Museum,
Calgary, Alberta, Ax70
Provenance: Found near
Ardmore, Alberta, Canada,
1959
References: Barsness 1977,
p. 25; Ewers 1986, p. 43,
pl. 14

Many cultures have produced sculptures of animals that are the main quarry of hunters. On the Plains, the principal food animal was the buffalo, and many early tribal groups carved buffalo to be used in ceremonies that "called the buffalo" and assured its availability as the tribe's main source of food, clothing, and shelter.

Most of these sculptures are associated with ancient or early historical sites; few have been documented among the historical tribes (Ewers 1986, pp. 123–26).

This spare yet sensitively carved figure captures the muscular mass of the buffalo with its large head and the great hump that rises over the shoulders. During the prehorse period bison were mostly hunted by large cooperative groups who built brush barriers and corrals where the herds could be trapped or sent over a cliff to be killed below. Buffalo-calling ceremonies were an essential element of Plains life, which so closely depended on these animals for survival. A similar buffalo figure, found near Carpio, North Dakota, is in the collection of the State Historical Society of North Dakota (2842).

EMM

**Pipe bowl**
Cheyenne (Tsistsistas),
ca. 1885
Pipestone
7½ x 4⅜ x 1¼ in
Amon Carter Museum,
Fort Worth, gift of Arthur
Woodward, Patagonia,
Arizona, 1966.18
References: Barsness 1985,
p. 81; Barness 1977, p. 37

This buffalo pipe shows the continuing importance of the buffalo to Plains life even after it had been hunted to near extinction by the Euro-American population. The sculptor skillfully indicated the basic form of the animal and added significant details of anatomy and even the texture of the buffalo's shaggy mane by engraving the surface with finely cut marks. (See Ewers 1986, pp. 57–61.)

EMM

Eugene Ridgely, Sr.
(Eagle Robe)
**Buffalo figure**
Northern Arapaho, 1991
Granite, petrified wood
4½ x 13¼ x 3 in
The Minneapolis Institute of Arts, the Christina N. and Swan J. Turnblad Memorial Fund, 91.92
Provenance: Purchased at the Northern Plains Tribal Arts exhibition, 1991, Sioux Falls, South Dakota

Eugene Ridgely, Sr. (Eagle Robe) was born on the Wind River Reservation in Wyoming. After service in the South Pacific in World War II he became a rancher, retiring in 1986. In this small sculpture Ridgely has captured the muscular presence of the buffalo by means of his chipping technique. Ridgely has said, "My art work is a personal expression that preserves the culture of the Arapaho people to be enjoyed and appreciated by my grandchildren, all children and the public."

EMM

**Buffalo cutout**
Teton Lakota, ca. 1860
Buffalo rawhide, black pigment
5¾ x 8¾ in
State Historical Society of North Dakota, 949
Provenance: Collected by Frances Densmore, Standing Rock Reservation, North Dakota, ca. 1911–14

Plains men made a variety of animal and human images that they cut from rawhide and used as personal amulets, parts of medicine bundles, or in sacred ceremonies such as the Sun Dance. Frances Densmore recorded the use of this buffalo representation and one in the form of a man, which were hung from the center pole of the Lakota Sun Dance Lodge to symbolize that both the enemy and the buffalo had been conquered with the help of divine intervention (Densmore 1918, p. 118, fig. 21, pls. 16, 17).

EMM

31

32

34

33

## 35

Humped-wolf
**Shield**
Crow (Absaroke), ca. 1850
Buffalo rawhide, native-
tanned leather, feathers,
pigments
21 in (diam)
The Minneapolis Institute
of Arts, the Christina N.
and Swan J. Turnblad
Memorial Fund and gift of
The Regis Corporation,
87.51
Provenance: Collected by
Lieutenant Stephen Seyburn
near Powder River,
Montana

Humped-wolf (or Hump)
was a mid-nineteenth-cen-
tury Crow warrior who
received this shield design
in a dream that was later
recounted by Knows His
Coups and Yellow Brow,
descendants of Humped-
wolf. According to the oral
tradition, Humped-wolf
saw this shield in a dream
while on a war expedition
against the Lakota. He was
caught in a blizzard on the
prairie and sought shelter
in the carcass of a buffalo.
When he slept he dreamed
his vision. After this experience he was known as Full-
mouth-buffalo (Lowie
1922, p. 409). Although
the details of the dream are
now lost, Knows His
Coups was able to describe
the meaning of the images
painted on the shield
(Wildschut 1975, pp.
67–68).

The green section on the
left represents summer, the
time of going to war, as
seen by the rows of flying
bullets aimed at the central
image of the bull buffalo.
The buffalo is shown uri-
nating, an observed detail
of natural behavior that is
associated with mating,
aggression, and the mark-
ing of territory. Wildschut
suggests that the urine
refers to the making of war
paint on raids when water
was unavailable. The owl's
feathers symbolize the
owl's ability to see at
night—a power that would
have been transferred to the
owner of the shield.
Another version of this
shield is in the National
Museum of the American
Indian (11/7678) (Wild-
schut 1975, pp. 67–68, fig.
29), and a third is in a private collection (see Dyck
1975, pp. 39–40). Crow
ceremonial objects were
sometimes made in as many
as four versions and pre-
sented to the dreamer's relatives (Lowie 1922, pp.
418–19).
EMM

**Shield cover and shield**
Crow (Absaroke), ca. 1850
Buffalo rawhide, native-
tanned leather, dyed horsehair, bird quills, buffalo
tail, wool, pigment
21¼ in (diam)
Peabody Museum of
Archaeology and Ethnology,
Harvard University, 15-34-
10/86249
Provenance: Gift of Charles
Peabody, 1915; purchased
from V. N. Thornburgh; collected from a Crow man
named White Arm

The buffalo was commonly
used on Plains shields as a
symbol of power derived
from dreams. This varia-
tion features a lone bull in
profile with representations
of its shaggy hair, curved
horns, protruding tongue,
and genitals. The dried tail
of a buffalo has been
attached to the shield as an
aspect of its ceremonial
power.
EMM

35

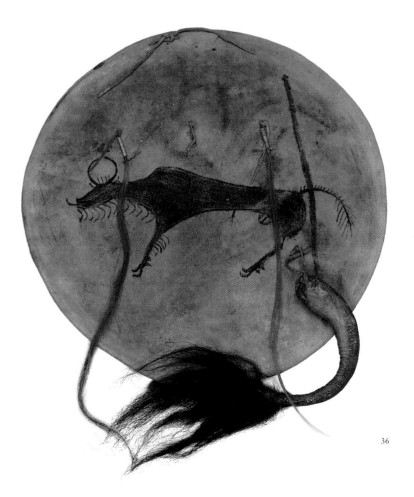

36

37

38

**Shield cover**

Crow (Absaroke), ca. 1850
Buffalo rawhide; native-
tanned leather; hawk feath-
ers; red, brown and black
pigment
21¼ in (diam)
Field Museum of Natural
History, Chicago, 71759
Provenance: Collected by
S. C. Simms, Museum
Expedition, Crow
Reservation, Montana,
1902

In this variant of the buffalo
shield, the animal is shown
suspended under a dark
storm cloud with six bolts
of zigzag lightning extending from the cloud to the
buffalo's hump and the
base of its tail. A similar
zigzag line of urine extends
from its body to the painted
circle around the edge of
the shield, which represents
a rainbow. The red marks
that fill the background
were described by Simms as
being rabbit tracks, but they
could also be hail, a natural
phenomenon often included
in warrior imagery, espe-
cially in conjunction with
thunder, lightning, and
storms.

EMM

**Shield**

Teton Lakota, ca. 1870
Muslin; feathers; horsehair;
porcupine quills;
willow; yellow, black, and
red pigment
18½ in (diam)
National Museum of the
American Indian,
Smithsonian Institution,
6/7911
Provenance: Collected by
Frances Densmore, Stand-
ing Rock Reservation,
South Dakota
References: Densmore
1918, p. 285, pl. 43

On this Lakota shield the
conventionalized frontal
image of a buffalo head is
used to represent the animal.
The head has been abstracted to a simple shape that
recalls the buffalo's massive
form, with additions of eyes,
nostrils, and a pair of powerful, curving horns. Wavy
lines ending in eagle feathers
come out of the mouth, and
a similar line encloses the
whole image in a frame of
spiritual power. Frances
Densmore recorded that this
shield was used in the dance
of the Lakota Buffalo Society
(*tatan'k watcipi*), whose
members wore headdresses
set with buffalo horns and
carried dance shields.
Membership in this and
other Animal Dreamer societies was limited to men who
had received dream visions
of the buffalo (Densmore
1918, p. 285).

EMM

**Drum**

Hunkpapa Lakota,
ca. 1865
Wood; hide; buffalo horns;
native-tanned leather;
yellow, black, and red paint
24 x 14⅛ in
National Museum of the
American Indian,
Smithsonian Institution,
23/2202
Provenance: Gift of John S.
Williams; collected by
William Michalsky, South
Dakota

This unusual prayer drum
was owned by Sitting Bull,
the great Lakota holy man
and war chief whose name,
Tatanka Yotanka, literally
means "sitting buffalo
bull." The design features a
yellow-faced buffalo with
staring red eyes, a shaggy
head, and sharp, curving
horns. Profile images of
buffalo are painted on
either side of the head but
have become worn through
use and are now barely visible. Two circular designs
with horns and lines of
power can also be faintly
seen in the top corners,
where they repeat the
major theme of homage to
this most important of all
Plains animals. The addi-
tion of actual buffalo horns
to the upper corners of the
drum transforms the entire
object into a metaphoric
image of the animal.
EMM

**Rattle**

Blackfeet (Siksika),
ca. 1865
Wood, buffalo hide
7¼ x 3⅜ x 2⅞ in
National Museum of the
American Indian,
Smithsonian Institution,
12/0321

Many of the Plains military
or Animal Dreamer soci-
eties used rattles as part of
their ceremonial rituals.
This rattle with the
engraved image of a buffalo
is of typical Plains manufacture. The hide was sewn
around a wooden handle
and set to dry, and small
stones or seeds were placed
inside. The large heart line
joining the buffalo's mouth
to its heart or lungs is a
conventional motif signifying spiritual vitality that
has its roots in Great Lakes
ceremonial art. (See Maurer
1977, nos. 69, 77, 122,
141, 155.)
EMM

**Drum**

Ute, ca. 1875
Wood; rawhide; red, black,
blue, and green pigment
15¼ in (diam)
The Denver Art Museum,
museum purchase,
1970.520
Provenance: Acquired from
Delbert Orr, Englewood,
Colorado

The Ute live on the western
Plains along the foothills of
the Rocky Mountains in
Colorado. This drum fea-
tures a boldly staring buffalo head with wavy lines
coming from its nostrils
and mouth indicating
breath and power. Around
the edge, four stylized buffalo feet, with characteristic
split hooves, honor the
sacred directions, from
which the buffalo will come
to feed the people.
EMM

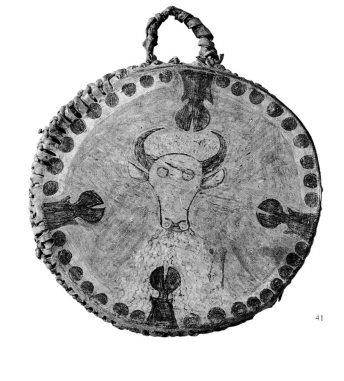

41

40

39

## 42

**Moccasins**
Lakota, ca. 1890
Native-tanned leather, rawhide, dyed porcupine quills, silk, glass beads
4 x 10½ x 4 in
American Museum of Natural History, 50-2909a,b
Provenance: Collected by Clark Wissler from the Crow Creek Lakota, 1902

Many Plains tribes had guilds of quillworkers, and later beadworkers, whose members were among the most respected women of the tribe (Mariott 1956).

They were expert in elaborately decorating items for use by priests and other ranking members of important social and military societies. This artist, using even stitches and tightly controlled contours, created a complex design of a blue buffalo head and blue geometric shapes against a vivid red background. Because dyed quills are subject to fading when exposed to light, it is unusual to see colors that have remained as strong as these.

EMM

## 43

Leo T. Arrowite
**Belt buckle**
Lemhi Shoshone, ca. 1990
Hide, dyed porcupine quills, glass beads, metal
21³⁄₁₆ x 3¾ in
The Minneapolis Institute of Arts, the John R. Van Derlip Fund, 91.63
Provenance: Purchased at Stewart's Trapline, Dubois, Wyoming, 1991

The belt buckle has become a major category of contemporary Plains Indian quillwork and beadwork. Many tribes make buckles for wear by their own people and for sale to

the outside market. The small scale of buckles necessitates tight folding of the quills. Here the artist has used his technical skill to create a powerful, ironic message, bringing together the American flag and the buffalo skull as a symbol of the American Indian. The use of the United States flag as a symbol by the Plains tribes is closely tied to the phenomenon of cultural identity and to icons of power (Pohrt 1975).

EMM

**Cradle decoration**
Lakota, ca. 1870
Native-tanned leather, porcupine quills, metal, cloth, horsehair
10½ x 43⅜ in
Omaha Public Library Collection, Joslyn Art Museum, Omaha, 567.1949
Provenance: Gift of General Rebeah S. Manderson, 1911; collected by Patrick Ryan, Chadron, Nebraska, ca. 1885
References: Hunt 1982, p. 154

This quillwork panel decorated the top section of a baby carrier. Each row features eleven animals. The

X-shaped designs at the ends of the rows represent spiders. Elk or deer heads follow the spiders. The next animals on the top row are big-horn sheep; on the bottom row they are buffalo. A thunderbird flanked by two smaller thunderbirds is in the middle of the upper row; in the center of the bottom row is a buffalo head. The designs represent a group of mythical and real animals that were central to the well-being of the child whose cradle they watched over.

EMM

44

42

43

**Tobacco bag**
Lakota, ca. 1875
Native-tanned deerskin,
glass beads, brass beads,
deer hooves
28 x 8½ in
The Cleveland Museum of
Natural History, 3202
Provenance: Collected by
Frederick N. Reed, late
1800s

The unusual range and
number of symbolic
designs on this bag indicate
that it must have been
made for use in ceremonies
pertaining to war. The
paired vertical symbols
beaded onto each side represent decorated pipe
stems, signifying war raids
led by the owner of the
object. On one side, a blue
buffalo head and a blue
anthropomorphic bird
holding a cresent moon
and a turtle are centered
below the pipe stems; four
equal-armed crosses or
stars on the bottom tabs
honor the cardinal direc-
tions. On the reverse, the
two pipe stems are
crowned by a blue crescent
moon, and the blue buffalo
head is flanked by two blue
horse tracks, which also
are symbols of war raids or
captured horses.
EMM

Walter Bone Shirt
**A Buffalo Society dancer**
Lakota, ca. 1890
Paper, ink, colored pencil
5 x 7¾ in
Private collection

This drawing comes from a
sketchbook of thirty pages
illustrating scenes from
everyday Lakota life, war,
and sacred ceremonies,
many of which were no
longer performed when the
drawings were made. The
drawings thus document
important rituals and
affirm the sacred life they
represent.

Like many Plains
groups, the Lakota had a
special society, known as
the *tatang ihanblapi kin*,
made up of people who had
received dreams of the buffalo. According to Clark
Wissler: "When they had
their dance, a shaman
would appear in the head
and skin of a buffalo. As he
ran about the camp a nude
young man stalked him,
while the cult followed
singing. . . . In the regular
ceremonies while the drumming is going on, the members bellow like buffalo and
some stamp a foot leaving
buffalo tracks upon the
ground" (Wissler 1912b,
pp. 91–92).

In this drawing by
Walter Bone Shirt, the
Buffalo Dreamer holds a
wavy hoop hung with four
eagle feathers as he dances
between two prayer ban-
ners. The ritual flight of
the buffalo is indicated by
the position of the run-
ning dancer's legs and the
animation of the feathers
and fringe that flow
behind him.
EMM

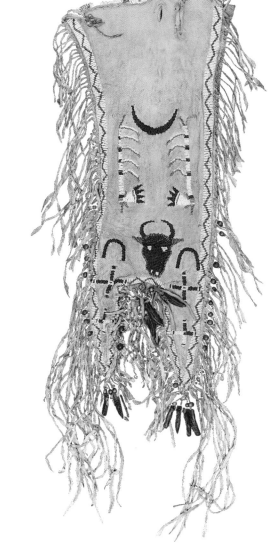
45

46

## 47

**Spoon**
Lakota, ca. 1900
Cow horn
13 x 2½ in
Montana Historical
Society, Museum
Collection, X82.44.24

The elk plays a significant role in the mythology, songs, social organization, and art of the Lakota people. "It is the elk, which is the emblem of beauty, gallantry, and protection. The elk lives in the forest and is in harmony with all his beautiful surroundings. He goes easily through the thickets, notwithstanding his broad branching horns. In observing the carcass of an elk it is found that two teeth remain after everything else has crumbled to dust. These teeth will last longer than the life of a man, and for that reason the elk tooth has become the emblem of long life. We desire long life for ourselves and our friends" (Densmore 1918, p. 176).

This horn spoon, with a handle in the form of an elk's head, is a magnificent example of Plains sculpture. The artist has beautifully rendered the elk's majestic antlers, slender muzzle, and delicate face. Early figurative spoons were made from the horns of bison and big horn sheep. After the depletion of the great buffalo herds and the forced relocation of the people to reservations, many carvers worked cow horns (Ewers 1986, p. 175).
AC

**Whistle**
Dakota, ca. 1880
Ash wood, sinew, red and yellow-orange pigment
27¾ x 2⅛ x 2⅞ in
The University Museum, University of Pennsylvania, Philadelphia, 45-15-1207
Provenance: Purchased by Charles H. Stephen, 1889

Among the Lakota the elk is closely associated with love and sexual passion. Young men in the pursuit of love sought the assistance of elk medicine to ensure their success. In imitation of the elk's whistling cry, suitors played wooden flutes and whistles. As Prince Maximilian zu Wied described in 1832, "The cry of the male elk, in the rutting season, is very singular. . . . It is a shrill whistle, which, for the most part, runs regularly up the scale, and then suddenly falls to a low, guttural note. The notes perfectly resemble a run upwards on the flageolet" (Thwaites 1906, 23:176).

One story tracing the origin of the courting flute tells of a poor young man rejected by the chief's daughter. In a dream he was visited by two elks in the form of handsome men. They gave him a flute, with instructions to return to camp and play among the lodges at night. When the young man did as he was told, all the women rose and followed him, including the chief's daughter. (See Powers 1986, p. 77.)

This carved elk whistle shows the bull elk in the act of heralding his mates. His mouth is open, and his antlers rest low on his outstretched neck. Unlike many elk flutes, which have brass tacks for eyes, this one has carved oval eyes.
AC

47

48

## 49

**Pipe bowl**
Lakota, ca. 1860
Stone
2½ x 1⅜ in
The Minneapolis Institute
of Arts, the Christina N.
and Swan J. Turnblad
Memorial Fund, 89.88

The image of a bull elk
with his outstretched neck
and antlers low on his
shoulders is carved in shallow relief on the underside
of this elbow-shaped pipe
bowl.

The circle or hoop (*cangle
skan*) to the left of the animal's foreleg may associate
this pipe bowl with the Elk
Dreamers' Society. Hoops
carried by dreamers in
dance performances were
made variously of twined
willow branches, fur, or
horsemint and other herbs.
Although not depicted in
this carving, a mirror was
sometimes suspended in the
center of the hoop by two
crossed cords representing
the four directions. The

mirror worked as a charm
or weapon from which the
dreamers could "shoot"
their elk power at all who
opposed them and also
bring "victims" under their
power. The hoop itself is
connected with the idea of
protection. Dreamers wore
this symbol to protect
themselves from the power
of other animal dreamers.
(See Wissler 1907, p. 42,
and Wissler 1912b, p. 87.)

Although we do not
know if this pipe was used
in elk ceremonies, Clark
Wissler in his discussion of
animal dreamer societies
noted the use of small
black pipes by Black-tailed
Deer Dreamers and yellow
pipes by Elk Dreamers
(1912b, p. 90). Perhaps the
carver of this pipe bowl
purposely chose an ochre-
colored stone.

AC

**Elk cutout**
Crow (Absaroke), ca. 1875
Rawhide, glass beads, com-
mercial cord
4 x 4½ in
Peabody Museum of
Archaeology and Ethnol-
ogy, Harvard University,
985-27-10/10464
Provenance: Bequest of
William H. Claflin, Jr.,
1985; collected by William
Wildschut, before 1929

Like many of the peoples of
the Upper Missouri, the
Crow have believed in the
power of love medicines to
win the affections of the
opposite sex. Both men and
women sought the charms
of a love medicine bundle
when courting. Love medi-
cine was also used to
restore the faithfulness of a
spouse and to regain love
lost (Wildschut 1975, p.
123). Medicines that
proved powerful in
courtship were often passed
down or lent to others for
their amorous pursuits.

Although not the only
animal to provide such

assistance, the elk is the primary giver of love medi-
cines, often appearing in a
dream to instruct the
would-be lover in the making of love charms such as
painted elk-hide robes,
courting flutes, headdresses, and cutouts like the one
seen here.

This small silhouette of
a bull elk, cut from raw-
hide, has a tiny yellow bead
for the eye and an orna-
mental pendant of blue
beadwork. It would have
been attached or suspended
by the loop of twisted cord
on its back (Wildschut 1975,
p. 130). A heart line, drawn
in blue, leads from the
heart to the mouth. Yellow
and blue are colors com-
monly seen on various forms
of Crow love medicine.

AC

49

50

## 51

## Moccasins

Lakota? ca. 1910
Deer hide, glass beads, porcupine quills
4 x 5 x 11 in
Museum of Indian Arts and Culture, Laboratory of Anthropology, Santa Fe, 25712/12

The quilled designs on these moccasins may be stylized deer or elk antlers or possibly a headdress adorned with antlers. Lightly dyed tan quills form the ears and outline the antlers, which are filled in yellow; the base of the form consists of small stepped blocks of purple and yellow. The background is a vibrant red.

This motif appears on various Plains objects, including pipe bags, quill-decorated robes, and baby carriers, but without a more specific attribution it is difficult to know its meaning. The size of the moccasins suggests they were worn by a man.

The moccasins may have been the property of an Animal Dreamer, worn to show membership in an Elk or Black-tailed Deer Dreamer Society. It is equally possible the design was worn by suitors as a love medicine to ensure success in courting. In Lakota culture the elk is endowed with special seductive powers, whereas the Cheyenne believe both the elk and the white-tailed deer provide the medicines (charms) that assist in the pursuit of love (Grinnell 1923, p. 134).

Perhaps the moccasins were made or worn by a person who chose the design to honor a special relationship with a guardian animal. Among the Dakota, the elk is a masculine symbol of beauty, virility, virtue, and charm (Deloria and Brandon 1961, pp. 5–6).
AC

## Fan

Dakota, ca. 1850
White pine; red, black, green, and blue paint
16½ x 11 in
Manoogian collection
Provenance: Collected by Lester Strawn, Ottawa, Illinois
References: Brasser 1987, p. 87

The incised painted imagery on this fan may connect it with a society of Elk Dreamers. A bull elk, carved to the left of the handle, is calling his mates, a harem of twenty-three cows. At the center of the fan is an elaborate composition of feathers and four thunderbirds. Brasser has interpreted the thunderbirds as representing lords of the four winds (Brasser 1987, p. 126). On the reverse, a central rosette motif is encircled by thirty-one women and three men.

The function of this object is unclear. Brasser has suggested that the fan is an early example of a "magical" mirror used by Elk Dreamers to "shoot" or flash their power at all whom they opposed (Brasser 1987, p. 126). Although Wissler, Densmore, and Fletcher all reported the use of actual mirrors at dreamer performances, Brasser proposes that the act of reflecting sunlight was not necessary but rather implied. The carved rosette served as the "mirror" from which "beams of elk medicine" were projected.

Another possibility is that the fan was used as elk medicine, a charm carried by suitors when courting. Flutes and mirrors were powerful love medicine charms. The mirrors carried by Elk Dreamers in ceremonies brought "victims" under the society's power (Wissler 1912b, p. 87). Again, the mirror is symbolic, not literal. The shape of the piece may show the influence of European-style fans.
AC

52

51

**Vest**

Lakota, ca. 1875

Hide, glass beads, porcupine quills

20 x 15½ in

Denver Museum of Natural History, Crane American Indian Collection, A.O.3585 Provenance: Mary A. and Francis V. Crane; collected by Julian D. Pyatt, South Dakota, before 1958

Among the Lakota and other Plains peoples, to dream of a particular animal has great significance, for it is through dreams that one may receive the supernatural powers of that creature. The bull elk (*hehaka*) is believed to possess extraordinary seductive powers over the females of its kind. To dream of the bull elk is to acquire this special ability to captivate females.

Men (and a few women) who dreamed of the elk joined the Elk Dreamers' Society, often acting out their dreams and "testing" their power in dance performances. At society feasts, Elk Dreamers sang songs and made medicine (*win c'uwa*) for attracting women.

For elk ceremonies, dreamers donned triangular masks of rawhide adorned with small branches representing antlers. They painted their bodies yellow and often painted their arms black from the elbow down and their legs black from the knee down. Dreamers carried hoops and mirrors from which to "shoot" their powers at rival dreamers (Buffalo Dreamers, Deer Dreamers, Heyoka Dreamers) and to bring "victims" (often women) under their influence. (See Wissler 1912b, pp. 85–88.)

The two figures depicted on the front of this beaded vest are Elk Dreamers in ceremonial dress. They wear rawhide masks with two eagle feathers added to represent ears and a third attached to the antler to give the wearer the ability to run as fast as the eagle flies (Densmore 1918, p. 178). Each carries a hoop with a single white feather and also a stick, probably used in the elk (*haka*) game. The red wavy lines on the dancers' bodies represent thunder, a sign that supernatural power is present (Wissler 1907, p. 47).

On the reverse of the vest is a man on horseback. He wears a full eagle-feather headdress and an officer's red military society sash signifying his high status. Above him is the symbol of the spiderweb, a four-cornered design depicted here in deep yellow. Like the elk, the spider (Iktomi) possesses a special ability to sway women, and its web offers protection from harm (Blish 1957, p. 199; Wissler 1907, pp. 48–49). (For more information on Elk Dreamer ceremonies, see Peter J. Powell's essay in this catalogue.)

AC

## 54

**Bag**
Lakota? ca. 1875
Native-tanned hide, glass beads
9⅛ x 12¼ in
Field Museum of Natural History, Chicago, 195791

The dream societies of the Lakota were composed of persons who had been visited by the same manifestation in a dream or vision. These organizations held feasts and ceremonies to test the medicine given to the members by their visionary patron.

The center figure on this beaded bag is an Elk Dreamer in ceremonial dress. For performances, Elk Dreamers painted their bodies yellow and wore masks of rawhide trimmed with branches representing antlers (see cat. no. 53). They carried hoops of twined branches with two cords crossed at the center.

The two flanking animals are more difficult to interpret. On the left is a deer, beaded in blue with a single line of black around the form. Black-tailed Deer Dreamers dressed similarly to Elk Dreamers with one important exception: they used the colors blue and black to adorn their bodies and costumes (Blish 1967, p. 200). Hoops carried by Black-tailed Deer Dreamers were constructed with a spiderweb design in the center (Wissler 1912b, p. 90).

The figure to the right is a wolf, beaded in pink with a green outline. Dreamers of this animal wore wolf skins over their backs and limbs. They painted their bodies white and their arms and legs red; the pink beads may represent these two colors in combination. This specific use of color suggests that the deer and wolf may refer to dream society members. Animal Dreamer societies often performed together at ceremonies held on Medicine Day, which would explain the presence of the three dreamers together.

The imagery on the reverse of the bag is enigmatic. A man riding a dappled horse follows or chases a buffalo. He wears a roach (porcupine hair headdress) and holds or waves two white feathers above his head.

AC

## 55

Silverhorn (Haungooah)
(ca. 1861–ca.1941)
**Visionary scene**
Kiowa (Gaigwa). ca. 1891
Paper, pencil, crayon
10¾ x 14¾ in
Field Museum of Natural History, Chicago, 67719.4
Provenance: Collected by Dudley P. Brown, Anadarko, Oklahoma, ca. 1899

This drawing is an enigmatic image of a mythological or visionary nature. A finely dressed man, holding his shield under one arm, appears to be placing small ornaments (possibly miniature shields, hair locks, amulets, or charms) on the antlers of a free-floating head of a supernatural anthropomorphic figure. The action and participants are undocumented.

AC

54

55

**Pipe stem**
Lakota, ca. 1880
Ash, porcupine quills, cotton cordage
24¾ x 1⅛ x 1⅛ in
Peabody Museum of Archaeology and Ethnology, Harvard University, 39-30-10/18206
Provenance: Collected by Henry M. Wheelright, 1901

Pipe stems carved with turtles and the heads of large mammals make up the majority of sculptural pipe stems. Though not all by the same hand, they share many characteristics of style and finish associated with the Lakota. This one has the head of a buffalo, a turtle, and the head of an elk, three animals found in Lakota stories (Ewers 1986, pp. 112–13).
EMM

**Pipe stem**
Dakota? ca. 1890
Ash
2 x 22½ in
The Denver Art Museum, 1964.232b
Provenance: Pat Warner, Oklahoma City, Oklahoma
References: Feder 1971a, fig. 44

Although many Plains tribes had animal pipe stems, most of those found in collections are Lakota. This one portrays two otters, carved in full relief to show the graceful curves and movement of their bodies. The carved stem might derive from the early tradition of decorating spiritually important stems with the actual heads and feathers of birds or parts of other sacred animals.
EMM

Green Grass Bull
**Pipe bowl and stem**
Blackfeet (Piegan), ca. 1880
Black-stained stone, wood
5 x 9¾ x 1½ in (bowl);
2⅜ x 1½ x 26⅞ in (stem)
Peabody Museum of Natural History, Yale University, 1986
Provenance: Given to George Bird Grinnell by Black-Coming-In-Sight-Over-The-Hill, Blackfeet Reservation, Montana, 1886–87
References: Ewers 1986, p. 82, fig. 60 (bowl), pp. 106–7, fig. 94 (stem); Maurer 1977, p. 189, cat. no. 249

A well-known Piegan pipe maker named Green Grass Bull made this complex pipe and stem for a fellow tribesman named Black-Coming-In-Sight-Over-The-Hill. This unique piece of sculpture features a man astride a stout animal that may be a buffalo. One end of the pipe is decorated with an eagle, the other with the head of a bear. On the stem are two eagles with outstretched wings. Green Grass Bull indicated to John Ewers that he had made some effigy pipes in his career but that most of his pipes were in the plain style typical of the Blackfeet (Ewers 1986, pp. 81–82, 107).
EMM

58

59

57

56

135

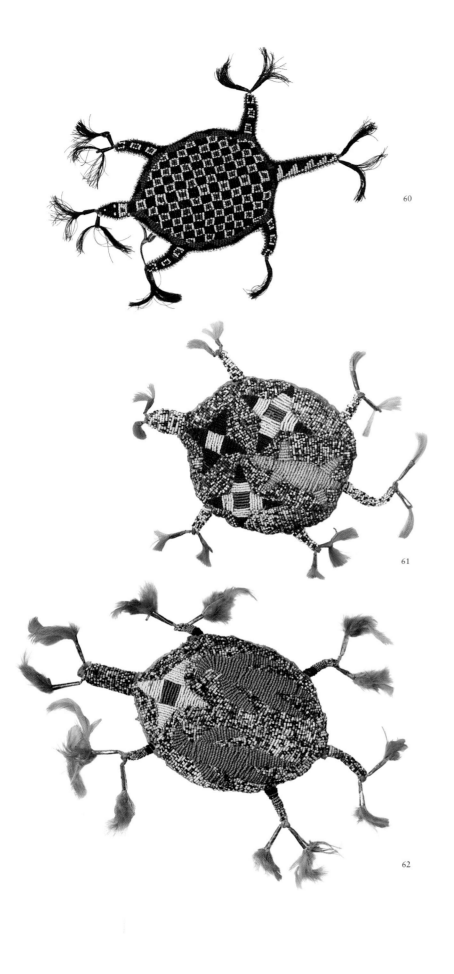

**Umbilical amulet**
Lakota, ca. 1875
Native-tanned leather, glass
beads, dyed horsehair,
metal, sinew, cotton thread
12 x 8½ x 1⅛ in
Peabody Museum of
Archaeology and Ethnology,
Harvard University,
13-48-10/85447

The dried umbilical cords
of infants were saved and
placed in an amulet case as
a protective medicine during the child's early years.
Girls had amulets in the
form of a turtle because of
the turtle's important role
in women's medicine. On
this unusually large and
finely made amulet small
"seed" beads delineate
details of the animal—its
feet, tail, head, and eyes
and the checkered pattern
on its shell. These amulets
are usually relegated to a
minor category of bead-
work by scholars, but they
should be more properly
appreciated as a broadly
practiced form of sculpture
in soft materials that has
thrived among Plains tribes
for hundreds of years.
EMM

**Pair of umbilical amulets**
Lakota? ca. 1875
Native-tanned leather, glass
beads, dyed horsehair,
metal, dyed feathers
12¼ x 9 x 2⅛ in;
15 x 10⅝ x 2 in
National Museum of the
American Indian,
Smithsonian Institution,
1/3344(2)
Provenance: Collected by
J. J. Steffen

These turtle-shaped umbilical amulets have multicolored bead backgrounds and
the unusual addition of representational graphic
imagery. One amulet fea-
tures two blue avian figures
with a red-centered, four-
pointed star above them.
The other shows a splayed-
out yellow animal sur-
rounded by three stars.
Graphic representational
imagery rarely is seen on
umbilical amulets.
EMM

**Umbilical amulet**
Assiniboine (Nakoda),
ca. 1860
Native-tanned leather,
sinew, cotton thread, glass
beads, brass beads, yellow
pigment
5¼ x 2½ x ⅜ in
Academy of Natural
Sciences, Philadelphia, on
loan to The University
Museum, University of
Pennsylvania, Philadelphia,
L84-1684
Provenance: Collected by
Amos H. Gottschall, Milk
River area, Fort Belknap,
Montana, 1896

Umbilical amulets like this
turtle were protective talis-
mans that ensured a child's
health and growth. These
small, colorful sculptures
were often suspended from
the top of a baby carrier,
above the child's head, as
sources of blessing and as
playful, visually stimulating
objects.
EMM

63

**Amulet**

Blackfeet (Siksika),
ca. 1880
Native-tanned leather, glass
beads, cotton
20⅞ in
Hearst Museum of
Anthropology, The
University of California at
Berkeley, 2-5482
Provenance: Donated by
Mrs. P. A. Hearst, 1901;
collected by J. Disbury of
Cluny, Alberta, Canada

This amulet represents the
rattlesnake, an animal that
is often found in Plains stories and myths. Amulets in
the form of animals were
commonly an integral ele-
ment of medicine bundles
or bundles associated with
ownership of a painted tipi.
Snake amulets were used by
the Hidatsa in rain cere-
monies, and Prince
Maximilian mentioned
snake pipe stems made by
the Blackfeet in the early
1830s. Snake amulets are
also documented as part of
certain healing medicine
bundles of the Crow
(Wildschut 1975, pp.
136–38, figs. 58, 59).
EMM

**Amulet**

Northern Cheyenne
(Tsistsistas), ca. 1860
Native-tanned leather,
sinew, glass beads, feathers
16 x 5 x 1½ in
The Kansas City Museum,
Kansas City, Missouri
40.607
Provenance: Collected by
Colonel Daniel B. Dyer,
Fort Reno, Oklahoma,
1885; owned by Dull Knife
References: Maurer 1977,
p. 163, cat. no. 198

Warriors sometimes car-
ried amulets whose power
had been received in dream
visions. These were important elements of their war
medicine. This brightly
colored light- and dark-
blue beaded lizard with
contrasting details in yellow, white, and red beads
was made for Dull Knife,
the great Northern
Cheyenne chief who was
also known as Morning

Star (ca. 1808–83). Morn-
ing Star had been an active
warrior but was also one
of the important chiefs of
his band of Northern
Cheyenne (Ohméseheso).
During the Indian wars of
1876 their village was
attacked and destroyed by
United States Cavalry led
by General MacKenzie.
Morning Star and other
survivors were later cap-
tured and confined at Fort
Reno, Oklahoma, where
this amulet was collected
by Colonel Dyer. The
Northern Cheyenne were
plagued with sickness in
this new and unfamiliar
land, and most of the
remaining men, women,
and children escaped to
begin a hard and futile
march north toward their
ancestral home. They were
soon recaptured and

interned at Fort Robinson,
Nebraska. In one last brave
attempt to return to their
homeland, the small band
of Cheyenne escaped again
in the winter of 1879, only
to be chased down on
January 9 in a final running
battle in which Morning
Star's band of men,
women, and children were
either killed or forced back
to confinement. Morning
Star died at Pine Ridge
Agency in 1883.
EMM

65

64

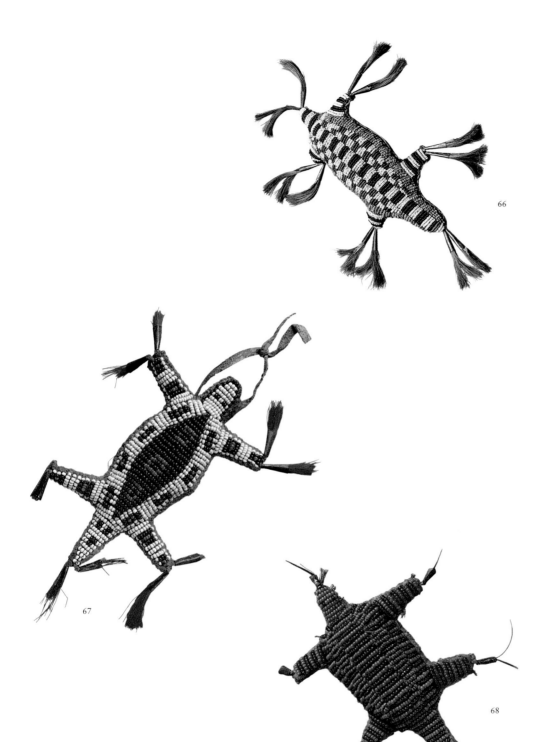

66

67

68

**Umbilical amulet**
Oglala Lakota, ca. 1900
Cotton, glass beads, dyed
horsehair, metal, sinew,
commercial cord
10½ x 7 x 1¼
American Museum of
Natural History, 50/2954
Provenance: Collected by
Clark Wissler on Pine
Ridge Reservation, 1902

**Umbilical amulet**
Sicangu Lakota, ca. 1900
Native-tanned hide, glass
beads, metal, traces of
feathers, commercial string
6¾ x 4½ x ¾ in
American Museum of
Natural History, 50.1/216
Provenance: Collected by
Emil W. Lenders, 1910

**Umbilical amulet**
Sicangu Lakota, ca. 1900
Native-tanned hide, glass
beads, dyed horsehair,
metal
7 x 5 x ¾ in
American Museum of
Natural History, 50.1/231
Provenance: Collected by
Emil W. Lenders, 1910

Among traditional Plains
peoples the practice of pre-
serving an infant's umbilical cord inside a small
amulet was rather wide-
spread. Such amulets often
took the form of lizards,
turtles, or snakes; the use of
amphibians may allude

to the infant's transition
from the watery environ-
ment of the womb to the
external world. According
to the Lakota medicine
man Lame Deer, lizards
and turtles were used
because they are strong and
long-lived, attributes that
families wish for infants as
well (Lame Deer 1972, p.
145). Amulets were
attached to babies' cradleboards, sewn to older children's clothes, and then
kept as part of personal
bundles throughout life.

Amulets seem sometimes
to have been made in pairs,
only one of them contain-
ing the umbilicus. Lame
Deer describes the "empty"
amulet as a decoy to "fool
the evil spirits." Although
many amulets have been
sold to outsiders, families
remove the umbilicus first.
All three of these amulets
show the rectilinear pattern
and extensive use of white
beads characteristic of
Lakota work.
LL

**Tipi model**
Kiowa (Gaigwa), 1904
Hide; wood; buffalo tail;
red, blue, black, and
yellow pigment
26 in
National Museum of
Natural History, Depart-
ment of Anthropology,
Smithsonian Institution,
245.045
Provenance: Collected by
James Mooney, Oklahoma,
1904
References: Ewers 1978a,
p. 32, fig. 29

This unusual tipi model
was commissioned by
Mooney in his efforts to
document Cheyenne and
Kiowa tipi and shield
motifs. According to
Mooney's notes, this tipi is
of a type called "quato-do"
and belonged to
Adalboingyato, a man of
the Kiowa Kingep band
who traditionally camped
in the northwest section of
the village circle. The tipi
has a dark blue groundline
and a series of white circles
on dark blue on the top of
the lodge, which represent
a starry sky. The body of
the tipi is painted with two
horned fishlike creatures,
one blue and one green,
with heart lines and indications of teeth and rib
bones. These are variants of
the underwater monster
found in the mythologies of
many Plains and Great
Lakes peoples.
EMM

69

**Dragonfly hair ornament**
Northern Cheyenne
(Tsistsistas), n.d.
Rawhide, sinew, paint, buttons, feathers
25⅝ (including tail) x 5⅜ in
National Museum of the
American Indian,
Smithsonian Institution,
24/2441
Provenance: Collected by
George Bird Grinnell in
Montana

**Shield cover**
Crow (Absaroke), ca. 1860
Hide, pigment, brass bells,
eagle feathers
19⅞ in (diam)
Field Museum of Natural
History, Chicago, 69633
Provenance: Collected by
S. C. Simms on Museum
Expedition, November–
December 1901, from Big
Medicine, grandson of the
original owner, Crow
Reservation, Montana

**Moccasins**
Lakota, 1880–1900
Bison hide, cloth, tin cones,
glass beads
10½ in
State Historical Society of
North Dakota, 86.234.102
Provenance: Gift of Usher
L. Burdick; obtained from
William Ward; collected at
Cherry Creek, Grand River,
Standing Rock Reservation,
North Dakota
References: Porsche 1987,
p. 47

The image of the dragonfly
was often used by warriors
throughout the Plains

because dragonflies are
quick and are difficult to
kill, and when they fly near
the ground they create dust
that makes them hard to
see. To acquire this protective power, warriors
adorned themselves with
the dragonfly image. It was
beaded onto moccasins, and
cutouts of it were used as
amulets.

This cutout (cat. no. 70)
was worn on the back of
the head with the eagle
plume hanging down
(Powell 1981, p. 352). The
button eyes add to the realism. Moccasins beaded
with the image of the dragonfly assured quick-footedness in battle. The wavy
beaded lines on these moccasins (cat. no. 72) are
associated with lightning
and power. Some men
painted the dragonfly on
their bodies or on their
shields (Grinnell 1962, p.
112). Catalogue number 71
has two dragonflies with
heart lines, which signify
their great powers. In the
center is a four-pointed
star, the morning star,
which figures so prominently in Plains mythology.
The dragonflies' antennae
are wavy lines pointed
toward the crescent moon.
This could indicate that, to
the owner of this shield
cover, the dragonfly has a
special relationship to the
powers above.
JDHC

70

72

Walter Bone Shirt
**Medicine Man**
Lakota, late 19th century
Paper, colored pencil, india
ink
5 x 7¾ in
Private collection

Although this drawing is labeled "Medicine Man," it is safe to assume that this is a woman wearing a dress and leggings. Over the dress she wears a robe decorated with the protective symbol of the dragonfly. She wears the headdress of the Strong Heart Military Society.

Although women were not members, they were allowed to carry paraphernalia of the Strong Heart Society if a relative belonging to the society was killed in battle (Densmore 1918, p. 321). A water boy's lance is stuck in the ground to her left.

A young man of ten to sixteen years of age who was in a war party often served as the water boy. A man who had had that task would kill a buffalo and make a water pail of its heart sac. Taking a stick about five feet long, he

would tie the pail at one and feathers at the other and then give this lance to the young man who was to act as water carrier for the war party. Later, the young man might discard the water pail and use the stick as a lance in battle (Wissler 1912b, p. 60).

The objects included in this drawing suggest that the woman could be in mourning for a member of her family who had served as a water boy in the Strong Heart Society and been killed in battle.

JDHC

73

**Robe with butterflies and morning stars**
Blackfeet (Siksika), 1844
Elk hide, pigment
83 x 92½ in
Folkens Museum-
Ethnografiska, Stockholm,
Sweden, 1854.2.27
Provenance: Possibly collected by Count Armand Fouché d'Otrante of France during his travels in the northern Plains region in 1842–44
References: Brasser 1988, p. 124; Raczka 1992, p. 69

This beautifully painted hide robe was worn by the holy woman in the Blackfeet Sun Dance, also known as the Medicine Lodge ceremony. As in most sacred Plains Indian ceremonies, a highly respected woman begins the Medicine Lodge ceremony. A Blackfeet man once said, "We look on the Medicine Lodge (Sun Dance) woman as you white people do on the Roman Catholic sisters" (Grinnell 1907, p. 268).

This Sun Dance robe is painted with alternating symbols of the butterfly or moth and the Maltese cross. Dreamers appeal to the power of the butterfly or moth as a messenger of the spirits (Wissler 1912a, p. 82), and the Maltese cross symbolizes the

morning star, an important element of Plains sacred ceremonies. This hide painting is unique in combining the pictorial imagery of the butterfly with the abstract geometric imagery of the morning star.

Blackfeet mythology includes many versions of how the Blackfeet were given the Medicine Lodge, one of which seems closely related to the images on this robe. A young man named Scarface wanted to marry a beautiful, wise, and true young woman, but she said he must first get permission from the Sun. Scarface looked for many days but couldn't find the lodge of powerful Sun. After passing many tests, Scarface was finally befriended by Morning Star, the son of Sun and Moon, who introduced Scarface to his father. Scarface asked Sun if he could marry the woman, and Sun took pity on him and agreed. Sun taught Scarface how to perform the Medicine Lodge ceremony and told him that only a woman could build the Medicine Lodge for Sun. If this woman were wise and true, Sun would be pleased and help (Grinnell 1907, p. 101).

The symbols of the butterfly and the morning star are painted on this robe because, like the butterfly, Morning Star acted as a messenger when he brought Scarface to Sun, who gave the Sun Dance to the Blackfeet.

The moth or butterfly is painted green, the color associated with the thunderbird, the most powerful of all winged beings. The symbols of the morning star are painted red, because it has sun power (Brasser 1988, p. 123). Four rows of symbols are painted on the hide, four being a sacred number among Plains tribes. The dotted rows may symbolize weasel tracks. According to another version of the origin of the Medicine Lodge, it was the weasel who instructed a woman long ago to paint this type of robe decoration (Wissler and Duvall 1908).

JDHC

74

## 75

Rain-In-The-Face
(Iromagaja)
(ca. 1835–1905)
**Grass Dance**
Hunkpapa Lakota, 1885
Paper, graphite, crayon
10 x 13 in
National Museum of the
American Indian,
Smithsonian Institution,
20/1628
Provenance: Bequest of
DeCost Smith; collected at
Standing Rock Reservation,
North Dakota
References: Ewers 1986,
p. 140, fig. 130

Rain-In-The-Face was a
noted warrior and chief of
the Hunkpapa. His name
derives from a battle
against the Gros Ventre
during which he fought all
day in rain that splattered
his red and black face
paint. He was in many battles, including the
Fetterman Fight of 1866
and the Battle of the Little
Big Horn in 1876 (Hodge
1912, pt. 2, 353). Here, he
depicts three warriors participating in a Grass Dance,
in which men often carried
objects associated with military societies and war
deeds. The dancer on the
right holds aloft a horse
effigy made to honor a
favorite mount killed or
wounded in battle. Rain-In-
The-Face and his war-horse
were both wounded in a
fight with the army near
Fort Totten, Dakota
Territory, in 1868, an
event he might have com-
menorated by carving a
horse effigy like the one in
this drawing.
EMM

## 76

**Horse effigy**
Teton Lakota, ca. 1880
Wood, leather, horsehair,
tin, red and blue pigment
10½ x 7½ x 34½ in
South Dakota State
Historical Society, Pierre,
74.2.122
Provenance: Collected by
Mary C. Collins, probably
at Little Eagle Station,
Standing Rock Reservation,
1884–1910
References: Coe 1977,
cat. no. 390; Ewers 1986,
p. 28, pl. 20

Horse effigies carved in
wood have been document-
ed among the Blackfeet,
Crow, Assiniboine, Gros
Ventre, and especially the
Lakota, who were the most
active sculptors on the
Plains. The effigies were
carried by warriors in victory dances to honor and
commemorate specially
trained and admired war-
horses considered to be
treasured companions who
shared the dangers and glo-
ries of battle (Ewers 1986,
pp. 139–43, pl. 20). Most
horse effigies concentrate
on describing only the head
of the animal, but in this
unusual example the entire
body is given form and life.
The horse is depicted leap-
ing through the air, its head
and neck extended and its
legs tucked up under its
lithe body. Horsehair has
been attached to the sculpture to indicate the mane
and tail. A lock attached to
the bottom of the bridle
represents an enemy scalp
taken as a trophy of battle.
EMM

## 77

**Horse effigy**
Oglala Lakota (catalogued
as Yankton Nakota),
ca. 1880
Wood, horsehair, brass
tacks, iron, leather, red and
black pigment
43 x 6¼ in (including tail)
American Museum of
Natural History, 50.1/515
Provenance: Collected by E.
M. Lenders, 1910

Most wooden horse effigies
are shown without limbs
because carving free-stand-
ing legs presented many
technical problems and the
wood tended to break at
the narrowest points of the
sculpture. This fine Oglala
"horse stick" captures the
animal running at full gal-
lop, its back flat, neck and
head extended, with the
alert ears, staring eyes, red
flared nostrils, and open
mouth of a powerful ani-
mal in the excitement of
battle. The body is painted
yellow to represent a dun-
colored horse, and the face
has a dark blue blaze.
Three large red triangles on
the body represent wounds
suffered by the horse in
action against the enemy.
Ewers reports several
sources that describe how
these effigies were not only
carried in dances but also
used by warriors to illustrate their experiences and
the counting of coups in
battle (Ewers 1986, pp.
139–42, fig. 132).
EMM

## 78

No Two Horns (He Nupa
Wanica) (1852–1942)
**Horse effigy**
Hunkpapa Lakota,
1900–1920
Wood, leather, pigment,
metal, hair
30 in
State Historical Society of
North Dakota, 86.234.180
Provenance: Collected by
Usher L. Burdick at Fort
Yates, Standing Rock
Reservation, North Dakota

This carved horse effigy
memorializes No Two
Horns's blue roan horse,
which was probably killed
in the Battle of the Little Big
Horn (State Historical
Society of North Dakota
1985). Blue roan is a combination of white and gray
that in a certain light looks
blue. The fatal bullet
wounds are represented by
inverted V shapes carved
into the horse's side and
painted red, similar to the
bullet wounds that No Two
Horns documented in many
of his drawings (cat. no.
173). No Two Horns used
his blue roan's death in battle, slightly varying in
theme, in all the art he produced. When portraying his
wounded horse, No Two
Horns added details such as
the bit and bridle, a scalp
attached to the jaw, and
horse hooves (cat. no. 169).
At one end of this horse effigy No Two Horns carved a
section that is meant to be
used as a handle.
JDHC

75

**Military society baton**
Southern Arapaho
(Inuna-ina), ca. 1891
Wood, brass tacks, eagle
feathers, leather
36⅞ x 3½ in
Academy of Natural
Sciences, Philadelphia, on
loan to the National
Museum of the American
Indian, Smithsonian
Institution, 16/7185
References: Ewers 1986,
p. 152, fig. 144

This military society baton
has the silhouette of a horse
carved at the end. Five
holes carved into the
horse's side and painted red
symbolize bullet wounds
suffered in battle. The
zigzag edge of the baton
could symbolize lightning.
Certain military batons
with lightning symbolism
would bring rain when
pointed toward the sky
(Kroeber 1983, p. 170).
JDHC

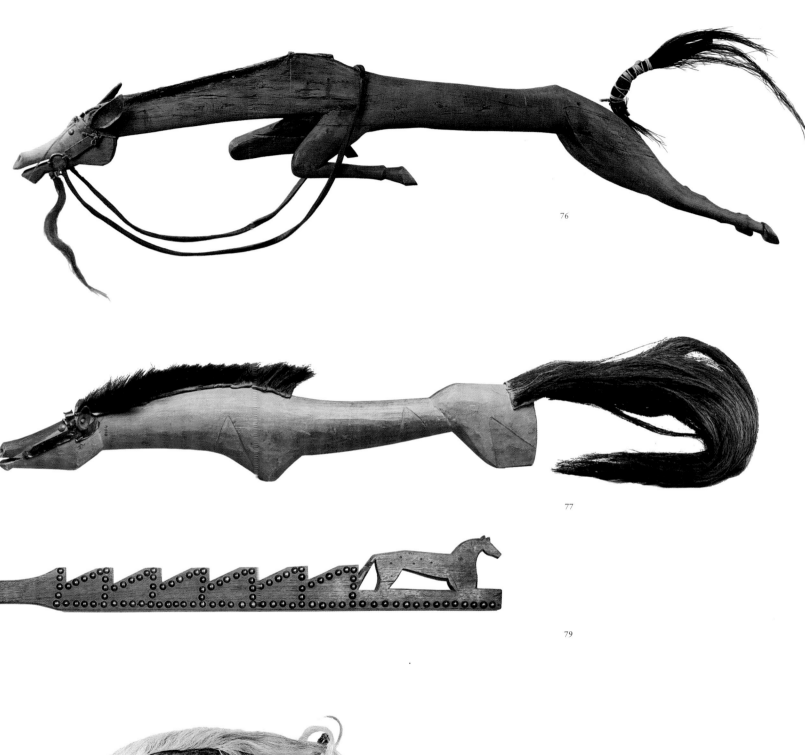

76

77

79

78

81

80

82

**Pipe bowl**

Santee Dakota, ca. 1840
Maple, metal
2½ x 1⅛ x 4⅝ in
The Minneapolis Institute
of Arts, gift of Jud and Lisa
Dayton, 89.42
Provenance: Collected by
Robert Camardo in
Minnesota

This unusual example of a
zoomorphic pipe is carved
of wood and has a metal-
lined bowl. The sculptor
used the flared bowl and
prow front commonly
found on Ojibwe and other
Great Lakes pipe bowls as a
base for the gracefully
arched neck and delicate
head of the horse and the
small head of the bear.

EMM

**Pipe bowl**

Lakota, ca. 1820
Slate
3⅞ x 1⅛ x 3⁷⁄₁₆ in
The University Museum,
University of Pennsylvania,
Philadelphia, NA 38376
Provenance: Gift of John
Wannamaker, 1901;
collected by George Catlin,
ca. 1832–39
References: Ewers 1986,
p. 64, fig. 34; Catlin [1844]
1973, pl. 98

This is one of the earliest
Plains pipes with the figure
of a horse. The horse is
carved to face the smoker
and strengthen the connection between it and the man
who used the pipe. Catlin
gave a description of the
process of carving pipes
from the red stone found in
ancient quarries in southwestern Minnesota and
often called Catlinite in his
honor. He wrote that
"Indians shape out the
bowls of these pipes from
the solid stone, which is not
quite as hard as marble,
with nothing but a knife.
This stone which is of a
cherry red, admits of a
beautiful polish, and the
Indian makes the hole in the
bowl of the pipe, by drilling
into it a hard stick, shaped
to the desired size, with a
quantity of sharp sand and
water kept constantly in the
hole, subjecting him therefore to a very great labour
and the necessity of much
patience" (Catlin [1844]
1973, 1:234).

EMM

**Tomahawk Society batons**

Arapaho (Inuna-ina),
ca. 1880
Wood, horsehair, red wool
cloth, feathers, leather, porcupine quills, brass tacks,
red pigment
41¾ x 13 x 2 in;
41¼ x 21¾ x 3⅛ in
National Museum of the
American Indian,
Smithsonian Institution,
14/1578(2)
Provenance: Collected by
William Wildschut

In their work among the
Arapaho, both James
Mooney and Alfred
Kroeber documented these
horse effigies as emblems
carried by members of the
Tomahawk Society
(hichăä´guthi), the third
highest ranked of the age-
graded Arapaho military
associations (Ewers 1986,
pp. 146–48). Mooney
recorded that when in battle these men "carried
sticks carved at one end in
the rude semblance of a
horse head, and pointed at
the other. In desperate
encounters they were
expected to plant these
sticks in the ground in a
line in front of the body of
warriors and to fight beside
them to the death unless a
retreat should be ordered
by the chief in command"
(Mooney 1896, pp. 87–88).

EMM

## 83

**Pipe bag**

Cheyenne (Tsistsistas) or
Arapaho (Inuna-ina),
ca. 1890
Native-tanned deerskin,
glass beads, pigment,
sinew, seeds
32 x 7 in
The Eiteljorg Museum of
American Indian and
Western Art, Indianapolis,
E82.50
References: Lanford 1990,
pp. 78–79

Beaded pipe bags most commonly bear geometric
designs. The earliest versions
showing representational
imagery date to the late
nineteenth century. This
example incorporates small
geometricized images into a
basically abstract design.

The quadrupeds here,
like those on the Cheyenne
cradle cover (cat. no. 84),
have been identified as deer,
perhaps because of their
erect tails, but more likely
represent horses, a far more
common image. The reverse
side bears small, highly
abstracted thunderbirds,
which are curiously oriented
sidewards.

LL

**Cradleboard and cover**

Cheyenne (Tsistsistas),
ca. 1900
Cotton, glass beads, wood,
metal, silk ribbons, iron
tacks, brass bells
48 x 13 x 7 in
American Museum of
Natural History, 50.1/637
Provenance: Collected by
Emil W. Lenders, 1910

This cradleboard displays
the classic Cheyenne structure of a soft, decorated
wrapper mounted on a
wooden panel with two
staves protruding at the
top. The framework made
it possible to prop the baby
and cradle securely upright
(see cat. no. 280). Decorated covers were often
made before a birth by the
mother's female relatives,
and a woman in a large and
wealthy family might
receive many such gifts.

Small quadruped figures
are a frequent motif on
cradleboard covers, both
quilled and beaded. These
have been variously identified as deer (Lanford 1990,
p. 75) and dogs (Prince
Maximilian zu Wied
described a Lakota cradleboard "entirely covered
with a ground of milk-

white porcupine quills, on
which figures of men, of a
vermilion color, and black
figures of dogs, and other
similar patterns, were most
tastefully embroidered, and
all of the most lively and
well-chosen colors"
[Thwaites 1906, 22 32]).
Conn (1986, p. 49) identifies similar motifs on a
Cheyenne cradleboard as
horses and indicates that
this associates the piece
with a baby boy. Central
Plains artists seldom
employed deer motifs and
showed dogs still less often.
Thus an association to
horses seems more likely.
Used on a baby cradle, the
horse motif would likely
reflect the family's wish of
a successful life for the
infant, including the prestige and material wealth
represented by horse own-
ership.

LL

84 83

Charles Chief Eagle
(b. 1961)
**Bag**
Oglala Lakota, 1991
Leather, glass beads, metal,
dyed horsehair
18½ x 15 in (with fringe)
The Minneapolis Institute
of Arts, the Ethel Morrison
Van Derlip Fund, 91.89

Charles Chief Eagle, from
Pine Ridge Reservation, is
one of the many contempo-
rary Plains artists who have
set aside the old divisions
of media by gender. In his
beadwork he uses traditional techniques and subjects.
EMM

**Moccasins**
Mandan (Numakiki),
ca. 1890
Native-tanned leather,
rawhide, glass beads,
porcupine quills
4 x 10 x 4 in
American Museum of
Natural History, 50/5375a,b
Provenance: Collected by
Clark Wissler, 1904

The U shape that decorates
these Mandan moccasins is
a commonly used Plains
symbol that represents
horse tracks. The tracks
have a number of possible
references, ranging from
the general designation of a
large number of animals to
the specific number of horses
taken on raids. Like the
human hand, the animal
track is a fundamental symbolic indentification used in
all periods of Plains art.
EMM

85

86

## 87

**Shield**
Hunkpapa Lakota,
ca. 1870
Native-tanned leather;
wood; red, black, and green
pigment
10 in (diam)
National Museum of the
American Indian,
Smithsonian Institution,
21/3663

The hide of this small
dream shield is stretched
over a wooden hoop rather
than a rawhide disk
because its purpose is to
serve purely as a talisman
of power, not an object of
physical defense. The
painter who created this
highly charged image
adapted his figures and
designs to the circular for-
mat for maximum visual
and emotional effect. The
vision centers on the alert,
prancing horse whose

raised tail and arched neck
connote energy and action.
The addition of buffalo
horns, the red dots of
sacred hail paint, and the
long red zigzag lines down
each leg indicate the spiritual nature of the animal.
Twenty-five red stars of
different sizes fill the sky
above the horse, and a red-
spotted rattlesnake travels
across the top of the scene
with typical undulating
movement. The snake is
balanced by an abstract
design of similar curve-
countercurve form that was
a convention of spirituality
in Lakota body painting
used on horses and
humans.

Clark Wissler reported
that the origin tale of the
Oglala Lakota Horse
Dreamers' Society featured
a thunder horse rising
through a great storm of
thunder, lightning, and
rain to reach the heavens
(Wissler 1912b, pp. 95–98).
This shield closely resembles the story, which provides a reasonable clue to
its association with Horse
Dreamer ceremonies.
EMM

**Buffalo-horse cutout**
Crow (Absaroke), ca. 1870
Rawhide, eagle bone,
native-tanned leather, blue
and white pigments
8⅝ x 11¾ in
National Museum of the
American Indian,
Smithsonian Institution,
15/5346
Provenance: Collected by
William Wildschut, Crow
Reservation, Montana

Success in war was closely
associated with the acquisi-
tion of power through spiritual assistance. The locus
of this power was the war
medicine bundle, of which
there were three major
types. The most powerful
were known by the princi-
pal object they contained,
such as a hoop medicine or
an arrow, and could be
replicated and used by
more than one person. The
second type of bundle contained individual war medicines received by a man in a
vision, no two of which
were alike. And the third
contained horse-stealing

medicine, to aid in capturing enemy horses (Wild-
schut 1975, p. 40). This
blue and white rawhide
cutout probably was made
for a war or a horse-
capture bundle. It com-
bines the body of a horse
with the feet, horns, and
protruding tongue of the
bull buffalo. The eagle
bone tied to it was a common ingredient of many
medicine bundles.
EMM

88

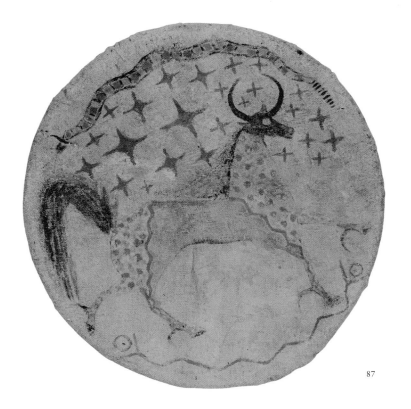

87

## 89

**Pipe bowl**
Spiro phase, Caddoan
culture, A.D. 1200–1350
Bauxite
10⅝ x 9½ in
The University Museum,
University of Arkansas,
Fayetteville, 47-2-1
Provenance: Excavated at
Spiro site, Oklahoma, in
1933
References: Hamilton
1952, pls. 9, 10; Brown
1976, pp. 256–58, fig. 53;
Maurer 1977, p. 67, cat.
no. 15

This pipe depicts a warrior
sitting with his hands on
his knees, in prayerful
meditation. A large hole
for the smoking mixture
was drilled in the back and
connected to a smaller

opening at the base of the
pipe, into which a hollow
stem was inserted to draw
the smoke.

The warrior is shown
wearing an elaborate headdress and has a long, fur-
wrapped hair braid. Small
shell maskettes of the Long
Nose God are attached to
his ears, and around his
neck is a large bead necklace that could have been
made of wood and copper.
He also wears a cloak covered with the pelts of small
animals such as ermine.
This pipe represents the
ancient tradition of warrior
imagery in cultures adjacent
to the Plains that provided
precedents for the development of Plains Indian art.
EMM

**Gorget**
Spiro phase, Caddoan
culture, A.D. 1200–1350
Shell
7⅛ x 7½ in
Oklahoma Museum of
Natural History, University
of Oklahoma, Norman,
B108-4
Provenance: Excavated at
Craig Mound, Spiro site,
Oklahoma
References: Philips and
Brown 1979, vol. 4, pl.
137; Brown 1976, p. 108

This shell pendant is carved
and engraved with the
image of two dancing war-
riors. Each wears the same
costume, which includes a
headdress with feathers and
a pendant that hangs down
over the face; earrings; a
necklace; and bracelets.
Their principal garment is a

kilt with an elaborate belt
hung with raccoon pelts.
They also wear cuffed moccasins and carry a gourd
rattle in one hand and a
small shield in the other.
The two warriors flank a
central post decorated with
painted designs, a shield,
and a raccoon, which is a
reference to a clan symbol
or tutelary spirit associated
with the special society to
which these men belonged.

The artist used a simple
linear style to indicate the
most significant details of
the dancers' anatomy and
costume. This principle of
representational imagery
was continued by histori-
cal Plains warrior-artists
in depicting similar scenes
of ceremony and war.
EMM

**Gorget**
Spiro phase, Caddoan
culture, A.D. 1200–1350
Shell
4¼ in (diam)
The Minneapolis Institute
of Arts, the William Hood
Dunwoody Fund, 91.37.2
Provenance: Collected by
Judge Claude Stone at
Temple Mound, Spiro site,
Oklahoma
References: Hamilton
1952, pl. 84, p. 208; Morse
1960, fig. 45

Shell pendants were worn
around the neck by high-
ranking individuals in
many early Woodlands cul-
tures as personal decora-
tions and signs of status. In
the Southeast, gorget pendants were carved with an
iconography that included
images of animals, warriors,

the sun, and human hands.
A hand inscribed with a
human eye is found as a
motif on a variety of ritual
objects from Oklahoma to
Alabama. To many Native
American groups the hand
is the ultimate signature of
the individual, and hands
were used as a symbol of
"coups," or achievements,
in nineteenth- and twentieth-
century Plains warrior art
(cat. nos. 224, 225) (Fundaburk and Foreman 1957,
pls. 17, 20, 23, 27, 28, 31,
32, 36).
EMM

91

90

89

## 92

## Wampum belt

Iroquois? ca. 1650–1800
Shell beads, fiber
41 x 1⅝ in
Société Musée du Vieil
Yverdon, 00.01.7

From the Atlantic coast to the Great Lakes, Native American peoples have used objects decorated with designs and images as a means of communication and as documentation of formal intertribal relationships. Among the most popular of these objects was the belt of tubular shell beads, which was used for formal diplomatic exchanges such as the ratifying of treaties and the declaration of war.

Examples from the seventeenth century, such as those preserved in the treasury of Chartres cathedral, testify to the long use of these belts. They are called *wampum*, after the Algonkian term for strings of shell beads used as currency and as signs of status.

The color, as well as the designs, of the large wampum belts used in official communications was significant. J. N. B. Hewitt reported that the Iroquois confederacy used belts made entirely of dark purple beads to notify each other of the death of a chief (Hodge 1912, pt. 2, p. 907). The wampum belt served as a device for delivering vital information and as a historical record of events and communal intentions.

The use of human figures on a wampum belt usually signified diplomatic relationships between groups, such as the famous seventeenth-century Penn Treaty belt (Speck 1925, pp. 12–16). This belt from the Vieil Yverdon collection is decorated with six human figures in white beads against a background of dark purple beads. The six nations of the Iroquois confederacy commonly used wampum belts in their many political activities, and this belt could very well be an affirmation of their alliance, each figure standing for one of the six tribes. This early use of representational imagery to symbolize and document important events in tribal history is a precedent for the use of symbolic images of communication in the cultures that developed on the Plains.

EMM

## 93

## Victory dance effigy

Lakota, ca. 1885
Wood, metal, red and black pigment
12⅞ x 2¼ x 1¾ in
The University Museum, University of Pennsylvania, Philadelphia, NA 4323
Provenance: Gift of Frances P. Lex, 1916; collected in 1889–90

Human effigy batons representing enemies killed in battle were carried in victory dances, especially by the Lakota. According to the Lakota historian Dr. Beatrice Medicine, "wooden clubs with carved heads were used in victory dances and in earlier times were adorned with scalps. Some of these sticks were long and served as staffs" (Ewers 1986, pp. 143–44). Like most Lakota victory effigies, this one has the distinctive front crest hairstyle worn by the Crow, the traditional enemies of the Lakota.

EMM

## War club

Hunkpapa Lakota, ca. 1890
Wood; brass tacks; iron nail; deerskin; feathers; leather; yellow, red, and black pigment
32 in
State Historical Society of North Dakota, 2594
Provenance: Collected by J. D. Allen, Fort Yates, Standing Rock Reservation, North Dakota
References: Ewers 1986, p. 135, fig. 123

The tradition of ball-headed war clubs with human or animal imagery is an old one that derives from tribes of the Great Lakes and Eastern Woodlands (see Feder 1971b, fig. 85; Coe 1977, fig. 69; Maurer 1986, fig. 7). The form was revived among the Lakota, especially at the Standing Rock Reservation, at the end of the nineteenth century (Ewers 1986, p. 135, fig. 123). These clubs were not used in battle but were made to be carried in victory dances as an emblem of a warrior's prowess. The carved head with its distinctive hairstyle represents a Crow or Arikara enemy who had been defeated in war.

EMM

92

93

94

## 95

**Pipe bowl**
Pawnee (Chahiksichahiks),
ca. 1830
Pipestone
2 x 4½ x 1¾ in
American Museum of
Natural History, 50.1/7352
Provenance: Collected in
"Sioux country, Upper
Missouri" (North or South
Dakota), 1913

There are at least six versions of this early style of pipe with an Indian seated on the shaft looking toward the bowl, which is carved in the form of a white man wearing a flat-brimmed hat. The earliest documented example was given to the artist George Catlin by a Pawnee who told him that "he could sit and look the white man in the face without being ashamed" (Ewers 1986, pp. 92–94). These pipes are an early example of how the Indians used representational art as a means of expressing their complicated and pressured coexistence with the white community.

EMM

## 96

**Pipe bowl**
Skidi Pawnee
(Chahiksichahiks), ca.
1860
Pipestone, wood
4¾ x 1¼ x 3½ in
Field Museum of Natural
History, Chicago, 59488
Provenance: Collected by
George A. Dorsey, Pawnee
County, Oklahoma, 1901
References: Ewers 1986,
p. 132, fig. 119

This simple L-shaped pipe bowl has a turtle carved on the shank and two human and two animal figures holding on to the rim of the bowl. The active poses imply a sense of narrative unusual in this type of sculpture. The male and female figures are dressed in European-style clothing, a seemingly incongruous touch added to an otherwise traditional vocabulary of Plains representational forms. When Dorsey collected it among the Skidi Pawnee on a Field Museum expedition in 1900 he was told that it was a "sacred pipe of peace or war." (See Ewers 1986, p. 132.)

EMM

**Pipe bowl**
Santee Dakota, ca. 1830
Pipestone, lead
3⅜ x 7¾ in
National Museum of
Natural History,
Department of Anthropology, Smithsonian
Institution, 26,22
Provenance: Transferred
from the War Department;
collected Missouri River
valley, before 1841
References: Ewers 1978b,
p. 54, figs. 3, 4; Ewers
1986, p. 22, pl. 10, and
p. 100, fig. 84

This is one of three elaborate pipes carved by a Santee sculptor in the early 1830s that feature delicately rendered figures and fine lead inlay of geometric designs and stylized buffalo hooves. This pipe shows a Santee chief seated at a table holding a jug that presumably contains whiskey. The artist has taken great care to indicate the chief's combed hair and the large medal hung around his neck that probably represents the bronze presidential peace medals given as gifts to prominent Indian leaders. A smaller figure of another Indian man is shown in front of the table, holding on to its legs. The pipe is inlaid with a buffalo-leg design on the shaft and a diamond and floral pattern on the bowl. The head and front paws of a dog are carved on the front of the shaft below the drum-shaped bowl. This theme of the role of alcohol in Indian life is a commentary on the liquor trade and its powerful and often demoralizing effects on the Native American population.

EMM

95

96

97

152

## 98

**Pipe bowl**

Lakota, ca. 1880

Pipestone

5⅛ x 1⅛ x 9⅝ in

Buffalo Bill Historical Center, Cody, Wyoming, NA 504.220

John C. Ewers has identified a similar scene on a Santee Dakota pipe as representing the trickster Iktomi (the spider) climbing the bowl of the pipe to escape a snake who curls around the shaft (Ewers 1986, pp. 96–97). The artist has used the traditional Lakota bowl shape as a stage for the story of this well-known mythical character, adding a strong element of visual narrative to a usually static form of pictorial representation.

EMM

## 99

**Pipe bowl**

Wahpeton Dakota, ca. 1880

Pipestone

4½ x 7¼ in

National Museum of the American Indian, Smithsonian Institution, 19/6757

References: Ewers 1986, p. 96, fig. 79

The sculptor of this elaborate Dakota pipe bowl used the traditional form as a means of visual display and pun. A turtle and a buffalo head are carved at the base of the shaft, and a turtle and a big-horn ram's head adorn the top of the bowl. The figure of a man wearing a European-style hat is carved as an integral element of the pipe shaft so that the bowl rises from his middle and is held between his hands like a huge phallus (Ewers 1986, p. 96).

EMM

**Pipe bowl**

Santee Dakota, ca. 1880

Pipestone, lead

4¼ x 1½ x 9¼ in

National Museum of the American Indian, Smithsonian Institution, 12/7533

Provenance: Gift of Franklin S. Smith

Plains men have been using the technique of lead or pewter inlay to decorate pipes since the early 1800s. The technique was first developed by Great Lakes pipe makers who must have learned metal-working skills from Europeans. It was principally used to add areas of geometric design in a silver color that contrasted beautifully with the red or black pipestone. To create the inlay, a channel with a beveled edge is cut into the stone and then filled with metal and finished to a smooth, even surface. To create representational images, the background is cut away and replaced by the metal so that the images are rendered in the color of the stone.

This pipe bowl and one at the Nebraska State Historical Society are among the most elaborate of inlaid pipes. The tall, slightly tapered bowl has four decorated sections. On the front is a large-scale, stylized floral pattern with close affinities to silk-ribbon appliqué. On the back of the bowl, facing the smoker, are depicted three European men with joined hands wearing top hats and frock coats, and below them are three large jugs, presumably containing whiskey. The left panel shows a pair of mammals sitting on their haunches, two seated men in the act of drinking, and two thunderbirds. The right panel shows a man in a European hat chasing another man on the run, the torsos and feathered heads of two Indian men facing each other, and at the bottom two European men talking with one arm raised as they are seated at a small table holding a jug of whiskey.

The pipe shank has a pair of buffaloes facing each other on the right side and an S-shaped design on the left. The top panel carries the name Charles Manaige, and the bottom panel, Thomas Robinson spelled backward. These men might have been the ones the pipe was made for.

Because its iconography has so many references to Europeans or Euro-Americans, this bowl could have been made for white traders or agents who were part of the bureaucracy of reservation life. This is reinforced by the frequent references to non-Indians and whiskey, the ill effects of which constitute one of the most serious social problems among contemporary Indian populations.

EMM

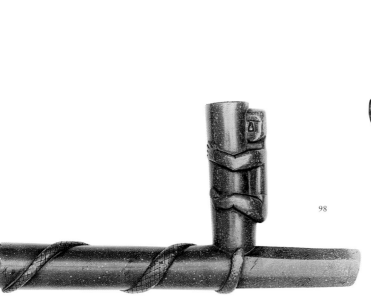

98

99

100

102

## 101

**Medicine bowl**
Sisseton Dakota, ca. 1860
Wood
1½ x 2¾ in
National Museum of the
American Indian,
Smithsonian Institution,
3/6836
Provenance: Collected by
L. Palm

Effigy bowls were primarily
an eastern Plains tradition
with roots in the Great
Lakes area and the ancient
Southeast, where ceramic
bowls decorated with ani-
mal and anthropomorphic
figures have been made for
hundreds of years. Most
large Dakota feast bowls
with anthropomorphic
heads facing the interior of
the bowl are reported to be
associated with the spirit of
E-ya, the glutton god, who
is honored at medicine
feasts (Ewers 1986, pp.
170–71). Small bowls like
this one were used for mix-
ing and administering medicines prepared by a spe-
cially trained person who
healed through herbal
remedies and prayer.
EMM

## 102

**Backrest banner**
Plains Cree
(Natimiwiyiniwuk),
ca. 1900
Native-tanned hide, buffalo
wool, wood, wool and
cotton cloth, glass beads
28 x 18⅞ in
Canadian Museum of
Civilization, V-A-502
Provenance: Purchased
from W. Fred Hammond,
Prairie Pioneer Museum,
Cupar, Saskatchewan, 1981;
acquired by collector from
Clifford Long Man, Gordon
Reserve, Touchwood Hills,
Saskatchewan, ca. 1900

Brasser (1984, pp. 56–63)
has shown that these beaded panels were once applied
to buffalo robes that covered the backrest beds used
by important shamans
known as *okihtcitawak,*
who had received visionary
powers that enabled them
to call the buffalo. These
dream visions of spiritual
power were allowed to be
illustrated on special ceremonial objects. This backrest banner features the
image of a man with a
heart line and outstretched
arms holding a pipe. He is
flanked by two bearlike
creatures who also have
heart lines. The separate
beaded disks were originally used to cover the eye
holes, and the longer beaded pieces covered the ears
of the buffalo robe.
EMM

101

**Visionary image**

Comanche (Niuam),
ca. 1880–89
Paper, pencil, ink, water-
color
6⅞ x 10 in
The Art Institute of
Chicago, gift of Richard A.
Lent in honor of Mr. and
Mrs. C. L. Lent,
1977.576.page 12
Provenance: Collected by
John A. Musser, post trad-
er, Fort Sill, Oklahoma, ca.
1880–89

This Comanche drawing
shows an Indian visionary
wrapped in a blanket and
holding an eagle-wing fan,
surrounded by a pack of
twenty-five wolves who
look at him with large,
staring eyes. The image
probably derives from a
dream in which the animals
appeared to the man with a
gift of power. Densmore
reported a wolf dream
received by a Lakota
named Brave Buffalo in
which he "met a pack of
wolves. They formed a circle around him, and as they
stood looking at him he
noticed that their nostrils
and paws were painted red.
They came toward him,
whereupon he grew dizzy
. . . after this dream . . .
he 'prayed to the wolves'
when he wanted to locate
game, and they always
told him where to secure it"
(Densmore 1918, pp. 179–80).
EMM

Yellow Nose (Hehúwésse)
(ca. 1852–after 1914)
**Visionary image**
Northern Cheyenne
(Tsistsistas), ca. 1880
Paper, graphite, watercolor,
crayon, ink
12½ x 7¼ in
National Anthropological
Archives, Smithsonian
Institution, 166,032
Provenance: Collected by
H. R. Voth from Spotted
Wolf, Cheyenne Reservation,
Darlington, Oklahoma,
1889

Yellow Nose was a Crow
who was captured as a boy
by the Cheyenne chief
Spotted Wolf and later
adopted. This powerful
visionary image shows on
the left a man with long,
flowing hair and a red
stroud breechclout whose
body is covered with blue
and red stars. He is receiving a pipe from a female
figure with long hair and
the legs of a buffalo who
resembles the Lakota's
White Buffalo Calf
Woman, one of the central
characters in Plains mythology, who is credited with
giving the sacred pipe to
the people. To the left of
these figures, a bald eagle
with a rattlesnake in its
beak sits in a tree as a witness to the sacred exhange.
EMM

103

104

105

106

**Two visionary images**
Southern Cheyenne
(Tsistsistas), ca. 1890
Paper, graphite, watercolor,
crayon
5⅝ x 8⅝ in
Buffalo Bill Historical
Center, Cody, Wyoming,
48.59.10; 48.59.8
Provenance: Gift of Mr.
and Mrs. Joseph Katz

These two visionary draw-
ings come from a sketch-
book of 124 drawings
attributed to four Southern
Cheyenne artists named
Sweetwater, Guilopin,
Kiowa, and Little Man.
The drawings are unusual
because they portray the
dreamer rising up from his
bed to receive the vision
that has been granted to
him by the Sacred Powers.
In one drawing a man with
long black braids and the
feet of an eagle points to a
horned owl and a small
animal sitting on an earth
lodge; a line of four
grasshoppers and a bee fly
above the scene. In the
other drawing a man rises
with open arms from his
willow backrest bed toward
a dream vision of a black
bear with a four-pointed
star around its head, a flying crane, and an animal
head surrounded by a ten-
pointed star.
EMM

## 107

**Rattle**
Lakota? ca. 1860
Hide, wood, stone, cloth,
red and yellow pigment
12¼ x 4⅛ in
Natural History Museum
of Los Angeles County,
A.7004.56
Provenance: Collected by
General Frank D. Baldwin,
ca. 1870–80

Globular hide rattles were
one of the emblems carried
by Plains military groups
such as the Strong Heart
Society (Densmore 1918,
pp. 320–22, pl. 45). Some
hide rattles examined in
museum collections have
images and designs cut into
them, but this example is
unusual for its variation of
forms. One side of the rattle is the figure of an eagle
or thunderbird with characteristic split tail and outstretched wings but with a
horned anthropomorphic
head. On the other side the
artist has depicted a four-
pointed star and a bear
paw. The rattle has been
stained red and the incised
lines filled with yellow pigment for symbolic value
and visual contrast.
EMM

## 108

**Rattle**
Lakota? ca. 1870
Wood, leather, dewclaws,
bird talons, brass bells, red
pigment
19⅞ x 2½ x 2¼ in
The University Museum,
University of Pennsylvania,
Philadelphia, 52-6-10
Provenance: Gift of Church
Training School,
Philadelphia, 1952

Rattles made of the split
dewclaws of buffalo, elk,
deer, or antelope were
emblems of office carried
by ranking members of
many Plains military societies. The unusual feature
of this rattle is the human
head with red horns and a
large red mouth with red
lightning lines of spiritual
power running from the
upper corners of the mouth
to the base of the horns.
The use of horns on
anthropomorphic figures is
usually associated with
supernatural beings, but a
secondary reference is to a
man wearing the buffalo-
horn headdress used in ceremonial activities and battle.
EMM

**Pouch**

Lakota? ca. 1860
Native-tanned leather,
cotton cloth, glass beads,
porcupine quills, metal,
yellow pigment
12¾ x 4½ in
Private collection

This small, yellow hide bag
with carefully pleated red
cloth trim was probably
used to hold personal medicine. It is distinguished by
the bold use of color and
the variety of the beadwork
decoration. Both sides of
the bag feature a horned
anthropomorphic torso
growing out of the body of
an eagle with outstretched
wings and tail. On one side,
this sacred composite figure
is made of small, dark red,
faceted beads outlined in
yellow with two light blue
diamonds on its body and
an eagle feather attached to
each hand. A white turtle, a
pink heart-shaped form,
and an elongated red and
green hourglass shape that
resembles the web symbol
of Iktomi, the spider, are

arranged above. On the
other side of the bag, the
horned bird-man has a pink
beaded head with red horns
and a light blue upper body
on dark red legs and tail
outlined in yellow beads.
Hoops with a pendant
eagle feather are on either
side of the figure, and two
red stars and an abstract
shape are arranged above
it. The complex iconogra-
phy combines sacred dance
regalia such as eagle feathers and hoops with images
from myths and visions.
EMM

107

108

109

**Moccasins**
Lakota? ca. 1800–1850
Native-tanned leather,
porcupine quills, glass
beads, metal ornaments,
cotton cloth
10 x 3½ x 3⅝ in
The Nelson-Atkins
Museum of Art, Kansas
City, Missouri (Nelson
Fund), 33-1182/1,2
Provenance: Acquired from
Fred Harvey, 1933

A supernatural being
known as Double Woman
(Anukite) has a prominent
role in traditional Lakota
religious belief. Among the
Oglala, one facet of Double
Woman is associated with
the origin of porcupine-
quill decoration. There is a
story of a young woman
who was taught the use of
quills by Double Woman in
a dream. Upon waking, she
in turn instructed others
and formed the quillwork-
ers guild. Because of this
association with Double

Woman, quilling is considered sacred (*wakan*). (See
Wissler 1912b, p. 93.)

When Double Woman
appeared to a person in a
dream, it was customary
for the dreamer to make a
feast and invite all who had
experienced the same manifestation. The dreamers
paraded through camp
flashing mirrors at others,
causing them to fall flat and
spit out black dirt and sage.
The parade was led by two
women considered to be
very *wakan,* whose pres-
ence embodied Double
Woman. These two women
"with sage in their hands,
hold the ends of a buffalo
hair cord to the middle of
which swings a small doll"
(Wissler 1912b, p. 94) or in
some cases a ball (Wissler
1907, p. 50).

On this pair of quilled
moccasins is the image of
Double Woman as
described by Wissler. The
women are joined by what
appears to be a cord, from
which dangles a circular
form, possibly a ball. The
figures, wearing long dresses, are treated as silhouettes with featureless faces
against a background of
vibrant red.

AC

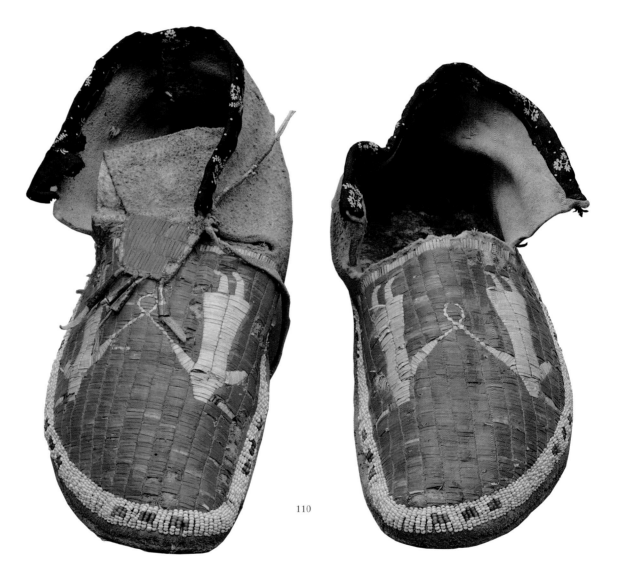

110

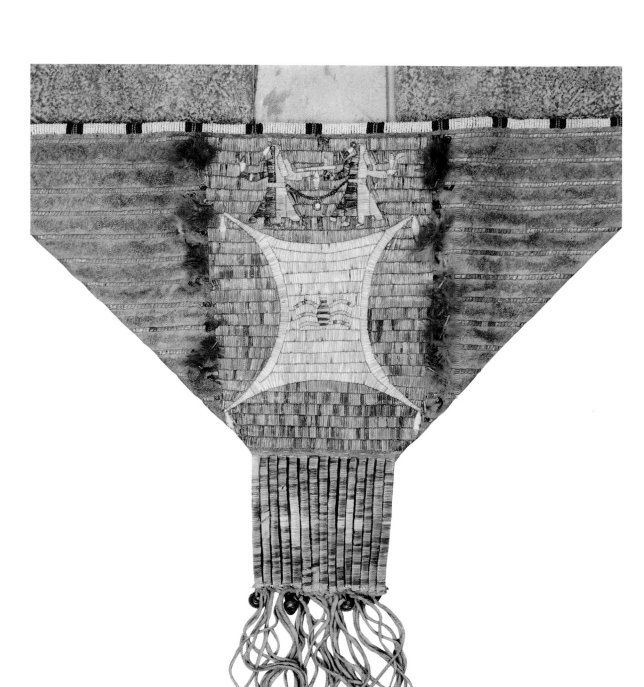

111

**Cradle cover**
Lakota, ca. 1880
Hide, porcupine quills,
glass beads, feather tufts,
brass bells
26 x 25⅜ x ½ in
National Museum of the
American Indian,
Smithsonian Institution,
9048
Provenance: Collected by
Joseph Keppler

Double Woman has many roles and associations in Lakota belief. One association is with the spider (Iktomi), through the ceremonial use of the spiderweb design.

Wissler, in his study of the protective designs of the Oglala, wrote of a secret ceremony carried out by certain women who had dreamt of Double Woman. For this observance, a child "is taken out to a lonely place, where a swing or hammock-like structure is made in the form of the spider-web design, supported by four corners, and the child is placed upon it. This is to bring good fortune to the child. A design of the spider-web might then be placed upon the robe of the child as a symbol of its having experienced the ceremony" (Wissler 1907, p. 50).

The spider, depicted here in the center of his web, is believed to have great wisdom and power. A spiderweb cannot be "destroyed by bullets or arrows (since they pass through it, leaving only a hole)," which may be the basis for the belief that the spiderweb has the power to protect people from harm (Wissler 1907, p. 48). This protective function may explain the use of the motif on a baby cradle.

Quilled above the spiderweb design is the conventional depiction of Double Woman as "two women tied together with a cord . . . from the middle of which hung a doll or ball" (Wissler 1907, pp. 49–50). Here a circular form or ball is suspended from the cord. The women appear identical except for the objects they carry. One holds a single feather, the other a bundle of sage or sweetgrass, and together they hold a pipe. The bodies of the figures are quilled in two parts, one side in purple and the other in yellow, perhaps to emphasize Double Woman's duality or her two faces.
AC

**Pipe bag**
Lakota, ca. 1870
Native-tanned leather, hide,
porcupine quills, shell, tin
cones
46 x 7 x 1⅞ in (including
fringe)
The University Museum,
University of Pennsylvania,
Philadelphia, CG010290-
2531

Double Woman was associated with the Elk Dreamers' Society and was represented at their ceremonials "by two women tied together by a cord . . . from the middle of which hung a doll or ball" (Wissler 1907, pp. 49–50). The imagery on this beaded pipe bag illustrates this association, with Double Woman on one side and two "dream" elk on the reverse.

Here Double Woman is depicted in the conventional form of two identical female figures joined at the waist by a blue cord. Their faces, as well as their bodies, are green; only their eyes and mouths are distinguished by a few white beads.

The two women hold between them a red pentagonal form with a rectangle of yellow in the center. This does not appear to be the doll or ball described by Wissler, but may instead represent a mirror used by a dreamer to flash "power" during dance performances (Wissler 1912b, p. 93). Two stylized shapes representing a dragonfly and a lizard appear above and below the figures.

On the reverse of the bag, the first elk is beaded in light blue and yellow and the second in navy blue. A small red circle, with an extended wavy line and feather, can be seen on the side of the first elk. Wissler, in his discussion of protective designs of the Oglala Lakota, explains this symbolic mark on mythical animals as the opening where the heart should be. "The conception seems to be, that an animal without a heart is immortal and supernatural" (Wissler 1907, p. 43).

AC

## 113

Oscar Howe (1915–83)
**Double Woman**
Yanktonai Nakota, 1971
Casein paints, paper
18¼ x 22¾ in
Lent by Adelheid Howe,
courtesy of Oscar Howe
Art Center, Mitchell, South
Dakota
References: Dockstader
1982, p. 45, fig. 66

The image of Double Woman is in essence a representation of ambiguity. Once a very beautiful supernatural being named Face (Ite), she was transformed into Double Face (Anukite), a being with one beautiful face and one horrid face as punishment for infidelity (Powers 1977, p. 55).

Double Woman may appear in several conventionalized forms: "a person with two faces, one beautiful, the other ugly; a single beautiful woman, most often a temptress; or two women who present alternative answers to a single question, often of a divinatory nature. The two women often change into black-tailed deer at the conclusion of dreams" (Powers 1977, p. 59).

Women who dreamed of Double Woman became skilled at quilling and tanning. It was also believed

that female dreamers acquired supernatural powers to seduce men. These women were known as deer women. Sexual contact with them was thought to be fatal; if a man came upon a lone woman in the forest or on the prairie he was supposed to avoid her, for she might be a deer woman (Wissler 1912b, pp. 92, 94).

Men who encountered Double Woman in dreams were often instructed to choose between male- and female-oriented implements. If the man chose the latter, he would live as a woman (*berdache*) (Wissler 1912b, p. 93).

Oscar Howe, in his master's thesis, offered the following interpretation of Double Woman: "The Double Woman . . . plays a dual role in traditional Sioux culture. She carved drawings on rocks which foretold future events, and acted as a temptress to lure men from camp to lose them or leave them unconscious. The moral being that man should have perfect control over his emotions, even in the presence of sheer beauty."

AC

**Pipe bag**
Lakota? ca. 1890
Tanned leather, glass beads, porcupine quills, feather tufts
36 x 8 x ½ in
The Thomas Gilcrease Institute of American History and Art, Tulsa, 8426-505
Provenance: Emil Lenders collection

Although not apparent at first glance, this beaded pipe bag depicts the mythical being known as Double Woman. Two female figures, one on each side of the bag, stand with their arms outstretched. A dark blue horizontal line leading from the hand of one figure wraps around the bag to meet the hand of the other. The rendering of the two women is virtually identical. Their bodies and cloth-

ing are depicted almost completely in red, a color associated with sacredness and sun imagery. In Lakota societies, a woman painted her hands and feet red to signify that she was entitled to participate in sacred ceremonies (Walker 1982, pp. 104–5).

Scarcely seen, at the far edge of the beaded panel, a small red rectangular form interrupts the length of the cord. This small block of color, divided across the middle by a row of white beads, may be the abstracted representation of the doll or ball usually associated with Double Woman, or it may be one of the mirrors used by Double Woman Dreamers in dance performances.

AC

114

113

161

Silverhorn (Haungooah)
(ca. 1861–ca. 1941)
**Five paintings of the
Medicine Lodge ceremony**
Kiowa (Gaigwa), 1902
Hide, pigment
Width: 50 in; 56 in; 52½ in;
56 in; 56 in
National Museum of
Natural History, Department of Anthropology,
Smithsonian Institution,
229, 894; 229, 895; 229,
901; 229, 896; 229, 897

Silverhorn (Haungooah)
was perhaps the most prolific and versatile Plains
artist of all time. Hundreds
of his drawings and paintings are preserved in public
and private collections. He
produced graphic works on
paper, hide, and muslin and
was a noted featherworker
and silversmith, working in
German silver. Building
upon the ledger art tradition that he learned in his
youth, Silverhorn developed his own distinctive
style, characterized by light,
airy figures and attention to
detail. He incorporated elements of naturalism and
perspective from Western
styles of art, particularly
after he had observed the
artist E. A. Burbank at
work, but remained committed to the basic narrative structure of Plains
graphic art. He in turn
influenced the young artists
who revitalized Plains
painting in the 1920s and
1930s. His nephew Stephen
Mopope, one of the artists
known as the Five Kiowas,
acknowledged Silverhorn as
his first art teacher.
Silverhorn's life spanned
the transition from the era
of nomadic bison hunting
to the Great Depression of
the 1930s. A master illustrator of Kiowa life and
culture, Silverhorn produced drawings of myth,
ceremony, and domestic life
as well as the classical subjects of warfare, hunting,
and courtship.

This series of hide paintings illustrating events of
the Medicine Lodge ceremony was the result of collaboration between
Silverhorn and James
Mooney, an anthropologist
with the Smithsonian's
Bureau of American
Ethnology. As early as
1894, Mooney had formulated a plan to document
Kiowa culture. In addition
to artifacts, sound recordings, and photographs, he
planned "to illustrate their
mythology and ceremonial
by a full series of aboriginal
drawings in colors on a sufficient and uniform scale by
the best artists in the tribe"
(Mooney 1894). However,
it was not until 1902, with
funds to produce an exhibit
for the upcoming Louisiana
Purchase Exposition, that
he was able to pursue this
aspect of the project. The
artist he hired was
Silverhorn, and the ceremony selected was the Kado,
or Medicine Lodge, the
Kiowa form of the Sun
Dance known throughout
the Plains. Mooney had
never witnessed the Kiowa
ceremony, which was vigorously opposed by the
Indian agents and had not
been performed since 1887,
but Silverhorn had come
into adulthood while it was
still the central event of
Kiowa religion. As game
was now scarce in the area
and hides difficult to
secure, Mooney made
arrangements to obtain art
supplies from Chicago.
Working with paints and
buckskins sent by a colleague of Mooney's at the
Field Columbian Museum,
Silverhorn produced this set
of paintings, described
by Mooney (1902) as
"unquestionably the finest
specimens of the kind ever
secured." There is no doubt
that Mooney helped to
define the form and content
of this series, but Silverhorn
brought to it his delicate
mastery of figural drawing,
his tradition of pictorial
storytelling, and his deep
understanding of the significance of each portion of
the ritual.

**Selection of the central pole**
(cat. no. 115). In the upper
register, a group of priests
await the return of two
warriors who have "counted coup" on the large cottonwood tree selected to
form the center pole of the
Medicine Lodge, thus
claiming it for the tribe.
Behind the priests sits the
woman, a Mexican captive,
whose office it is to cut
down the tree. In the lower
register, the keeper of the
Taime, a sacred image,
makes an offering of smoke
before the image is removed
from its wrappings (also by
a Mexican captive) and
exposed to view during the
course of the ceremony.
The framework of poles
marks where the Medicine
Lodge will be constructed.
The use of captives ensures
that no harm will befall
tribal members if errors are
made during these ritual
activities.

**The sham battle to capture the central pole** (cat. no. 116). Warriors of the various military societies, armed with shields and coup sticks of leafy willow branches, stage a spirited mock attack upon the women and other warriors who defend the central tree behind a breastwork of branches. The warrior at the far left brandishes the notched quirt of a warrior society leader. The women joining the attack may represent the honorary female members of a military society.

**Erecting the center pole within the camp circle** (cat. no. 117). In the upper corner, tracks and a carcass tell the story of the hunt to secure the sacrificial strip of buffalo hide to bind offerings at the top of the Medicine Lodge pole. At the bottom, the pole itself is felled by the captive woman and measured by the Taime priest. In the center, the pole, with offerings attached, stands within the camp circle, represented by the hereditary painted tipis of the prominent families of the tribe. Position within the camp circle defined the social relations among various members of the Kiowa tribe; the tipi designs represented spiritual relations between the Kiowa and the world of the supernatural.

116

117

118

**Building the Medicine Lodge** (cat. no. 118). With the center pole in place, women bring in additional uprights and leafy branches to complete construction of the circular Medicine Lodge. They are escorted by warriors beating hand drums, and all are singing. Two couples mounted double on horseback in the foreground represent the many warriors who take young women up behind them and ride double around camp until late in the day. This annual gathering of the whole tribe was an opportunity for courtship and the arrangement of marriages.

**The Medicine Lodge and the peyote ceremony** (cat. no. 119). The figures on the left represent the participants and the ritual equipment of the Medicine Lodge—the decorated center pole; the pipes, fan, and rattle of the dance; the closed Taime box; and the box as it is opened during the ceremony to expose the sacred image. A Buffalo Dancer appears at the far left, and two pledgers with their upper bodies painted are shown in front and rear view holding bunches of sage and eagle-bone whistles. A warrior in a horned bonnet holds a red shield, one of a series dedicated to the Taime. Mooney identified the mounted figure at the top as "a member of a warrior society in full Sun Dance equipment." The remaining scenes are of a peyote ceremony, a ritual that became prominent in the years when the Medicine Lodge ceremony was no longer held. At the lower right, four peyote leaders approach the ceremonial tipi. The faintly penciled word "By" connected to the first man suggests that this is a self-portrait of the artist. Behind the tipi are two men with ritual equipment including a large peyote button. At the upper center is the peyote tipi, with a woman waiting outside to hand in water at dawn. To the right of this, as if inside the tipi, the participants are seated in a semicircle around the central fire and the crescent-shaped altar upon which rests the sacred peyote.

CG

119

Richard West (b. 1912)
**Cheyenne Sun Dance, First Painting of the Third Day**
Cheyenne (Tsistsistas), ca. 1949
Paper, watercolor
24½ x 35 in
Philbrook Museum of Art, Tulsa, 49.20
References: Wade 1986, fig. 77

The Cheyenne artist Richard West studied art at Bacone Junior College in Muskogee, Oklahoma. The art department there had been started by Acee Blue Eagle and developed by teachers like Woody Crumbo, who were proponents of the Oklahoma and Santa Fe styles of painting. West went on to become director of the art department at Bacone from 1947 to 1970 and guided generations of young artists. Much of his own painting has been devoted to scenes from Cheyenne ceremonial life. He records and evokes the power of dances, rituals, myths, and stories, depicting with ethnographical correctness the details of the costumes and objects that are a record of the sacred ways he portrays with respect and honor.
EMM

**A Sun Dance camp**
Cheyenne (Tsistsistas), ca. 1890
Paper, crayon, ink, pencil
8½ x 13¾ in
National Anthropological Archives, Smithsonian Institution, 154,064-C
Provenance: Received from Mildred McLean Hazen, Washington, D.C., 1892

This drawing illustrates a Plains Sun Dance camp—a circle of tipis enclosing the ceremonial ground centered on the Sacred Pole of the Sun Dance Lodge. Eight Sun Dancers are shown from the back as they face the pole, wearing long skirts, breechclouts, and keyhole-shaped hair ornaments. Their bodies are covered in sacred paint, and two of the men wear their shields on their backs. Other eagle-feather headdresses, two shields, and a bow lance are also displayed in the lodge. The drummers and singers are positioned to the right of the dancers as the assembled crowd gathers to witness the ceremony and join in its blessings. All are dressed in their finest clothing, which includes robes with beaded strips and the striped Navajo chief's blanket that was such a popular trade item among Plains tribes. Both men and women hold umbrellas, a prized and very practical item that provided shade during the long hot days of summer.

In 1897 the federal government banned the Sun Dance as part of its effort to assimilate Indians into American society at large by denying them the right to speak their native languages or perform their religious ceremonies. This official policy of cultural genocide continued for thirty years, depriving Native Americans of the knowledge and information they used to pass from one generation to the next by their ancient tradition of oral learning. The Indian Reorganization Act of 1934 finally assured the Indian people that they could follow the religion of their ancestors. Father Peter J. Powell (1970, p. 171) reports that around 1957 the Cheyenne began to create books of drawings to be used to instruct future generations in the detailed rituals of the sacred ceremonies. In this way the old traditions are perpetuated through the continuing belief of the people as expressed through the medium of representational imagery.
EMM

120

121

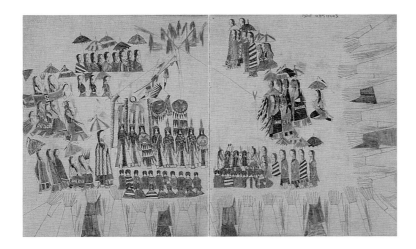

**122**

Wohaw (Gu hau de)
(1855–1924)
**A Sun Dance vision**
Kiowa (Gaigwa), ca. 1875
Paper, pencil, crayon
8¾ x 11¼ in
Missouri Historical Society,
1882.18.46
Provenance: Donated by
Mr. and Mrs. James Barry
(Frances Grady's parents),
1882; collected by Frances
and John Grady, Fort
Marion, St. Augustine,
Florida, 1877
References: Harris 1989,
pp. 80–81

The southern Plains war-
riors who were sent to
prison at Fort Marion were
encouraged to make draw-
ings of their life, but few
chose to illustrate traditional
religious activities. In this
powerful scene, however,
Wohaw drew a Kiowa man
dressed and painted for the
sacred Sun Dance. He
stands in front of the Sun
Dance Lodge, whose brush-
covered sides surround the
decorated center pole. A tipi
used in this complicated ceremony stands on the west
side of the lodge. The Sun
Dancer raises his arms and
lifts his face to the sky,
where he sees a vision of the
sun, moon, morning star,
and two great thunderbirds.
One thunderbird holds two
arrows in its talons and the
other shoots a line of power
from its eyes to an unusual
figure of a man covered
with eagle feathers.
EMM

**123**

Silverhorn (Haungooah)
(ca. 1861–ca. 1941)
**A peyote ceremony**
Kiowa (Gaigwa), ca. 1891
Paper, pencil, crayon, ink
10¾ x 14¾ in
Field Museum of Natural
History, Chicago, 67719.4
Provenance: Collected by
Dudley P. Brown,
Anadarko, Oklahoma,
ca. 1899

This drawing comes from a
set of four sketchbooks
with 256 illustrations made
by the Kiowa artist
Silverhorn, the most prolific
draftsman of his time (cat.
nos. 115–119) (Wiedman
and Greene 1988, pp. 32–41).
It illustrates part of the peyote ceremony that devel-
oped in the late nineteenth
century and remains a
major element of Native
American religion. A man
dressed in his finest attire in
the Kiowa style—yellow
painted hide shirt and leggings trimmed with long
twisted fringe—stands next
to the Peyote Lodge and
raises his right hand as a
salute to the sun, moon,
and morning star.
EMM

**124**

Walter Bone Shirt
**A Lakota Sun Dancer**
Lakota, ca. 1890
Colored pencil, india ink,
paper
5 x 7¾ in
Private collection
Provenance: Possibly
Rosebud Reservation

This image of a Lakota Sun
Dancer comes from a book
of thirty drawings that
illustrate scenes of war,
camp life, and especially
men and women in ceremo-
nial regalia. This drawing
shows a man with an eagle-
feather headdress and a
long yellow and blue Sun
Dance skirt. He also wears
arm bands, and eagle feathers are suspended from his
wrists and ankles. The
dancer faces the sacred center pole of the Sun Dance
Lodge, which has blue and
red flags and eagle-feather
staffs at its base and
rawhide figures of a horned
man and a horse suspended
from its top.
EMM

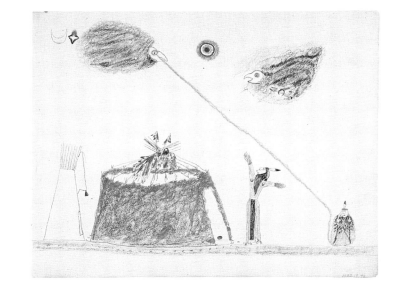

122

123

124

Yellow Nose (Hehúwésse)
(ca. 1852–after 1914)

**Ghost Dance**

Cheyenne (Tsistsistas),
1891
Deerskin, colored ink
39 x 49⅝ in
National Museum of
Natural History,
Department of
Anthropology, Smithsonian
Institution, 165,127
Provenance: Produced for
the Chicago World's Fair,
1892
References: Mooney 1896,
pl. 109; Alexander 1916,
10:150–51; Minneapolis
Institute of Arts 1976, p. 84

The extreme cultural stress
and physical privation
Plains people endured in
the early reservation period
gave rise to a number of
millenarian movements
prophesying a return to former times when there were
no whites in North America
and game was abundant.

Of these the most wide-
spread and best known was
the Ghost Dance move-
ment, which began in
Nevada around 1889 with
the visionary experiences of
a Paiute man, Wovoka
(Jack Wilson). News of
Wovoka's prophesies trav-
eled quickly among Plains
peoples, extending as far
north as the Lakota and as
far south and east as the
Cheyenne, Arapaho, and
Pawnee groups in
Oklahoma.

Wovoka preached coop-
eration and social harmony
in anticipation of the end of
the present world, and he
assured his followers that
regular performance of a
circle dance would hasten
the moment. The nature of
the dance varied from place
to place, but among many
peoples it included the
induction of trance. It is this
practice that is represented
on a hide painted in 1891
for the anthropologist
James Mooney, principal
recorder of the Ghost
Dance, by the Cheyenne
artist Yellow Nose.

Here a group of figures
is surrounded by a circle of
male and female dancers (in
many Plains areas men and
women dancing together
was unprecedented before
the Ghost Dance). Two of
the women carry babies on
their backs, and women's
hairstyles note a distinction
between Cheyenne (braid-
ed) and Arapaho (loose). At
the lower center a woman
dancer holds a stuffed crow,
an important Ghost Dance
image, and several people in
the circle wave handker-
chiefs. A number of dancers
wear belts decorated with
disks of German silver.

At the center several
people, shown supine on
the ground, have already
entered a trance; George
Sword, who had witnessed
the Ghost Dance, com-

mented that "the persons
dropped in dance would all
lie in great dust the dancing
make" (Mooney [1896]
1965, p. 42). One man, at
left, holds a shinny stick;
another (inverted, upper
left) holds a hoop, or
baqati wheel. A woman
(upper right) has raised her
arms in trance and dropped
her dotted shawl. At the far
right a medicine man, one
arm extended, helps a
dancer achieve a trance.
Mooney ([1896] 1965, p.
177) comments that the
painting gives a good sense
of Cheyenne and Arapaho
Ghost Dance practices of
the period.

LL

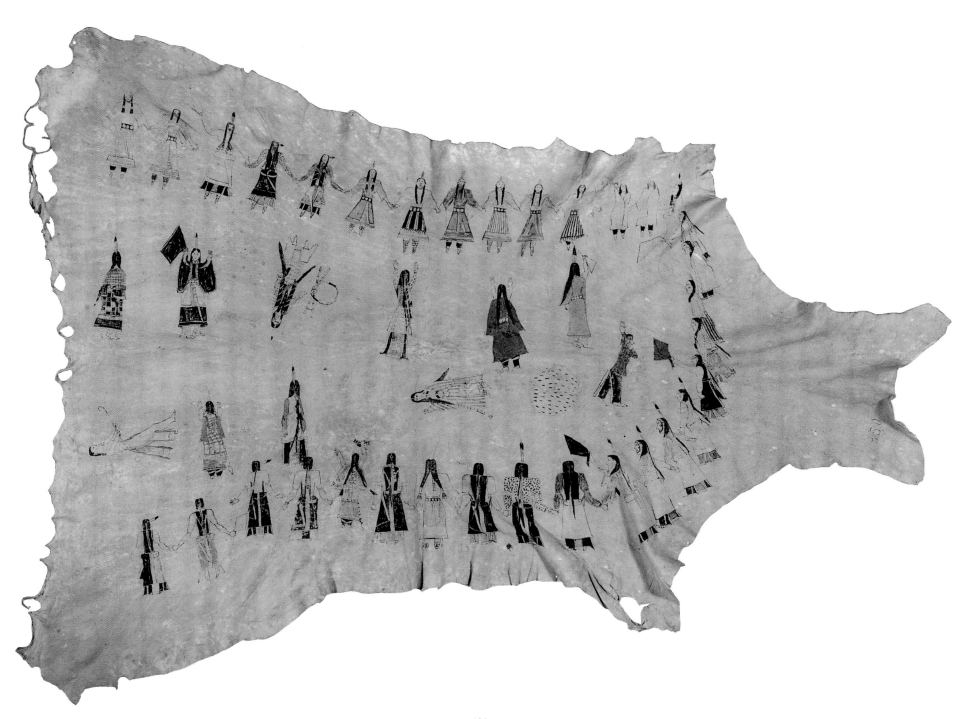

125

**Ghost Dance dress**
Arapaho (Inuna-ina),
ca. 1890
Native-tanned hide, eagle
feathers, pigment
57½ x 35 in
Logan Museum of
Anthropology, Beloit
College, 30449
Provenance: Collected by
Albert Green Heath from
Little Crowe in Oklahoma,
ca. 1915; acquired by the
Logan Museum from the
Heath estate, 1956
References: Minneapolis
Institute of Arts 1976,
p. 42; Josephy 1991,
fig. 6, p. 5

The imagery of this Ghost Dance dress is primarily astral. Two rows of circular stars define the top border of the yoke, above a crescent moon in the center and clusters of Maltese crosses representing the morning star. These images, particularly the morning star, may be an allusion to the dawning of a new era. Wovoka described eloquently how the old world would simply be rolled up, revealing a fresh new world free of hunger and persecution. The addition of eagle feathers, a traditional honoring symbol, probably reflects the idea that eagles transported Ghost Dancers who were in a state of trance to the other world, where they saw their deceased relatives and glimpsed the world to come.
LL

126

127

**Ghost Dance dress**
Arapaho (Inuna-ina),
ca. 1890
Native-tanned deerskin,
glass beads, pigment, tin
cones
58 x 41 in
The Eiteljorg Museum of
American Indian and
Western Art, Indianapolis,
E80.77
References: Eiteljorg 1981,
p. 56; Conn 1982, p. 117

Some Ghost Dance clothing is
notable for its elaborate and
detailed decoration. This
example, like cat. no. 128, is
fully painted and features narrow bands of beadwork at
the hem and the metal tinklers used by southern Plains
Ghost Dancers. The representation of stars as cinquefoils
rather than Maltese crosses or
four-pointed forms suggests
an ultimate source in
American flags and military
paraphernalia. At the yoke is
a figure of a woman flanked
by eagles. She holds a pipe in
her right hand and a branch,
possibly a sage bundle, in her
left. There is a feather in her
hair and two cruciform stars
above her.

According to Conn
(1982), this dress is one of
seven Pawnee examples
made to fulfill a Ghost
Dancer's dream of seven
identically dressed women
dancers; unfortunately he
cites no source. The iconography and coloration
suggest an Arapaho
attribution.

LL

## 128

**Ghost Dance dress**
Arapaho (Inuna-ina), 1890s
Native-tanned hide, eagle
feathers, fur, cloth, metal,
animal horn, pigment, glass
beads
62½ x 47 in
Field Museum of Natural
History, Chicago, 70726
Provenance: Collected by
George Dorsey in 1901 in
Oklahoma from the wife of
Black Coyote
References: Minneapolis
Institute of Arts 1976,
pp. 40–41

Although Ghost Dance ide-
ology emphasized a revival
of older, precontact cultural traditions, it also permitted a considerable number of innovations. One of
the most remarkable was
the role accorded to
women, whose visions
carried authority and who
danced hand in hand with
men in the circle (see cat.
no. 125). The number of
women's Ghost Dance
dresses extant, and their
elaborate decoration,
attests to the prominence
of women as participants
in the movement.

This brightly painted
dress combines conventional Ghost Dance imagery of
birds, stars, and pipes with
the more unusual image of
human hands, in other contexts a representation of
coups. Each side displays
four hands, alternating in
red and green, perhaps
traced directly onto the
dress, and small four-pointed stars in the palms of
each. In the center of each
yoke is a vertical pipe, from
which streams a pattern of
hail. The dress is unusual in
its extensive trimming, with
beadwork at the neck and
waist and metal tinklers at
the hem.
LL

**Ghost Dance dress**
Oglala Lakota, before 1907
Cotton muslin, pigment
52¼ x 49¼ in
American Museum of
Natural History, 50/3055
Provenance: Collected by
Clark Wissler on Pine
Ridge Reservation, 1902–7
References: Wissler 1907,
pp. 38–39, figs. 14 and 15;
Minneapolis Institute of
Arts 1976, pp. 68–69

The protective function of
Ghost Dance clothing,
which Lakota people interpreted as invulnerability to
bullets, is linked to that of
shields. Clark Wissler
notes that in earlier times
shields were said to dis-
tract enemies and draw
their fire, thus sparing the
carrier's body, but that this
method of protection is
inappropriate for some-
thing worn on the body.
Nevertheless, he records,
Ghost Dancers refer to the
triangular painted bib area
of shirts and dresses as the
"shield" (Wissler 1907, p.
38), and he argues for a
connection between the
images used on this area
and earlier shield designs.

This dress, one of a num-
ber commissioned by Wissler
between 1902 and 1907,
was made well after the
Wounded Knee massacre as
a re-creation of a dress said
to have been worn in that
encounter. Unfortunately
Wissler did not note the
names of the painters.

According to his expli-
cation of the design, here
the front "shield" area is
given over to celestial
imagery; the red area is a
thundercloud, and the
descending green line indicates lightning descending
from the heavens. The
upper back bears the eagle,
and here the triangle and
extending line are said to
represent a rattlesnake. The
large front panel combines
dragonflies and star
imagery; the back shows
bison tracks and a butterfly
in addition to dragonflies
and stars. On the proper
right side rainbows arc
across the width of the
panel, with swallows above
and below and a single turtle above. The left side is
decorated with lizards.

Hail patterns are scattered
over the entire surface.

The iconographic struc-
ture of the garment is
unusually complex. The
astral imagery refers to the
coming of a new universe,
in which the problems of
the present world vanish.
The remainder of the dress
is concerned with the
process of that transformation—how Indian people
survive their struggle with
whites. The animals represented all either have a flit-
ting motion and are thus
able to avoid the hail of
bullets surrounding them
(swallows, butterflies, and
dragonflies) or are hardy
and long-lived (turtles,
lizards, and buffalos).
Their power to avoid dan-
ger is invoked on behalf of
the wearer of the dress.
LL

129

128

## 130

Attributed to Little Wound
**Ghost Dance shirt**
Oglala Lakota, 1890–91
Cotton muslin, pigment,
commercial leather
34¼ x 32½ in
The University Museum,
University of Pennsylvania,
Philadelphia, 45-15-283
Provenance: Purchased by
Charles H. Stephens,
August 19, 1917, on Pine
Ridge Reservation from the
daughter of Yellow Bear
(son of Little Wound)

In terms of Ghost Dance
theology and practice
there was considerable
regional variation among
adherents. The notion that
Ghost Dance clothing
made the wearer invulner-
able to bullets was held
most clearly among the
Lakota. In George Sword's
account: "They said that
the bullets will not go
through these shirts and
dresses, so they all have
these dresses for war"
(Mooney [1896] 1965, p.
42). In fact the iconography of much Ghost Dance
material is concerned with
the need for protection.
Images of hail, for exam-
ple, refer to showers of
bullets (a threat, it must be
noted, associated in its origin with whites, whom
Ghost Dancers expected to
eradicate). Despite this,

the clothing seems to have
been worn primarily for
dancing, not for battle.

This shirt shows a pat-
tern of hail around the
neck. On the front a four-
pointed star, echoing a
spiderweb pattern, is anthro-
pomorphized by the addi-
tion of a small head (and
partially transformed into
a five-pointed design).
Dragonflies flank the neck
opening, invoking for the
wearer the associative
power of the insect's darting flight. On the back a
large bird shoots power
from its claws and beak,
the power lines carrying
down the sleeves of the
shirt. Wissler (1907) notes
that bird images typically
appear on the back of
Ghost Dance clothing and
that these represent eagles,
probably because eagles
were said to conduct the
unconscious dancer to the
other world.

Charles H. Stephens
purchased the shirt in 1917
from the wife of Joe Paints
Yellow. Her grandfather,
Little Wound, was a mod-
erate associated in the internal and external struggles
that led up to the Wounded
Knee massacre, and the
shirt may have belonged to
him. Little Wound's father,
Bull Bear, had been killed
by Red Cloud in 1901 in a
leadership dispute.
LL

## 131

Attributed to Red Hawk
**Testing the Ghost Shirt**
Lakota, ca. 1885
Paper, ink, pencil, crayon
7½ x 12¼ in
Milwaukee Public Museum,
2063
Provenance: Collected by
Captain R. Miller at
Wounded Knee, South
Dakota, December 29,
1890

Drawings related to the
Ghost Dance are relatively
uncommon among Plains
works on paper. A ledger
book from the Milwaukee
Public Museum, collected
on the battlefield following
the Wounded Knee mas-
sacre (see cat. no. 267),
contains a number of Ghost
Dance–related subjects.
This example shows a
mounted figure riding
through a shower of bul-
lets; the horse, its tail tied
up for battle, is painted
with dragonflies, an image
connoting avoidance of
danger. The rider wears
beaded moccasins and leg-
gings and carries a sidearm
at his waist and a rifle in
one hand. The "ghost
shirt" seems rather to be a
cape: a hide painted with
Ghost Dance imagery of an
eagle and stars and worn
over his shoulder.

The inscription seems to
allude to the Lakota belief
in the protective function of
Ghost Dance clothing. But
because the writer's identity
is unknown, it is not clear
whether the title was given
by the artist or by the
Lakota owner of the book
or by a white at a later
time. In 1900, when the
book entered the
Milwaukee collections, the
catalogue noted that it was
"painted and written by
Red Hawk." The drawings
are by several hands, however, and the book includes
two lists of Indian names,
presumably those of the
artists. Thus, although the
relation of the drawing to
the Ghost Dance is clear,
the name of the artist and
the precise subject remain
obscure.
LL

## 132, 133

**Two dolls in Ghost Dance
costume**
Oglala Lakota, ca. 1900
Native-tanned hide, pig-
ment, human? hair, feath-
ers, glass beads, porcupine
quills
12⅛ x 6 x 2¼ in;
14⅛ x 6¼ x 1¼ in
National Museum of the
American Indian,
Smithsonian Institution,
9/7607 (male), 9/7608
(female)
Provenance: Collected by
Mrs. Emma Dow on Pine
Ridge Reservation

Regrettably little is known
about the making and
intended use of Ghost
Dance dolls such as these.
Although they may have
been made for children to
play with, it seems likelier
they were made for gift or
sale to European Ameri-
cans. Sewn with consider-
able care and skill, they are
dressed in detailed repro-

ductions of Ghost Dance
clothing, with many highly
important motifs drawn or
painted on them. The man's
"shield," or bib, bears a
solar image in front and a
crescent moon in back. The
front of his shirt shows an
eagle, and the flaps of his
leggings are decorated with
dragonflies and forked
lightning. The upper por-
tion of his shirt has a pattern of hail encircling his
shoulders. The woman's
dress bib has eagle images
front and back, while
another eagle is placed midway down the back of the
dress. Beaded bands encircle the dress, and she wears
a necklace, belt, and leggings of beads. Both figures
wear beaded moccasins,
and their facial features are
rendered in beads as well.
LL

131

174

130

132

133

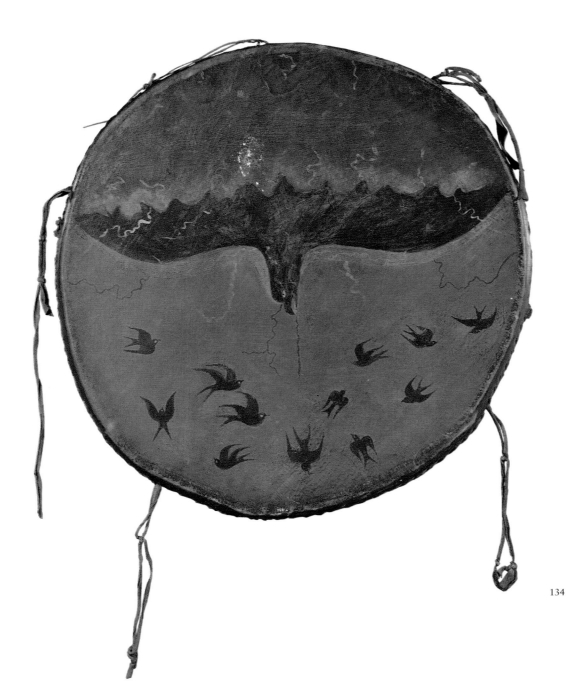

134

**Ghost Dance drum**
Pawnee (Chahiksichahiks),
1890s
Wood, rawhide, pigment
23 x 3¾ in
Field Museum of Natural
History, Chicago, 71856
Provenance: Collected by
George Dorsey in Okla-
homa, Pawnee County,
1902
References: Lesser 1933,
pp. 264–65; Walker Art
Center and The
Minneapolis Institute of
Arts 1972, no. 654;
National Geographic
Society 1974, facing p. 26

The Lakota's disastrous
encounter in 1890 with the
United States Army at
Wounded Knee, on Pine
Ridge Reservation, brought
most Ghost Dance activity
and proselytizing to a halt,
although aspects of belief
and practice were quietly
continued. Elsewhere
among Plains people, how-
ever, the Ghost Dance continued for a time. As it
brought hope for a return
to earlier ways of life, the
Ghost Dance also stimulated people to revive older
cultural forms that had
fallen into disuse. Traditional music and dance

underwent a revival among
Arapaho and Pawnee, for
example, as did the playing
of hand games, which
involved betting on the
location of hidden stones.

Among Pawnee people
the hand game revival
transmuted into games
directly connected to Ghost
Dance. Individuals received
variant hand-game rules
and practices in visions,
and although the general
play resembled earlier versions, great emphasis was
placed on ritual and
ceremonial aspects of the
games (Lesser 1933,
p. 155). Having dreamed of
a game, a person would
assemble a bundle of necessary paraphernalia and
stage the game according
to the detailed requirements
of the vision.

This drum forms a part
of a hand-game bundle that
belonged to George Beaver,
who was well known as a
medicine man. The bundle
also included four drum
supports, eight tally sticks,
two bows and two arrows,
two rattles, and a feather
ornament. His game was
originally played in a dark-
blue tent decorated with
dot patterns representing
hail, and the bundle items,
along with a pipe, would
have been laid out in ritual

order before the beginning of the game. Pairs of players from the two competing "teams" would try to out-guess one another, and in the intervals between games the participants would sing Ghost Dance songs and dance, accompanied by the drum.

Lesser, working from his own examination of one face of the drum and Dorsey's unpublished field notes, identifies the large swooping bird as an eagle with streaks of lightning, or, metaphorically, a thunderbird, and the smaller birds as red-breasted swallows, which flock together before a storm (Lesser 1933, pp. 264–65). The eagle's wings are intended to suggest looming storm clouds, and these birds, together with the hail patterns on the tent, represent the power of the game to produce rain. The beat of the drum likewise alludes to thunder. Crows and eagles were specifically associated with Pawnee Ghost Dance hand games, sometimes representing the competing teams (Lesser 1933, p. 157). Although George Beaver was affiliated with the Crow side, his use of the eagle on his drum probably derived from a dream. The use of black, green, and blue on

the image associates it with the north in hand-game iconography. On the reverse side is a much simpler image of a four-pointed star. That side was said to be used during the ceremony if the game was played at night, whereas the more complex image was used for afternoon games.

Although Ghost Dance hand games resembled earlier versions in many respects, they required more ritual paraphernalia and knowledge, and they did not involve betting. The game was nonetheless played with great intensity: in the early days "losers cried desolately and the winners were jubilant" (Lesser 1933, p. 157). It is clear that the game functioned as a metaphor for the broader issues that the Ghost Dance itself represented: hope, risk, chance, death, and rebirth.

LL

**Vest**

Lakota (collected as Blackfeet [Siksika]), before 1910
Native-tanned hide, glass beads
37½ x 18⅛ in
Ethnographic Museum, University of Oslo, Norway, 21.168
Provenance: Collected by Christian Leden in Alberta, Canada, 1910–11

This vest, although collected as Blackfoot, shows Lakota and Pawnee characteristics in its beading technique and imagery. On the front, celestial imagery of stars and crescent moons hovers above trees and opposed male and female elks. The animals and trees are united by a groundline, an unusual feature of beadwork imagery probably derived from Euro-American sources. On the back, two pairs of birds fly above abstract star designs. The forked tails of the central birds identify them as swallows, and these, together with the emphasis on astral imagery on the vest as a whole, suggest an association to the Ghost Dance.

LL

135

177

**Ghost Dance cape**
Arapaho (Inuna-ina),
ca. 1890
Cotton, pigment
69 x 86 in
American Museum of
Natural History, 50/352
Provenance: Collected by
A. L. Kroeber after 1899
References: Kroeber 1907,
pp. 433–34; Kroeber 1900,
fig. 45

This large painted cloth,
catalogued as a cape or
banner, has no known par-
allel in the typology of
Ghost Dance forms. Its
formal arrangement is
highly symmetrical. An
arcing rainbow, associated
with roads or trails in
sacred cosmology, spreads
from corner to corner, and
its extremities support
pipes, a highly potent symbol in both traditional
Arapaho religion and in
Ghost Dance ideology.
Two large opposed birds,
whose beaks shoot power
lines to the upper corners,
cling to the center of the
rainbow trail. Two smaller
birds are shown in flight,
and the upper portion of
the cloth is filled with
astral imagery.

According to Kroeber
(1907), the painting represents the dream of a man
who "was middle-aged at
the time of the ghost
dance." The painter saw in
his dream a man dressed in
black silk; the visionary

being knew all his thoughts
and showed him "the new
world that was to be." He
was led to stand on a rainbow in the sky, from
which he could see the
earth and the heavens. The
small red triangles in the
lower corners represent the
earth. He also saw the
crow and the eagle (the
bird resembling a parrot),
whose voices, shown as
wavy lines, reached up to
the stars. Lesser birds (the
magpie and the bullbat) fly
toward the center.

Two pipes rest on the
rainbow, one of red catlinite and the other of black
soapstone, which Kroeber
(1907) notes was consid-
ered more sacred. Like the
voices of the birds, and
the actions of the birds in
Ghost Dance ideology, pipe
smoke is a means of com-
munication with the world
above.
LL

136

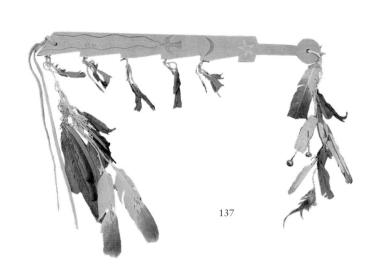

137

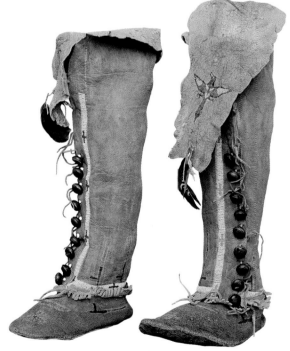

138

**Ghost Dance baton**

Cheyenne (Tsistsistas) or
Arapaho, ca. 1891
Mirror, glass beads, brass
bells, sinew, wood, leather,
hawk and magpie feathers
22 x 27½ in
The Cleveland Museum of
Natural History, 8514
References: Josephy,
Thomas, and Eder 1990,
p. 1, fig. 1

This military society–style
baton has carved symbols
associated with the Ghost
Dance. One side shows the
crescent moon and stars
and a bird with green,
black, and yellow wavy
lines that represent power
coming from its head. On
the other side are another
bird and a man holding a
pipe in his right hand and a
cedar branch in his left. The
cedar tree is often used as a
symbol of sacredness
because of its "never-dying
green," powerful fragrance,
and dark red heartwood
(Mooney 1896, p. 809).
The figure holding the pipe
and cedar branch is also
seen in Arapaho Ghost
Dance dresses (cat. no. 127).
JDHC

**Ghost Dance boots**

Arapaho (Inuna-ina),
ca. 1890
Native-tanned leather,
brass bells, feathers, glass
beads, pigment
19 x 10¾ x 4 in
American Museum of
Natural History, 50/623
Provenance: Collected by
A. L. Kroeber after 1899;
possibly belonged to
Short Name

Although the principal
functional application of
Ghost Dance imagery was
on shirts and dresses, such
imagery appears on many
other types of objects as
well. Here a pair of
woman's high boots is
heavily decorated with
motifs associated with the
Ghost Dance: Maltese
crosses representing stars at
the toes, a crescent moon
and rainbow at the instep,
sacred pipes about the
ankles, a turtle and eagle at

the backs of the ankles. On
the top flaps are magpies,
important in Ghost Dance
iconography because they
are associated with the
western region that was
the home of Wovoka, the
Paiute Ghost Dance
prophet, and because
Paiute Ghost Dance cos-
tumes made use of magpie
feathers. The combination
of astral symbols with
images of certain animals is
common on Ghost Dance
materials.

Even the choice of the
red background probably
has symbolic connotations.
Mooney cites a Cheyenne
Ghost Dance song that
refers to red paint: "The
crow/ . . . He brings it to
me/ . . . The red paint/ . . .
It will make you strong"
(Mooney [1896] 1965,
p. 277). The inclusion of
brass bells is unusual; a
tenet of Ghost Dance ideology among northern Plains
people was the avoidance
of imported Euro-American
goods, and metal in particular was excluded. Although
southern Ghost Dancers
wore metal jewelry and
belts, few items of Ghost
Dance clothing have
attached metal. The bells
may thus have been added
at a later time.
LL

**Pipe bag**

Arapaho (Inuna-ina), after
1890
Native-tanned hide, glass
beads
31⅞ x 6¾ in
Foundation for the
Preservation of American
Indian Art and Culture,
Inc., Chicago
References: Maurer 1977,
cat. no. 240

Ghost Dance clothing and
paraphernalia often show
blended iconography, integrating the symbolic vocabulary of the dance into
more traditional religious
imagery. In the case of this
pipe bag, for example,
many of the devices
appeared singly on older
objects, but their combination here strongly points to
an association to Ghost
Dance. One side of the bag
bears a crescent, a raven,
and descending lines of
power—a set of celestial
images. The other side is
concerned with the terres-
trial: a tree and four turtles.
The crescent moon, the
star, and the raven are particularly frequent as Ghost
Dance motifs, but the bag
alludes to Arapaho cos-
mogonic myth as well.

In the Arapaho version
of creation, a being in
human form walked on the
primal water, holding a
sacred pipe. After many
attempts, the being merged
with a turtle and with the
pipe to form a ducklike

creature that brought earth
up to the surface of the
water and thus created the
universe (Harrod 1987,
pp. 50–51). In Arapaho
thought, the body of the
turtle echoes the form of
the universe because its legs
define the four directions;
directionality is also of
great importance in pipe
ceremonies. The impor-
tance of the number four is
reiterated in the four turtle
images. Allusions to the
formation of the universe in
the context of the Ghost
Dance are a means of
describing the renewal of
the world that the dance
will bring about—the pristine state of creation will be
achieved.
LL

139

**The arrest and death of Sitting Bull**
Hunkpapa Lakota,
1900–1915
Muslin, paint
70 x 72 in
State Historical Society of North Dakota, 941
Provenance: Possibly collected by Frances Densmore at the Standing Rock Reservation, North Dakota

Following the Battle of the Little Big Horn, Sitting Bull and his followers escaped to Canada, only to return under adverse conditions in 1881 to live on the Hunkpapa reservation at Standing Rock. Sitting Bull was an assertive leader feared by the whites, especially during the events involving the Ghost Dance troubles in 1889 and 1890. The civilian and government leaders had created a highly emotional and volatile situation in Dakota Territory as a means to crush Indian resistance once and for all.

The Indian agent at the Standing Rock Reservation, Major James A. McLaughlin, ordered the arrest of Sitting Bull because he felt he was a dangerous "malcontent." Trying to avoid a confrontation between the police and Sitting Bull's band, McLaughlin set the date of arrest for December 20, the day that rations were issued and the people would be gathered at the agency. When Sitting Bull told McLaughlin that he would attend the Ghost Dance at Pine Ridge with or without McLaughlin's approval, the date of arrest was moved to December 15. Forty-three regular and special Indian police rode into Sitting Bull's camp that morning to arrest the Hunkpapa holy man.

The Indian police pressured the Ghost Dance followers and arrested many of their leaders. The people looked to Sitting Bull, a man known for his spiritual strength, for advice. The scene in the upper right corner of the painting depicts Sitting Bull praying at the Ghost Dance center pole. This prayer reads "Father look at me and be kind to me."

In the center of the painting, Sitting Bull is taken from his log cabin by three Indian policemen— Brown Wolf, High Eagle, and Red Tomahawk. During the arrest, Sitting Bull's band gathered around the police and a skirmish ensued. The lower section of the painting shows Sitting Bull on the ground, bleeding from wounds and defended by many of his followers wearing Ghost Dance shirts. Other followers can be seen running to safety. It was a costly fight, in which Sitting Bull, seven of his followers, and six Indian police died.

The creator of this painting illustrated the events that led to Sitting Bull's death by showing many events occurring at the same time. To follow a chronological order, the viewer must start in the upper right corner of the muslin, with Sitting Bull at the Ghost Dance center pole, and move to the left, where the Indian police arrive and dismount. The artist's rendering of their fine horses shows that the government gave the Indian police the finest equipment (State Historical Society of North Dakota 1984, p. 49). Then the scene moves down to the arrest of Sitting Bull. Finally, the lower section shows Sitting Bull dying of his wounds.
JDHC

140

## 141

Wohaw (Gu hau de?) (1855–1924)

**Allegorical drawing of a man between a buffalo and a domesticated bull**

Kiowa (Gaigwa), 1877
Paper, pencil, colored pencil
8¾ x 11½ in
Missouri Historical Society, 1882.18.1
Provenance: Collected at Fort Marion, Florida, in January 1877 by Frances and John Grady; gift of Mrs. James Barry (Mrs. Grady's mother) to the Missouri Historical Society, 1882
References: Petersen 1971, pp. 90–91, 209, color pl. 9; Ewers 1978a, pp. 33–34; Harris 1989, pp. 128–29; Berlo 1982, p. 13, fig. 15; Berlo 1990, p. 136, fig. 5; Barsness 1977, pp. 92–93

This well-known drawing has been published repeatedly as a representation of the dilemmas faced by Plains peoples in the late nineteenth century. The artist was known as Wohaw, the name inscribed above the central figure, but this was likely a mispronunciation or a nickname given him before he was sent to Fort Marion. Although Wohaw is said to be a Kiowa term meaning "beef," it may be a creolized term in imitation of drovers' cries (Petersen 1971, p. 213, n. 1). According to descendants, his name may have been Gu hau de (Wolf Robe) (Harris 1989, p. 14).

Wohaw seems to have derived the basic design of this image from a painted tipi made by a Kiowa man, Screaming on High, who was also transported to Fort Marion and died there shortly after arrival (Ewers 1978a, p. 34). On the tipi a domesticated bull and a buffalo stand on either side of the door opening; the bull exudes a cloud of power. Wohaw may very likely have seen the tipi in use in Kiowa territory before 1875. He has elaborated the theme considerably, adding the central, perhaps autobiographical, figure as well as the opposed tipi and church, bison herd and plowed field. Harris interprets the pattern of dots beside the tipi as peyote buttons, but this seems unlikely, since the image is so indistinct and because no Native American Church imagery has been documented before 1891. The bison herd and the plowed field are logical as parallel means of sustenance.

LL

## 142

Oscar Howe (1915–83)

**Calling on Wakan Tanka**

Yanktonai Lakota, 1962
Paper, casein paints
24 x 31½ in
The University Art Galleries, The University of South Dakota
Provenance: Collected by Lender, ca. 1966
References: Dockstader 1982, p. 43, fig. 46

Oscar Howe's career spanned four decades, during which he became the most famous Plains Indian artist of his time. His work was widely exhibited and published in the general art world as well as in the Indian community, and he became the first Plains artist to bridge the gap between traditional Indian values and the world of contemporary art. Howe was born on the Crow Creek Reservation in South Dakota and attended the Pierre Indian School as a boy. From 1935 to 1938 Howe studied with Dorothy Dunn at the Santa Fe Indian School.

After serving in the army during World War II, Oscar Howe began his long career as an art teacher at Dakota Wesleyan University and then at the State University of South Dakota in Vermillion. He taught hundreds of students, among them Herman Red Elk (cat. no. 206), Robert Penn (cat. no. 4), and Arthur Amiotte (cat. no. 301). His own work was exhibited in over fifty one-man shows, included in a host of catalogues, books, and articles, and given numerous awards.

Howe developed a personal style that allowed him to express the traditions and spirituality of the Lakota through contemporary media. His work is marked by a radial energy that unites the pictorial elements visually and thematically. In his own words: "It has always been my version of Indian traditions to make it my own way, but every part comes from Indian and not white culture. I have been labelled wrongly a Cubist. The basic design is *Tahokmu* (spider web). From an all-Indian background I developed my own style" (Dockstader 1982, p. 15).

*Calling on Wakan Tanka* is a visionary scene of three men in a circle of fire offering prayers to the Great Spirit through the sacred pipe ceremony. Howe's "spider web" design unites the painting visually and expresses the principle of natural harmony and spirituality that is at the heart of Plains culture. Oscar Howe not only brought a Lakota vision to the world at large, he also worked tirelessly to legitimize and support the right of Indian artists to express an independent creative vision based on traditional values.

EMM

## 143

Red Cloud (1840–ca. 1906)

**Vision painting and battle scenes**

Cheyenne (Tsistsistas), 1904
Muslin, pigments
68⅝ x 101¾ in
Field Museum of Natural History, Chicago, 96809
Provenance: Collected by James Mooney, Darlington, Oklahoma, 1904

This large painting combines the ceremonial and biographical traditions of Plains art to illustrate important events in the life of a Northern Cheyenne warrior named Red Cloud. The bottom half shows scenes from a vision that features three tipis painted with stars, the sun and moon, and a frieze of running buffalo with heart lines around the bottom. An eagle or hawk sits on top of the lodgepoles. Between the tipis are a spirit buffalo painted with a heart line and images of the morning star, crescent moon, and sun, and the figure of Buffalo Man, painted with the same astral symbols and carrying a pipe. Buffalo Man is surrounded by four disks, and both he and the spirit buffalo have indications of the breath of life coming from their mouths and nostrils. The vision painted on the tipis was given to Red Cloud by Buffalo Man in a dream.

The top half of the painting shows scenes of three battles in which Red Cloud fought against the Crow. On the right, Red Cloud wears a black shirt and a bandolier of German silver disks. He has a quiver strapped across his chest and holds a bow in his left hand as he counts coup on his enemy with a quirt. In the second scene, Red Cloud has dismounted from his horse to scalp the Crow warrior he has shot with an arrow. The third scene, on the left, depicts a fight between Red Cloud and two Crow, one of whom he has shot with a rifle and scalped before attacking the other and wounding him fatally with an arrow in the body. These events probably took place in 1863 when Red Cloud took part in a battle in which an allied force of Northern Cheyenne, Northern Arapaho, and Lakota fought a two-day encounter with the Crow (Mooney 1903–6).

EMM

141

142

143

**Warrior's shirt**

Upper Missouri, Mandan (Numakiki)? ca. 1800–1830
Native-tanned leather, human hair, porcupine quills, sinew, red and black pigment
55x 30 in
Peabody Museum of Archaeology and Ethnology, Harvard University, 90-17-10/49309
Provenance: Received from the American Antiquarian Society of Worcester, Massachusetts, in 1890; possibly acquired from Roderick McKenzie, ca. 1819
References: Minneapolis Institute of Arts and Walker Art Center 1972, p. 127

This shirt honors the bravery and prowess of a warrior who counted coup on two armed enemy and killed thirty-four. The hero's exploits were painted on the shirt, which was worn on special occasions such as victory dances, military society gatherings, and other social functions. The figures are drawn in an archaic style whose simple forms, minimal outlines and details, and conventionalized hourglass-shaped figures are characteristics of ceremonial art.

The victorious warrior is shown on horseback in the lower left corner. Being the only mounted figure emphasizes his status and power, also implied by his red genitals. A dotted line connects the rider to the column of figures above him, and a trail of horse tracks brings him back down the second line of figures on the right. The hands touching the shoulders of the first two figures in the left column, one of whom holds a bow and arrow and the other a flintlock rifle, show that the mounted warrior has counted the highest of coups on them—touching an armed enemy with his bare hand. The other six figures have feathered lances drawing blood from wounds in their chests, indicating that they have been killed. In the row of figures on the right, the artist has included details that convey important information about the status or identity of the dead enemy. The two figures at the top of the row were men of power, bravery, and status, as indicated by the war shield hung with eagle feathers held by the top figure and by the red sash, an emblem worn by warriors of proven ability and high rank in the military societies that were a principal feature of all Plains tribes. The medallion of black-dyed buckskin sewn onto the center of the shirt is decorated with a delicately worked quill design of two concentric rings of oval forms. These represent the eagle feather and the feather headdress design that was also painted on robes (cat. no. 305). The second figure from the bottom is singled out by his buffalo-horn headdress, perhaps denoting membership in a Buffalo Bull warrior society. A flintlock rifle is also shown, above his shoulder.

The back of the shirt has a similar arrangement of coup designs featuring two rows of ten warriors killed in battle by the owner of the shirt, two with arrows and eighteen with a lance. A similar quilled rosette is sewn in the center of the back, and quilled strips of rectangular and circular forms in white, yellow, orange, and red cover the shoulder and arm seams. The shirt is also decorated with locks of human hair—gifts from warrior companions signifyng that they honored and trusted the shirt's owner as their leader and friend. The inner cuffs of the sleeves and the collar are stained red from the body paint worn by the owner when he used this garment of honor and accomplishment.

EMM

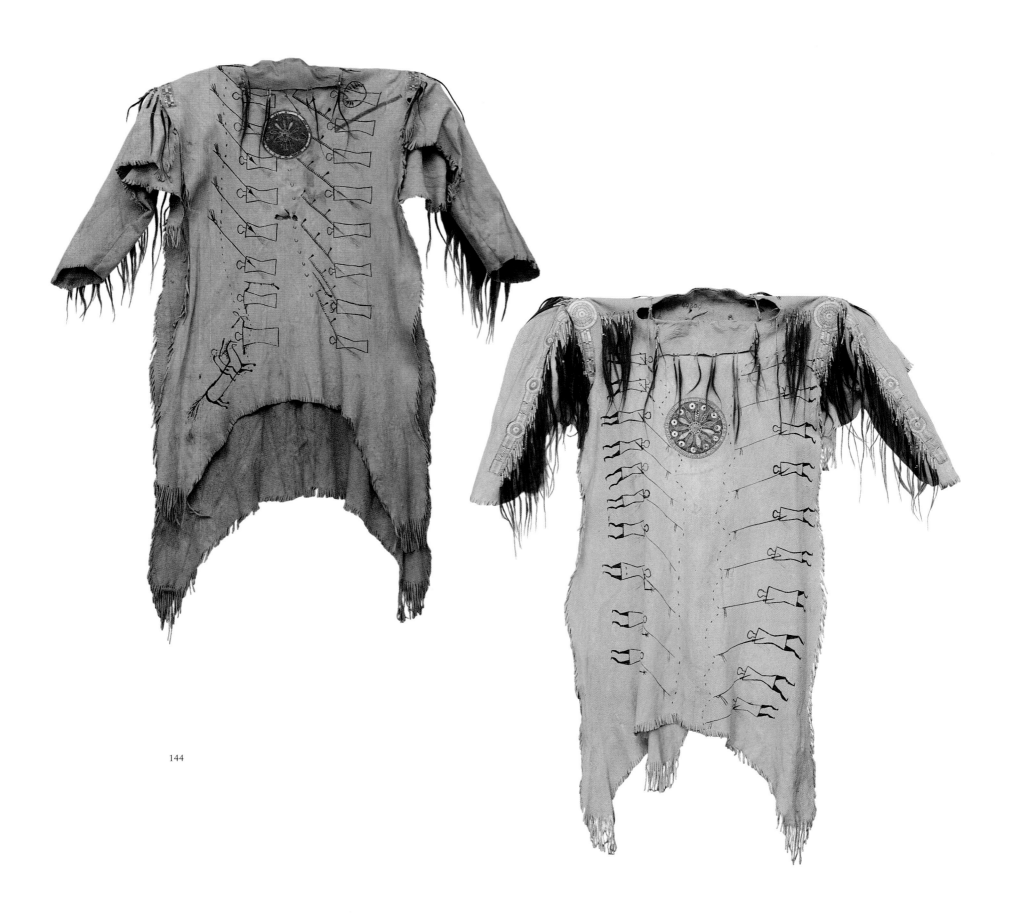

144

**Warrior's shirt**
Mandan (Numakiki) (catalogued as Santee Dakota?),
ca. 1830
Native-tanned leather; porcupine quills; sinew; glass beads; red ochre; black, green, and red pigment
35½ x 53½ in
Bern Historical Museum, Ethnography Department, N.A. 15
Provenance: Accessioned in 1890; collected by Lorenz Alphons Schoch in Missouri Territory, July 1837
References: Thompson 1977, p. 158, figs. 85, 86

This rare example of an early nineteenth-century warrior's shirt painted with biographical themes was collected by a Swiss mer-

chant who worked in the important trading center of St. Louis from 1833 to 1842. In 1837 he visited encampments of the Shawnee, Delaware, Kansas, Kickapoo, and Potawatomi, prairie tribes that often had commerce with the Plains peoples along the west bank of the Missouri River. This Upper Missouri–style shirt must have come to the prairie groups through their extensive trade system.

The shirt is constructed of two softly tanned skins that have been left untrimmed. It is decorated

with dyed and plaited porcupine quill strips, light blue pony beads, and lengths of fringe along the seams of the arms. The painted figures represent the battle record of coups counted or enemies killed by the great warrior who owned the shirt. On the front are four rows containing twenty-one highly stylized warriors, whose long tapering bodies and abstracted legs and arms are indicated with a simple bold line. The figures have no suggestions of faces and are differentiated and individualized only by their

hairstyles, weapons, military regalia, and clothing. They are armed with bows and quivers full of arrows, flintlock rifles with powder horns and red cloth shot pouches, tomahawks, knives, and spears. Weapons directed at a figure from above represent the weapon with which that enemy was touched or killed, for example, the bow that touches the shoulder of the striped figure on the right in the top row. Two of the defeated warriors are shield men; the last figure on the left of the top row is a distinguished

officer of a military society, as shown by his horned headdress and the red and white sash trimmed with eagle feathers. The man next to him wears a long red frock coat with what might be a pattern of body paint showing underneath.

The back of the shirt documents fourteen enemies defeated in battle, including three men wearing long frock coats and a man with a horizontally striped body that could indicate body painting or a decorated shirt. This figure

and the one next to it wear their hair in the front-crest style associated with the Crow and Arikara.

Documented biographical paintings of this period are extremely rare. The close resemblance between these figures and the ones painted on the Mandan robe collected by Lewis and Clark in 1805 strongly supports a Mandan attribution for this important example of early Plains painting (cat. no. 147).

EMM

145

**Warrior's shirt**
Mandan, ca. 1830
Native-tanned leather, porcupine quills, dyed human hair and horsehair, blue and white glass beads, brown pigment
47¼ in
Canadian Museum of Civilization, VH2 (73/66/187)
Provenance: Purchased from Arthur Speyer, Jr., in 1973; Arthur Speyer, Sr.; J. F. G. Umlauff, Hamburg, Germany

This painted war shirt was accompanied by a label saying it was Mandan and collected in 1832, an attribution of tribal style and date that is supported by its construction, decoration, and painting. The figures of the defeated warriors are painted in the same graphic style and with the same depictions of weapons as the shirt from Bern (cat. no. 145), but this shirt has hairlocks instead of leather fringe, a different quill pattern, and more pony beads. It also has horse tracks and images of twelve human heads painted on each sleeve.

EMM

146

**Robe with war exploits**
Mandan, 1797–1805
Native-tanned buffalo hide;
dyed porcupine quills;
black, red, green, yellow,
and brown pigment
94 x 102 in
Peabody Museum of
Archaeology and Ethnology,
Harvard University, 99-12-
10/53121
Provenance: Gift of the heirs
of David Kimball, 1899;
Boston Museum; Peale
Museum, 1828–50; Christian
Jacob Hutter, Pennsylvania,
1828; possibly Lieutenant
George Christian Hutter;
Thomas Jefferson,
Monticello, 1805–26; collect-
ed by Lewis and Clark, 1805
References: Ewers 1939,
p. 26, pl. 22

This buffalo robe painted
with scenes of war is the
earliest securely documented example of Plains bio-
graphical art. It was collected by the famous Lewis and
Clark expedition to the
Upper Missouri area in
1804–5. The first winter
quarters of the expedition
were located at Fort
Mandan, an outpost for
trade and military protection located on the west
bank of the Missouri River
near the mouth of the Knife
River in central North
Dakota. In their records
that spring, Lewis and
Clark made an inventory of
Indian objects they had collected and sent as gifts to
President Thomas Jefferson
at Monticello. The ship-
ment included this robe,
which was described as a
"buffalo robe painted by a
Mandan man representing
a battle fought eight years
since [ca. 1797] by the
Sioux and Recaras against
the Mandans, Menitarras
and Ah-wah-har-ways,
Mandans &c on horse
back" (Willoughby 1905,
p. 634). The robe had an
interesting subsequent history, passing from Jefferson
to the Charles Willson
Peale Museum in
Independence Hall,
Philadelphia, and then to
the Boston Museum and
eventually to Harvard's
Peabody Museum in 1899.

As described by its col-
lectors, this robe illustrates
an unusually large battle
involving the combined
forces of five northern
Plains tribes, the "Sioux
and Recaras" against an
allied force of "Mandans,
Menitarras and Ah-wah-
har-ways" (Mandan,
Hidatsa, and Amahami, a
Siouan tribe that became
incorporated with the
Hidatsa around 1835). It
was a battle between the
semisedentary Mandan,
Hidatsa, and Amahami,
who combined buffalo
hunting with agriculture
and lived in villages of large
earth lodges, and the
nomadic Lakota, their traditional enemy. While at
first glance the arrangement
of figures looks random
and chaotic, a closer examination reveals a narrative
structure that organizes the
sixty-four figures into a
possible combination of
twenty-two episodes of
individual and group com-
bat. Two groups of war-
riors in the upper right are
united by a dotted line that
indicates a relationship of
action, but most of the
groupings are made by the
implied sequences of narrative as the warriors face or
strike at one another.

Whereas the figures of
the warriors and horses are
delineated by a system of
simplified conventional
forms, the individual
images are particularized by
details of hair, costume,
and military equipment.
The hide shows twenty men
mounted on horses differ-
entiated by their body color
and two different styles of
manes, one clipped and one
indicated by a scalloped
line. Twelve of the warriors
carry shields and five wear
different kinds of military
society sashes that mark
them as officers of high
rank. The combatants are
armed with various
weapons, including bows
and arrows, spears, knives,
axes, and flintlock rifles
with the accompanying
powder horns and red cloth
shot pouches. A mounted
warrior with an eagle-
feather headdress and a red
shield in the lower left section has a pipe drawn in
front of his face to show his
role as a leader in this battle; in the section above him
are two men with the feathered bow lance that was a
military society emblem of
rank.

A close analysis shows
at least two personal styles
of drawing figures and
horses, suggesting that the
robe was painted by two
men, probably comrades-
in-arms who had participated in the great battle. This
style of biographical art can
also be seen on shirts (cat.
no. 145) and on the very
similar robe and shirt in the
collection of the Musée de
l'Homme in Paris.

Robes decorated with
battle scenes were worn
only by warriors of great
experience and reputation.
Karl Bodmer drew this portrait (fig. a) of an unidenti-
fied Piegan warrior wearing
a biographical robe during
the summer of 1833 while
visiting Fort McKenzie on
the Upper Missouri River.
He accurately described the
archaic style of early
Blackfeet warrior art that
continued as the most conservative style of Plains
painting well into the twentieth century.

EMM

Cat. no. 147, fig. a
Karl Bodmer, Swiss (1809–93),
*Piegan Blackfeet Man*, 1833, watercolor and
pencil on paper, 12⅜ x 10 in, Joslyn Art
Museum, Omaha, Nebraska, gift of the Enron
Art Foundation, NA148

147

Mato Tope (Four Bears)
(ca. 1800–1837)

**Robe with Mato Tope's exploits**

Mandan (Numakiki),
ca. 1835
Native-tanned buffalo hide;
red wool cloth; sinew; dyed
porcupine quills; horsehair
and human hair; red,
brown, yellow, and black
pigment
63 x 82¾ in
Bern Historical Museum,
Ethnography Department,
N.A. 8
Provenance: Accessioned in
1890; collected by Lorenz
Alphons Schoch, Missouri
Territory, July 1837
References: Thompson
1977, pp. 152–54, fig. 78

This is one of two surviving
robes painted with his war
exploits by Mato Tope, the
famous Mandan chief. (cat.
no. 149). (The other was
collected by Prince
Maximilian zu Wied and is
in the Linden Museum,
Stuttgart.) It illustrates
eight of the battles fought
by this noted warrior. They
can be interpreted today
because we have the narrative given by Mato Tope in
1832 to George Catlin.
Catlin devoted ten pages
and four illustrations in his
book to a transcription of
Mato Tope's oral account

of the scenes. Following
Plains custom, let us begin
at the east (right) side of the
robe and move clockwise.

The first scene shows
Mato Tope charging at a
large group of Assiniboines,
represented by the mass of
round heads shown
entrenched in a defensive
position near a Mandan village. Mato Tope has black
body paint and striped legs
and face, an eagle feather in
his hair, and a red military
society sash over his shoulder. With his left hand he
fires a flintlock rifle at a
fleeing Assiniboine, wounding him in the shoulders.
The man had fired at Mato
Tope but his gun burst and
is now lying on the ground.

The second scene shows
Mato Tope wearing an
eagle-feather trailer and
leggings that are red on the
inside and horizontally
striped on the outside. He
is badly wounded and
bleeding, abandoned by his
party on the field of battle,
an unusual and frowned-
upon action. He stands
over the body of a
Cheyenne warrior in a red
frock coat, whom he has
killed. The tracks above
the fallen enemy's head
represent the thirty

Cheyenne foe who fought
in the battle.

The next scene repre-
sents the culmination of
Mato Tope's most famous
fight, which took place during a large engagement of
Mandan against Cheyenne.
The Cheyenne chief chal-
lenged Mato Tope to single
combat with rifles on
horseback. When Mato
Tope's powder horn was
shot away, the two turned
to their bows and arrows
until their quivers were
empty. The Mandan's horse
was then killed from under
him, and the two warrior-
chiefs met in close combat.
Mato Tope was wounded
twice in the hand by the
Cheyenne's knife before he
wrested it away and killed
him with it. (See Catlin
1844, 1:152–53.)

The next illustration
shows Mato Tope with two
eagle feathers in his hair
and the lower half of his
face and his body painted
red. He uses a lance hung
with eagle feathers, which
represent coups, to strike a
Cheyenne chief who had
challenged him to individual combat. The next scene
shows a fallen Cheyenne
chief with a long eagle-
feather war headdress and a
shield trimmed with eagle
feathers lying on the
ground next to his horse.
During the fight the
Cheyenne's wife bravely

rushed forward to help her
husband and was also
killed.

In the scene above this,
Mato Tope wears his eagle-
plume headdress as he leads
his war-horse, which carries
his large red shield and
wears its own crest of eagle
plumes. The scene refers to
his going alone to an
Ojibwe village to avenge
the murder of a Mandan.
He stayed hidden for six
days without food and
finally attacked the village
and killed the two Ojibwe
women, shown on the
ground in front of him
wearing black dresses. He
escaped his pursuers and
returned, adding another
daring episode to his war
credits.

The single figure of
Mato Tope wearing his
characteristic red paint and
holding his eagle-feather
shield and lance represents
one of his bravest engagements. Several hundred
Minitaris and Mandans
were attacked by a large
body of Assiniboines and
retreated to a better position. Mato Tope was the
only one who held his
ground, firing his rifle and
killing one of the enemy.
The four rows of tracks in
front of Mato Tope repre-

sent the enemy; the marks
behind him indicate his
own people who retreated
and the many bullets flying
around his body. It was in
this engagement that he
earned his name, because
the Assiniboine said he
charged them like four
bears (*mato tope*)!

Mato Tope's painting
style on this robe is quite
different from the stark,
two-dimensional linearity
typical of Mandan painting
just thirty years before.
Mato Tope combined ele-
ments of European style,
such as interior coloring
and shading and a sense of
three-dimensional form,
with the conventional poses
of early Plains art. In doing
so, he demonstrated his
own artistic ability and his
willingness to experiment
with pictorial style and
introduce changes to a very
conservative tradition.
EMM

148

Mato Tope (Four Bears)
(ca. 1800–1837)
**Battle with a Cheyenne**
Mandan (Numakiki),
ca. 1833–34
Paper, pencil, watercolor
12 x 15½ in
Joslyn Art Museum, Omaha,
Nebraska, gift of the Enron
Art Foundation, R17
Provenance: Gift of the
Enron Art Foundation,
1986; Northern Natural
Gas Company (Enron Art
Foundation), Omaha,
Nebraska, 1962; M.
Knoedler and Company,
Inc., New York, ca. 1960;
collection of Schloss
Neuwied, Germany, ca.
1845; collected by Prince
Maximilian zu Wied, Fort
Clark, North Dakota,
1833–34

Mato Tope (Four Bears)
was the most distinguished
warrior and the most highly
respected and well-liked

chief of his time. He was
interested in knowing the
whites who visited nearby
Fort Clark, among whom
were the artists George
Catlin and Karl Bodmer.

Catlin spent about three
weeks with Mato Tope in
the summer of 1832 paint-
ing portraits of him and
illustrating his war regalia,
especially a robe painted by
Mato Tope with twelve
scenes of his most impor-
tant battles; versions of this
robe still exist in the collections of the Linden
Museum, Stuttgart, and the
Bern Historiscal Museum.
Catlin described Mato
Tope as follows: "This
extraordinary man, though
second in office, is
undoubtedly the first and
most popular man in the
nation. Free, generous, elegant, and gentlemanly

in his deportment—hand-
some, brave and valiant"
(Catlin [1844] 1973,
1:145).

A year later Mato Tope
developed an even stronger
relationship with the Swiss
artist Karl Bodmer, who
accompanied Prince
Maximilian zu Wied on a
trip to the Upper Missouri
and spent the winter of
1833–34 at Fort Clark.
Bodmer, whose artistic talents surpassed Catlin's,
made drawings of Mato
Tope, including these two
portraits. One portrait
(fig. a) shows Mato Tope in
his full regalia as a notable
who was the head of the
Dog Society and leader of
the annual Okipa festival,
which was the Mandan's
major religious ceremony.
The other (fig. b) shows
him holding a tomahawk
and wearing body paint

and the insignia of his
many victorious deeds in
battle. The yellow hand
painted on his chest means
that he had taken prisoners,
and the horizontal lines
painted on his arms are
marks of coups he had performed. The eagle feathers
in his hair are emblems of
coups, the split turkey
feather indicates an arrow
wound, and the yellow-
dyed owl feathers show his
membership in the Dog
Society. The six painted
wooden sticks with brass
nails in the ends represent
bullet wounds, and the
wooden knife recalls his
most famous battle, with a
Cheyenne chief. All of these
symbols demonstrate that
the Plains warrior used personal adornment as well as
painted clothing to signify
his accomplishments.

Through the documen-
tation of Catlin and Bod-
mer, Mato Tope became
the first well-known war-
rior-artist of the Plains.
Unfortunately, he suffered a
terrible death during a
smallpox epidemic that dec-
imated the Mandan in
1837, a tragic victim of one
of the introduced diseases
that killed millions of
Native Americans after the
arrival of Europeans in the
fifteenth century. (See also
Ewers 1981a, pp. 52–77.)

During the winter of
1833–34, Bodmer devel-
oped an especially close
relationship with Mato
Tope, who spent hours
watching him draw and
paint. Knowing of Mato
Tope's own artistic skills
and interest in the media
and techniques of European
visitors, Bodmer gave Mato

Tope a gift of paper, pencils, and watercolors. This
drawing of Mato Tope (on
the left) locked in mortal
hand-to-hand combat with
a Cheyenne chief is
described in catalogue number 148. A comparison of
the drawing with the ver-
sion painted on the robe in
Bern shows how Mato
Tope was able to use the
fine pencil line to indicate
small details like the colored fringes on his striped
leggings or the fine lines of
his hair and eagle-feather
headdress. The brush and
watercolors also allowed
him to suggest different textures and to show effects
such as his red body paint
or the complexly painted
leggings of his foe.
EMM

**Cat. no. 149, fig. a**
Karl Bodmer, Swiss (1809–93),
*Mato Tope, Mandan Chief,*
1834, watercolor on paper,
16½ x 11⅛ in, Joslyn Art
Museum, Omaha, Nebraska,
gift of the Enron Art
Foundation, R16

**Cat. no. 149, fig. b**
Karl Bodmer, Swiss (1809–93),
*Mato Tope, Mandan Chief,*
1834, watercolor on paper,
13¾ x 11 in, Joslyn Art
Museum, Omaha, Nebraska,
gift of the Enron Art
Foundation, NA117

149

**Warrior's shirt**
Upper Missouri, ca. 1840
Native-tanned leather; dyed porcupine quills; horsehair; red, yellow, black, and brown pigments
34⅝ x 22¼ x 23¼ in
National Museum of Natural History, Department of Anthropology, Smithsonian Institution, 403,344-A
Provenance: Gift of Robert L. Dwight, 1965

By the 1830s a strong market had developed for the purchase or trade of fine Indian objects, especially decorated and painted clothing. Then, as now, scenes of battle were most popular. This shirt was probably made by a Plains warrior-artist for that market.

The front of the shirt is decorated with two quilled rosettes, a square bib with hairlocks, a series of dark circles, and seven figures of warriors (three in the top row and two each in the second and third rows). The bodies of the men are drawn in the same conventionalized style used since the early years of the century and typified by the Lewis and Clark robe. But here the torsos and heads are detailed, as on Mato Tope's robe (cat. no. 148). Two of the men wear feather headdresses and one carries a shield. All of them have the typical range of arms— flintlock rifles, bows, arrows, and an axe. The marks painted along the lower border indicate the tracks of people and horses related to the battles described above.

The back also has quilled rosettes and battle scenes. Two warriors are in the top row and three in the row beneath. The man holding the shield with a horse painted on it has been wounded in the right shoulder by a knife, and his opponent has suffered a spear wound in the left thigh. In the bottom scene, the warrior on the right has been hit with an arrow in the right thigh but has managed to kill his two opponents with a rifle shot through the chest. The shoulders and arms of the shirt have expertly plaited quill strips sewn to cover the seams, and each sleeve is painted with black horizontal stripes, which were often used to indicate the number of coups the warrior had counted against his enemies.

This shirt was made by a man who proudly regarded it as a testimony to his achievements as a warrior; it was collected by a non-Indian who saw it as a cultural souvenir that supported his romantic notion of the noble savage. This well-preserved 1840s war shirt still has its original biscuit-colored hide, bright quills, and body colors. Older objects may be in excellent condition if they were properly stored, away from air pollutants and light, soon after being collected. (See Honour 1975b.)
EMM

150

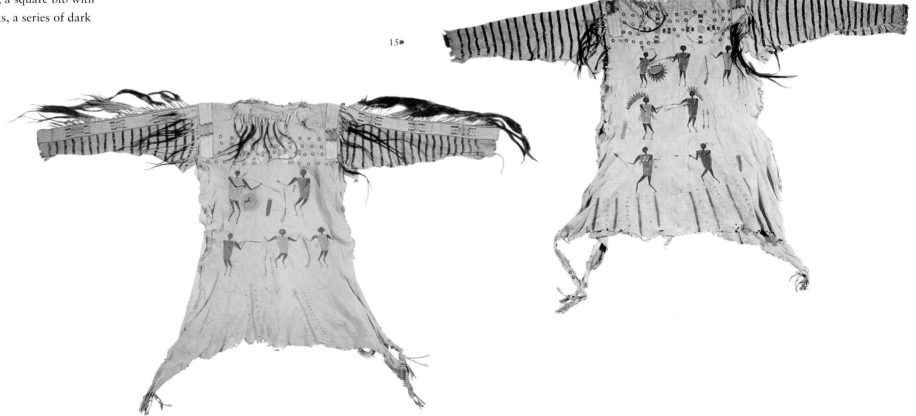

**Robe with war exploits**
Upper Missouri, ca. 1835
Native-tanned buffalo hide;
brown, red, yellow, and
green pigment
72 x 80 in
National Museum of
Natural History,
Department of Anthro-
pology, Smithsonian
Institution, 2130
Provenance: Transferred
from the War Department,
1866

This early example of a
warrior's biographical robe
is typical of the mid-1830s
style in its combination of
late eighteenth-century conventional figure design with
a greater use of detail in the
depiction of clothing and
weapons and a fuller use of
color and texture to define
body paint, accessories, and
horses. The robe is divided
into five horizontal zones in
which the action and narrative sequences go from right
to left, following the system
used by almost all Plains
artists. The forty-eight
human figures, two horses,
and one bear together make
up the historical events represented on this robe.

The image of a warrior
wearing a red deer-hair
roach headdress with a single eagle feather and a long
braid, a black and red shirt,
red breechclout, and black
fringed leggings appears
seven times; this man is
obviously the main character
in these exploits as well as
the person who painted or
owned the robe. In the top
row he is seen three times.
Starting from the right he is
shown with a pipe in his
right hand, signifying that he
was the pipe-carrier or
leader of the raid. He holds
a flintlock rifle in his left
hand and shoots a naked
warrior holding a rifle and a
ramrod in front of a set of
lodgepoles with no cover.
The wounded man collapses
backward with the force of
the bullet, an unusual, closely observed action for a
work of this period. The five
rudimentary half figures
next to the pipe-carrier are
part of a story that involves
the grizzly bear with a red
heart line two rows below,
which is tied to the figures
by a dotted line that denotes
tracks. The hero is next seen

with his pipe and rifle moving toward a small figure in
a long red frock coat. In the
third scene he stands with
bow and arrow, having been
wounded twice in the legs by
gunshots from two enemies,
including one carrying a
shield and a red and black
military society sash, who is
wounded with an arrow.

In the second row the
principal warrior is first
shown counting coup with
his bow on a warrior he has
just shot with an arrow. To
the left he shoots another
man with an arrow, and in
the row below he faces the
charge of a man with hair
bunched on his forehead
riding a large red horse with
a feathered bar under its
chin. The hairstyle and the
halter-decoration war medicine are both associated
with the Blackfeet (Keyser
1991, pp. 261–67). On the
far left of the row, the warrior has been wounded in
the stomach by a bullet as
he fights with his enemy. In
the seventh episode the warrior stands alone holding
his rifle and ramrod in his
left hand and his red-

bowled pipe and a quirt in
the other. The eight U-
shaped designs next to him
are horse tracks, representing horses captured in a
raid on the enemy.

The other scenes refer to
events in the lives of his warrior friends, who probably
belonged to the same military society and fought
together. The robe is unusual for the amount of detail
describing the clothing, body
paint, and military paraphernalia of the combatants,
including accurate renditions
of fox- or wolf-pelt headdresses, feathered shields,
military society sashes, and
the long European-style
frock coats that were popular trade items in the first
half of the nineteenth century. The eleven objects drawn
on the right side are quirts
surrounded by horse tracks
that symbolize war raids in
which the robe's owner was
a major participant or
leader.

EMM

151

**Tipi liner with scenes of battle**

Cheyenne (Tsistsistas),
ca. 1875
Native-tanned buffalo hide;
red, yellow, black, and
brown pigment
114 x 123 in
American Museum of
Natural History, 50.2/2641
Provenance: Collected by
Colonel J. M. Andrews,
1924

This large tipi liner, made
of several hides sewn
together, was hung from
the poles on the inside of a
lodge to block drafts and
act as a dew cloth. It is covered with seven rows of
battle scenes showing
Cheyenne warriors fighting
the Crow and other Indian
enemies. By the third quarter of the nineteenth century, Plains warrior-artists
had become increasingly
interested in using more
detail in the representation
of figures, horses, clothing,
and military equipment.
They also were developing
a style in which they depicted men and animals in full
action, described by a
greater variety of poses and
movements. In this robe
the pictorial organization
and sense of narrative are
basically the same as in
early robes, but the additional details make for a
more energetic scene of
action and convey more
factual information about
the participants. Large liners like this were probably
used in the tipis belonging
to the military societies,
whose members' exploits
were honored in the painted scenes of battle.

EMM

152

**Tipi liner with scenes of battle**

Cheyenne (Tsistsistas), 1904

Hide; red, white, brown, yellow, black, and blue pigment

74¾ x 135½ in

Field Museum of Natural History, Chicago, 96808

Provenance: Collected by James Mooney, Darlington, Oklahoma, 1904

This painting of battle scenes is half of a large tipi liner collected by James Mooney while he was working with the Cheyenne in Oklahoma. Mooney had been commissioning model painted shields and tipis to document the making of these objects, an important aspect of southern Plains life that had all but disappeared by the turn of the century. The extensive use of commercial paints, including white, which was not used by traditional artists, suggests that this magnificent example of Cheyenne warrior art was also created at Mooney's request.

On this half of the liner are five rows of painted figures representing battles fought with the United States Army and with enemy tribes. The top row probably represents the battle known as the Platte Bridge Fight, which took place in the summer of 1865 when the Cheyenne, Arapaho, and Lakota joined forces to attack the Immigrant Trail and the steady flow of whites through their territory (Grinnell 1955, pp. 216–29). On the right, four cavalrymen are retreating from the ambush set for them by the assembled warriors. Each is touched by a lance to indicate that he was killed in this part of the battle. Next to the cavalrymen, an officer and a warrior are locked in hand-to-hand combat. Their horses lie dead on the ground along with weapons and the Cheyenne's war headdress with buffalo horns and eagle feathers. At the left edge, the main body of soldiers stands in front of their tents firing to cover their comrades' retreat from the bridge.

The next three rows of figures represent individual fights between the Cheyenne and their Pawnee, Crow, or Shoshone enemies. The Pawnee can be identified by their scalp-lock coiffure and high-topped black moccasins. The Crow and Shoshone both favored the forehead crest hairstyle seen on the three men to the left of the third row. Also in the third row are scenes of a Cheyenne scalping a woman and of another woman killed by a lance. In Indian warfare there was often no differentiation by sex or age; all persons were liable to be legitimate enemy targets.

The bottom row shows events from the Battle of the Little Big Horn, in June 1876. On the right is a pile of soldiers' bodies lying where they died. The bows above them are signs of coups that were counted on them in the fighting. To the left is a scene of the terrors of war in which two Cheyenne hold down a wounded trooper to kill him. At the end of the row, the artist depicted one of the many acts of bravery that day: a Cheyenne Warbonnet man is wounded by a bullet in the hand as he charges into a group of riflemen.

This painted liner is the type that would have been used in one of the large double tipis made especially for the military societies.

EMM

153

One Bull
**Custer's War**
Hunkpapa Lakota, ca. 1900
Muslin; pencil; blue, red,
yellow, brown, and black
pigment
39½ x 69¼ in
Mandan Indian Shriners, El
Zagel Temple, Fargo,
North Dakota
Provenance: Collected at
Fort Yates, Standing Rock
Reservation, North Dakota

One Bull, a Hunkpapa warrior of Sitting Bull's band, was among the hundreds of Indian men who participated in the Battle of the Little Big Horn on June 26, 1876. Because it was the most serious loss of any United States Army engagement with the Plains Indians, the battle and the army commander, Major General George Armstrong Custer, became part of the legend of the American West. For many years afterward, this battle remained a source of anger and shame for the Seventh Cavalry and the white population in general. Newspapers across the United States decried it as a massacre and used it to stir passions against the Plains people.

By the turn of the century the pacification and subjugation of the Plains tribes were complete. White travelers and collectors showed a renewed interest in acquiring Indian-made objects, and the Indians themselves gained new confidence to portray historical events that had previously been too sensitive but could now be the subject of a popular item to sell to whites. This painting, entitled *Custer's War*, is a synopsis of the Battle of the Little Big Horn that includes descriptions of the events as recalled by the artist.

The five great camp circles of the principal groups of Lakota and Cheyenne are identified on the left, and scenes from the long day's fighting are distributed around the composition. In stark contrast to these vignettes of action are the more simply drawn rows of heads and torsos at the lower left, which represent Indians killed in the battle. An inscription at the bottom center says that the work was drawn by One Bull and witnessed by Gall and Tatanka Yotanka (Sitting Bull), two famous chiefs who were major figures in the event. (Another version of this painting by One Bull is in the collection of the Sioux Indian Museum, Rapid City, South Dakota.)

EMM

154

Standing Bear (Mato Najin) (1859–1934)

**Events leading to the Battle of the Little Big Horn**
Minneconjou Lakota, ca. 1899
Muslin; pencil; red, blue, yellow, green, and black pigment
72 x 72 in
Foundation for the Preservation of American Indian Art and Culture, Inc., Chicago, gift of Dorothy C. and L. S. Raisch
Provenance: Joe Bauxar; in-laws of Elbridge Ayer Burbank; probably collected by Elbridge Ayer Burbank, probably on Pine Ridge Reservation, South Dakota, ca. 1899–1903
References: Maurer 1977, p. 162, cat. no. 196

This painting of the events leading up to and including the Battle of the Little Big Horn is one of the most elaborate and visually complex historical narratives in Plains art. In his essay in this catalogue, Father Peter J. Powell gives a detailed account of the many scenes, which include an Elk Dreamers' Society Dance, Sitting Bull's Sun Dance, the Lakota encampments, and the battle itself (cat. nos. 156–166). Despite the number of figures and objects, the artist maintained a sense of visual clarity and readability that allows us to follow the narrative even though the painting connects events that took place over several weeks. The artist also incorporated elements of European representation, such as showing figures from different points of view and in a variety of poses, that make the crowd scenes easier to read in terms of relative space and distance.

EMM

155

Red Horse
**The Battle of the Little Big Horn**
Minneconjou Lakota, 1881
Paper, pencil, colored pencil
24 x 36 in
National Anthropological Archives, Smithsonian Institution, 2367-A
Provenance: Collected by Charles E. McChesney, M.D., Acting Assistant Surgeon, U.S. Army, Cheyenne River Reservation, South Dakota, 1881
References: Mallery 1889, pp. 563–66, pls. XL, XLIII, XLIV, XLVII

Red Horse was a Minneconjou warrior who fought in the Battle of the Little Big Horn. This single most famous military event in the history of the Indian wars was part of a larger campaign designed to sweep the free tribes from the Plains. In the spring of 1876 three army columns totaling about 2,500 men went into action in the large area that now includes southeastern Montana and the adjoining areas of Wyoming and North and South Dakota. Unaware that General George Crook's men had fought a hard engagement at Rosebud Creek, just a few days' ride south, Custer and about 500 men of the Seventh Cavalry moved toward the Little Big Horn River, or what the Indians call the Greasy Grass, because of activity reported there. On the morning of June 25, Custer approached the valley and saw an encampment of hundreds of tipis. In a fatal miscalculation, the experienced Civil War and Indian wars veteran underestimated the numbers he was facing and divided his troops into three groups. Three companies of about 115 men under Captain Frederick W. Benteen were sent off to scout the hills overlooking the Indian position. Three companies of some 140 men under Major Marcus Reno were ordered to attack the southern end of the village. Custer and his officers did not realize until too late that they were facing the largest Indian encampment ever recorded on the Plains, over 7,000 Lakota, Cheyenne, and Arapaho, including as many as 2,500 warriors, all of whom had suffered at the hands of the army. It was Custer and the Seventh Cavalry who had killed and mutilated so many of the women and children at the Washita in 1868, and the Indians had many scores to settle. Reno's troops were quickly routed, and when Benteen's men rode up they were desperately digging a defensive position on the hills above the river. Red Horse himself described this part of the battle: "The day was hot. In a short time the soldiers charged the camp. . . . The women and children ran down the Little Bighorn river a short distance into a ravine. The soldiers set fire to the lodges. All the Sioux now charged the soldiers and drove them in confusion across the Little Bighorn river. . . . On a hill the soldiers stopped and the Sioux surrounded them" (Mallery 1889, p. 565).

Meanwhile, Custer took five companies of about 210 men and rode north behind a ridge above the village. The troopers were widely scattered on the hill, and though they fought hard they were soon surrounded. Within an hour they had all been killed. The survivors of Reno's and Benteen's troops had established a position that they maintained despite repeated attacks throughout most of the next day. Then the attack was abruptly broken off as scouts reported large columns of infantry marching toward the villages. The battle was over and the United States Army had suffered its worst defeat in the history of the Western Campaigns.

In 1881, just five years after the battle, when it was still a very emotional issue, Red Horse was persuaded by Dr. McChesney to make the largest of the many pictorial accounts of the fighting. Red Horse produced forty-two large drawings that are generic descriptions of the action rather than accounts of specific events. The six drawings shown here are representative of the groups in the set, which includes five pages of soldiers approaching the villages (cat. no. 156), five drawings of tipis that represent the Indian encampments (cat. no. 157) (two tipis in this drawing are identified as belonging to the Yearling and Roman Nose), five scenes of Indians charging, five drawings of Indians fighting with cavalry (cat. no. 158), five drawings of dead cavalry horses, five of dead Lakota warriors (cat. no. 159), five of dead and mutilated soldiers (cat. no. 160), and six drawings of Indians leaving the battleground with captured horses (cat. no. 161). The whole set of drawings was sent by McChesney to Colonel Garrick Mallery, who was preparing his monumental study on the picture writing of the American Indian. In that book he published illustrations of ten of the drawings and devoted four pages to their explanation, including a long account of the battle given by Red Horse (Mallery 1889, pp. 563–66).

Red Horse was a talented and versatile artist who could indicate great numbers by filling the entire picture plane with tipis of similar scale (cat. no. 157) or with the outlined figures of mutilated bodies piled against the edges of the page (cat. no. 160). He also used descriptive details in an accurate and sensitive way, as in his careful descriptions of Indian shields, clothing, and headdresses. Red Horse's talents as a creative draftsman are best shown in the scene of battle (cat. no. 158), in which he created a complex yet comprehensible web of figures and action that gives a sensation of the excitement and confusion of battle.

EMM

156

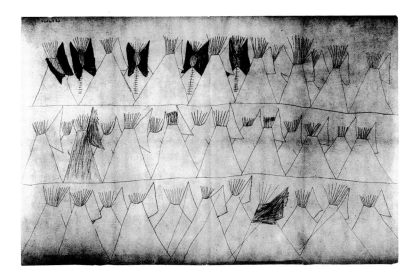

157

158

159

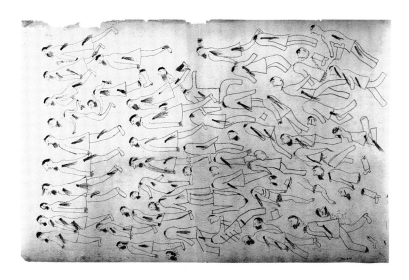

160

161

Yellow Nose (Hehúwésse)
(ca. 1852–after 1914)
**Four drawings of the Battle
of the Little Big Horn**
Cheyenne (Tsistsistas),
ca. 1885
Paper, colored pencil,
pencil, watercolor, ink
12½ x 7¼ in
National Anthropological
Archives, Smithsonian
Institution, 166,032
Provenance: Transferred
from the Bureau of Ameri-
can Ethnology; collected by
the Reverend H. R. Voth
from Spotted Wolf,
Cheyenne Reservation,
Darlington, Oklahoma,
before 1889
References: Powell 1981,
illus. pp. 537, 539, 541, 543

Yellow Nose was a Ute who
was captured by the Chey-
enne at the age of four and
adopted by the famous
chief Spotted Wolf. Yellow
Nose grew up to be "all
Cheyenne" and a noted
warrior leader. He was also
one of the most extraordinary painters of his time.

These four drawings are
selected from a ledger book
containing 106 drawings by
Yellow Nose, Spotted Wolf,
and others. What distin-
guishes Yellow Nose as an
artist is his ability to portray the frenzied action of
battle by depicting complicated movements as if they
were frozen in time.

The first drawing (cat.
no. 162) shows a Cheyenne
warrior who has been shot
while charging a group of
soldiers lying on the ground
in a defensive position. His
yellow war-horse has been
struck by three bullets and
has crashed to the ground
with blood gushing from its
mouth. The warrior,
wounded in the arm and
the side while taking his
German silver bridle from
the dead horse, begins to
walk away from the troops,
an act of bravery and control that was expected from
a shield-bearing warrior.

In the second drawing
(cat. no. 163) two
Cheyenne warriors show
their bravery by charging a
group of soldiers, whose
rifles are visible on the right

162

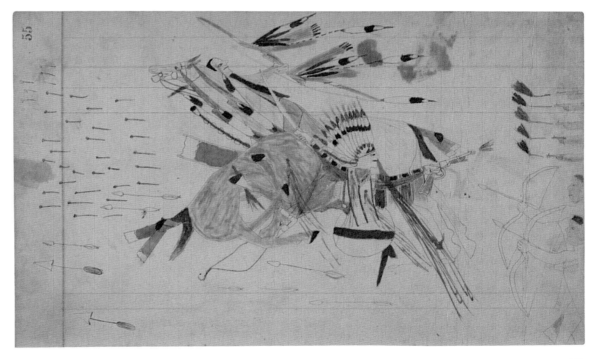

163

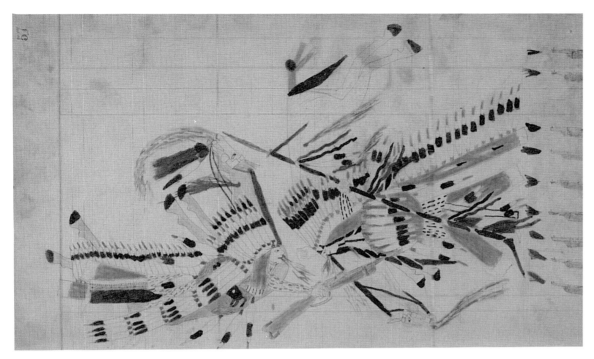

164

165

edge of the paper, and two Indians with bows and arrows, who represent the Crow and other Indian scouts who fought with the Seventh Cavalry. A war chief wearing an eagle-feather headdress and carrying a painted shield, a carbine, and a saber has been fatally wounded along with his horse. As they fall to the ground his companion charges back to the Indian lines brandishing his specially decorated military society bow as the bullets and arrows fly past him.

The third drawing (cat. no. 164) is the most challenging of the series. It depicts two Cheyenne warriors with eagle-feather headdresses and long feather trailers. They also carry sacred vision shields with elaborate feather decoration, which add to the complexity and visual texture of the scene of action as men and horses fall under a fusillade of soldiers' bullets. The warrior on the right carries one of the otter-fur-wrapped lances of the Elkhorn Scrapers Society. The man on the left is Yellow Nose, identified by the tadpole designs on his leggings. The

sense of action and movement is accentuated by the strong use of color and black accents that help animate the drawing.

The fourth drawing (cat. no. 165) illustrates Yellow Nose performing his most famous action of the battle, his capture of a United States flag and use of it to count coup on Custer's troops, who had dismounted and were fighting bravely on the hill above the river. According to Cheyenne oral history: "Yellow Nose came riding in among them. One trooper was carrying a flag. As he saw Yellow Nose coming, he jumped on his horse and started to run. Yellow Nose was too quick for him . . . he grabbed the flag out of the trooper's hand . . . he charged ahead, striking soldiers right and left with the flag, counting coup on them, touching the soldier horses as well, claiming them as his own. . . . He was a great man now, for he was first to charge in among these soldiers" (Powell 1981, p. 1024).
EMM

Yellow Nose (Hehúwésse)
(ca. 1852–after 1914)

**Portrait of a warrior woman**

Cheyenne (Tsistsistas),
ca. 1885
Paper, pencil, colored pencil, ink, watercolor
12½ x 7¼ in
National Anthropological Archives, Smithsonian Institution, 166,032
Provenance: Collected by H. R. Voth from Spotted Wolf, Cheyenne Reservation, Darlington, Oklahoma, 1889

War was a man's activity among Plains tribes, but there were a few women who actively participated in battles. This drawing shows one of these Cheyenne fighting women. She enters the field of battle wearing only a long red stroud breechclout tucked under a cartridge belt. Her long, dark hair flows behind her as she rushes the enemy holding a breech-loading carbine. This may be an image of Yellow Haired Woman (Heóvaee), who participated in the battle of Beecher's Island in 1867 and in the great fight with the Shoshone the following year (Powell 1981, pp. 134–35).

EMM

**Fight between Indians and the army**

Kiowa (Gaigwa)? ca. 1890
Paper, pencil, crayon
7 x 12 in
Texas Memorial Museum, 1988-21
Provenance: Acquired from Lilly Tips (wife of Carlos); Carlos Tips, Frankfurt, Germany; Dr. Edward H. Tips, Austin, Texas; collected by Hermann Schild, U.S. Indian Commissioner, Dakota, Arkansas, 1895

This drawing is from a book containing a variety of scenes of battle and camp life. It shows a group of six Indian warriors fighting four soldiers who have dismounted and are firing their rifles from a defensive position dug for protective cover. The artist has learned the European style of depicting figures from different angles to show their relative positions in the scene. This type of perspective drawing was an innovation in traditional Plains art. It began to be used as the native artists had more opportunity to see Euro-American imagery.

EMM

166

167

168

Attributed to Old Bull
(Tatanka´-Ehan´ni)
(b. 1845)
**Exploits of Old Bull**
Hunkpapa Lakota, ca. 1910
Muslin, ink, pencil
36 x 48 in
Mandan Indian Shriners,
El Zagel Temple, Fargo,
North Dakota
Provenance: Collected at
Fort Yates, Standing Rock
Reservation, North Dakota

This drawing depicts the exploits of a Hunkpapa Lakota man known as Old Buffalo or Old Bull. The story begins at the lower right corner and continues in a clockwise direction. The labeling and the lines that separate the different scenes were probably added by the collector in an attempt to make the story easier to understand.

In the coldest part of the winter, known as the "wood-cracking moon," in the year 1873, a group of Crow warriors, enemy of the Lakota, sneaked into Old Bull's camp and captured horses. Although the snow was deep, Old Bull and his friends formed a war party and pursued the raiders. After eleven days they reached the Crow camp; that night they quietly entered the camp and took fifty-three horses. They walked their horses all that night, on the way back to their village. This event is labeled "No. 1" on the muslin painting.

The next morning Old Bull noticed that the Crows were in pursuit, following the horse tracks in the snow. Old Bull's war party took up a defensive position in a rocky ravine, where they fought a long, hard battle. Many horses were killed, as shown in the scene labeled "No. 2." Old Bull's party included a fifteen-year-old boy who was shot in the back with an arrow during the battle. After the war party fought off the Crow, Old Bull made a travois for the boy and the group traveled many days to reach their village, which is seen in the area labeled "No. 3." During the trip Old Bull cared for the injured boy and became very close to him. When they finally reached the village, Old Bull found the boy's parents and left the boy with them. The next morning the boy died. From then on the boy was known as Wana´gli ya´ku, or Brings the Arrow, because he brought the arrow home in his body (Densmore 1918, p. 412).

Old Bull used many typical Plains conventions to tell his story. In scene "No. 2," he drew the Crows lined up with rifles to show that they were numerous, and all the injured horses are drawn with legs and neck outstretched. Other Hunkpapa artists used similar conventions in their drawings (cat. no. 171).
JDHC

No Two Horns (He Nupa Wanica) (1852–1942)
**Tipi cover with battle exploits**
Hunkpapa Lakota, ca. 1915
Canvas, paint
86 x 169½ in
Mandan Indian Shriners, El Zagel Temple, Fargo, North Dakota

No Two Horns was an accomplished Hunkpapa warrior and artist. He produced work in a variety of graphic media and also sculpture (cat. no. 78). His drawings record his own important military exploits and those performed by noted men of the Lakota. This tipi follows that pattern. It is painted with fifteen battle scenes that include horse raiding, counting coup, and other military activities. These exploits feature prominent Lakota such as Crow Ghost (Kangi Wanagi), Bear Heart (Mato Chante), Sitting Bull (Tatanka Yotanka), Two Bears (Mato Nopa), Grey Whirlwind (Wamni Yomni Hota), No Two Horns (He Nupa Wanica), Red Bow (Itazipa Luta), Red Hail (Wasu Luta), One Buffalo (Tatanka Wajina), and Chief Grass or Used-as-a-Shield (Waha´canka-ya´pi) and his son Pézi or Charging Bear (Mato-Wata´kpe). Some of these stories have been documented, while others have been lost in oral tradition.

No Two Horns painted his thunderbird shield on the rear of the tipi to signify that it was his. One battle exploit painted on the tipi has been documented by No Two Horns in ledger drawings. It shows No Two Horns wounded in the legs while firing his rifle and holding his shield (cat. no. 173). He is fighting beside his dying blue roan horse, which lies bleeding from eight wounds, its neck twisted to illustrate that it has been broken. The horse is painted with wavy power lines and has a medicine pouch tied around its neck. No Two Horns carved similar horse effigies with similar details including the bridle and the tongue hanging out of the side of the horse's mouth (cat. no. 170).

Another exploit shows his father, Red Hail, riding down an enemy who is on foot. This horse is also painted with wavy lines on the legs and neck and has a medicine pouch tied around its neck. Two arrows have been shot at Red Hail, one hitting his foot and the other going past him. Two wounds are shown on his foot, indicating that the arrow pierced completely through. Red Hail holds an empty quiver under his left arm and a bow in his hand. He holds a long staff with his right hand, which he uses to count coup on his enemy. The enemy warrior's hairstyle and face paint indicate that he is either Crow or Assiniboine.

He has two body wounds from Red Hail's arrows. He stands ready to fire another arrow as Red Hail counts coup on him.

Along the bottom border of the tipi another scene features an unknown Lakota man and One Buffalo. These two men are mounted on one horse, escaping from the enemy under a hail of bullets. One Buffalo is riding in the rear and has taken a bullet in the back. His horse lies dead of bullet wounds. To the right are three enemy men, aligned in profile, firing their rifles. Behind the enemy are horse tracks, indicating that they were mounted. One Buffalo apparently had his horse shot from under him, and his friend rode to his rescue. No Two Horns used the same conventions to show a similar exploit on a ledger drawing (cat. no. 174).

Painted in the lower left corner of the tipi is an exploit of Sitting Bull. Sitting Bull is seen here scalping an enemy, probably a Crow. The Crow bleeds from a bullet wound in the stomach. Below each man is his rifle. Behind Sitting Bull his horse awaits his command.

Red Bow's 1865 capture by General Alfred Sully's forces is documented on the left center of the tipi. Here General Sully is shown on a cavalry horse capturing Red Bow by grabbing his horse's reins. No Two Horns has illustrated the cavalry horse by detailing its horseshoes and the distinctive style of its cavalry saddle. Red Bow holds his bow and arrows as he is led away by General Sully.

General Sully and his forces were sent into Dakota Territory to arrest the Indians involved in the Great Sioux Uprising of 1862, which had left hundreds of whites dead in Minnesota. His forces indiscriminately attacked Indian villages throughout Dakota Territory. At the Battle of White Stone on September 3, 1863, 156 Indian men were taken prisoner. Many, including Red Bow, served sentences at Fort Snelling, Minnesota (Sully 1974, p. 178). It is doubtful that General Sully himself captured Red Bow. No Two Horns shows him taking Red Bow to illustrate that it was forces under his command that captured the Lakota warrior.

This tipi was made for the tourist market or for a white friend of No Two Horns. Traditional styles and techniques were used.

JDHC

No Two Horns (He Nupa Wanica) (1852–1942)
**Horse effigy**
Hunkpapa Lakota, ca. 1900
Wood, horsehair, leather, metal, blue and red pigment
34 in
State Historical Society of North Dakota, 1403
Provenance: Collected by the Reverend Aaron McGaffey Beede, Fort Yates, Standing Rock Reservation, North Dakota

No Two Horns was a Hunkpapa warrior who fought in many battles including the Little Big Horn engagement of 1876 (cat. nos. 156–161). An accomplished draftsman and sculptor, No Two Horns is known to have carved at least five horse effigies, including this one of a dying horse with its tongue hanging out of the left side of its mouth and five red triangles representing the fatal wounds received in battle. In the Lakota language this horse effigy was described as a *ta sunka kan opi wokiksuye*, or "sacred-memorial-of-his-horse-killed." Like other Lakota carvers, No Two Horns developed the elegant pictorial convention of having a horse's leg extend directly from the outstretched neck, thus using the front and rearmost parts of a galloping horse to represent its entire body. The object hanging from the bridle represents an enemy scalp, which was often tied to a war-horse as a trophy of battle.

EMM

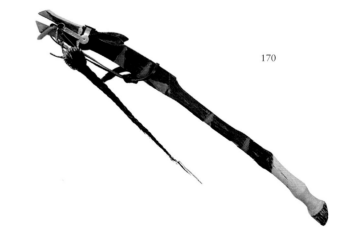

170

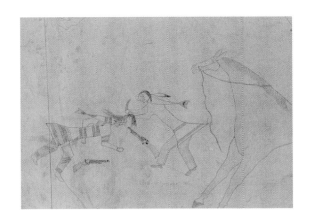

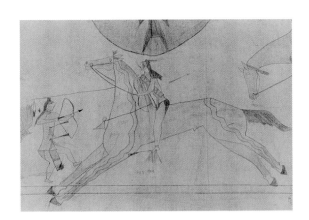

169

No Two Horns (He Nupa Wanica) (1852–1942)
**Six scenes of war exploits**
Hunkpapa Lakota, 1900–1915
Paper, pigments
8 x 10 in
State Historical Society of North Dakota, 9380-AA; 9380-W; 9380-FF; 9380-GG; 9380-JJ; 9380-QQ
Provenance: Collected by the Reverend Aaron McGaffey Beede at Fort Yates, Standing Rock Reservation, North Dakota

No Two Horns, son of Red Hail and cousin of Sitting Bull, was an experienced Hunkpapa warrior. At fourteen years of age he was a member of a war party against the Assiniboine, and at nineteen he killed his first bear, a high honor among Plains Indians. No Two Horns claimed to have served as a scout for Custer, although there is no official record that he did. When Custer went against Sitting Bull, No Two Horns went to his cousin's side. No Two Horns had two horses shot from under him in battle, one while fighting the Crow and the other in the Battle of the Little Big Horn. After Little Big Horn he escaped with Sitting Bull to Canada. In the 1880s he returned to Standing Rock Reservation, where he produced most of his art, working up until his death at the age of ninety (State Historical Society of North Dakota 1985).

No Two Horns was an accomplished sculptor and draftsman. His themes were usually his own warrior exploits, but he occasionally documented exploits of other noted men in his tribe. He made many effigy horse sticks in honor of the blue roan that he lost in battle. These drawings, which were found loose, probably came from a book that No Two Horns owned. Many of the scenes are similar and were probably drawn for the tourist market.

In catalogue number 171, No Two Horns has slipped into the camp of the Crow, enemies of the Hunkpapa, to capture a horse. Although No Two Horns illustrated only one horse, the tracks behind the horse may indicate that he actually took many horses. No Two Horns proudly displays his Kit Fox Society lance so all can see his society affiliation.

In catalogue number 172, No Two Horns, identified by his shield (cat. no. 7) counts coup, using his quirt, on an enemy, probably a Crow. No Two Horns has painted his face with wavy lines like those on his shield, which give power in battle. Power lines are also drawn on the neck and legs of his war-horse to give his favorite mount invincibility. The scalp tied

to the horse's head shows that the horse has achieved honor in battle. A well-trained war-horse runs the enemy down so the rider can count coup.

No Two Horns has his blue roan horse shot from under him and is wounded in the leg in catalogue number 173. His horse is bleeding from the nose and mouth, a clear sign that the wounds are fatal. No Two Horns falls to the ground holding his military society quirt (cat. no. 5) in his right hand and his rifle in his left. It is believed that these events took place during the Battle of the Little Big Horn against Custer. No Two Horns drew many variations of this exploit. He honored the blue horse in several effigy horse sticks (cat. nos. 78, 170).

No Two Horns is shown rescuing his friend in battle (cat. no. 174). The pompadour hairstyle and red face-painting on the figures on the right suggest that the ememy are Crow. Their vertical alignment indicates great numbers of them, and the horse tracks indicate that they were mounted. No Two Horns's comrade was injured when his blue horse, pictured at the right, was shot from under him. The horse tracks, beginning

at the lower left and moving clockwise, indicate the path that No Two Horns took to rescue him. No Two Horns rode back into the line of fire, represented by the rifle flash marks, to rescue his friend and was wounded in the leg while firing three shots at the enemy (note the three flash marks pointing toward the Crow). Once again, No Two Horns's horse has power lines on its head and legs and a scalp mounted on its head. The pouch around the horse's neck is probably filled with herbs, meant to give the horse supernatural protection in battle.

In catalogue number 175, No Two Horns shows Magpie, a Strong Heart Society warrior (cat. no. 177), falling to his death in battle. The Crow warriors are shown in a circle with flash marks coming from each man. This indicates that Magpie was surrounded by the Crow and caught in a hail of bullets. Magpie is identified by the bird drawn above his head. Name glyphs like this are commonly seen in Plains Indian ledger art. A line is usually drawn from the person's mouth to the glyph, as if the name were spoken. No Two Horns repeats the magpie's legs along this line to show that the magpie is flying out of Magpie as he dies.

In catalogue number 176, No Two Horns describes an exploit of his cousin, Sitting Bull, identified by his name glyph. During a battle against the Assiniboine, Sitting Bull, wearing a Strong Heart Society headdress, is impressed by the bravery of an Assiniboine. Sitting Bull runs into a hail of bullets and captures this enemy. Sitting Bull adopted this brave Assiniboine and gave him the name Little Assiniboine, which was later changed to Jumping Bull (cat. no. 181). A later collector is probably responsible for the "S. B." and "Hohe" written under the figures. The initials are for Sitting Bull, and Hohe is the Lakota word for Assiniboine.

JDHC

171

174

172

175

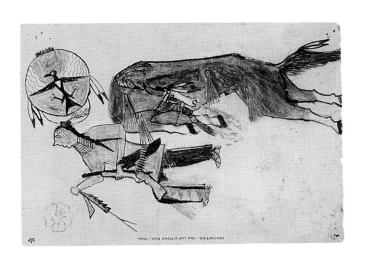

173

176

Sitting Bull (Tatanka Yotanka) (1834–90)

**Four autobiographical drawings**

Hunkpapa Lakota, 1882
Paper, ink, pencil, crayon, watercolor
8¼ x 13 in
National Anthropological Archives, Smithsonian Institution, 1929-B
Provenance: Collected by Lieutenant Wallace Tear, Fort Randall, Dakota Territory, 1882
References: Stirling 1938, p. 44 (nos. 12, 13), p. 45 (no. 14), p. 48 (no. 20)

Sitting Bull is history's most famous Plains Indian, known for his prowess as a warrior, his role as a chief and leader of the Hunkpapa, and especially among Indians for his strong medicine and spiritual power. His father, who was also known as Sitting (buffalo) Bull, was a sub-chief who schooled his son well. First noted for his ability in hunting buffalo calves at the age of ten, the young Sitting Bull accompanied his father on a war raid when he was fourteen and counted his first coup against the Crow. He took an active part in the Plains wars of the 1860s and fought in many engagements against the army and enemy tribes, especially the Crow. By 1870, Sitting Bull was given credit for sixty-three coups, an extraordinary testimony to his courage and tenacity. His reputation continued to grow until his coming onto the reservation in 1881. In the days between the battles of the Rosebud and the Little Big Horn, in June of 1876, Sitting Bull made a sacrifice at a Sun Dance that is described in Father Powell's essay. His vision foretelling the outcome of the Custer fight gained him more prominence among his people as a holy man and a seer. After the fighting, he led the western group of the camp on a march south, during which they were attacked by General Miles's troops. Sitting Bull and a large group then escaped to Canada, where they stayed until he surrendered at Fort Buford in 1881 under a promise of amnesty. This song was sung by Sitting Bull after his surrender: "A warrior I have been, now it is all over, a hard time I have" (Densmore 1918, p. 459).

These four drawings were made by Sitting Bull at Fort Randall just one year after his surrender. They are selected from a book of twenty-two drawings known as the Smith

177

178

179

180

Record, which illustrates and describes selected incidents in the great warrior's career, mostly against other Indians (Stirling 1938). In the first drawing (cat. no. 177), Sitting Bull shows himself wearing a horned headdress and a military society sash and carrying his vision shield painted with the figure of an eagle. The headdress is similar to headdresses worn by ranking members of the Strong Heart Society, which was created by Sitting Bull, Gall, and Crow King. In this scene of 1859 he charges a Crow warrior who has just wounded him in the leg. In Sitting Bull's own words: "Here is where I got wounded in leg and got off of horse and killed this man. No prisoners in that fight. This is 'Stand and Kill' Crow Chief" (Stirling 1938, p. 44). In the second drawing (cat. no. 178), Sitting Bull is thirty years old and is shown on horseback wearing his Strong Heart Society headdress and a coat made from Hudson's Bay blankets. Sitting Bull shows himself riding down a young Assiniboine warrior whom he took prisoner. Impressed by his bravery and character, he adopted this young man named Jumping Bull and brought him into his family. In the next drawing (cat. no. 179), Sitting Bull, age thirty-three, wears a war cape and, using his quirt carved in the zigzag shape of lightning, counts coup on a Minitari chief named Bull Head. Sitting Bull captured this man and then sent him home with presents as a gesture to make peace with the Minitari and the Assiniboine. In the last drawing (cat. no. 180), Sitting Bull wears an eagle-feather headdress and trailer as he kills a Crow warrior with his lance.

Sitting Bull's drawings are the slow, careful work of an unsure draftsman, but in several drawings like this one he took pains to depict a dark gray dappled horse that must have been a special favorite. The full, sleek flanks, the carefully combed mane and tail, and the alert face are all signs of his feelings for this beautiful animal.

EMM

211

Four Horns

**Five drawings from the life of Sitting Bull**

Hunkpapa Lakota,
ca. 1870
Paper, ink, watercolor
7¾ x 10½ in
National Anthropological Archives, Smithsonian Institution, 1929-A
Provenance: Collected at Fort Buford, Dakota Territory, 1870
References: Stirling 1938, p. 11 (nos. 7, 8), p. 19 (no. 24), p. 23 (no. 31), p. 33 (no. 52)

In 1870 Sitting Bull made a series of autobiographical drawings along with his adopted son, Jumping Bull. Fifty-five of them were then copied by another Lakota warrior-artist named Four Horns, a common name that was also used by Sitting Bull before 1857. A Yanktonai man later brought them to Fort Buford, where they were purchased by Assistant Surgeon James Kimball. Another set, now lost, was purchased at the same time, showing that as early as 1870 the Lakota were producing biographical drawings for sale and trade to whites, even though this was in a time of open hostilities.

A comparison of the first two drawings by Four Horns (cat. nos. 181 and 182) with their counter-

parts of the same events drawn by Sitting Bull (cat. nos. 178 and 179) shows that Four Horns closely followed the details of Sitting Bull's models, but he had a more graceful control of line and was more sensitive to the design of the drawing on the page. Whereas Sitting Bull signed his name in English in the Smith drawings, Four Horns used the more traditional name glyph of a drawing of a seated bull buffalo to signify his hero. In the first drawing Sitting Bull captures the young Hohe or Assiniboine warrior Jumping Bull, who would become his adopted friend. The second drawing shows Sitting Bull counting coup on a Crow warrior with his zigzag quirt, which is here decorated with a fox pelt, possibly a reference to the Kit Fox Warrior Society. The enemy is shown falling forward with a bleeding wound in his chest.

The third drawing (cat. no. 183) shows the artist at his best, depicting a scene of action and excitement from 1869. Sitting Bull wears his Strong Heart Society headdress and carries his eagle shield; his horse is decorated with a long scalp lock hanging from the bridle. They are shown charging into a group of Crow warriors

who had taken a defensive position behind some rocks, symbolized by the circle drawn around the figures. As Sitting Bull rides through a storm of bullets to strike the enemy with his bow, the Crow warrior fires a rifle into his face, but misses. Thirty Crow were reported killed in this fight.

The fourth drawing (cat. no. 184) illustrates an event that took place in June of 1863 when Sitting Bull engaged in a skirmish with a wagon train from General Sibley's command on the Missouri River near the mouth of Apple Creek. Sitting Bull charged the wagons under heavy fire; here he is shown counting coup on a wagoneer, who holds a long whip, and then making off with his saddled mule. In the final drawing (cat. no. 185) Four Horns shows Sitting Bull as a young man riding off with two horses captured in a raid. He uses the unusual technique of placing the Sitting Bull name glyph on the back of the second horse and uses a line running from the buffalo to the man's mouth to show their direct relationship.

EMM

181

182

183

184

185

186

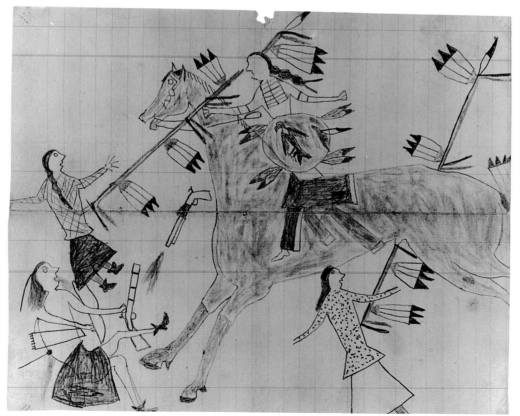

187

**Short Bull** (b. 1845)
**Battle scene**
Sicangu Lakota, ca. 1885
Paper, ink, crayon,
watercolor
7⅛ x 10 in
Mark Lansburgh collection,
Santa Fe
Provenance: Collected by
Natalie Curtis-Burlin, ca.
1922

Short Bull was a Sicangu
warrior active during the
Ghost Dance period. In
1890 he visited the prophet
Wovoka at Pyramid Lake,
Nevada, and returned to a
position of prominence
among the Lakota, who
were involved in the ceremonies of this important
pan-Indian religious movement. In this battle scene,
from a sketchbook of thir-
ty-nine drawings, Short
Bull depicts a Lakota warrior wearing a horned
headdress, a black shirt,
and leggings with black and
white beaded strips. This
warrior is falling from his
wounded horse as they
charge a group of three
Crow armed with bows and
a rifle. The horse, painted
with the wavy power lines
that the Lakota often used
as a sacred design, is bleeding heavily from a bullet
wound in the flank. Its neck
and head are carefully fore-
shortened to show the awk-
wardness of its fall as the
rider tumbles forward,
dropping his military society
lance wrapped in otter fur.
EMM

**Crazy Horse fighting the
Pawnee**
Oglala Lakota, ca. 1877
Paper, pencil
6⅝ x 8 in
The Denver Art Museum,
gift of Hugh R. Gibson,
John H. Gibson, and Mrs.
Warren Jones, 1986.581.4
Provenance: Collected by
George P. Wallihan at Fort
Robinson, Nebraska, 1877

Crazy Horse was a greatly
respected leader, warrior,
and medicine holder of the
Oglala, whose strength in
helping his people resist the
white invaders earned him
a great reputation. An
active and fearless war
leader, he was involved in
battles with enemy tribes
and the United States Army
from the 1850s until his
surrender in 1877. Crazy
Horse was known as a dis-
tant, spiritual man who
nonetheless was generous
and protective. He led his
Oglala warriors in many

major offensives, including the Little Big Horn, where he personally led a charge that cut off Custer's line of retreat.

After a long running fight against General Miles's troops, he was forced to surrender to save the lives of the people he had sworn to protect. Crazy Horse was placed under arrest on September 7, 1877, at Fort Robinson, Nebraska; he was shot and killed when he tried to free himself. This drawing shows him with an eagle shield and feathered lance attacking a Pawnee warrior and two women who wear the high-topped black moccasins associated with that tribe.

EMM

Yellow Horse
**Two scenes of battle**
Northern Cheyenne (Tsistsistas), ca. 1865
Paper, pencil, ink, watercolor
8 x 12 in
Foundation for the Preservation of American Indian Art and Culture, Inc., Chicago, gift of Dorothy C. and L. S. Raisch, Doreen Mimura Neog, and Florence Ely Hunn, Chicago, ca. 1930
References: Maurer 1977, pp. 164–65, fig. 99a and c

The Yellow Horse drawings are among the oldest warrior ledger drawings, which mark the introduction of paper as a material for the Plains artist. Yellow Horse is identified by the name glyph just behind his head. His considerable skill at drawing can be seen in these two scenes, which combine a sure depiction of human and animal form with an engaging sense of action. In the first (cat. no. 188), Yellow Horse is shown wearing military clothing captured in an earlier engagement as he charges in among a group of four cavalry troopers to count coup even as they fire at him with their pistols. In the second drawing (cat. no. 189), Yellow Horse is seen riding down a bearded white man who has fallen to the ground.

EMM

Attributed to Big Cloud
**Counting coup**
Cheyenne (Tsistsistas), ca. 1880
Paper, graphite, colored pencil
7 11/16 x 12 5/16 in
The Minneapolis Institute of Arts, gift of Jud and Lisa Dayton, 89.41

This is a rare early example of a Cheyenne warrior's drawing that shows an interior view as well as an indication of landscape. The warrior has dismounted from his horse, which has its tail tied up for war and is entering a house, where he counts coup on an Indian woman with his bow after having struck an Indian man and a white man with his quirt. His name glyph in the form of a mounted rider is shown just above his head. Beyond the roof and smoking chimney the artist has added a landscape with a distant ridge line covered with trees and brush.

EMM

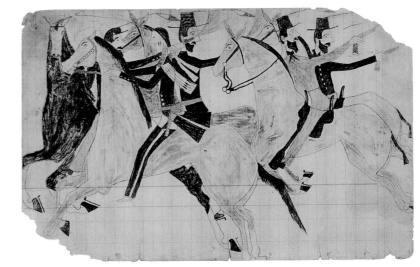

188

189

190

215

191

192

White Swan
**Two drawings of war exploits**
Crow (Absaroke), ca. 1895
Paper, pencil, watercolor
15 x 20 in
Seton Memorial Library, Philmont Scout Ranch, 84.2.3; 84.2.4
Provenance: Collected by Ernest Thompson Seton, Crow Reservation, Montana, 1897
References: Seton 1897, 6:84; Cowles 1982, pp. 55–57, figs. 4, 6

White Swan, a Crow warrior and a brother of Curley's, also signed on as a scout for the army. He was wounded with Reno's forces at the Little Big Horn. Although he was often an unsure draftsman, he became the most prolific Crow warrior-artist of his time, painting many scenes of Indian life until his death in 1905.

In the first drawing (cat. no. 191), White Swan shows himself on the ridge above the Lakota camp on the Little Big Horn River. He has dismounted and is kneeling with a telescope looking at the activity in the village. The second drawing (cat. no. 192) depicts White Swan shooting a Lakota warrior with arrows during the fight by the Little Big Horn. Both these drawings and the one done by his brother Curley (cat. no. 193) are typical of the Crow style, which is generally stiffer and more angular than the style of the Lakota, Cheyenne, Kiowa, and others.
EMM

Curley
**Portrait of a Grass Dancer**
Crow (Absaroke), ca. 1887
Paper, pencil, crayon, watercolor
12½ x 7¾ in
Montana Historical Society, gift of Charles I. Beason, X15.01.03
Provenance: Collected by Charles I. Beason at Raw Hide Creek, near Meeteetse, Wyoming, winter 1886–87

The Crow warrior Curley gained fame by being one of the Indian scouts who rode with Custer's Seventh Cavalry and survived the Battle of the Little Big Horn. This drawing was collected from him in the late 1880s as he was camped with about twenty lodges at a site south of the Crow Reservation. It depicts a man wearing the dance bustle associated with the Grass Dance, a ceremony popular with all the Plains tribes during the late nineteenth century.
EMM

193

**Warrior's robe**
Blackfeet (Siksika), ca. 1880
Native-tanned deerskin;
red, black, and brown
pigment
61 x 66 in
Royal Ontario Museum,
Toronto, Canada, 975.73.6
Provenance: Acquired from
the Provincial Museum of
Ontario (Normal School);
Edith M. Curzon (the col-
lector's daughter); collected
by Sarah Curzon, Blackfeet
Reserve, Alberta, Canada,
1862–98
References: Boyle 1904, pp.
55–57

The painting of biographical war scenes on hide and
later muslin was widely
practiced by Blackfeet
men, who continued to use
an archaic style of drawing
well into the twentieth century. The narrative scenes
on this robe are divided by
the long, undulating body
of a plumed rattlesnake,
also found on Blackfeet
painted tipis (Ewers 1981b,
p. 44, fig. 10). In the top
half a stylized figure with
outstretched hands that
resemble the style used in
petroglyphs is shown run-
ning off a herd of horses.
Scenes of combat between
two warriors on foot and
two sets of mounted war-
riors are joined on the left
by images of goods such as
arrows, bags, an axe, and
a powderhorn. The scenes
below the serpent include a
horned lizard, a man driving off ten horses, and
three battles involving
many warriors, among
them a group that has dismounted and taken up a
defensive position defined
by a circle drawn around
them.

EMM

194

Chief Washakie
(1804–1900)
**Autobiographical exploits**
Shoshone-Flathead,
ca. 1865–75
Native-tanned elk hide,
pigments
36 x 48 in
The Newark Museum, gift
of Mrs. F. F. Longley,
1950, 50.2330
Provenance: Collected by
Mrs. John S. Loud (wife of

Colonel John Loud), Fort
Washakie (?), Wyoming

Charlie Washakie (b. 1873)
**Exploits of Chief Washakie**
Shoshone, ca. 1890
Native-tanned deer hide,
pigments
64 x 80 in
Wyoming State Museum,
62.31.189
Provenance: Gift of J. K.
Moore, Jr., Cheyenne,
Wyoming

Chief Washakie spent his early years in Montana with the Flathead tribe of his father. After his father's death, he and his mother moved to Wyoming to live with her tribe, the Wind River Shoshones. Washakie's reputation as a warrior grew as he matured, and he became chief of the Shoshones by the late 1840s. Chief Washakie actively sought amicable relations with the whites by encouraging members of his band to help local white ranchers recover livestock and to help the local Mormon church. He allowed settlers traveling on the Oregon Trail safe passage through Shoshone territory and later signed a treaty giving Union Pacific Railroad the right-of-way through his land. Chief Washakie willingly agreed to settle his band permanently on the Wind River Reservation in 1869. He allowed his warriors to be used as scouts for the United States Army against the Lakota, Cheyenne, and Arapaho. His troops later helped the army pursue Crazy Horse, the famous chief of the Oglalas. After the death of one of his sons, Chief Washakie converted to Christianity. When he died in 1900, he was buried with full military honors at the Wind River fort, which was renamed in his honor.

His son Charlie assumed the responsibilities of Shoshone chief after his father's death, mostly greeting white dignitaries visiting the reservation.

Chief Washakie made approximately ten hide paintings, and Charlie probably produced twice as many. Chief Washakie's influence is often apparent in Charlie's hide paintings, both in style and in subject as the hide-painting tradition was passed from one generation to the next.

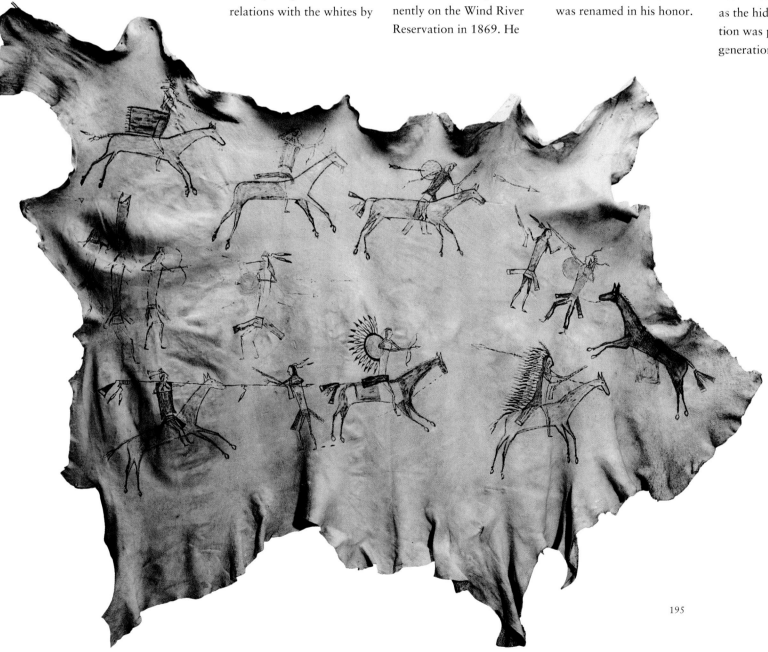

195

Chief Washakie's figures of horses and people are elongated, often with the bodies much larger than the legs. This style, adopted by his son, became a distinctive style of Wind River artists. Chief Washakie paid careful attention to details that were relevant to the subject. Charlie Washakie drew more realistically proportioned horses than his father, which might be attributed to Charlie's attending government school until the age of nineteen.

Charlie Washakie's hide paintings often featured accounts of his father's battle exploits. In the paintings shown here, Chief Washakie illustrated eight of his own exploits, and Charlie used five of his father's exploits. Three events are documented in both paintings.

On Charlie Washakie's hide painting, a collector drew numbers to identify each exploit. Number one shows Chief Washakie in battle against the Blackfeet when he was shot in the face with an arrow. This can be seen in Chief Washakie's hide painting in the center right. It is the best known of all Chief Washakie's exploits and the easiest to identify.

In another scene, Chief Washakie was in a battle against the Lakota and his horse was wounded. Chief Washakie, wearing a horned warbonnet and leading his horse, counts coup on and kills many Lakota. This exploit can be seen at the lower right of Charlie Washakie's painting and at the middle right on Chief Washakie's.

Finally, at the upper left, Chief Washakie shows a fight against the Arapaho, in which he fled and was pursued by the enemy. This is repeated in Charlie Washakie's painting, also at the upper left.

The horse on the extreme lower left of Charlie Washakie's painting is different from the others, but comparison with the horses in Chief Washakie's hide shows that the father drew horses in this style, and he might have added this one to his son's work (see Stewart 1991).

JDHC

196

George Bull Child
(b. 1891)
**The Baker Fight, 1870**
Blackfeet (Piegan),
ca. 1930
Native-tanned hide, ink,
paint
24 x 37⅝ in
The Denver Art Museum,
1985.106
Provenance: Collected by
L. D. Bax at Browning,
Montana, ca. 1930
References: Conn 1986,
cat. no. 90, p. 102

George Bull Child was one of the most active Blackfeet artists of the period from about 1920 to 1950. During that time he produced a variety of painted hides and muslins for trade and sale to the white collectors' market that developed with the increased tourism brought by the railroad. The scene depicted by Bull Child shows not the so-called romantic life of the Plains warrior but rather one of the many instances in which the United States Army attacked a civilian village, following the government policy of decimating the Indian population by killing them or driving them into captivity. This robe shows the Baker Fight, which took place on the Marias River in 1870. Cavalry troopers charge the Blackfeet village, represented by eleven tipis, nine of which are painted with dream visions and heraldic images. One has the blackbird design of the Kicking Woman family (cat. no. 22). The bodies of the massacred men, women, children, and even infants wrapped in their cradles lie dead on the ground. (See Ewers 1983, pp. 52–61 and Ewers 1958, pp. 236–53.)

EMM

197

New Bear (Above)

**Battle scene**

Probably Hidatsa (catalogued as Gros Ventre [Haaninan]), 1884
Paper, pencil, ink, commercial pigment
8⅛ x 25⅛ in
Eastern Montana College Library, Special Collections, Charles H. Barstow Collection of Indian Ledger Art, 1930.58
Provenance: Collected by Charles H. Barstow, Bureau of Indian Affairs clerk, at Crow Reservation, Montana, March 20, 1884
References: Heidenreich 1985

The Gros Ventre are a northern Plains tribe also known as the Atsina, or Gros Ventre of the Prairie, who are related to the Arapaho and have their roots in the northern Great Lakes area. Since 1889 the Gros Ventre have shared the Fort Belknap Reservation with the Assiniboine. This double sheet depicts a running battle between eight Lakota pursued by a group of Crow warriors. The scene is unusual in the number of combatants and the vivid blues, reds, yellows, and pinks New Bear used to color the warrior's shirts and horses. It is inscribed as being "drawn by 'Above' Captain of Crow Indian Police/Crow Agency. M.T. Territory, March 18th, 1884" and was undoubtedly made for sale to whites who were visiting the reservation.

EMM

198

White Bear
**Battle between the
Cheyenne and the
Shoshone**
Cheyenne (Tsistsistas),
1885
Paper, graphite, colored
pencil
16½ x 28¾ in
Montana Historical
Society, Museum
Collection, X61.16.03
Provenance: Gift of Mrs.
Frances Jurgens Tobie,
1961

In this unusually large
drawing a group of
Cheyenne warriors attacks
an enemy village. White
Bear has identified some of
the Cheyenne by name,
including Brown Bear,
High Wolf, Crow
Necklace, Small Shield,
Twins, Sack-to-Gather, and
Big Crow. They charge the
enemy through a storm of
flying bullets. The enemy—
Shoshone, Crow, or
Arikara—are shown with
their distinctive crested
coiffure as they lie behind a
ridge line overlooking their

camp so that only their
upper bodies are visible.
The notes indicate that
Twins was killed and
Brown Bear was wounded
twice in this fight. This
drawing might represent a
battle that took place in
November of 1876 when a
group of Northern Chey-
enne attacked a Shoshone
village. As described by
Powell, the Shoshone war-
riors fought from behind
breastworks and many died
on both sides, including
Twins, who was shot

through the chest (Powell
1981, p. 1051). The draw-
ing was made by White
Bear when he was incarcerated in the territorial prison
in Deer Lodge, Montana,
for burning a rancher's
house in retaliation for his
attack on their chief, Black
Wolf. After serving a year,
White Bear was pardoned
and released.
EMM

White Bear Woman and
Red White Buffalo
**Dress**
Mandan (Numakiki),
ca. 1884
Muslin, pigment
52 x 55 in
American Museum of
Natural History, 50.1/5352
Provenance: Collected by
Gilbert Wilson, 1909, from
Beaver, a Mandan woman
(a member of Three Band)
who was given the dress by
White Bear Woman
References: Wilson
1905–12, pp. 130–33

This dress was made by
White Bear Woman and
painted by her husband,

Red White Buffalo. It
shows the exploits of the
men in the wearer's family.
When it was collected, it
had been given to Beaver
by its previous owner. The
front of the dress records
the exploits of White Bear
Woman's brother, Lean
Bear, and the back records
the exploits of Red White
Buffalo. The five wound
marks refer to Lean Bear's
battle injuries. One wound
is drawn in a different
shade of red, indicating that
the bullet did not completely
pass through the body.

In the two exploits in
the top row on the front of

199

the dress, Lean Bear is mounted on a horse and chasing the enemy while under fire, indicated by the reverse horse tracks and flash marks. In the bottom row, Lean Bear is counting coup on two enemy warriors. In the exploit shown on the left, Lean Bear is the second to count coup on the enemy, as indicated by the line above the wounded enemy's head. In the exploit on the right, the enemy has had coup counted on him twice before Lean Bear, indicated by the two lines above his head.

On the back of the dress, the top row shows Red White Buffalo shot through both arms by the Lakota, waiting to be rescued by a friend on horseback. At the bottom left, Red White Buffalo is hitting a woman with his lance. On the bottom right, Red White Buffalo counts coup on a man who has been counted coup against twice before.

Red White Buffalo's exploits are also represented by abstract designs on the sleeve. The horseshoe marks around the sleeve indicate that Red White Buffalo had a horse shot from beneath him. The rows of inverted horse shoes signify horses captured. The vertical lines mean that he was a member of a war party, the horizontal lines that he was a leader of the party. Red White Buffalo thus led a total of three war parties and captured twelve horses but failed to capture three horses The horizontal bar with the anthropomorphic figures indicates that Red White Buffalo was a leader of a war party and killed many enemies (Wilson 1905–12, pp. 130–33).

JDHC

**Dress**
Lakota, ca. 1900
Native-tanned deerskin, glass beads
51¾ x 39⅜ in
Hearst Museum of Anthropology, The University of California at Berkeley, 2-10054
Provenance: Collected and donated by Mrs. P. A. Hearst, 1916

Among the Lakota, women whose relatives had been killed in battle had the privilege of wearing dresses depicting scenes of combat from the lives of those warriors (Densmore 1918, p. 367). At first the scenes were painted on hide and then on muslin dresses, but with the growing popularity of pictorial beadwork at the turn of the century, Lakota women began to create beadwork renditions of these special dresses. In this example the traditional turtle-by-the-shore-of-the-lake design is combined on the front with the image of a pair of warriors with eagle-feather headdresses, beaded vests, and Strong Heart Society banners riding on red and white pintos. On the back of the yoke is another pair, with headdresses and coup sticks on yellow horses. The use of warrior imagery on a reservation-period dress shows the continuing social importance of this theme to Plains women and their peer group communities.

EMM

201

200

223

**Vest**
Lakota, ca. 1890–1900
Native-tanned hide, glass
beads, cotton cloth, sinew,
cotton thread
18½ x 18¾ in
The University Museum,
University of Pennsylvania,
Philadelphia, NA 2421
Provenance: Donated by
Mrs. Archibald Barklie,
1915; collected by General
Frank C. Armstrong
References: Flint Institute
of Arts 1975, p. 145,
no. 195

**Vest**
Lakota, ca. 1890–1900
Native-tanned hide, glass
beads, cotton cloth, sinew,
thread
19⅜ x 20 in
Lisa and Jud Dayton
Provenance: Collected by
Alexander Petrie, Sheridan,
Wyoming, 1906

Beginning in the 1890s,
Lakota women began to
develop a new style of decoration in which whole garments and objects were
covered in beadwork. The
beaded pictorial vest was a
popular item worn by
Indian men (cat. no. 135)
and made for sale to the
growing market of white
collectors. Catalogue number 202 features an excep-
tionally animated scene of
four mounted warriors
counting coup on their enemies. Three of them wear
Strong Heart Society headdresses. This vest also has
renditions of United States
flag cavalry guidons, a popular theme in reservation-
period art.

The second vest (cat. no.
203) shows seven Lakotas
wearing eagle-feather headdresses and holding coup
sticks and weapons. On the
back of the vest, a Lakota
mounted on a yellow horse
is about to strike a Crow
with his saber—a specific
war coup uncommon on
pictorial vests.

EMM

202

203

David P. Little (Oyate Wachinyapi) (b. 1953)
**To Serve in Defense of Our Nation**
Oglala Lakota, 1989
Color coupler print
8 x 12 in
The Minneapolis Institute of Arts, the John R. Van Derlip Fund, 92.9.1
Provenance: Purchased from the artist

David Little is a veteran who served with the United States Marines during the Vietnam War. After returning home to Pine Ridge, Little began his work as a photographer portraying themes in contemporary Lakota life. This balanced still life of military gear features an eagle feather—a warrior's talisman of protection and spiritual sustenance—centered between helmet, M-16, and bayonet. American Indians have served in every war fought by the United States since the War of Independence in 1776. Service in the armed forces is considered an honorable and valued act. It is supported by the military societies that still exist among many Plains tribes, such as the Black Hills Veterans Society, an all-Indian group to which Little belongs.

EMM

**Warriors**
Cheyenne (Tsistsistas), ca. 1880
Paper, ink, crayon
7 x 8½ in
National Anthropological Archives, Smithsonian Institution, 154,064-C
Provenance: Received from Mrs. Mildred McLean Hazen, Washington, D.C., 1892

These four warriors are probably dressed for a military society function or some event other than war, because their horses' tails are not tied up and, though the men are armed, none of them is painted or carries war medicine. The mounted men have shields and lances decorated with eagle feathers and a cavalry guidon. The man to the right also carries a bow case and quiver on his back. He and one of his companions wear European hats hung with an eagle feather—a fashion common in the later nineteenth century. All of the men wear European cloth shirts, have woolen blankets folded around their waists, and wear cloth leggings. In the late eighteenth and early nineteenth centuries, the adoption of European goods was often driven by the desire to own objects of status that were rare and therefore desirable. But the use of these goods soon increased as they became more varied and readily available through trade. When availability was combined with the severe loss of game and therefore of hides, people turned to cloth clothing and used their traditional hide costumes only for special occasions and ceremonies. The one major exception was moccasins, which continued as the favored footwear of men and women.

EMM

204

205

Herman Red Elk (1918–86)
**Robe with biography of a Lakota warrior**
Yanktonai Lakota, 1965
Buffalo hide, earth pigments
69 x 80 in
U.S. Department of the Interior, Indian Arts and Crafts Board, Sioux Indian Museum and Crafts Center, Rapid City, South Dakota, R-67.4.1

Provenance: Commissioned by the lender, 1965

Herman Red Elk was born on the Fort Peck Reservation in Poplar, Montana. After graduation from the Chemawa Indian School in Oregon he joined the army and served during World War II. He attended workshops at local schools and studied with Oscar Howe at the University of South Dakota in 1964 and 1965. In 1963–64 he worked on a project researching the techniques and materials of traditional Plains painting on hide, using bone brushes and earth pigments prepared in the old ways. He was also active as a teacher working with the Sioux Indian Museum from 1969 to 1985. In describing his work as an artist, Red Elk said, "I enjoy painting; trying to recapture and preserve the very early traditions of our Sioux of the Plains—their religion, their ceremonies, and their many ways of expressing themselves in their various art media."

This hide is Red Elk's version of the autobiography of George Saves Life, with scenes of war, horse capture, courting, and an Elk Dreamers' Dance.
EMM

206

Martin Red Bear (b. 1947)
**Akicita Wasté (Good Soldier)**
Oglala Lakota, 1991
Acrylic, canvas
36 x 36 in
The Minneapolis Institute of Arts, the John R. Van Derlip Fund, 91.96
Provenance: Purchased at Northern Plains Tribal Art exhibition, Sioux Falls, South Dakota, 1991

Martin Red Bear was born on the Rosebud Reservation and went to school on the Pine Ridge Reservation, where he now treaches humanities and art at the Oglala Lakota College. In 1969, he entered the army and there got his first experience in painting. Red Bear served with the Fifth and Fourth Infantry Divisions, during his tour of duty in Vietnam. *Akicita Wasté* (Good Soldier) is his tribute to the men and women who served in the armed forces during the Vietnam War. Red Bear used details to give information to the viewer, just as the nineteenth-century warrior-artists did in their drawings and paintings.

As interpreted by the artist, the top of the painting is formed by the sacred hoop that represents the continuity of life. It is decorated with the insignia of units from the five branches of the armed forces that served in Vietnam. The center of the circle is divided vertically, with an American flag on one side and on the other the symbol of the POWs (prisoners of war) and MIAs (missing in action) that many feel are still unaccounted for. A faceless soldier holding an M-16 rifle represents all the men who fought in the war. The hoop is flanked by star quilt designs, representing beauty and life, and hung with four feathers painted yellow, black, red, and white, which honor the four directions and the four races of humanity that fought in the war. Below the hoop is a buffalo skull, an essential element of Plains sacred ceremonies. The top of the skull is marked by a line of animals and dancers. Figures of a buffalo (the giver of life), a bald eagle (America) and a golden eagle (the Indian), and a bear (courage and bravery) are interspersed with four dancing warriors adorned with eagle feathers. On their shields are the insignia of the four airborne units that fought in the war. From left to right they are the 82nd Airborne Division, the 173rd

Airborne Brigade, the 101st Airborne Division, and the Special Forces Airborne. Below these are two warriors on horseback, who represent the 1st Cavalry Division (on the left) and the 11th Armored Brigade (on the right). The shields on the buffalo skull honor the many support units, such as supply, engineers, and medical.

In combining traditional Indian symbols with modern military iconography, Martin Red Bear has made a powerful contemporary statement of an old cultural theme—the honoring of the warrior. "As far back as Lakota history tells us," he says, "we as Lakota people have always honored our warriors. Like all American tribes we still pay a special respect to our soldiers. In this painting honor is given to all who served during the Viet Nam Era. We were all a mixture of cultures and became as one. The honor that is shown in the painting *Akicita Wasté* is given from a cultural, aesthetic and a sincere personal point of view." EMM

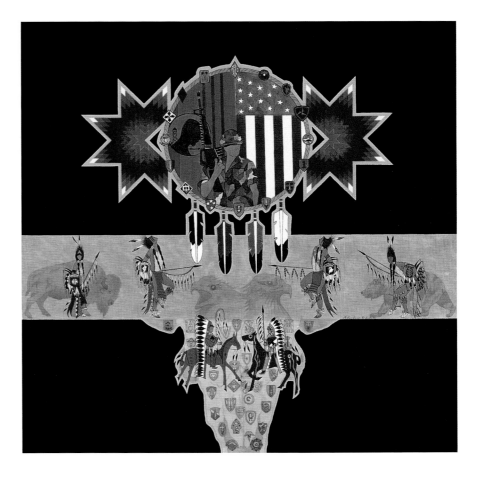

207

208

Dixon Palmer (Tsain-sah-hay) (b. 1920)
**Little Bluff tipi**
Kiowa (Gaigwa), 1992
Canvas, paint
18 ft (diam)
The Minneapolis Institute of Arts
Provenance: Commissioned for the exhibition

Dixon Palmer was born in Anadarko, Oklahoma. At age twelve he began his involvement as a traditional dancer and costume maker. After serving in combat with the Forty-fifth Division in World War II, he returned to Oklahoma to continue his work as a dancer, winning national competitions. He painted his first tipi in 1955 and made his first copy of the Little Bluff tipi in 1973. Little Bluff (Tohausen) is revered as the most famous of the Kiowa chiefs. A distinguished warrior and diplomat, he died in 1866 after serving as head chief of his people for thirty-three years. Little Bluff kept what is regarded as the first Kiowa picture calendar, or winter count, which he drew on a buffalo hide.

According to James Mooney, this battle tipi was the best-known painted tipi among the Kiowa at the turn of the century (Ewers 1978b, p. 14). The design was given to Little Bluff by Sleeping Bear, a Cheyenne leader, as a gift to mark the negotiation of a lasting peace between the two tribes in 1840. In the fall of 1864, Little Bluff gave the rights to this design to his nephew, who was also known as Little Bluff. He and his family used the tipi for years and renewed it several times. Around 1881 the second Little Bluff gave the right to renew the tipi to one of his sons, who continued to live in it until the father's death in the winter of 1891–92. By that time, the painting was almost worn away, and the lodge was considered to be the last painted tipi in the tribe. A model of it was made for James Mooney by Charley Ohettoint, a son of Little Bluff II, who had been one of the warriors imprisoned at Fort Marion from 1875 to 1878. Sometime between 1916 and 1918 Ohettoint also made a full-scale version for his family's use, the last version made before Palmer's effort in 1973 for the Museum of the Southern Plains exhibition "Painted Tipis by Contemporary Plains Artists."

The tipi is divided into two sections, one with stripes and the other with representational images. The yellow stripes were on the tipi when it was received from the Cheyenne and may be references to battle honors. The alternating black stripes were added by Little Bluff to honor fifteen successful war expeditions that he led in which enemy scalps were taken without loss to his Kiowa warriors. Black is the traditional color of victory for the Plains tribes, who painted their faces black during celebrations of achievement in war. The series of twelve tomahawks hung with eagle feathers was added by Heart Eater, a Kiowa friend of Little Bluff's who died in 1853, a great warrior known for his many coups using the tomahawk. The eight lances decorated with red cloth and eagle feathers represent coups made by another warrior, Sitting-On-A-Tree, who was also a contemporary of the Kiowa chief. The upper portion of the north side of the tipi cover (the door always faces east) was reserved for the image of a war event in which the Kiowa were surrounded by their enemies but still managed to escape. This scene, which was changed each time the tipi was remade, always consisted of a single warrior encircled by the enemy. The large battle scenes on the main section of the north side were also changed with each renewal, to represent important achievements in the continuing military history of the tribe. The original tipi was made of the tanned hides of fourteen buffalo and had twenty-two poles. The first

Little Bluff was said to renew this famous lodge each year after the summer hunt (Ewers 1978b, pp. 13–17). Tipis painted with battle scenes were also used by the Lakota and other Plains tribes.

A version of this famous tipi, painted by Dixon and George Palmer in 1974, is used by a contemporary Kiowa Veterans group known as the Kiowa Black Leggings Society (*ton-kon-gah*). The north side contains battle pictures that illustrate the war records of men who fought in World War I, World War II, Korea, and Vietnam, using modern equipment such as tanks. It is a powerful reminder of the vital role still played by the military society in the life of the Plains warrior.

EMM

208

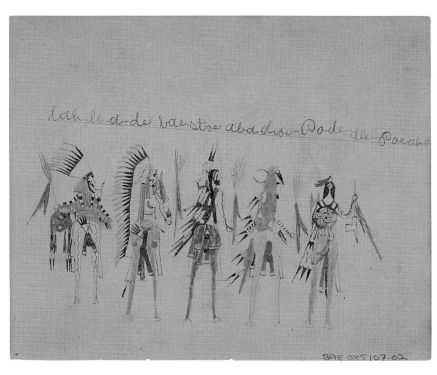

209

210

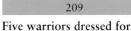

**209**

**Five warriors dressed for battle**

Cheyenne (Tsistsistas),
ca. 1880
Paper, ink, colored crayon
7 x 8½ in
National Anthropological
Archives, Smithsonian
Institution, 154,064-C
Provenance: Received from
Mrs. Mildred McLean
Hazen, Washington, D.C.,
1892

All Plains tribes had military societies whose members acted as tribal police, maintaining order in camp, on the march, and especially during the buffalo hunt. The warriors of these groups were bound together by rules and strong feelings of comradeship and mutual support. Each society had its own organization, dances, regulations, dress, and emblems of rank. Grinnell noted that there were six warrior societies among the Cheyenne and that most, but not all, of the able-bodied men of the tribe belonged to one or more of them. These societies were the Kit Fox (*wóhkseh'hetaniu*), the Elkhorn Scrapers (*him'oweyuhk'is*), the Dog Soldiers (*huta'mita'ni*), the Red Shields (*mahohe'was*), the Crazy Dogs (*hota mi massau*), and the Bowstrings (*him'a tauo'his*) (Grinnell 1923, 2:48).

The artist used the interesting method of showing the five warriors from the rear, an unusual approach that allowed him to depict the war regalia worn by each man. The figure on the right is the leader of the group, since he carries the pipe. He has a shield on his back and war medicine in the form of a bird attached to his hair, and lightning lines are painted down each arm. His horse's tail has been tied up for war with a long piece of red stroud cloth having the characteristic undyed white edge. While the leader gazes ahead, his four companions look at him. They all wear their own personal regalia, which includes an animal-skin headdress that could be a Kit Fox emblem, a sash that could be a Dog Soldier sash, eagle-feather headdresses, a war shirt, and another shield. Their horses' tails are tied up, as was the custom, and the two horses on the left are painted with sacred protective designs. The four warriors all carry a short branch, perhaps the willow coup sticks used in the sham battle to capture the central pole of the Sun Dance Lodge, an event documented among the Kiowa by Silverhorn (cat. no. 116).
EMM

**210**

Walter Bone Shirt
**Warrior in a military society dance**
Lakota, ca. 1880
Paper, ink, colored pencil
5 x 7¾ in
Private collection

This drawing shows a Lakota warrior performing in a military society dance. He wears a headdress with buffalo horns and eagle feathers that could be from the Strong Heart Society. In one hand he carries a painted baton cut with the zigzag line of lightning and in the other a pole with a scalp and two eagle feathers. The bottom half of his face is painted with the head of a buffalo, and lightning lines are painted down his arms and legs. These are the same type of lines painted on Lakota war-horses and seem to be associated with bringing power and endurance in battle (cat. no. 172).
EMM

**Two scenes from a military society dance**
Arapaho (Inuna-ina),
ca. 1880
Paper, graphite, colored pencil
7¾ x 12⅜ in (each sheet)
Gaylord Torrence

**Women dancing with military costumes**
Arapaho (Inuna-ina),
ca. 1880
Paper, graphite, colored pencil
7¾ x 12⅜ in
Gaylord Torrence

The double-page drawing shows members of a military society dancing in front of their lodge. Many of the warriors carry objects of rank, such as long poles painted or wrapped in cloth and hung with eagle feathers, and they shake ring-shaped rattles to accompany their singing. Two of their leaders are shown on horseback directing the movements of the dancers as they proceed through the village. The direct frontal view captures the full effect of the dance as the men fulfill one of their important ceremonial obligations.

On the single sheet are six women holding or wearing military society emblems or weapons belonging to male relatives killed in battle. In this way the women join in the ceremonies of the society and gain honor for themselves and their families by respecting the achievements of those who gave their lives as soldiers of their people.
EMM

211

212

213

214

215

216

**Eagle-feather headdress**
Arapaho (Inuna-ina),
ca. 1890
Eagle down and owl feathers, hide, glass seed beads, hair, ermine hide, wool, sinew, cotton cloth
12 x 39 x 14 in
Peabody Museum of Archaeology and Ethnology, Harvard University, 49-44-10/32675
Provenance: Gift of Henry Seton, 1945–50; collected by Seton, 1935–36

The eagle-feather headdress has been depicted in many forms in Plains Indian art (see the essay by George Horse Capture in this catalogue). Indians wearing a "feather head-dress" first appeared in European art as early as the sixteenth century (Honour 1975a, p. 4). This image of the Plains Indian has become synonymous with Indians of every region.

In the traditional Plains world, the eagle-feather headdress was worn only by men of accomplishment and respect. To wear the feathers of the eagle, the greatest bird of all, is to honor the bird and to honor the wearer. Truly great men wear headdresses that have trailers of eagle feathers attached to the back. When a headdress with trailer is worn, the energy of the eagle is felt not only on the head but throughout the entire body.
JDHC

**Eagle-feather headdress**
Blackfeet (Siksika),
ca. 1890
Eagle feathers, deer hide, glass beads, wool fabric, sinew
24 x 22 x 25 in
Peabody Museum of Archaeology and Ethnology, Harvard University, 61-1-10/39010
Provenance: Gift of William W. Howells, 1961; collected by Amelia Elizabeth White (?)

Feather headdresses usually have a strip directly below the feathers and above the forehead that is decorated with a beaded band. Usually geometric patterns are found on this band and occasionally pictorial images. Beaded onto this warbonnet's band are a star and a horned figure, probably a buffalo.

When a man wearing a warbonnet like this one comes toward the viewer, it looks as though the feathers are standing on end, completely around the head, making a circle. This image of the warbonnet has been transferred to other media in Plains Indian art (see the essay by George Horse Capture, in this book).
JDHC

Attributed to No Two
Horns (He Nupa Wanica)
(1852–1942)

**Buffalo Society headdress**

Hunkpapa Lakota, 1900
Bison hide, horn, raptor
feathers, red pigment
40 x 16 in
State Historical Society of
North Dakota, 10353
Provenance: Collected by
David Fuller at Standing
Rock Reservation, North
Dakota

In many Plains tribes, men
who had visions or dreams
of the buffalo could join
the Buffalo Society. These
men wore headdresses
made of a buffalo head and
hide and imitated the buffalo while reenacting their
vision in the Buffalo Dance
(Densmore 1918, p. 285).
In most of these cere-
monies, a young man
"hunted" one of the buffalo men, ritually killed him,
and painted him red to
symbolize the blood of the
animal (Wissler 1912b,
p. 91).

JDHC

**Moccasins**

Mandan (Numakiki)?
ca. 1860–80
Native-tanned hide, porcu-
pine quills, cotton, cork
9¼ x 2½ in
State Historical Society of
North Dakota, 9951
Provenance: Collected by
Daniel Webster Longfellow
at Fort Berthold
Reservation, Montana
(Longfellow was storekeep-
er at the Fort Berthold
Reservation from 1876 to
1880)

The sunburst motif associated as an honor symbol
with eagle-feather head-
dresses appears with some
frequency on quilled and
beaded moccasins, but the
depiction on these moc-
casins of a full headdress
with feathered trailer is
unique. The artist displayed
particular skill in the fine-
ness of the quilling and in
the composition, placing
the elongated motif on the
vamp of the shoe with evident care.

    Sized to fit a man's feet,
the moccasins were proba-
bly made by a female relative of the wearer in recognition of the honor his
deeds had brought to the
family. They show evidence
of much use, and the soles
were recovered with cork at
a later date.

LL

Red Paint family

**Honor pouch**

Oglala Lakota, ca. 1940
Hide, cotton thread, porcu-
pine quills, sinew, ribbon,
seed beads, ink
18¼ x 10½ in (with fringe)
South Dakota Art Museum,
gift of the Reverend and
Mrs. Frank Thorburn,
85.1.59
Provenance: Given to the
Reverend Frank M.
Thorburn, Episcopal
Mission, Pine Ridge
Reservation, South Dakota,
by the Red Paint family
References: Hail 1983, p. 41

Plains Indians from all generations consider serving
their community or country
by going to war a high
honor. When a family
member goes to war and
returns, the family offers
tribute to the soldier, not
by receiving gifts but by
giving gifts in his honor. In
the old days, it was com-
mon to give horses away
when a young man
returned from his first war
party. At the first large
gathering, this young man
would receive his manhood
name, appropriate to his
deeds of valor (Densmore
1918, p. 362).

When Amos Red Paint
returned from World War
II, a victory dance was held
for the returning veterans.
The Reverend Thorburn
received this pouch from
the Red Paint family so that
he would remember Mr.
Red Paint and honor him.
The upper portion of the
pouch has the letter *V*
beaded onto it, a reference
to the World War II slogan
"Victory." On the other
side of the pouch is a
quilled Christian cross.
The Red Paint family were
members of Mr. Thorburn's
church.

JDHC

218

217

**Bow**
Lakota, ca. 1880
Wood, sinew
49 in
State Historical Society of
North Dakota, 81.32.4

Pretty Bear
**Four arrows**
Yanktonai Nakota,
ca. 1920
Wood, feathers, metal
22 in
State Historical Society of
North Dakota, 5426.1–4
Provenance: Collected from
the artist, Cannon Ball,
North Dakota, 1930

Usually long bows were
used for warfare and
shorter bows for hunting.

When George Catlin visited
the Plains in the 1840s he
commented that when
Plains Indians were armed
with bow and arrows there
was "no set of mounted
men of equal numbers so
effective and invincible in
this country" (Catlin 1857,
pp. 33–34). It was said a
skilled Lakota man could
shoot five arrows before
the first arrow hit the
ground. In battle, the bow
was quicker and more
effective than the muzzle-
loader and the cap and ball
revolver (Hamilton 1972,
pp. 108–9).

Bows were also used for
hunting buffalo at close

range. The hunter, mount-
ed on his best horse, would
ride close to the buffalo
and fire arrows into the
animal. It was said that a
"good" bow would send
the arrow into the buffalo
so that the tip would stick
into the flesh. An "excellent" bow would send the
arrow deep into the animal
so that only the feathered
end would stick out, and a
"fine" bow would send the
arrow completely through
the animal.

Plains bows were usual-
ly made from cherry, plum,
or crab apple wood. The
bowstring was made from
buffalo bull sinew, twisted
tightly and then dried
(Densmore 1918, p. 427).
JDHC

No Two Horns (He Nupa
Wanica) (1852–1942)
**Kit Fox Society bow lance**
Hunkpapa Lakota, 1900
Wood, eagle feathers, steel,
red and blue cotton
64½ x 3 in
State Historical Society of
North Dakota, 10491
Provenance: Collected by
David Fuller at Standing
Rock Reservation, North
Dakota

The bow lance was the
trademark of the Kit Fox
Society of the Hunkpapa,
named because of the
"active and wily" character
of its members in battle
(Wissler 1912b, p. 14). It is
a decorated bow with a

spearhead at one end. It
was used as a weapon, a
coup stick, and a society
banner. When in battle,
society members often
drove the bow lance into
the ground and fought by
it, knowing it had powers
to protect them (Powell
1981, p. 990). No Two
Horns was a member of the
Kit Fox Society. Although
associated primarily with
the Kit Fox Society, bow
lances were used by other
Plains military societies as
well.
JDHC

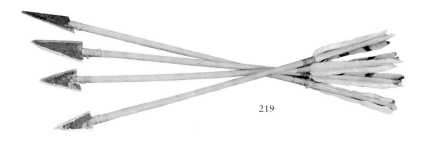

219

219

220

White Eagle (Wanbli Ska)
**Soldier society lance**
Hunkpapa Lakota,
before 1933
Paint, brass tacks, wood,
horsehair, cloth, feathers,
string
65½ x 21 x 1¼ inches
American Museum of
Natural History, 50.2/3440
Provenance: Collected by
H. Scudder Makeel from
Red Woman (Winyan Luta)
(89 years old) at Wood
Mountain, Saskatchewan,
Canada, 1933; given to
Red Woman by her brother
White Eagle

White Eagle belonged to
two military societies, the
Badger Society and the
Sotka Yuha Society. After
White Eagle retired from
the Badger Society, its
members allowed him to
keep this lance in remem-
brance of his brave deeds in
battle.

This type of lance,
sometimes called a crooked
lance, was used by many
military societies across the
Plains. In battle, bearers of
such a lance would use it to
count coup on the enemy.

Today, the tradition of
using a crooked lance as
military society identification is gone. The crooked
lance has instead become a
Native American "flag"
symbolizing the whole of
Native American tradition.
In powwows across the
Plains, the opening cere-
monies feature the crooked
lance and the United States
flag, carried together as
symbols of honor that
reflect the Native Ameri-
cans' dedication to their
country and to their people.
JDHC

**Drumstick**
Lakota, ca. 1875
Wood, native-tanned deer-
skin, porcupine quills
23¼ x 1¼ x 1¼ in
Academy of Natural
Sciences, Philadelphia, on
loan to The University
Museum, University of
Pennsylvania, Philadelphia,
L84-2368
Provenance: Collected by
Amos H. Gottschall near
White River, South Dakota

**Shell gorget**
Lakota, ca. 1885
Shell, hide, metal, pigment
3¾ in (diam), 1½ in deep
The University Museum,
University Pennsylvania,
Philadelphia, NA 4301
Provenance: Gift of Lydia
T. Morris, 1915; collected
in 1885

Wounds received in war-
fare are reminders of past
accomplishments, and
clothing, jewelry, and other
objects are adorned with
symbols that signify these
battle honors (cat. no.
200). The head of this
drumstick is divided into
thirds, and each section has
an illustration skillfully rendered in quillwork. The
first depicts two wounds,
the second shows an
anthropomorphic figure,
and the third has a pipe
with a feather attached and
a horse track. The hairstyle
and the red coloring on the
face suggest the figure
could be a Crow, an enemy
of the Lakota. The use of
an enemy's image on a

drumstick may parallel representations of enemies on
dance batons (cat. no. 94).
From the illustrations on
the drumstick, a story
could be told—the owner,
possibly a pipe carrier for
his society, went to war
against the Crow and was
wounded twice in battle.

The tradition of shell
gorgets is an ancient one,
and for many generations
shells have been traded
from tribe to tribe to be
used as gorgets. This shell
gorget has five symbols

that indicate the owner has
been wounded five times,
probably by bullets. When
a bullet penetrates the flesh,
the flesh surrounding the
wound swells. This swelling
is represented by the half-
circle shape carved above
each bleeding wound.
JDHC

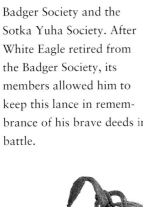

223

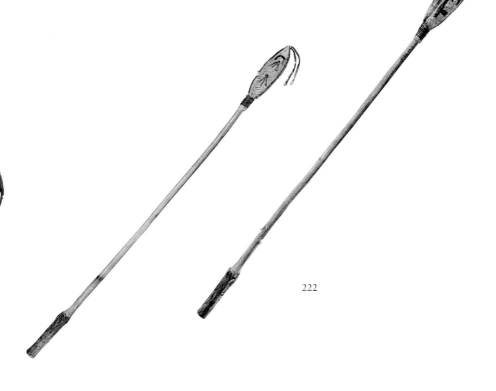

222

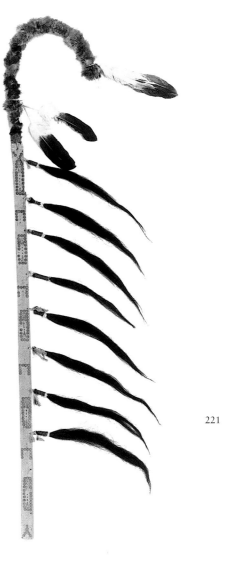

221

**Warrior's shirt**
Oglala Lakota, ca. 1890
Native-tanned hide, hair,
glass and metal beads,
sinew, blue-green and
yellow pigment
32¼ x 67 in
Bern Historical Museum,
Ethnography Department,
Si 40/I
Provenance: Collected by
E. W. Lenders, before 1910
References: Thompson
1977, pp. 175–76, fig. 120

This fine warrior's shirt
shows the persistence of the
hand motif as a prime symbol of the warrior even in
the days of reservation life,
when the tribes were no
longer fighting. Rather than
a notation of specific battle
honors, the blue and green
beaded hands are a general
reference to war and bravery. Like the United States
flags that alternate with
them, the hands are generic
references to power. The
combination of hands and
flags on this shirt bespeaks
the changing systems of
social identity that the Plains
tribes adopted as they came
to terms with their new circumstances as virtual wards
of the government that had
been their mortal enemy just
a few years before. An old
label that accompanied the
shirt attributes it to a man
named Red Tomahawk. A
man by that name was one
of the Lakota police who
arrested and shot Sitting Bull
in December 1890.
EMM

224

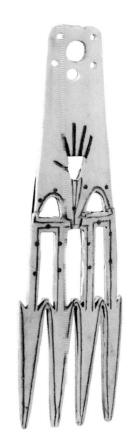

226

**Moccasins**
Arapaho (Inuna-ina),
ca. 1880
Native-tanned hide, glass
beads, cotton cloth,
rawhide
11⅛ x 3¾ in; 9½ x 3½ in
National Museum of the
American Indian,
Smithsonian Institution,
10/4447(2)
Provenance: Presented by
John J. White

**Roach spreader**
Pawnee (Chahiksichahiks),
ca. 1830
Elk antler, metal
7½ x 2¼ in
The Denver Art Museum,
museum purchase,
1968.354

The importance of human
hand imagery as a symbol
of achievement in battle is
demonstrated in these two
objects of warrior clothing.

The moccasins have
hands made with the dark
blue, green, red, and yellow
beads favored by Arapaho
women beadworkers. They
would have been worn in
victory dances that celebrated a warrior's achievements.

The roach is a headdress
made of a long, narrow
"brush" of deer or porcu-
pine hair that was worn on
the top of the head. The
spreader fit the middle of
the roach and was used to
hold it open and to secure
upright feathers (in the
holes drilled in the end).
Roaches originated among
the people of the Wood-
lands and the Prairie but
were adopted by many
Plains tribes. This early
Pawnee example has four
arrow or spear points and
a human hand as signs of
war and the counting of the
highest coup—touching an
enemy in battle.

EMM

225

**Pipe bag**

Oglala Lakota, ca. 1870
Native-tanned deerskin,
glass beads, porcupine
quills, sinew
32 x 6 in
Peabody Museum of
Archaeology and Ethnology,
Harvard University, 985-
27-10/59449
Provenance: Bequest of
William H. Claflin, Jr.,
1985; William H. Claflin,
Jr., 1930–85; William R.
Morris, 1930; collected
from U.S. Army sources
(including General Cook),
1878–93

**Pipe bag**

Pawnee (Chahiksichahiks)?
ca. 1860
Native-tanned hide, glass
beads, blue and black
pigment
30⅛ x 7½ in
The Denver Art Museum,
museum purchase, 1950.98
References: Feder 1971a,
fig. 12

The pipe is intimately tied
to the life of the Plains
man as a medium of prayer
that affects all activities,
especially war. Pipes were
smoked before and after
battles to ask for protection
and to fulfill the obligatory
rites that were an element
of all war medicine. The
leader of a war expedition
was entrusted with carrying
the pipe as a symbol of his
leadership and responsibility to his fellow warriors.

The Oglala Lakota pipe
bag (cat. no. 227) is decorated with the images of
two pipes with blue stems
and red bowls, which indicate that the owner of the
bag was the leader of two
war parties. The yellow
heads with blue eyes and
mouths represent an enemy
warrior killed on each of
these expeditions. The lines
coming from the tops of the
heads are references to
hairlocks or scalp locks,
which were removed from
slain enemies as tokens of
victory and power. These
images could also recall the
ancient practice, followed
throughout the Americas
and indeed throughout the
world, of decapitating enemies killed in battle.

The Pawnee bag (cat.
no. 228) is an older object
decorated with powerful
war symbols. The two
heads are stark and grim
reminders of enemies killed,
and the four yellow cres-
cents are horse tracks that
signify the number of horses
taken from the enemy. The
red beads under each track
could also be a sign that the
owner of the bag had four
horses wounded in battle.
On the reverse side, the
main beaded panel features
two striking images of dark
blue hands with yellow
fingernails and red beaded
squares on the palms. The
hand is usually a sign of the
highest coup, touching an
enemy in battle with the
bare hand, although hands
were also taken as battle
trophies to be displayed in
victory dances (Powell
1981, pp. 980–81). These
beaded bags were made
by women relatives of the
victorious warriors and
demonstrate the close relationship that women had to
the ceremonies of war.
EMM

**Pipe bag**

Cheyenne (Tsistsistas),
ca. 1875
Native-tanned leather, glass
beads, dyed cow tail, metal,
deer hooves
18⅞ x 6¼ in
Hearst Museum of
Anthropology, The Univer-
sity of California at
Berkeley, 2-4888
Provenance: Collected
by Colonel H. L. Scott,
ca. 1876–97
References: Storm 1972,
p. 100

Each Plains tribe had a
style of decorative quillwork and beadwork to
embellish clothing and
objects used in secular and
ceremonial activities.
Because tobacco and the
smoking pipe were impor-
tant parts of a man's personal spiritual bundle, they
were treated with care and
respect. This elegantly proportioned bag is typical of
the "stripe style" made by
Cheyenne women from the
mid-nineteenth century to
the present. The repetition
of geometric units in
sequences of four honors
the sacred four directions
and the awareness of spirituality which that concept
represents. The three elongated diamond shapes with
white bottom sections and
dark red tops are another
reference of blessing, symbolizing eagle feathers.
EMM

227

228

229

**Robe with scenes of battle and horse capture**

Crow (Absaroke), ca. 1875
Native-tanned buffalo hide, brown and red pigment
80 x 90 in
The Minneapolis Institute of Arts, gift of Lisa Dayton, 89.91
Provenance: Collected on the Crow Reservation, Montana, ca. 1985

Since the early nineteenth century the Crow people of Montana have been known for their finely decorated costumes and boldly painted shields. Though they seem to have produced fewer painted hides than the Cheyenne, Lakota, or Blackfeet, this robe demonstrates that the Crow practiced the tradition of pictorial representation of warrior narratives with considerable skill.

The scenes of action are divided into four horizontal zones, with the principal movement being from right to left. They describe personal combat and the capturing of horses from the enemy, the two major preoccupations of the Plains warrior. The Crow warriors, such as the man on a horse in the top row upper right, can be identified by the characteristic front hair crest that stands up brushlike on their foreheads. This man holds a curved coup stick as a sign of his achievements in war. He rides down a man holding a bow and arrow and wearing a capote, or winter coat, made of Hudson's Bay blankets that was also favored by the Crow. Just to the left, a Crow warrior on foot wearing blanket leggings and carrying a bow in one hand and a rope in the other drives off a herd of eleven horses. The artist has done a masterly job of representing the moving herd by overlapping the horses' necks and heads and carefully delineating their intermingled legs.

Linear details and color identify the salient attributes of the dozens of figures and horses painted on the robe. Details such as the horned war headdress with eagle-feather trailer worn by the mounted warrior on the right, or the war shirt with black and white beaded strips on the mounted warrior to the left, help show the tribal affiliation and rank of the participants. In the same way, the short black hair and black breechclout of the man being attacked by the horned-headdress man show him to be a Pawnee, one of the traditional enemies of the Crow.

Most painted hide robes and shirts with sharply defined images were collected immediately after they were made. This robe, however, shows the natural patina and wear of an object that was used and honored for generations.
EMM

230

Pretty Hawk (Oh'Zan)

**Tipi liner with scenes of
horse raids and battle**

Yankton Nakota,
ca. 1864
Native-tanned buffalo hide,
sinew, pigment
91 x 158½ in
Peabody Museum of
Archaeology and Ethnology,
Harvard University,
12-48-10/84298
Provenance: Museum pur-
chase, 1912; collected from
the Lakota in 1876

Tipi liners of hide and later of canvas were tied to the poles on the inside of the tipi so that they just touched the ground. They functioned as dew cloths and as a barrier to the cold winds that frequently blow across the plains. Ordinary liners were undecorated or painted with geometric borders. However, the liners of military society lodges—double-sized tipis that housed gear and served as meeting places for the men—were often painted with the exploits of the most famous members of the group, as a record of their achievements as brave warriors.

This large liner, made of several buffalo hides sewn together to form a large curved screen, is covered with figures of warriors and horses. When it was installed in the military society lodge, it formed a background of action for the very men who recounted the events it depicted. The liner is named for Pretty Hawk, the warrior identified by the black hawk name glyph that appears five times in scenes of war and horse raiding. His warrior friends are identified by their clothing or regalia, like the man with the horned headdress who carries a fur-wrapped lance with a curved end. This lance is a respected emblem of the *blotaunka,* the group of officers selected to serve with the leader of a war expedition (Wissler 1916, pp. 56–58.

This liner is its exceptional for its size, its early date, and the profusion of figures covering its surface. The groups of horses are especially well conceived— the artist overlapped the running animals so that the ranked heads and milling legs give the effect of movement and action. For its dynamic effect to be fully appreciated, the liner must be seen on a curved surface approximating the inner wall of the tipi, whose arc gives visual energy to the scenes of action.

EMM

231

Yellow Horse
**Raiding for mules**
Cheyenne (Tsistsistas),
ca. 1865
Paper, pencil, watercolor
8 x 12 in
Foundation for the
Preservation of American
Indian Art and Culture, Inc.,
Chicago, gift of Dorothy C.
and L. S. Raisch, Doreen
Mimura Neog, and
Florence Ely Hunn
References: Maurer 1977,
p. 164, fig. 199b

The coming of the army
and white settlers to the
Plains brought goods as
well as conflict. In this
drawing, Yellow Horse is
seen riding off with a herd
of mules, probably taken
from the army, which used
the sturdy animals for draft
as well as riding. The artist
has skillfully indicated the
movement of the animals
by overlapping the forms
and using color to separate
them as they are shown galloping across the page.
EMM

Swift Dog (Sunka Lu-zahan)
(1845–1918)
**Two drawings of Swift Dog
capturing horses**
Hunkpapa Lakota,
ca. 1870
Paper, ink, crayon, water-
color
8¼ x 13½ in
Mark Lansburgh collection,
Santa Fe
Provenance: Collected by
Paul Dyck from Kills
Enemy (Kte-To´ka Wiscasa),
brother of Swift Dog, 1935

By the eighteenth century
horses had become an
essential part of Plains
Indian life, extending the
range of the nomadic buffalo hunters and in general
allowing them greater
mobility. Because the possession of horses was vital
and horses were highly valued, capturing them from
the enemy gave wealth and
prestige while at the same
time depriving the foe. As
an act of bravery and
honor, the taking of horses
equaled the wounding or
killing of an enemy in battle,
and many expeditions had
horses as their goal. Men
often undertook horse raids
on foot, expecting to walk
for many days before finding an enemy camp.
Certain men acquired great

232

reputations for their ability to get horses from their enemies, usually with spiritual assistance from some type of horse medicine (Wildshut 1975, pp. 92–93). Warriors who returned from a successful raid often gave horses as gifts to their relatives and celebrated their victory with songs like the Lakota horse capture song in which Two Shields sings "Older sister, come outside, horses I am bringing back" (Densmore 1918, p. 362).

Swift Dog was a Hunkpapa warrior of great bravery whose drawings combine a graceful line with a sense of action that adds vitality to his autobiographical scenes. In catalogue number 234, Swift Dog is mounted on his horse. The horse's tail is tied up for war, and a scalp is attached to its bit. Swift Dog wears a beaded shirt, painted leggings, and a red stroud breechclout that trails in the wind, giving animation to his movement. He holds a stick with an eagle feather as he leads two horses that were prob-

ably taken from an enemy camp, as they both have eagle feathers attached to them. The black thunderbird in the upper right corner is probably a name glyph, and the eleven horse tracks refer to the total number of horses taken in the raid. In catalogue number 233, Swift Dog is seen walking out of an enemy camp with three horses, one saddled and the other two prepared for war. This is a great act of bravery—entering a hostile camp and capturing horses that have been tied to their owners' tipi lodges! Swift Dog holds a sacred bow lance, an emblem of leadership that was used in the military societies of many Plains tribes, especially the *tokola*, or Kit Fox Society (Wissler 1916, pp. 14–23).

EMM

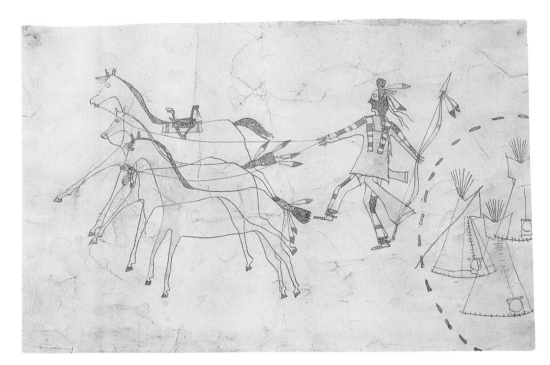

233

234

243

Al Chandler (Good Strike)
(b. 1936)
**Painted tipi**
Gros Ventre (Haaninan),
1991
Canvas, paint, brass
18 ft (diam)
The Minneapolis Institute
of Arts
Provenance: Commissioned
for the exhibition

Al Chandler paints tipis to express himself artistically while staying within the limitations of traditional tipi design. This tipi was executed in traditional northern Plains style, with the lower section red and the upper section blue. Within these colored sections are white circles, possibly representing stars, and along the lower border a rainbow encircles the entire tipi. The design is similar to that of the Kicking Woman family tipi (cat. no. 22).

In the middle section of this tipi are two animals important in traditional Plains Indian life, the horse and the buffalo. Two buffaloes are seen in profile on the north and south sides; the back is painted with a mounted warrior chasing four horses. The warrior wears a breastplate and a warbonnet with trailer. His horse has a feather tied to its mouth and painted horse tracks on its rump, signifying that the owner has captured many horses. The four horses the warrior is pursuing are red, yellow, white, and blue.
JDHC

235

244

New Bear (Above)
**Buffalo hunt**
Probably Hidatsa
(catalogued as Gros Ventre
[Haaninan]), ca. 1884
Paper, ink, commercial pig-
ment
8 x 13¾ in
Eastern Montana College
Library, Special
Collections, Charles H.
Barstow Collection of
Indian Ledger Art, 1930.60
Provenance: Collected by
Charles H. Barstow,
Bureau of Indian Affairs
clerk, Crow Reservation,
Montana
References: Heidenreich
et al. 1985

This drawing depicts a typical buffalo hunt. The
hunter has just shot two
buffaloes and is drawing an
arrow from the quiver
strapped to his back. Both
of the shot buffaloes are
bleeding from the mouth,
an indication that they
are mortally wounded.

Two tribes were histori-
cally referred to as Gros
Ventre, the Gros Ventre of
the Prairie and the Gros
Ventre of the River. They
speak separate languages
and live in different areas
on the Plains. Today, these
two tribes are called the
Gros Ventre and the
Hidatsa, respectively. The
Gros Ventre are related to
the Arapaho, and the
Hidatsa are related to the
Crow. Considering this, it
is probable that New Bear
was Gros Ventre of the
River, or Hidatsa.
JDHC

236

Wohaw (Gu hau de?)
(1855–1924)
**Buffalo hunt**
Kiowa (Gaigwa), 1877
Paper, pencil, colored
pencil
8¾ x 11¼ in
Missouri Historical Society,
1882.18.24
References: Harris 1989,
pp. 42–43, no. 8

Wohaw (Gu hau de?)
(1855–1924)
**Scene of buffalo butchering**
Kiowa (Gaigwa), 1877
Paper, pencil, colored
pencil
8¾ x 11¼ in
Missouri Historical Society,
1882.18.5
References: Harris 1989,
pp. 44–45, no. 9; Berlo
1982, p. 11, fig. 9

Wohaw (Gu hau de?)
(1855–1924)
**Men cooking meat**
Kiowa (Gaigwa), 1877
Paper, pencil, colored
pencil
8¾ x 11¼ in
Missouri Historical Society,
1882.18.37
References: Harris 1989,
pp. 46–47, no. 10; Berlo
1982, p. 11, fig. 10

Like most sketchbooks, an album of drawings by the Kiowa artist Wohaw now at the Missouri Historical Society contains numerous images related to buffalo hunting, making clear the primacy of the buffalo as a means of sustenance in the life of Plains people before confinement to reservations. Wohaw shows, among other scenes, hunters intermingling with a herd of bison; one man shoots an animal with a pistol, while the remaining four use bows and arrows (cat. no. 237). In another image (cat. no. 238), he describes the aftermath: butchering a carcass, work which was done by women. Here the immediacy of the scene is made clear by the cluster of horses, from which hunters have dismounted, and the two mountain-lion quivers strewn on the ground. A third drawing (cat. no. 239), one of Wohaw's most complex works, shows an elaborate landscape of receding hills and trees. In the foreground horses graze and warrior paraphernalia is hung on brush, while at the center a man roasts or smokes buffalo ribs. Two other warriors, one smoking a pipe, sit to one side. In the background, just at the horizon, a buffalo head and two men in profile can be seen. As Harris suggests (1989, p. 46), this drawing may represent a sequence of events in time.

LL

237

238

239

**Tipi liner with hunting scenes**
Arapaho (Inuna-ina),
ca. 1920
Canvas, pencil, pigment
34½ x 104 in
American Museum of
Natural History, 50.2/4319
Provenance: Collected by
Mrs. A. B. West, 1939

The Plains Indians lived by hunting the game, especially the buffalo, that was plentiful before European Americans divided the great herds with railroads and hunted out entire regions by the 1870s. The tribal hunt was organized and controlled by the military societies so that the maximum amount of game could be obtained to feed the people. After the men and boys had completed the dangerous job of hunting the buffalo on horseback, the entire camp joined in the hard work of skinning, butchering, moving the carcasses to camp, and drying the meat and preparing the hides. This liner gives a complete visual description of the activity, beginning with the hunters shooting the buffalo with arrows in the lower right. The huge animals are skinned and butchered on site, and then the hides and meat are carried back to camp on horseback and on the dog- or horse-pulled travois, made of two poles that formed a platform for transporting heavy loads.

To the left of the hunt scene, the artist shows the men returning to the village with buffalo hides over their saddles. Some lead another horse, probably one trained to engage in the dangerous chase in which both man and horse were often killed. The camp circle shows a ring of tipis, including many painted with heraldic and dream images. A Buffalo Society dancer wearing a buffalo headdress and tail and carrying a long spear walks inside the circle as a mother admonishes her young son, who holds a toy bow and arrows. Two Wolf Dancers in animal skins bend over to make their characteristic movements just outside the bottom of the tipi circle; to the left an Elk Dancer wearing a horned mask and carrying the hoop of the society blows a bone whistle. In between the Elk Dancer and the Buffalo Dancer a woman can be seen taking the hair off a buffalo hide. Above her, a kneeling woman scrapes the flesh from a staked-out hide with a special tool. To her right is half of a hide staked out and painted with a characteristic Arapaho parfleche design. Farther to the right is a large buffalo robe painted yellow with a feather circle motif in the middle. The camp scene also includes a kettle cooking over the fire and a group of five dogs pulling travois.

EMM

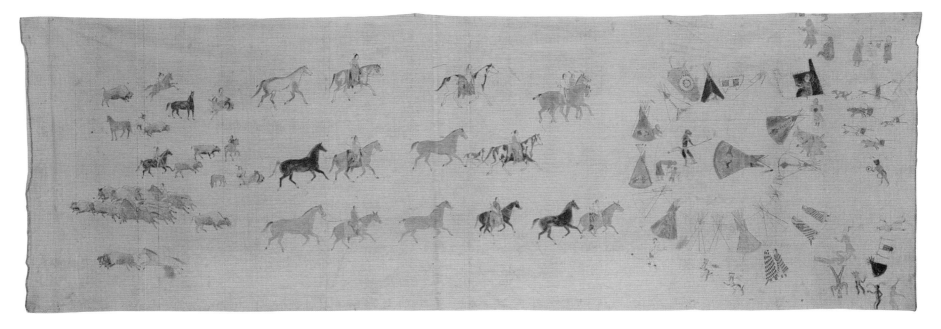

240

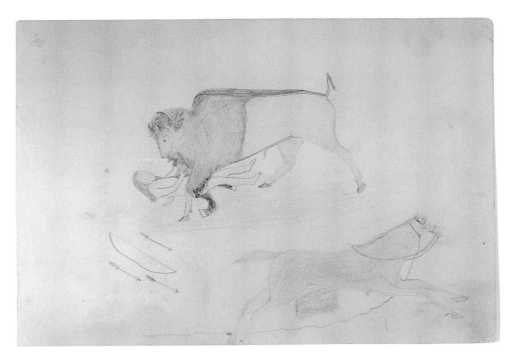

241

242

**Two hunting scenes**
Comanche (Niuam),
ca. 1880–89
Paper, pencil, ink, water-
color
10 x 14½ in
The Art Institute of
Chicago, gift of Richard A.
Lent, in honor of Mr. and
Mrs. C. L. Lent,
1977.576, page 16B;
1977.576, page 16
Provenance: Collected by
John H. Musser, post
trader, Fort Sill, Oklahoma,
ca. 1880–89

The dangers of buffalo
hunting were many, and
each year a few men of
each tribe were killed in
accidents with these large,
aggressive animals. In catalogue number 241, a
hunter has been thrown
from his horse and is being
trampled and gored by an
enraged bull. Catalogue
number 242 shows a war-
rior fighting a mountain
lion with a knife as one of
his friends tries to shoot
the animal from behind a
tree. Surviving such
attacks was considered an
honor, and men often were
given credit for counting
coup on dangerous ani-
mals like large felines or
bears.

EMM

Ahsit (White Man)
(1853–1931)
**Painted fan**
Southern Cheyenne
(Tsistsistas), 1878–79
Wood, cotton, silk,
pigment
10½ x 17 in
American Museum of
Natural History, 1/4616
Provenance: Collected by
P. Schuyler, ca. 1895;
Armstrong Institute,
Hampton, Virginia

The Cheyenne Ahsit was
imprisoned at Fort Marion
and subsequently attended
the Hampton Institute for
one year. There he and the
other former Fort Marion
inmates produced a large
number of drawings and
decorated items, but only a
few survive. Like the
ceramics, painted fans
were sold and also given as
gifts to supporters of the
school. The fans were said
to be "decorated in a way
to keep a whole congrega-
tion awake through a hot
Sunday sermon" (Petersen
1971, p. 262).

One side of the fan
shows a buffalo-hunting
scene and is inscribed with
the artist's name ("Cheyenne,
Ahsit [cipher] English
name, Whiteman"); on the
reverse two mounted men
armed with lances pursue a
green deer.

LL

**Model tipi**
Cheyenne (Tsistsistas),
ca. 1900
Leather, porcupine quills,
pigments
31½ x 53½ in
American Museum of
Natural History, 50.1/6500
Provenance: Collected by
Mrs. Walter Shirlaw, 1912

Model tipis were sometimes made as toys for Plains children, but most of those found in collections were made for the growing market of museums and private collectors. James Mooney commissioned a set of model painted tipis from the Kiowa, which was exhibited at the 1893 Columbian Exposition in Chicago. In 1901 he commissioned another project—a set of Cheyenne tipis for the St. Louis World's Fair of 1904. This not only established the tipi model as a desirable collector's item among non-Indians, it also gave Indian artists another salable object type to add badly needed income to the reservation economy. The men soon found that their former principal occupations of war, horse raiding, and hunting were the most sought-after subjects among collectors, because they illustrated the non-Indian's romantic view of native life.

This model tipi cover shows scenes of hunting that would never have been found on a full-sized tipi. There are examples of battle scenes on tipis but not images of hunting, which indicates that this painting was done specifically for sale to outsiders. The painting shows seven warriors, who are dressed for battle as much as for the hunt. Two of the horses have their tails tied up for war, and some of the men carry military insignia, including the man on foot at the left, who wears an eagle-feather headdress and carries a decorated saber. Two hunters shoot buffalo with their bows and arrows while others hunt an elk or a white-tailed deer and a bighorn ram. A particularly adventurous man is shown attacking a grizzly bear with a tomahawk. The artist took advantage of the curving wall of the erected tipi to give dynamism to this scene of the chase.
EMM

243

244

**Dress**
Hunkpapa Lakota,
1875–80
Buckskin, pigment, beads,
tin cones
48 x 44 in
State Historical Society of
North Dakota, L641
Provenance: Collected by
David Toro at Standing
Rock Reservation, North
Dakota; owned by Pretty
White Cow (niece of
Sitting Bull)
References: State Historical
Society of North Dakota
1984, p. 23

The beaded yoke of this
dress has a U-shaped
abstract design in its center
that refers to the turtle, a
female protective symbol
commonly used on Lakota
dresses. The lower section
has hunting scenes drawn
on front and back. The
front features two women,
one killing a buffalo and
the other butchering a buffalo. The back shows two
women, one on horseback
killing a bear and the other
on foot hunting an ante-
lope. It is not known
whether these are the
exploits of Pretty White
Cow or if she is the artist.
Among many Plains tribes
there were women referred
to as "manly hearted
women," women who
took on the responsibilities
that traditionally were
men's, such as hunting
and warfare, as shown on
this dress (Medicine 1983,
p. 271).
JDHC

**Boys hunting rabbits**
Comanche (Niuam),
ca. 1880–89
Paper, pencil, ink,
watercolor
10 x 14 in
The Art Institute of
Chicago, gift of Richard A.
Lent in honor of Mr. and
Mrs. C. L. Lent, 1977.577
Provenance: Collected by
John H. Musser, post
trader, Fort Sill, Oklahoma,
ca. 1880–89

Boys were encouraged to
begin practicing their skills
with the bow and arrow at
an early age, in preparation
for their role as hunters. In
this scene five young boys
hunting rabbits for the family larder are gaining valuable experience in the art of
stalking and hitting a rapid-
ly moving target. Four of
the boys seem to be suc-
cessful, but the one on the
left crouches down and
cries, a young casualty of
the game. By the age of ten
many boys were already
joining the buffalo hunt,
where they were assigned
to seek out and shoot
calves.
EMM

245

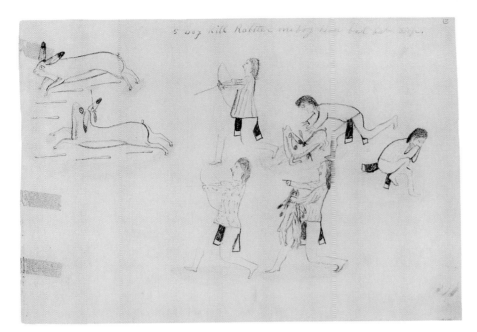

246

247

Blackbear Bosin (1921–80)
**Prairie Fire**
Kiowa (Gaigwa)–Comanche
(Niuam), ca. 1953
Paper, watercolor
23 x 33¾₆ in
Philbrook Museum of Art,
Tulsa, 53.7
References: Wade 1986,
fig. 178; Dockstader 1966,
fig. 218

Blackbear Bosin represents a generation of Plains artists that continued the Oklahoma and Santa Fe style of painting developed in the 1920s and 1930s. The movement was inspired by Mrs. Susan Peters, who worked as a field matron for the Kiowa Agency in Anadarko, Oklahoma, from 1916 through the 1930s. Mrs. Peters organized art classes to encourage the young people to express themselves and their Indian world. In 1926 Peters introduced her students to Edith Makier and Oscar B. Jacobson, professors of art at the University of Oklahoma at Norman. These teachers actively supported the work of the young artists. Monroe Tsatoke, Stephen Mopope, Spencer Asah, James Auchiah, and Jack Hokeah enrolled at the university and began a group known as the Five Kiowas. Their subject matter was scenes from traditional Kiowa life, especially dancers and ceremonies. They used tempera or casein paints to get flat areas of color, which they defined by a clear use of line. These men were active participants in Kiowa ceremonial life, and this close association with traditional ways gave their imagery an authenticity that takes it beyond the decorative nature of the style.

Blackbear Bosin continued the Oklahoma Kiowa style, which was also supported at the School of American Indian Art in Santa Fe, New Mexico. *Prairie Fire* is one of the best-known works of the period. Its stylized vision of a past world is energized by the complex pattern of smoke and flames that threatens the running antelope, the hunters on horseback, and the more naturalistically drawn wolves skulking through the bushes in the foreground.
EMM

Attributed to Cadzi Cody (Codsiogo) (1866–1912)

**Buffalo hunt and Wolf Dance**

Shoshone, 1885–95
Antelope hide, ink, paint
48 x 34 in
Heritage Plantation of Sandwich, Sandwich, Massachusetts, 1980.3.1

Codsiogo was born in 1865 and had his name changed to Cadzi Cody in tribal enrollment records in 1900. Relatively unknown to his contemporaries, Cadzi Cody probably produced more hide paintings than any other Plains Indian artist (Alexander 1938, p. 10). As with other Wind River Shoshone artists, the major subject of Cadzi Cody's hide paintings was the Wolf Dance, which was popular on the Wind River Reservation during his time. This painting shows Cadzi Cody's rendition of the Wolf Dance with a United States flag serving as a center pole. The Wind River Shoshones called this dance *tásayùge*, but whites referred to it as the Wolf Dance or the War Dance (Lowie 1915, p. 822). War parties were often symbolized as wolves, and when a war party returned, a dance was held (Weitzner 1979, p. 290). Eventually this dance was transformed into the Grass Dance, with men wearing warbonnets with long streamers and feather bustles.

Cadzi Cody included a scene of the traditional buffalo hunt to make the painting more salable to the white tourists visiting the reservation to observe the Sun Dance. The tourists constituted a new market for traditional Native American arts, especially scenes of dancing, hunting, and warfare. With this outside market for images of Indian ceremonialism, Cadzi Cody replaced the flag with a center pole from the Sun Dance. As the demand for his work grew, he began using stencils to draw the buffalo, which allowed him more flexibility and speed. Cadzi Cody used the tradition of hide painting as both a cultural statement and a means of economic survival.

JDHC

248

249

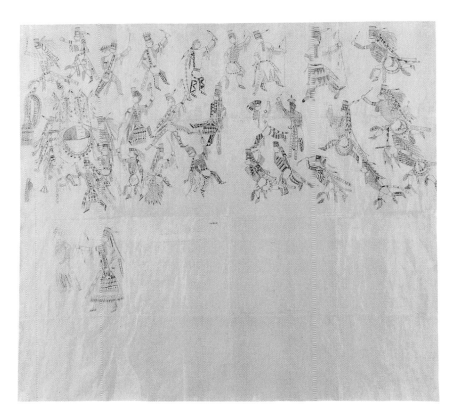

Elk Head
**Exploits of Elk Head**
Gros Ventre (Haaninan),
ca. 1883–85
Pencil, paper
39 x 36 in
Montana Historical
Society, Museum
Collection, X82.49.01 a,b
References: Montana
Historical Society 1976,
p. 54

Elk Head made these draw-
ings of Gros Ventre life
while incarcerated in the
territorial prison at Deer
Lodge, Montana, for
murder. On one side of the
paper, men dressed in
southern Plains–style
turbans perform the war
dance (Powell 1981,
p. 832). They are holding
their weapons as they
dance, probably recalling
former exploits. In the
upper right corner of the
drawing, eight singers sit
around a large drum.
Directly below them is a
man touching another
dancer with a staff, probably a reenactment of counting coup on the enemy. The
carefully detailed surface
textures of the dance costumes illustrate the different types of beadwork and
patterning.

On the reverse side Elk
Head drew several individually labeled scenes that are
probably autobiographical.
In the center is a Lakota
shooting at Elk Head's
mother while she carries
Elk Head as a baby. Above
this scene are various battle
exploits, including Elk
Head mutilating Lakota
enemies and killing Lakota
warriors who have taken
Gros Ventre scalps. The
lower section illustrates
scenes associated with
camp life—Elk Head hunt-
ing buffalo, deer, and elk
by a group of painted tipis,
and a man carrying a bull
boat and then sitting and
paddling. Like the figures
on the other side, these
wear southern Plains–style
clothing. Since the Gros
Ventres are from the northern Plains, Elk Head may
have been illustrating
scenes of a visiting group.
JDHC

New Bear (Above)
**Men going to a dance**
Probably Hidatsa (catalogued as Gros Ventre [Haaninan]), ca. 1880
Paper, ink, commercial pigment
8½ x 12½ in
Eastern Montana College Library, Special Collections, Charles H. Barstow Collection of Indian Ledger Art, 1930.63
Provenance: Collected by Charles H. Barstow, Bureau of Indian Affairs clerk, Crow Reservation, Montana

Dancing has always been an important part of Plains Indian life. Women and men participate in formal dance ceremonies that are performed for social as well as ceremonial occasions. Dances were an important part of dream cults and military societies and were held to celebrate victories in war and the making of alliances. During the reservation period men's dances became especially important, because in some ways they replaced the ritual activities and vital cultural expression that had focused on the military societies. As war and raiding for horses were removed from men's lives, the dance became a prime expression of Indian male identity.

In this drawing, New Bear shows a scene that was common during the late nineteenth century and that can still be witnessed at powwows today. A group of carefully painted and adorned men are walking to the dance ground, wrapped in their blankets and holding their tomahawks and feather dance bustles. They all wear the deer-tail headdresses known as roaches, which incorporate eagle feathers extending from the top of the crown.

The bustles show that they are going to perform a version of the Grass Dance, a spirited male performance that spread from the Omaha of the prairie throughout the Plains during the reservation period. The inscription on this drawing identifies the dancers as being either Gros Ventre of the River (Hidatsa) or Sioux (Lakota). Because of the generic nature of the decoration and the widespread use of similar Grass Dance costumes, it is difficult to make a precise tribal identification.
EMM

New Bear (Above)
**Women dancing**
Probably Hidatsa (catalogued as Gros Ventre [Haaninan]), ca. 1883
Paper, ink, commercial pigment
7¾ x 9¾ in
Eastern Montana College Library, Special Collections, Charles H. Barstow Collection of Indian Ledger Art, 1930.66; 1930.67
Provenance: Collected by Charles H. Barstow, Bureau of Indian Affairs clerk, Crow Reservation, Montana

In the most traditional style of Plains women's dances, the participants move with a slow, stately rhythm that emphasizes control, continuity, and beauty. Dances of this type are popular with all tribes and are still performed at powwows throughout the West. In these drawings, New Bear illustrates two groups of Hidatsa, or Gros Ventre of the River, women performing a line dance. Their dresses, leggings, and moccasins are painted black, red, white, and yellow. They wear their hair in two long, wrapped braids that hang down in front, and all but two of the women have circular patches of vermilion painted on their cheeks, a fashion still followed today. Long decorative strips hang from the women's bodices and the backs of their collars. Among the Gros Ventre of the Prairie, women had an important role in the eight sacred dances of the people, one of which was the Women's Dance (*benoht-cao'we*), in which the women wore feathered headdresses (Cooper 1957, pp. 242–252).
EMM

Horace Poolaw (1906–84)
**Fancy War Dance, Craterville, Lawton, Oklahoma**
Kiowa (Gaigwa), ca. 1928
Gelatin silver print
8³⁄₁₆ x 11⅝ in
The Horace Poolaw Photography Project, Stanford University
References: Marriott and Poolaw 1990, p. 24, cat. no. 50

As a young man Horace Poolaw worked in Anadarko, Oklahoma, as an assistant to a landscape photographer and later as assistant to the owner of a portrait studio. He continued to make photographs until the end of his life, documenting his own family occasions as well as more public events. He is the only known professional Native American photographer of his generation, and the long span of his career adds further interest to his work.

This photo was made at the Craterville Indian Fair, an event that featured dances and reenactments for white tourists. A close view of a dance performance, it shows the extent to which elements of the fancy-dress powwow costume were already established at an early date. Dance has already moved out of an internal religious or social context and become a staged event for outsiders. Although some of Poolaw's photos of this period showing costumed Kiowa people have a self-conscious stiffness, the man in this image seems absorbed in his movements and unaware of the photographer.
LL

250

253

251

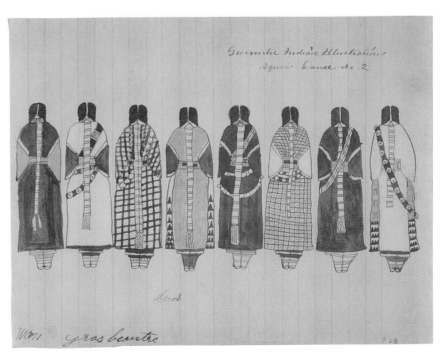

252

Bear's Arm (Loc´-pitz-he-a´-lish)

**An Indian camp**
Hidatsa (Minitari),
ca. 1910
Cardboard, watercolor
10 x 15 in
State Historical Society of
North Dakota, 12004
Provenance: Collected by
Orin G. Libby, Fort
Berthold Reservation,
Montana

Bear's Arm painted this scene to recall daily life in the days of freedom on the northern Plains. The village is near fresh running water for drinking, cooking, bathing, and swimming (a favorite children's pastime). Horses graze at the edges of the camp and in meadows just beyond. The time is just after a successful buffalo hunt, when hides are spread out on the ground to be scraped and the thinly sliced sheets of buffalo meat have been hung on the wooden racks to dry so they can be stored for later use. Shields on tripods and military society crooked lances are placed outside the warriors' tipis as people rest in the shade of their lodges or walk about to visit. Although the nostalgic elements and the absence of non-Indian goods recall the past, this is the kind of traditional Plains camp that is still brought together for special ceremonial occasions. By placing the village within a fully described landscape and using the technique of overlapping forms and perspective, Bear's Arm adapted elements of European representational style to depict a scene of traditional Plains life.

EMM

254

### A Cheyenne village

Cheyenne (Tsistsistas),
ca. 1880
Paper, pencil, ink, crayon
7 x 8½ in
National Anthropological
Archives, Smithsonian
Institution, 154,064-C
Provenance: Received from
Mrs. Mildred McLean
Hazen, Washington, D.C.,
1892

Scenes of tipi encampments
were very popular in Plains
drawings after the 1870s
because such encampments
were a prominent feature of
life on the open prairie. The
magnificent effect of many
tall, stately, conical lodges
set against the landscape
and the sky can still be witnessed during the great ceremonies and tribal fairs on
the Plains. In this drawing,
a Cheyenne tipi village is
set up on both banks of a
tree-lined river. The artist
created a pictorial order of
horizontal scenes stacked
one upon the other to indicate the foreground,
midground, and so on,
back to the horizon. The
empty immediate fore-
ground borders a line of
nine tipis painted with
visionary and hereditary
designs that include
abstract symbols and representational images such as
the stars, sun, and moon.
The tops of the tipis bristle
with a mass of fine lines
that represent the tapered
ends of the fourteen to
twenty lodgepoles around
which the tipi covers are
wrapped. In a traditional
Plains camp, the tipis were
arranged in one or more
circles. An individual's
place was determined by
family, clan, and military
or dream society member-
ship. The artist has represented the circle by overlapping the right edge of each
tipi to suggest a depth relationship of objects in space.
Most tipis were not painted, so the presence of many
decorated lodges must signify a special event. The
scene could also be imagi-
nary, made to illustrate the
great painted lodges from
the past that had all but
disappeared by the time
this drawing was made. A
wooden wagon is drawn
up in front of the tipis,
making an eerie frame for
the buffalo head painted on
the tipi behind it. A shield
and an eagle-feather headdress are set up on a tripod
to the left of the lodges.

A tree-lined stream is
shown behind this group of
tipis, and a low hill sepa-
rates the trees from another
camp with six painted
lodges. The hill must have
some particular special significance, because four
shields on tripods and four
banners are set on it. The
flat, empty plain runs from
the back of these lodges to a
line of low mountains, and
beyond that is a flat horizon
line—a complicated spatial
setting indicated with an
intelligent and economic use
of line.

EMM

## 256

Roan Eagle
**Moving camp**
Oglala Lakota, ca. 1890
Paper, pencil, ink, water-
color
7¼ x 12³⁄₁₆ in
The Minneapolis Institute
of Arts, the Putnam Dana
McMillan Fund, 90.107

The traditional life of most
Plains tribes was nomadic.
Temporary camps were reg-
ularly moved in the never-
ending search for the herds
of buffalo and other large
game animals on which the
tribes depended for food,
shelter, and the other necessities of life. Before the
introduction of the horse,
household goods were car-
ried by humans and by dogs
with packs or dragging a
tipi-pole travois. The horse
provided greater mobility
and carrying power, as illustrated in this typical camp
moving scene. A woman
carries a small child on her
back as she leads a horse
whose saddle is strapped
with packages. The long tipi
poles are tied to the saddle
to form a travois, a convenient platform to carry the
heavy tipi cover, hide robes,
blankets, and other bulky
items. An infant can be seen
securely nestled on the
travois. In most Plains tribes
the women owned the tipis
and camp goods, and it was
their job to move them and
set them up at the new
campsite.
EMM

256

## 257

Wohaw (Gu hau de)
(1855–1924)
**Two men departing on an
expedition**
Kiowa (Gaigwa), 1877
Paper, pencil, colored pencil
8¾ x 11¼ in
Missouri Historical Society,
1882.18.21
Provenance: Gift of Mrs.
James Barry (Mrs. Grady's
mother) to the Missouri
Historical Society, 1882;
collected at Fort Marion,
Florida, in January 1877 by
Frances and John Grady
References: Harris 1989,
pp. 62–63

Although the convention of
horse tracks to suggest
action over time is common
in Plains drawings, this
motif is infrequent in
Wohaw's work. Here, how-
ever, he shows the foot-
prints of both people and
horses. A man wearing
a dark blanket has left the
tipi, caught his horse, and
led it up to the lodge. A
man with a shield has
approached from a differ-
ent direction, and a woman
in a red calico dress has
emerged from the tipi carrying a quiver, lance, and
bow. A shield and a lance,
perhaps those of the man
with the horse, hang from a
bush in the background.
    The men are leaving on
an expedition, perhaps, as
Harris suggests (p. 62), for
war, but more likely hunting. Some drawings in
Wohaw's notebooks seem
to suggest a narrative
sequence, and this image is
directly followed by one of
two men with similar dress
and accoutrements killing a
buffalo. The interpretation
of the drawing as preparation for hunting is rein-
forced by the flowing tail
of the horse; horses' tails
were tightly bound with
cloth for battle, a convention shown elsewhere in
the Wohaw book (see
Harris 1989, pl. 13).
LL

## 258

Howling Wolf (Honanistto)
(1850–1927)
**Scene of a Cheyenne camp**
Southern Cheyenne
(Tsistsistas), ca. 1876
Paper, ink, crayon, pencil
8¾ x 11¼ in
Field Museum of Natural
History, Chicago, 83999
Provenance: Made at Fort
Marion, St. Augustine,
Florida, ca. 1876–77

While he was a prisoner at
Fort Marion, the Cheyenne
warrior Howling Wolf
worked with a friend
named Soaring Eagle to
produce a sketchbook of
eight elaborately rendered
scenes that contrast life at
Fort Marion with life on
the Plains. In this drawing
Howling Wolf uses newly
learned techniques of perspective, overlaps objects to
indicate their relative position in space, and shows
figures from different
angles, all of which adds to
the sense of the circle that
is the essence of a Plains
camp. A group of men and
women are seated inside a
ring of seven tipis. Shields
are hung on poles next to
two of the lodges, and
many of the women wear
the black and white hori-
zontally striped blankets
that were coveted items
traded up from the Navajo
in Arizona.
EMM

## 259

Buffalo Meat (Oewotoh)
(1847–1917)
**Going in to trade**
Cheyenne (Tsistsistas),
1876
Paper, ink, graphite,
colored pencil
8¾ x 11¼ in
Amon Carter Museum,
Fort Worth, 1965.48.1.7
Provenance: Purchased
from the Old Print Shop,
Inc., 1965; given by the
artist to Captain Richard
H. Pratt, Fort Marion,
Florida, 1877

Buffalo Meat, a Southern
Cheyenne warrior, was sent
to a federal prison in St.
Augustine, Florida, as punishment for acts of war and
violence against the white
population. He was arrested on April 3, 1875, and
returned to the reservation
three years later. The strategy of the prison was one
of rehabilitation and acculturation, including education and the opportunity
for prisoners to make souvenirs to sell to tourists.
Buffalo Meat was one of
the men who excelled at
drawing; he gave this book
of camp life, hunting, and
scenes of travel to the commandant of the prison.
    In this drawing Buffalo
Meat gives a lively account
of a group of Southern
Cheyenne going in to trade
with the non-Indian set-
tlers who owned one of the
stores or trading posts that
were located around the
western forts and later the

government reservation agencies. The two men at the top of the composition wear cotton shirts, hats, and vests, European-style clothing that had become the fashion among the Plains tribes by the mid-1870s. They also wear blankets neatly folded around their waists and the other traditional Indian garb of leggings, breechclouts, and moccasins. The first man carries a pipe and pipe bag and rides a white mule, while his friend leads two pack horses loaded with goods for trade, probably furs, hides, or decorated clothing. The men are traveling with two women holding gaily colored umbrellas and dressed in their finest clothes and ornaments, including long dentalium shell earrings and chokers and long belts decorated with nickel silver disks. The woman on the yellow and white horse leads the horse of her daughter, who is dressed in a miniature version of her mother's finery.

Trade had always been an important aspect of Plains Indian life. Before the coming of the whites, the Indians had established extensive systems that linked the continent. Jablow notes how the trade between Indians and whites in the eighteenth and early nineteenth centuries constituted the core of both the Indian economy and the European westward expansion (Jablow 1951). This trade quickly became an important part of Plains Indian life as the people grew more dependent on non-Indian goods for their livelihood. By the early eighteenth century, guns, powder, and shot had become increasingly vital elements of war. Demand for these was soon followed by a growing demand for metal cooking pots and pans, steel knives, cotton and wool cloth, and items of personal decoration such as colored glass beads, pigments, and nickel silver ornaments. During the reservation period this list continued to grow as fewer needs could be satisfied with traditional materials, which were disappearing with the loss of game on the open plains.

EMM

257

258

259

**Beaded suitcase**

Minneconjou Lakota,
1902
Commercially produced
suitcase of leather and
metal; deerskin, glass beads
13¾ x 18½ x 8¾ in
Ruth M. O'Dell
Provenance: Gift to present
owner from Cheyenne
River Reservation family
References: Lessard 1990,
pp. 56–57, fig. 5; Pohrt
1975, p. 71, cat. no. 78;
Sotheby's, New York, June
12, 1992, no. 147

In this virtuoso example of
beadwork, the artist has
enveloped the surface of a
manufactured suitcase with
beaded deerskin. The top
and ends show a pattern of
alternating crossed flags
and five-pointed stars, and
each side bears a complex
and detailed pictorial scene.
One, a representation of a
woman standing by a meat-
drying rack outside a tipi,
seems very close in content
and composition to certain
drawings showing scenes of
domestic life. Smaller figures of a man smoking and
a boy playing with a dog
appear below the rack,
while a golden eagle flies
above and the date 1902 is
included at the center of the
top edge.

On the reverse side we
are shown what appears to
be a specific episode, in
which an Indian man wear-
ing facial paint and a Euro-
American man in military
dress shake hands. Each
holds the reins of a horse.
Above the white man's
horse an eagle flies, while
in the upper corner is a
wounded buffalo. Between
the two animals are the
initials M. G. This personal
identification further rein-
forces the idea that the
scene may represent a
biographical event. Despite
the difficult medium of
beadwork, the artist has
included fine detailing on
the woman's clothing and
jewelry, the horse equip-
ment, and even the tipi
pegs.

Surviving examples of
beaded suitcases are rare,
although an early photo-
graph in the Burdick collection catalogue shows a
number of examples dis-
played at a reservation fair
(Porsche 1987, p. 25).
Dennis Lessard (1990,
pp. 54–63) has suggested
that the suitcase is part of a
corpus of work produced
on the Cheyenne River
Reservation, perhaps by the
same artist. Also in the
group are several other
objects in this exhibition:
two tipi bags (cat. nos. 270
and 271) and a pipe bag
(cat. no. 269). Another
beaded suitcase from a private collection (and recently at auction [Sotheby's,
New York, June 12, 1992])
closely resembles this one
in its pictorial style. It is
inscribed "Nellie Gates 54
yrs. to J. A. Archambault
1907," suggesting that
Nellie Gates was the
maker. A photo by Frank
Fiske in the North Dakota
Historical Society showing
a seated woman with the
present suitcase in front of
her is labeled "Nellie Two
Bears Gates, Fort Yates
N.D." and lends further
support to the attribution.
The inscription "MG" here
may refer to a member of
Nellie Gates's family.

LL

260

**Two tipi bag panels**
Minneconjou Lakota, ca. 1885
Native-tanned deerskin, glass beads, sinew, linen, cotton thread
9¼ x 16¼ in; 9¾ x 16 in
The University Museum, University of Pennsylvania, Philadelphia, NA 5494a,b
Provenance: Purchased by Mrs. M. A. Thompson, Fairfax, South Dakota, 1916
References: Lessard 1990, p. 61, fig. 10

As the reservation period continued, scenes of camp life became frequent subjects in representational beadwork. This was a major change from the gender-specific divisions of art in traditional Plains life, in which the making of representational images was men's work and the creation of abstract, geometric designs was the pursuit of women. On some examples of pictorial beadwork a drawing can be seen underneath the beads; possibly a man drew the images and they were then beaded over by a woman (Maurer 1977, no. 197, p. 163). Whatever the case, the tradition of pictorial beadwork became a widely followed convention during the early decades of the twentieth century. The panels shown here decorated tipi bags—or rectilinear pouches of soft, tanned leather used to hold a variety of personal and household goods. One panel shows two men riding double, who have come to visit a man and a woman in front of their tipi. The man wears an eagle feather in his hair, and the woman has a beaded robe wrapped around her waist and holds a bucket in her hand. The other panel shows two women seated on the ground with a friend standing between them. A cooking pot hangs from a forked stick to the left of the three tipis, which presumably belong to the women. The artist developed a spot-stitch technique that allowed her to indicate fine details by using one row of small seed beads. She combined this control over the medium with a strong sense of contrasting color to depict minutiae such as the women's long dentalium shell earrings and the elktooth dress worn by the standing figure. Dennis Lessard has made a convincing case that the work of this artist and other work of the same style was created by Minneconjou Lakota from the Cheyenne River Indian Reservation in west central South Dakota from about 1885 to 1900 (Lessard 1990, pp. 54–63).
EMM

261

**A cloth trader**
Cheyenne (Tsistsistas),
ca. 1880
Paper, pencil, ink, crayon
7 x 8½ in
National Anthropological
Archives, Smithsonian
Institution, 154,064-C
Provenance: Received from
Mrs. Mildred McLean
Hazen, Washington, D.C.,
1892

**A trading party of Navajo**
Comanche (Niuam),
ca. 1880–89
Paper, pencil, ink, water-
color
10 x 14½ in
The Art Institute of
Chicago, gift of Richard A.
Lent in honor of Mr. and
Mrs. C. L. Lent, 1977.576
page 39
Provenance: Collected by
John H. Musser, post trad-
er, Fort Sill, Oklahoma,
ca. 1880–89

For thousands of years the
native peoples of North
America maintained an
extensive trading system
that linked the continent.
Intertribal and interregional
trade was also an impor-
tant means of communica-
tion, bringing ideas, technical knowledge, art styles,
songs, and dances, as well
as goods, from one area to
another. Tanned buffalo
hides were actively traded
by the Plains tribes to the
agriculturists in the earthen
lodge villages along the
Missouri River or through
the southern Plains to Taos
and the Rio Grande pueb-
los. From ancient times,
rare items of personal
adornment and ceremonial
importance were among the
most often traded goods.
There was a steady trade
from the Pacific Northwest
for the long, white dentalium shells used in making
earrings and necklaces.
Rare earth pigments in
reds, blues, and yellows
were also a highly sought-
after commodity. The horse
had a significant effect on
the intertribal trade of
tanned and painted buffalo
robes, dried meat, leather
clothing, and horses from
the nomadic hunters of the
west to the agriculturalists
of the east for products
such as dried corn, beans,
squash, and tobacco. The
horse allowed men to hunt
independently; previously
the women had been essen-
tial in forming the sur-
rounds that led the buffalo
into the killing area. With
the aid of horses, men
could kill more animals,
and women could spend
more time preparing the
hides. The result was an
increase in tradable goods
and greater prosperity for
the family (Jablow 1951,
pp. 20–21). The women
artists who made and decorated the fine clothing and
painted the robes for trade
were thus producing for a
market outside the tribe
long before the non-Indian
collecting market developed
in the second half of the
nineteenth century.

The Cheyenne drawing
(cat. no. 262) shows men
trading wool and cotton
cloth to a group of women
who sit in a semicircle
around them. One of the
men presents his goods to
the customers as the other
two sit smoking a pipe and
discussing the action. Four
red and black blankets and
breechclouts are set up next
to these men as if in a store
window. The women are
drawn in profile or from
the back, and the third figure from the right wears a
so-called second phase
Navajo chief's blanket,
with its characteristic horizontal stripes in natural
white and dark brown with
geometric blocks in red.
This is the type of blanket
that would have been
obtained from the Navajo
traders in catalogue num-
ber 263.

The Comanche drawing
(cat. no. 263) shows a
party of Navajo with pack
mules bringing woven tex-
tiles, such as blankets and
saddle pads, and other
goods from the high
deserts of Arizona to the
southern plains of Texas.
From there the Comanche
would themselves trade
some of these goods to the
tribes from the central and
northern Plains and the
prairie.

EMM

262

263

Buffalo Meat (Oewotoh)
(1847–1917)
**Self-portrait**
Cheyenne (Tsistsistas),
ca. 1879
Paper, ink, crayon, water-
color
6¾ x 4⅜ in
Oklahoma Historical
Society, State Museum of
History, 1042.3
Provenance: Collected by
Frank H. Taylor, Fort
Marion, Florida, 1878
References: Petersen 1971,
p. 228

Buffalo Meat was twenty-
eight years old, with a wife
and child, when he was
arrested by the army under
a charge of being one of the
"ringleaders" of a group of
Southern Cheyenne war-
riors that had been active
on raids against army and
civilian sites in the
Oklahoma Territory. He
was arrested at the
Cheyenne Agency, Indian
Territory, on April 3, 1875,
and arrived at the prison in
St. Augustine, Florida, on
May 21, 1875. He spent
three years there in "rehabilitation confinement" and
was released to return to
his home on the reservation
on April 11, 1878. He had
a long and active life serving as a chief of his tribe, a
policeman, laborer, team-
ster, and delegate to a
Washington conference. He
was also active as a worker
and a deacon in the Baptist
church. This self-portrait
was done at the age of thirty, while he was still a prisoner at Fort Marion trying
to adjust to a life that was
totally different from the
world he knew. The draw-
ing shows him as he was
before imprisonment, a
young warrior dressed in
the height of fashion carrying an acculturated combination of status symbols—a
European hat and an eagle
feather, a printed cotton
shirt and fringed leather
leggings. He holds a pipe
and pipe bag in one hand
and a multicolored umbrel-
la in the other. Buffalo
Meat demonstrates his
drawing skill by depicting
his horse from the front, a
technique of foreshortening
that he learned from his
teachers at Fort Marion.
Buffalo Meat died of tuberculosis at his home near
Kingfisher, Oklahoma, in
1917 at the age of seventy
(Petersen 1971, p. 228).
EMM

264

266

Etahdleuh Doanmoe
(1856–88)
**Scene of two riders**
Kiowa (Gaigwa), ca. 1880
Paper, crayon, watercolor
8¼ x 12 in
National Anthropological
Archives, Smithsonian
Institution, gift of E. P.
Upham, 1916, 290,844

In his time at Fort Marion
Etahdleuh became a particular protégé of the commandant, Captain Pratt. Pratt
arranged for him to continue
his studies at Hampton
Institute and then employed
him at the Carlisle Indian
School. In 1880 Pratt
arranged for Etahdleuh to
work at the Smithsonian
Institution in Washington,
D.C., for several months as
an informant on Kiowa language and culture. He may
have made this drawing at
that time.

Because of its relation to
the mounted warrior
depicted on the Hampton
Institute's ceramic jar (cat.
no. 266)—and because of
the difficulty of working on
a curved surface—it is reasonable to speculate that
the drawing served as a
sketch for the jar. If the
drawing was made during
his time in Washington,
however, it postdates the
jar. It may be that both
images derive from a third,
unknown source.
LL

Etahdleuh Doanmoe
(1856–88)
**Painted jar**
Kiowa (Gaigwa), 1878–79
Terra-cotta, paint
6⅜ x 4⅛ in
Hampton University
Museum, 00.1926
Provenance: Hampton
Normal and Agricultural
Institute, ca. 1878
References: Petersen 1971,
pp. 136, 262–64; Hultgren
1987, pp. 32–39

Educational reform move-
ments of the late nineteenth
century placed considerable
importance on manual
training as well as intellectual development, and this
approach also manifested
itself in Indian educational
policy, with the additional
purpose of helping students
turn their cultural heritage
to profit. The same basic
principle continued from
the marketing of Fort
Marion prisoners' drawings
to the formation of the
Santa Fe Indian School (see
cat. no. 283).

Students often decorat-
ed commercially produced
items. Luther Standing
Bear, one of the first
pupils at the Carlisle
Indian School in
Pennsylvania, remembers
being given wooden plates
to paint (Standing Bear
1928, p. 146), and stu-
dents at the Hampton
Normal and Agricultural
Institute also produced
large quantities of such
work for sale and as gifts

to financial supporters.
On this manufactured
vase Etahdleuh, a Fort
Marion prisoner who
entered Hampton in 1878,
has painted a standing
warrior, a tipi, and a
mounted Kiowa man.
The rider carries an eagle-
feather fan and wears
southern Plains–style
leggings.

The equestrian image is
strikingly close to an
Etahdleuh watercolor on
paper (cat. no. 265) showing two figures on horse-
back. The standing figure
bears some resemblance to
a watercolor at the
Massachusetts Historical
Society (Petersen 1971, pl.
34). The Hampton archives
note that the vase was
"painted by E. Tahdleuh in
the Industrial Sewing Room
in charge of Miss Galpin."
LL

265

Attributed to Red Hawk
**A courting couple**
Lakota, ca. 1885
Paper, pencil, crayon, ink
7⅜ x 12¼ in
Milwaukee Public
Museum, 2036
Provenance: Collected by
Captain R. Miller, Wounded
Knee Creek, South Dakota,
January 8, 1891

Courting was a popular
subject in many sketch-
books during the early
reservation period. Here, a
young warrior riding his
finest horse comes to visit a
handsomely attired single
woman. They both carry
the parti-colored umbrellas
that were such a fashion on
the Plains during the late
nineteenth century. The frequency of courting scenes
in drawings and beadwork

(cat. nos. 269, 270) clearly
indicates that the social
process of finding a mate
and establishing a family
was an honored part of
Plains life. This drawing is
from a book that was taken
from the body of a dead
Lakota warrior on the
killing ground at Wounded
Knee, on the Pine Ridge
Reservation in South
Dakota. On December 29,
1890, at the height of the
white hysteria over the
Ghost Dance, Si-Tanka (Big
Foot) and his camp of
Minneconjou Lakota were
attacked by an overwhelm-
ing army force, and more
than three hundred men,
women, and children were
massacred. This sounded
the death knell for Indian
freedom on the Plains.
EMM

Clara Archilta (b. 1912)
**Panel**
Kiowa-Apache-Tonkawa,
1984
Seed beads, glue, masonite
20 x 16 in
U.S. Department of the
Interior, Indian Arts and
Crafts Board, Southern
Plains Indian Museum and
Crafts Center
References: Southern Plains
Indian Museum 1986

Beadwork, like many forms
of art, is continually changing as artists find new
approaches to their work.
Here Clara Archilta has
modified the technique of a
traditional medium. In most

beadwork, the beads are
sewn onto cloth or hide, but
Archilta has used liquid
adhesive to attach threaded
beads to a hard, flat surface.

This panel is suffused
with color and pattern. By
integrating small areas of
color in the foreground, the
artist has given depth and
texture to the landscape.
The imagery is a conven-
tional Plains subject with
one interesting difference,
the depiction of motion.
The angle of this horse
would not be seen in earlier
Plains pictorial works. The
artist may have developed
this approach by working
with photographic images.
AC

267

268

**Pipe bag**

Minneconjou Lakota,
ca. 1885
Native-tanned hide, glass
beads, porcupine quills,
metal, dyed horsehair
32¼ x 7½ in
The Denver Art Museum,
museum purchase,
1948.156
Provenance: Collected by
Victor J. Evans
References: Conn 1982,
p. 112, fig. 83; Lessard
1990, p. 55, fig. 1

**Tipi bag**

Minneconjou Lakota,
ca. 1885
Native-tanned hide, glass
beads, metal, dyed deer
hair
17 x 20 in
Cranbrook Institute of
Science, 8603
Provenance: Collected by
Edgar M. Height, 1890
References: Lessard 1990,
p. 56, fig. 2; Maurer 1977,
p. 173, cat. no. 214

This pipe bag (cat. no.
269) by the Cheyenne
River master beadworker
must have been collected
very soon after it was finished, because it is so well
preserved and lacks indications of wear or use. The
scenes on both sides of the
bag depict a courting couple. On one side, the
young woman stands in
front of her tipi dressed in
fine clothes, including an
elk-tooth dress, long dentalium earrings, and a
beaded buffalo robe
around her waist. The

other side shows her suit-
or, a young warrior with
an eagle feather in his hair
as a sign of achievements
in war. He is wrapped in
an elegantly beaded or
quilled buffalohide robe
and holds an eagle-wing
fan and a cavalry saber
with two eagle feathers
suspended from its hilt. He
has brought a gift of six
fine horses to show his
worthiness and seriousness
as a prospective husband.

The Lakota woman
from the Cheyenne River
Reservation who made the
tipi bag was a master of
pictorial beadwork who set
a standard that still inspires
contemporary pictorial
beadworkers (cat. no. 276).
Her intricately designed figures show the salient features of a form or design,
such as the elk-tooth-
decorated blue stroud
dresses worn by the two
women on the horse to the
left. The three suitors on
the right have eagle feathers
in their hair. Two of them
carry eagle-feather fans,
and the man standing
between the two horses is
resplendent in his decorated
robe, long trailer of metal
disks, and a cavalry saber
hung with four rows of
eagle feathers.

EMM

269

270

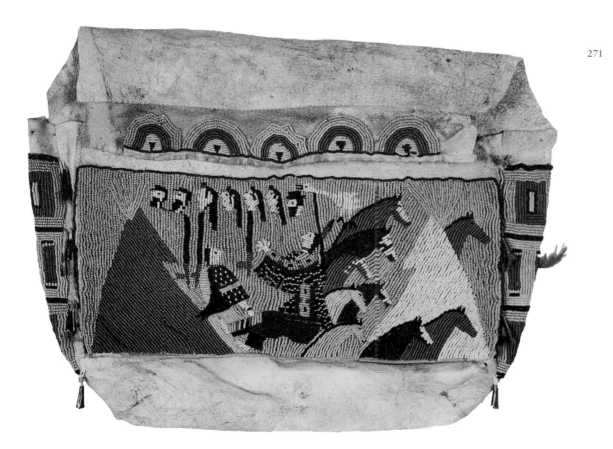

271

**Tipi bag**
Minneconjou Lakota,
ca. 1885
Native-tanned hide, glass
beads, metal, dyed deer
hair
18 x 20 in
National Museum of the
American Indian,
Smithsonian Institution,
6/0325
Provenance: Collected by
Joseph Keppler

In this Cheyenne River–style
bag, the pictorial beadwork
illustrates a camp with two
tipis, a herd of nine horses,
and a man sitting on the
ground telling the story of
his war honors to a woman
sitting in front of him. The
man has been identified as
White Swan, a Minneconjou
chief who was active as a
leader from 1866 to 1900.
White Swan's name glyph
appears over his head, and a
series of seven heads is seen
next to it. The heads with
hats and beards represent
white men, probably sol-
diers killed in battle; the
other four heads, with the
forehead crest hairstyle, are
most likely Crow enemies
killed by White Swan. The
three pipes with blue stems
and red bowls indicate that
White Swan was the leader
of three war expeditions in
which two Crow and one
soldier were killed. A recita-
tion of war honors was a
regular part of a courtship,
in which a warrior described his accomplishments.
EMM

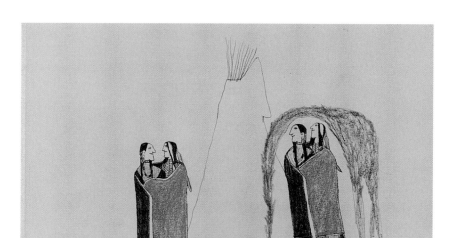

273

This man
Indian Kiowa
write me and
Koba

272

Wild Horse (Koba)
(1848–80)
**Courting couples**
Kiowa (Gaigwa), ca. 1875
Paper, pencil, ink, crayon,
watercolor
7¾ x 12½ in
National Anthropological
Archives, Smithsonian
Institution, 39-C
Provenance: Formerly in the
collection of the Bureau of
American Ethnology,
donated by the collector's
widow, Mrs. Mary B.
Reynolds, Washington,
D.C., 1945; collected by
Burnet S. Reynolds at Fort
Marion, St. Augustine,
Florida, ca. 1875

Koba was a Kiowa war-
rior with experience in
horse raids and war before
he was taken prisoner and
sent to Fort Marion at the
age of twenty-seven. After
three years under the strict
discipline and rigorous
acculturation programs of
Captain Pratt, the zealous
officer in charge of the
Indian prisoners, Koba
volunteered to go to the
Hampton Institute in
Virgina to learn the
English language and be
schooled in Christianity,
farming, and at least one
manual trade. Koba was
praised as being "one of
the brightest and most
promising among the
scholars" and was admit-
ted to the program
(Petersen 1971, p. 131).
He spent a year at
Hampton and then moved
to Lee, Massachusetts,

where he was employed as
a farm worker. From there
he went to the Carlisle
Institute in Pennsylvania
for a year before returning
to the reservation in
Oklahoma in the fall of
1880. He died later that
year of consumptive
tuberculosis.

In this drawing Koba
shows himself and a young
lady wrapped together in a
blanket, a traditional courting custom of the Plains
tribes. The man would
approach a woman he
wanted to talk to and wrap
his blanket around them as
a formal sign of his
courtship intentions. The
woman could simply refuse
or could stay with him,
talking for hours. This type
of courting ritual was performed publicly and often
with others there as unoffi-
cial chaperones.

EMM

Wohaw (Gu hau de?)
(1855–1924)
**Courting couples**
Kiowa (Gaigwa), 1877
Paper, pencil, colored pencil
8¾ x 11¼ in
Missouri Historical Society,
1880.13.41
References: Harris 1989,
pp. 58–59, no. 16; Berlo
1982, pp. 10–11, fig. 11

In traditional Plains society,
courtship and marriage
were strictly regulated by
older adults. Marriages
were generally arranged
between families, but the
wishes of the principals
were usually taken into consideration. A young man
could attract a woman's
attention by strolling in
front of her family's tipi,
hoping to catch her alone
and envelop her in his
blanket for conversation.

In this drawing made by
the Fort Marion prisoner
Wohaw, two couples stand
near a tipi, one under a shade
arbor, suggesting the summer
season. The clothing and jewelry of both men and women
are shown in considerable
detail. Courtship as subject
matter for drawings seems to
begin with the Fort Marion
artists, who produced many
such scenes; it is not represented in earlier ledger books
(Harris 1989, p. 58). The
images may have developed
from the prisoners' loneliness,
from European Americans'
interest in the quaint and
exotic, or from both factors.

LL

Buffalo Meat (Oewotoh)
(1847–1917)

**A newly married man
receiving his friends**

Cheyenne (Tsistsistas),
1876

Paper, ink, graphite,
colored pencil

8½ x 11¼ in

Amon Carter Museum,
Fort Worth, 1965.48.1.4

Provenance: Purchased
from the Old Print Shop,
Inc., 1965; given by the
artist to Captain Richard
H. Pratt, Fort Marion,
Florida, 1977

In traditional Cheyenne
society a man was expect-
ed to court a young
woman for one to five
years before he could
expect an offer of marriage
to be accepted by her and
her family. Marriages were
carefully negotiated, and
the groom was expected to
provide horses and other
valuable goods in
exchange for the daughter
whose presence and labor
had been part of her family
system. Grinnell reports
that a newly married man
was expected to show that
he was a good provider by
bringing back plenty of
meat from the hunt. "If he
failed himself to kill
enough meat, his friends
made it a point of honor to
see that his horses were
loaded. . . . A part of it
was cooked and a feast
given to his friends, his

wife asking some old man
to call out the names of the
husband's friends, inviting
them to the feast"
(Grinnell 1923, pp.
145–46).

Buffalo Meat's drawing
describes just such a scene.
The artist sits in front of his
painted tipi dressed in his
finest clothes and holding
an eagle-feather fan. His
bride is just coming out of
their lodge to bring her
husband his pipe and pipe
bag, which he will use at
the feast for a smoke of
prayer and welcome. A
wooden rack behind the
tipi is hung with a sun
shade made from a striped
Mexican blanket. Buffalo
Meat's five male friends are
also dressed in their best
visiting clothes, including
woolen blankets decorated
with wide beaded strips
and two finely woven
Saltillo blankets traded up
from Mexico. Three of the
men, including Star and
Little Chief, carry eagle-
wing fans; the other two
have sabers whose hilts are
hung with long cloth sashes
decorated with eagle feathers. All of the men have
long trailers of nickel silver
disks hanging down their
backs and wear chokers
and breastplates made from
tubular bone beads.

EMM

Old White Woman

**Courting couple**

Cheyenne (Tsistsistas),
ca. 1880

Paper, graphite, colored
pencil, ink

7 x 11 in

Collection of Jonathan
Holstein

The Cheyenne use of a blanket in courtship was adapted
from a Lakota practice
known as *sina aopemai ina-
jinpi*, "standing wrapped in
the blanket" (Grinnell 1923,
p. 132; Powers 1980, p. 45).

When a young Cheyenne
man wished to court a
young woman formally, he
would wait for her outside
her lodge, wrapped in a
blanket or robe and possibly
carrying love medicine of
the white-tailed deer. When
the young woman passed
by, the suitor would place
his arms around her, enve-
loping her in the courting
blanket. With their heads
hidden from view, the couple would quietly talk within the privacy of the blanket.
The woman could, at any
time, reject a suitor by breaking away from his embrace.

In this drawing the artist
depicted torsos rather than
full-length figures, an unusual touch that enhances
the intimate tone. The artist
has reduced the complex,
irregular form of the blanket into a simple block of
color. The overlay of the
profile on the front of the
face is also unusual in early
Plains drawing.

AC

275

274

Todd Yellow Cloud Agusta
**Baby bonnet**
Oglala Lakota, 1991
Cotton fabric, glass beads
6¼ x 4¾ x 5¾ in
The Minneapolis Institute
of Arts, the Christina N.
and Swan J. Turnblad
Memorial Fund, 91.93
Provenance: Purchased at
the Northern Plains Tribal
Arts exhibition, Sioux Falls,
South Dakota, 1991

Beaded baby bonnets are a
classic example of an acculturated form. In nineteenth-
century Euro-American
society, headgear was virtually an omnipresent con-
vention of dress—an indi-
cator of social class and an
area for display of prestige
that extended even into
infants' clothing. Plains
Indian women took the
bonnet form further still,
entirely covering the surface with quilling or beadwork that is elegant but
could hardly have been
comfortable. Probably such
bonnets were not for daily
wear.

This finely beaded con-
temporary example com-
bines large star and flag

motifs on the center strip
with narrative scenes on the
side panels. On the proper
left side a woman sits cross-
legged beside a cooking pot,
a meat-drying rack in the
background and a horse's
head looming over her. On
the right panel a young man
wrapped in a quilled robe
leads a cavalcade. These
images draw on late nine-
teenth-century examples, all
of which are included in this
exhibition: the cavalcade
derives from a pipe bag at
the Denver Art Museum
(cat. no. 269), and the seated
woman closely follows the
design on a tipi bag from the
University Museum,
University of Pennsylvania
(cat. no. 261). The star and
crossed-flag motif is close to
that on the sides of a beaded
suitcase (cat. no. 260). All
three early works were published by Dennis Lessard
(Lessard 1990) in an article
attributing the style to the
Cheyenne River Reservation.
Lessard's publication has
stimulated the interest of
several contemporary bead
artists (see also cat. no. 85).
This example received the
South Dakota Governor's
Award at the Northern
Plains Tribal Arts exhibition.

In his history of the
Ghost Dance, Mooney
notes that the infant

Zitkala-noni, one of the
few Lakota survivors of
Wounded Knee, was wear-
ing "a little cap of buckskin, upon which the
American flag was embroi-
dered in bright beadwork"
when she was found by
United States soldiers next
to her mother's body in the
aftermath of the battle
(Mooney [1896] 1965, p.
132). His inclusion of this
detail suggests that he was
not insensitive to the
painfully ironic appearance
of the flag motif in those
circumstances.
LL

276

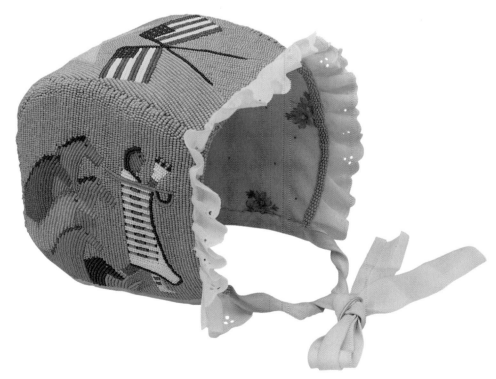

277

278

279

Horace Poolaw (1906–84)
**After the Peyote Meeting,
Mountain View, Oklahoma**
Kiowa (Gaigwa), ca. 1930
Gelatin silver print
8 x 11¹¹⁄₁₆ in
The Horace Poolaw
Photography Project,
Stanford University
References: Marriott and
Poolaw 1990, p. 27, cat.
no. 64

Peyotism swept across the
southern Plains around the
turn of the century, and by
1920 was formalized into
the Native American
Church. Incorporating elements of Christian belief
into a more traditional
Plains religious structure and
adding the ingestion of peyote as a sacred ritual practice, the Native American
Church continues to play an
important cultural role for
many Plains people. Here
participants in a night-long
peyote ceremony are gath-
ered outside a tipi on the following morning, resting,
smoking, and talking.
Several of the men are lying
down, perhaps still recover-
ing from the effects of the
drug. Despite the formal
grouping of the figures in the
background and the symme-
try of the composition, the
photograph has an intimate
quality absent in Poolaw's
more public views.
LL

Horace Poolaw (1906–84)
**Kiowa Group in American
Indian Exposition Parade,
Anadarko, Oklahoma**
Kiowa (Gaigwa), 1941
Gelatin silver print
12¾ x 9⅞ in
The Horace Poolaw
Photography Project,
Stanford University
References: Marriott and
Poolaw 1990, p. 26, cat.
no. 62

The Craterville Indian
Fair, a white-owned tourist
attraction, closed in 1929;
perhaps business declined
because of the Depression.
The next year, however, a
group of Indian people in
nearby Anadarko estab-
lished the American Indian
Exposition, which still
takes place there every
year. In this parade photo,
Kiowa women and men
ride on a car, their elaborate costumes and self-dis-
play fulfilling outside
expectations of tourist
pageantry. Probably the
photos that visitors took
home with them looked
very much like this one,
even though Poolaw was
for many years the official
photographer for the exposition.
LL

Horace Poolaw (1906–84)
**Carnegie Indians Baseball
Team, Carnegie, Oklahoma**
Kiowa (Gaigwa), ca. 1933
Gelatin silver print
7¹⁵⁄₁₆ x 11⅜ in
The Horace Poolaw
Photography Project,
Stanford University
References: Marriott and
Poolaw 1990, p. 23, cat.
no. 46

In prereservation times,
men worked cooperatively
in hunting bands and war
parties, but games or team
sports were largely the
province of boys. When
traditional means of social
interaction were no longer
available, new ways developed, including introduced
sports. Here a team of
adult men from the small
Oklahoma town of
Carnegie are assembled in a
standard-format team pic-
ture following a game. The
man in a brimmed hat at
the center is probably the
manager. The uniforms,
equipment, and labeled
valise indicate a considerable degree of organization;
probably the Indians played
on a local small-town
circuit.
LL

Horace Poolaw (1906–84)
**Bryce Poolaw, Anadarko, Oklahoma**
Kiowa (Gaigwa), 1947
Gelatin silver print
8⅞ x 5¼ in
The Horace Poolaw
Photography Project,
Stanford University
References: Marriott and
Poolaw 1990, cat. no. 6

Besides his extensive documentation of contemporary Kiowa lifeways, Horace Poolaw also recorded the lives and events of his family. Here his youngest child, Bryce, smiles at the photographer from the security of his cradleboard. The photo appears to have been made at night, probably at a family or social event. By 1947, many Kiowa parents probably used manufactured baby equipment, but in families conscious of the importance of the past, traditional clothing and accoutrements would have made an appearance, particularly on special occasions.

LL

Horace Poolaw (1906–84)
**Evelyn Saunkeah, Lucy Apheatone, Nell Saunkeah, Vivian Saunkeah, Rainy Mountain Church, Mountain View, Oklahoma**
Kiowa (Gaigwa), ca. 1930
Gelatin silver print
8⅜ x 11⅜ in
The Horace Poolaw
Photography Project,
Stanford University
References: Marriott and
Poolaw 1990, p. 19, cat.
no. 19

The four young girls in this picture were attending a Christmastime camp meeting sponsored by the Rainy Mountain Baptist Church. Their clothing and posture, the Christmas presents in their arms, even the occasion itself all suggest the strong influence of the outside world among Kiowa people in the 1920s and 1930s. At the same time, the tents in the background (part of the temporary church encampment), the pattern of cyclical ceremonial times for which people gathered from some distance, even the practice of gift exchange all have deep roots in the traditional Plains ways of life.

LL

David P. Little (Oyate Wachinyapi) (b. 1953)
**Three Lakota Girls in Their Dancing Dress**
Oglala Lakota, 1990
Color coupler print
8 x 10 in
The Minneapolis Institute of Arts, the John R. Van Derlip Fund, 92.9.2
Provenance: Purchased from the artist

The creation and wearing of traditional costume has always been one of the major expressions of cultural identity of the Plains Indian people. Among contemporary Plains tribes, traditional dress is worn on special occasions such as coming-of-age ceremonies, school graduations, and weddings, as well as at the powwows that are growing in number and popularity. Families will commit a great deal of time and resources to the making of fine clothing and jewelry for their children so that they can grow up within a strong Indian cultural environment.

Photographer David Little's portrait of three Lakota girls shows their pride and excitement in wearing the clothes that are an integral part of their cultural heritage. The girls' names also reflect the importance of tradition. From left to right they are Her Good Day (Ta Anpetu Waste Win), Rattling Woman (Sinte Hla Win), and Good Cedar Woman (Hante Waste Win). Traditional Indian names contribute to a strong sense of identity as a member of a Native American family.

EMM

280

281

282

283

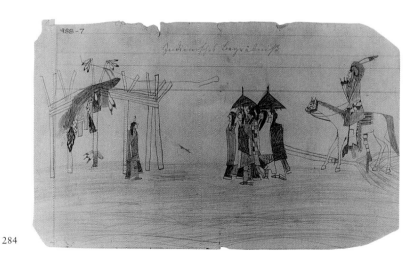

284

Oscar Howe (1915–83)
**Dakota Teaching**
Yanktonai Nakota, 1951
Watercolor, paper
14 x 21³⁄₁₆ in
The Philbrook Museum of
Art, Tulsa, 51.8
Provenance: Purchased
from the artist at the Sixth
Annual Contemporary
American Indian Painting
Exhibition, 1951
References: Dockstader
1982, p. 26, ill. p. 50

As Oscar Howe's artistic
style matured, he began to
integrate new expressive
means into his work. This
development was contro-
versial because it broke the
boundaries of convention-
ally defined "Indian" art.
Howe became an eloquent
spokesman for the right of
Native American artists to
draw from both traditional
and contemporary sources.

*Dakota Teaching* is one
of his last works before this
dramatic shift in style.
Painted in broad, flat areas
of color, the work shows
an older man seated on a
hide outside a decorated
tipi. He holds an eagle
feather in his hand, and a
number of small imple-
ments are scattered beside
him. At the left, a boy and
a girl hold what appear to
be eagle-bone whistles. In
its balanced composition
and gentle tone, the picture
emphasizes the importance
of elders as teachers and
the value of tradition.

LL

**A Plains burial**
Kiowa (Gaigwa), ca. 1885
Paper, pencil, crayon
7 x 12 in
Texas Memorial Museum,
1988-7
Provenance: Acquired from
Lilly Tips (wife of Carlos),
1964; Carlos Tips,
Frankfurt, Germany; Dr.
Edward H. Tips, Austin,
Texas; collected by
Hermann Schild, U.S.
Indian Commissioner,
Dakota, Arkansas, 1895

Burial and mourning rites
were important in traditional Plains cultures and are
still followed with the
utmost care and respect.
This drawing shows a
funeral oration being delivered by a friend or relative
of the deceased, whose
body has been carefully prepared and placed on the
burial scaffold. Bodies were
also put on platforms in
trees, in caves, or in crevices
in the rocks or were placed
on the ground and covered
with large piles of stones.
Clothing and objects of personal value were often
buried with their owners,
but most belongings were
redistributed to other members of the tribe, a practice
still followed in the "give-
away" ceremony, in which
blankets and household
goods are distributed following the funeral. The
Plains people have a strong
concept of an afterlife. The
Cheyenne, for example,

believe that "the spirit of
the dead man found the
trail where the footprints all
pointed the same way, followed that to the Milky
Way, and finally arrived at
the camp in the stars, where
he met his friends and relations and lived in the camp
of the dead" (Grinnell
1923, p. 160).

EMM

Blue Thunder
**Winter count**
Upper Yanktonai Dakota,
ca. 1931
Muslin; red, yellow, and
blue pigment
35 x 134 in
State Historical Society of
North Dakota, 86.234.22
Provenance: Collected by
Usher Lloyd Burdick
References: Porsche 1987,
p. 78

Among the Dakota, calendar histories like this one are known as winter records (*waniyetù wowápi*) or winter counts (*waniyetù yawápi*). In this context the term "winter" denotes the entire year from one winter to the next. James H. Howard (1976) noted that the introduction of a standard orthography for the Dakota language (Santee dialect) in 1852 led to a gradual growth in literacy in the native language, which resulted in the use of the written word rather than a pictograph to describe an event. While many keepers of the winter counts maintained the visual record, others completely abandoned pictographs in favor of a written document.

Blue Thunder, the man responsible for this winter count, was a scout and camp crier from the Standing Rock Reservation. The count is primarily Upper Yanktonai, with the addition of events pertaining to the Blackfeet and Hunkpapa bands of the Teton Lakota. Blue Thunder painted four versions of this winter count, which documents the years from 1785 to 1913. This one has been extended by a group of pictographs that brings the history up to 1931. These later images appear to have been done by as many as four different persons. In the main body of work, a direct, bold line was used to define the images as clearly as possible. Blue Thunder's pictographs cover a wide range of subjects, including many figures of Indian men and women, warriors, Animal Dreamer Dancers, and animals. Many winter counts are still maintained as an important aspect of traditional Plains life.

EMM

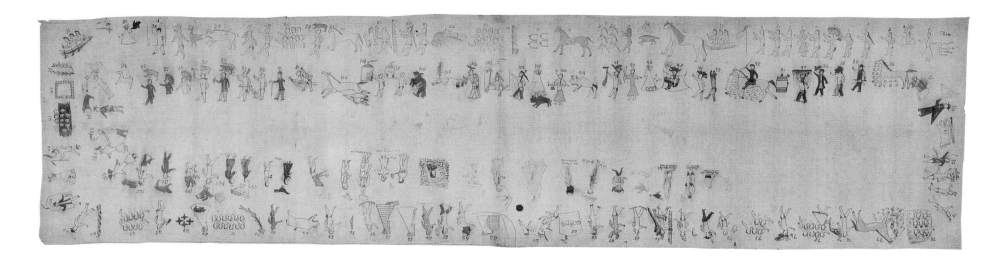

285

Attributed to Swift Dog
(Ta-sunka-duza) (1834–1925)
**Winter count**
Hunkpapa Lakota,
ca. 1912
Muslin cloth; blue and
black ink; red, yellow, and
green pigment
35 x 53 in
State Historical Society of
North Dakota, 791
Provenance: Collected by
the Reverend Aaron
McGaffey Beede, Fort
Yates, Standing Rock
Reservation, North
Dakota, ca. 1930

Winter counts are calendrical histories that were kept by many tribes throughout the Plains as a means of codifying the historical record of the people and as a sequenced structure to determine the relative passage of time. A symbol, object, or simple scene served to represent an entire year. These pictographic images illustrated the most important or unusual event of the year. Garrick Mallery, one of the first scholars to study winter counts, was told that among the Yanktonai Dakota the " 'Keeper of the Count' was responsible for the perpetuation of the history . . . with this counsel of the old men of his tribe, he decided upon some event or circumstance which should distinguish each year as it passed, and marked what was considered to be its appropriate symbol or device upon a buffalo robe kept for the purpose. The robe was at convenient times exhibited to other Indians of the tribe, who were thus taught the meaning and the use of the signs as designating the several years" (Mallery 1889, p. 266).

This winter count is a copy of an older document associated with a Lakota man named High Dog. Following Lakota tradition, the responsibility for maintaining the history was passed on from one generation to the next. When it was collected, this version documented 114 years of Lakota history, from 1797–98 to 1911–12. The collector was the Reverend Mr. Beede, who served as the director of Episcopal mission work in North Dakota from 1901 to 1917. Beede worked with Hunkpapa elders to transcribe an explanation of the pictographs. For example, the horse with two riders falling from its back (no. 8) illustrates the year 1805, when the Crow attacked a Lakota village in a major battle in which some of the Crow warriors were mounted two on one horse. The year 1911–12 is remembered as the time when children had measles and a bright comet appeared in the skies. All of Swift Dog's drawings are clearly rendered for maximum visual impact. (See Howard 1960, pp. 335–416, pls. 45–47.)

EMM

286

**Cradleboard**

Oglala Lakota, before 1910
Tanned hide, wood, cotton,
glass beads
41 x 11½ x 13 in
American Museum of
Natural History, 50.1/1269
References: Pohrt 1975,
pp. 44–45

Unlike most Lakota baby
carriers, this one includes
the supporting boards
used by Cheyenne and
other southern peoples.
The cover is certainly one
of the most complex and
ambitious examples of
Plains pictorial beadwork
extant. Even the staves
are wrapped in beads;
during the florescent
period of beadwork
Plains women jokingly
claimed to be able to
bead anything that would
stand still.

   The outer surface
depicts an important
moment in the life of the
Oglala leader Red Cloud:
returning home from an
1871 trip to Washington,
D.C., to meet with the
president and other gov-
ernment officials, he was
given a gift of horses by
his escort, Major ("Genl.")
Smith (see pp. 52–56). At
that moment in the diffi-
cult history of Lakota relations with the American
government, things seemed
relatively peaceful,
although they deteriorated
quickly thereafter.

287

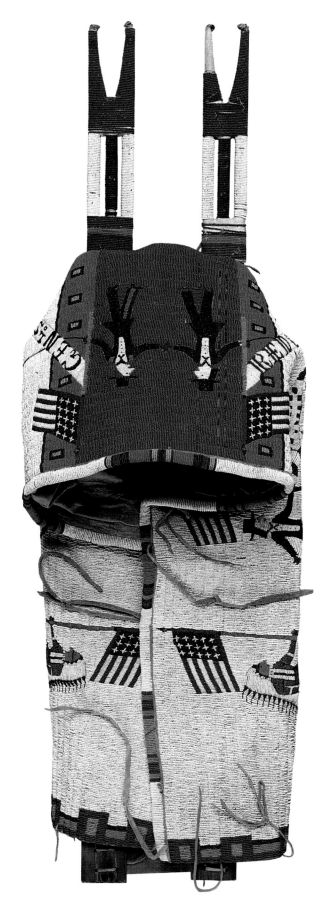

Depictions of historical events occur with some frequency in drawing books, but they are highly unusual in beadwork and still less common on cradleboards. The use of this scene on a cradle probably made some years after the event may represent a wish for a stable future for the infant. It is possible that the cradle was made within Red Cloud's family, perhaps even as late as the time of his death in 1909, although little information about provenance survives. The clothing worn by the two men and their followers seems to correspond with the skirted frock coat worn by army officers in the 1870s and 1880s (Shelly Madson, personal communication, June 1992). If the cradle is indeed of a later date, one might speculate that the image is based on earlier photographs.

LL

287

Howling Wolf (Honanistto)
(1850–1927)
**Three autobiographical scenes**
Southern Cheyenne
(Tsistsistas), ca. 1876
Paper, pencil, crayon
8¾ x 11¼ in
Field Museum of Natural
History, Chicago, 83999
Provenance: Made at Fort
Marion, Florida, ca.
1876–77

The 1870s were difficult
years on the southern
Plains. Efforts at building a
lasting peace between
Indians and whites were
constantly disrupted by
incidents of violence on
both sides. The army was
trying to keep supply routes
open and maintain the safety of the whites who were
moving through or settling
in the territories of
Oklahoma and Texas, the
ancient homelands of the
Kiowa, Comanche,
Southern Arapaho, and
Southern Cheyenne.
Catalogue number 288
shows a large group of
Indian men and women sit-
ting in a large circle on the
parade ground of an army

fort. The only whites present are the lone army officer, the bearded man wearing a hat and talking to an
Indian man in the center of
the scene, and the man driving the wagon that has just
deposited the large pile of
goods on the ground.
Howling Wolf illustrates
one of the many occasions
when the army and the
government agents tried to
barter goods for the co-
operation of the southern
Plains tribes and their
promise to keep the peace.
The whites have offered
cloth, metal buckets, axes,
and two rifles. As the short
figure holding a pipe in the
center of the circle calls out
names, people come for-
ward to receive their allot-
ment of goods. Four men
are shown by dotted lines
to be returning to their
families with gifts of buckets and cloth. The man on
the left is smoking a pipe—
a sign of his peaceful
intentions.

Unfortunately there
were many instances in
which the more militant
and aggressive of the warriors could not be con-
trolled, and a continuing
series of hostile acts resulted in strong military action.
In December of 1874,
Lieutenant Richard H.
Pratt of the Tenth Cavalry
was detailed to investigate
the situation and conduct
hearings to determine who
were the most dangerous
warriors in the area. In the

288

289

Howling Wolf.

290

following months, seventy-two Indian men were arrested on charges ranging from murder to being a "ringleader" of the resistance. In the spring of 1875 the men were sent by train to Fort Marion in St. Augustine, Florida, which would serve as their prison for the next three years.

Pratt, who had made the investigation and arrest, was promoted to captain and put in charge of the group on its journey to Florida and assigned to act as their commandant in prison. The scene depicted in catalogue number 289 shows the Indian prisoners on the trip; the three images of trains indicate the many times they had to stop on the journey. In the center the prisoners are shown sitting on the ground in front of army barracks. A detail of soldiers with fixed bayonettes stands guard while two others bring them cups of water to drink. Catalogue number 290, an ambitious view of land and water, shows the transfer of the prisoners from a train to a steamboat that will take them to Fort Marion. The Indian men are standing on the deck of the boat with their guards. The prisoners attracted a great deal of attention on their trip and during their imprisonment at Fort Marion. Pratt eventually allowed them to sell drawings and crafts to visitors and even staged a hunt in which three Indians on horseback killed a bull with arrows for the amusement of the crowd.

The cultural shock of the trip and prison must have been tremendous for these men who had spent their lives as freely moving buffalo hunters. Howling Wolf's drawings show his ability to observe and record the details of an unfamiliar world with the same accuracy that he applied to scenes from his traditional environment. It is interesting that he drew a cross on the train engine and the two large vessels (cat. no. 290), showing how closely he associated the Christianity of Captain Pratt and his other teachers with the circumstances of his transportation and captivity.

EMM

Zotom (1853–1913)

**Four autobiographical scenes**

Kiowa (Gaigwa), 1876

Colored pencil, paper

8½ x 11 x ½ in

Taylor Museum for Southwestern Studies, Colorado Springs Fine Arts Center

Zotom was one of seventy-one men arrested and sent to prison at Fort Marion, Florida, in 1875. Like many of his fellow prisoners, he earned money and a measure of fame by producing sketchbooks of drawings and painted ceramics and fans for sale to tourists and the surrounding St. Augustine community. On one occasion when Zotom was commissioned to duplicate one of his sketchbooks, a delay in the work prompted Captain Pratt to write, "Zotom is very slow with the duplicate book because the lady visitors have flooded us with fans to paint, and his reputation gives him the lion's share" (Petersen 1971, p. 66). The drawings shown here are from a sketchbook containing fourteen.

Catalogue number 291 is a simple linear composition of pup tents erected alongside a small building. Several soldiers appear both in and out of the tents, some with only their feet visible. Scenes such as this were commonplace at Fort Marion and the forts where the prisoners were held before they arrived in Florida. In catalogue number 292, a row of army officers is viewed from behind. The eleven men in the center appear identical in form and dress.

Catalogue number 293 illustrates both the interior and the exterior of a building, presumably the one where the prisoners received academic instruction and vocational training. Through the symmetrically placed windows the viewer can see inside the rooms, where four female school teachers seem to be instructing the prisoners seated on benches. This drawing is an exercise in depth and perspective. Although objects farther away usually appear smaller, here the artist chose to draw the men in the foreground smaller and the women in the background larger, so the women can be clearly seen.

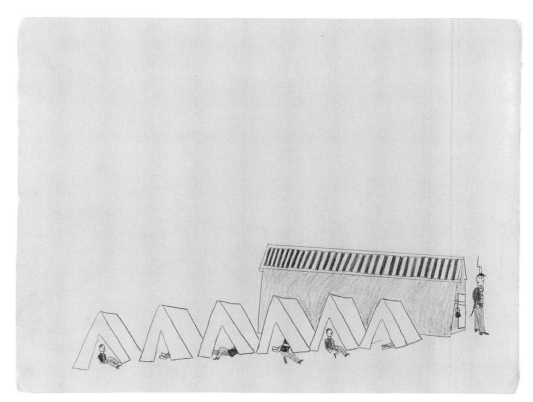

291

292

293

294

Catalogue number 294 appears to be the interior of a church, with symmetrically arranged lamps, doorways, pews, and windows. Once again the artist tackled the difficult task of showing depth and spatial relationships. The clergyman, who in actuality is the farthest away, is drawn quite large, looming over the people in the foreground. Perhaps this hieratic rendering was used purposely by the artist to signify the clergyman's status.

Following his release from Fort Marion in 1878, Zotom spent three more years in the East pursuing additional education and religious training. By 1881 Zotom, baptized Paul Caryl Zotom, had become an ordained deacon of the Episcopal church and had returned to Indian Territory to establish an Episcopal mission among the Kiowa, Comanche, and Kiowa-Apache (Petersen 1971, p. 179).

Like many of the men held at Fort Marion, Zotom found his return to his people difficult. Caught between the white man's ways and the ways of their people, these men found little acceptance in either world. Scrutinized by church leaders out of fear he would leave the "white man's road" and "return to the blanket," Zotom struggled in his service to the Episcopal church and later the Baptist church. By his death in 1913, he was practicing peyotism, the syncretic religion later known as the Native American Church (Petersen 1971, p. 190).

Zotom produced most of his artistic work while at Fort Marion. Tipi models painted for the anthropologist James Mooney almost twenty years later constitute his only works after his release from Fort Marion (Petersen 1971, p. 190).

AC

**Indian policemen**
Assiniboine (Nakoda),
ca. 1897
Paper, ink, crayon
5⅛ x 8 in
Glenbow Museum,
Calgary, Alberta
985.221.131
Provenance: Collected by
Dr. O. C. Edwards, Indian
Department physician,
Ottawa, Canada

The governments of the
United States and Canada
established Indian police
forces to maintain order on
the newly formed Plains
reservations. Just as the
*akicita* warrior societies
provided a force for maintaining public order in the
traditional Plains camp, so
did the Indian police orga-
nize former warriors to act
in this capacity in their new
environment. The police-
men were issued military
uniforms, arms, and badges
of authority. The police
were for the most part
accepted by the people, but
incidents like the arrest and
killing of Sitting Bull by
Red Tomahawk and the
other Lakota Indian police
in December of 1891 led to
angry resentment and dis-
trust. Plains reservations in
the United States are still
patrolled by Indian police
organized by the Federal
Bureau of Indian Affairs.
EMM

295

296

297

Wohaw (Gu hau de?)
(1855–1924)
**Pair of double portraits**
Kiowa (Gaigwa), 1877
Paper, pencil, colored pencil
8¾ x 11¼ in
Missouri Historical Society,
1882.18.34
Provenance: Collected by
Frances and John Grady in
St. Augustine, Florida,
1877; given to the Missouri
Historical Society by Mr.
and Mrs. James Barry
(Frances Grady's parents),
1882
References: Harris 1989,
pp. 90–91, no. 32

Although a number of Plains
drawings contain detailed
representations of physiog-
nomy and costume, Wohaw's
execution of this drawing is
unique. The artist has
arranged two pairs of figures, one of Kiowa soldiers,
one of American soldiers,
and surrounded each with a
decorative frame. Although
superficially similar, the
American soldiers are differentiated in small details: the
color of their shakos, belts,
and pant stripes and the
addition of a strap across the
shoulder of one. The Kiowa
portraits show more detail,
and more distinction in
detail, than the images of the
whites do. Wohaw seems to
be conveying two points:
that there are parallel systems of distinction in dress
in both societies, and that
Kiowa and American sol-
diers should be thought of in
equal terms.
LL

**A cowboy**
Kiowa (Gaigwa)?
ca. 1885
Paper, pencil, crayon
7½ x 12 in
Texas Memorial Museum,
1988-17
Provenance: Acquired from
Lilly Tips (wife of Carlos),
1964; Carlos Tips,
Frankfurt, Germany; Dr.
Edward H. Tips, Austin,
Texas; collected by
Hermann Schild, U.S.
Indian Commissioner,
Dakota, Arkansas, 1895

In the mythology of the
American West, the pairing
of cowboy and Indian typifies the limited view of
Plains Indian life held by
most citizens in the domi-
nant culture. Stockmen, or
"cowboys," played a significant role in the history of
the modern Plains begin-
ning with the great cattle
drives of the 1860s and
continuing with the estab-
lishment of ranching as a
major industry that still
thrives in many areas.
Contact between the ranchers and the Indians was
often short and violent as
the two groups competed
for grazing and rights of
territorial occupation. This
drawing demonstrates the
Indian artist's keen powers
of observation and ability
to use details to describe
the important identifying
characteristics of subject,
whether from his own cul-
ture or a foreign one. This
cowboy wears the tradi-
tional wide-brimmed felt

hat and bright red bandana
as he puffs on his curved-
stem pipe. He also wears a
long trail coat and a pair of
leather chaps over his high-
heeled riding boots. He
holds the reins and a quirt
in one hand as he prepares
to throw his lariat at a
steer, indicated by tail and
hindquarters as it runs off
the page. The cowboy uses
an elaborate saddle fitted
with silver mounts and a
double girth for roping. His
horse has a carefully braided mane, wears iron horse
shoes, and is branded.
EMM

Unknown student from Carlisle Indian School
**Scene of school enrollment**
Crow (Absaroke), 1891
Paper, pencil, colored pencil
7⅞ x 9⅞ in
Eastern Montana College Library, Special Collections, Charles H. Barstow Collection of Indian Ledger Art, 1930.51
Provenance: Collected by Charles H. Barstow, Bureau of Indian Affairs clerk, Crow Reservation, Montana
References: Heidenreich et al. 1985, p. 14, ill. p. 15

Charles H. Barstow, clerk at the Crow Agency from 1878 until 1898, encouraged artistic activities at the agency and collected examples of work. A group of sixty-six drawings from his collection, now at Eastern Montana College, are annotated by the collector. Most show scenes of warfare or domestic life, but a number address themes of Indian–white relations.

The most unusual of these is a drawing that, according to Barstow's notes, was made by "boys from Carlisle Indian School." It shows a rotund man and an Indian policeman confronting a woman who holds a young girl by the hand. Barstow's rather benign interpretation reads as follows: "Major Wyman U.S. Ind. Agent at Crow Agency Mont. with his chief of Police 'Boy that Grabs' trying to get Indian children for the school. A Crow Indian squaw leading her little girl by the hand to deliver her to the Capt. of Police." It is not hard, however, to read in the woman's aggressive stance and gesture, and in the seemingly satirical depiction of Wyman, a dispute over the girl's schooling. While still a student at Carlisle, the Sicangu Lakota Luther Standing Bear recruited children for the school from the western reservations, and his accounts make clear the difficulty in persuading parents to give over their children to an institution where the rate of illness and death was known to be high and where authorities attempted through severe discipline to eradicate traditional language and culture (Standing Bear 1928, pp. 162–66).

LL

Frank Calico
**Page of school notebook**
Oglala Lakota, 1890s?
Paper, ink, colored pencil
10½ x 8 in
Collection of Richard A. and Marion D. Pohrt
Provenance: Arthur Abraham, Flint, Michigan; collected on Pine Ridge Reservation about 1905 by an unknown schoolteacher

This example of school-work combines drawing and penmanship exercises. It appears to be the work of someone around the age of ten. It is hard to know whether the text was the work of Frank Calico himself or was copied or dictated; its principal theme is a careful distinction between horses "that are heavey [sic] and can work," which are preferred by whites, and horses that "have small bodies and can run very fast and long time," which Indians want. The central figure of his drawing is a man wearing an eagle-feather headdress and carrying a coup stick, but the horses seem to be the large, bulky type that "can plow new ground" rather than warriors' mounts. A secondary theme is proper care for horses; animal husbandry was taught in schools and by government agents, but travelers' accounts in prereservation days suggest that general principles of horse care had always been well understood (Roe 1955, pp. 251–52).

LL

298

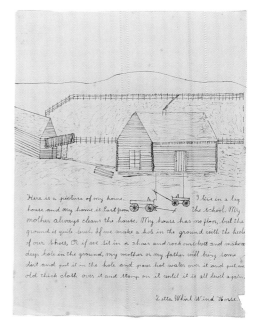

299

300

Zetta Whirl Wind Horse
**Page of school notebook**
Oglala Lakota, 1890s?
Paper, ink
10½ x 8 in
Collection of Richard A.
and Marion D. Pohrt
Provenance: Arthur
Abraham, Flint, Michigan;
collected on Pine Ridge
Reservation about 1905 by
an unknown schoolteacher

While Frank Calico's drawing (cat. no. 299) serves as
embellishment to his text,
Zetta Whirl Wind Horse's
careful and elaborate drawing overshadows the brief
paragraph. It shows the
outside of her family's log
home, including a fenced
pasture, an outbuilding,
two empty wagons, a few
logs on the ground, and the
suggestion of a gateway,
but her writing concen-
trates almost exclusively on
the floor of the house.
From the level of detail
included, we may guess
that she produced the text
herself. Both drawing and
text can be read as a proud
assertion to her teacher of
the cleanliness and order of
her household. Such draw-
ing and writing exercises
reveal both the intentions
of reservation schools and
the concerns and strategies
of the pupils as they
attempted to integrate the
two spheres of their lives.
LL

Arthur Amiotte (b. 1942)
**Prince Albert**
Oglala Lakota, 1989
Collage, acrylic, canvas
20 x 24 in
The Minneapolis Institute
of Arts, the Ethel Morrison
Van Derlip Fund, 90.78

One of the most prominent
contemporary Plains
artists, Arthur Amiotte has
worked in a variety of
media and styles. Trained
in university fine arts programs, he studied briefly
with Oscar Howe. Amiotte
has been a fine arts teacher
at the secondary and uni-
versity levels through
much of his career and has
published and lectured
internationally.

Like much of his work, this
collage draws on Lakota
history and his own family
heritage. *Prince Albert*
combines fragments of
turn-of-the-century tobacco
advertising and packaging
with engravings, family
photos, and text in an ironic commentary that relates
tobacco use, the English
royal family, and Lakota
family traditions and comments critically on white
appropriation and misuse
of Native American culture.

Amiotte's great-grand-
father, Standing Bear,
appears in the lower left
corner; he was for a time a
member of Buffalo Bill's
Wild West show, toured
Europe, and performed
before Queen Victoria, who
appears in multiple images
in the opposite corner. She
in turn is connected to her
consort, Prince Albert, who
provides the link to tobacco. The large central image
is a painting of Chief
Joseph, again taken from
advertising, and along the
bottom edge the artist has
drawn heads with name
glyphs taken from the Red
Cloud census drawing now
in the collections of the
Smithsonian Institution.

In the upper right corner
is a photo of Amiotte's
grandfather, George
Mestith, and beside him, on
paper replicating that of
ledger books, is Amiotte's
wry text: "Us Indians and
us cowboys and us Indian-
Cowboys still like Bull
Durham best. We still
remember and like Albert's
wife, Victoria. She own's
Grandmother's land up
north. Some of our relatives
still live there in Canada."
A companion piece, *Bull
Durham*, is in the museum
at St. Joseph School,
Chamberlain, South
Dakota.
LL

301

Jaune Quick-To-See Smith
(b. 1940)

**Sources of Strength**

Salish-Cree-Shoshone, 1990
Paper, pastel, ink
29¼ x 41¼ in
The Minneapolis Institute
of Arts, the Christina N.
and Swan J. Turnblad
Memorial Fund, 92.64

Jaune Quick-To-See Smith
is one of the Native
American artists who have
been able to bring their
work into the mainstream
of the American and
European contemporary art
market. She is represented
in museums around the
country and has had many
well-reviewed exhibitions,
both here and in Europe.
Smith's very personal style
combines powerful, ener-
getic drawing with a variety
of images that reference,
but do not copy or roman-
ticize, the art created by
past generations of Indian
artists. Raised on the
Flathead Reservation in
Montana, Smith is also an
eloquent and dedicated
advocate of Native
American rights, which she
expresses in her numerous
lectures, panel discussions,
and interviews. In an essay
on the 1987 exhibition
"Women of Sweetgrass,
Cedar, and Sage," Smith
wrote about the role of
women in Native American
art: "Bringing forth the old
forms and materials, building on them, and revitaliz-
ing them is a process that
Indian women have done
for eons. Like New York
artists incorporating and
reacting to Western art history, we respond to our
visual history while crossing into new territories"
(Smith 1987, p. 37). In
*Sources of Strength*, Smith
presents a variety of
images—horse, feather,
bear, thunderbird, hand,
flower, tipi, and human figure. Some are expressed in
traditional forms, such as
the bear and thunderbird
on the left, some in a personal style animated by an
active line, such as the
horse in the lower right or
the petroglyphlike figures in
the upper left. They are
brought together and vital-
ized by a layered zigzag
structure that recalls the
similar lines used in early
Plains ceremonial art to
depict lightning, thunder,
and spiritual power.
EMM

302

Amelia Iron Necklace
(1867?–1936)
**Bilingual English-Dakota
hymnal with beaded cover**
Lakota, ca. 1932
Native-tanned deerskin,
glass beads, muslin, sinew
5½ x 4 x 1 in
South Dakota Art Museum,
gift of the Reverend and
Mrs. Frank Thorburn,
1985.1.33
Provenance: Gift of Amelia
Iron Necklace to the
Reverend Frank Thorburn,
Wakpala, Standing Rock
Reservation, ca. 1931
References: Hail 1988, p. 46

Among missionized Plains
women, liturgical clothing
and paraphernalia became
an area for expression of
Christian religious devotion
and display of needlework
skills, continuing an indigenous tradition of decorated
objects for ceremonial use.
Encouraged by clergy and
religious, artists produced
large numbers of vestments,
altar hangings, and other
items. Some rendered
Christian images directly,
while others incorporated

aspects of traditional Plains
iconography.

Mrs. Amelia Iron
Necklace of Standing Rock
Reservation beaded this
hymnal cover as a gift to the
Reverend Frank Thorburn
of the Episcopal mission at
Standing Rock around
1931. The images combine
allusions to her personal life
with an assimilationist view
appropriate for presentation
to a missionary priest.
Thorburn recorded her
interpretation of the work:
"The front red beads with
eagle are for the Dakota.
We are all Americans. The
date is my husband's death,
1928. The back is white for
the English. The horse was
his favorite that he rode to
church carrying his books.
The middle of the back is
brown, a mixture of red and
white; the two, Indian and
white, have to learn to live
together and sing together"
(Hail 1988, p. 46).

LL

Emerson Spider (b. 1921)
**Medallion necklace**
Oglala Lakota, 1972
Cut glass beads, tanned
leather
3¾ in (diam)
U.S. Department of the
Interior, Indian Arts and
Crafts Board, Sioux Indian
Museum and Crafts Center,
Rapid City, South Dakota,
R-72.2.3
Provenance: Collected by
the lender, 1972
References: Southern Plains
Indian Museum 1986

This beaded medallion
necklace, with its
mosaiclike portrait of
Christ, is the work of the
Oglala artist Emerson
Spider, of the Pine Ridge
Reservation. The symmetrical beadwork pattern on
the cord is a reference to
peyotism and the Native
American Church. Peyote
beadwork designs—repeti-
tive patterns of zigzags
arranged to create a rainbow effect—are found on
gourd rattles, fans, staffs,
and other objects used in
peyote ceremonies. Beads
are painstakingly sewn, one
at a time, with either a
"peyote" (gourd) stitch or
a "Comanche" (brickwork)
stitch (Wiedman 1985,
p. 42).

Peyotism is a synthesis
of Native American and
Christian symbolism and
spirituality. A peyote ceremony or meeting involves
prayer, song, meditation,
and the consumption of
sacramental peyote but-
tons. Adherents of pey-
otism follow an ethical
code called the Peyote
Road, which "emphasizes
brotherly love, care of the
family, self-reliance, and
avoidance of alcohol" (Hail
1983, p. 182).

Originating among the
Apache, Kiowa, and
Comanche of the southern
Plains in the late nineteenth
century, the peyote religion
was formally established as
the Native American
Church in Oklahoma in
1918. Although it is
believed to be the largest
intertribal religion in North
America today (Wiedman
and Green 1988, p. 34),
only five percent or less of
the Christian Oglalas on
the Pine Ridge Reservation
are known to practice the
peyote religion (Powers
1986, p. 189).

AC

304

303

**Robe with feather design**
Lakota, ca. 1870
Native-tanned buffalo hide;
red, yellow, blue, and
brown pigments
90 x 120 in
The University Museum,
University of Pennsylvania,
Philadelphia, NA 3985
Provenance: Collected by
James H. McLaughlin,
1911

Buffalo-hide robes were the
principal outer garment of
both men and women. On
hides for winter use the
heavy hair was left, but it
was removed from robes
made for warm weather.
The hides were prepared by
women. The long and ardu-
ous tanning process utilized
the brain of the buffalo
and resulted in a very soft
and durable leather. A
woman produced on aver-
age about ten hide robes
per year, which were used
for clothing and bedding
or traded to outsiders for
other goods.

This robe design is asso-
ciated with men because
the central design element
is a geometric stylization of
the eagle feather, the fundamental symbol of a war-
rior's spirit and achievements. The feather designs

are arranged in concentric
circles that create a form
based on the rear view of
an eagle-feather headdress,
one of the principal
insignia of the successful
warrior. As George Horse
Capture notes in his essay
in this book, the close relationship of this painted
design to a ceremonial
object gives it a special
meaning that is continued
in the contemporary star
quilt (cat. nos. 308, 309).
The radiating lines of the
circular design associate
this pattern also with the
sun, an extension of meaning that is consistent with
Plains iconography and
world view. Most feathered
circle robes have some sort
of border design. Here
eagle-feather fans are
painted in each corner;
often the borders are geometric.

In Karl Bodmer's paint-
ing (fig. a), a Hidatsa warrior named Two Ravens
wears over his left shoulder
a summer robe painted
with the feather circle
design. This painting, done
in 1834, documents the
early use of this magnificent
painted garment.
EMM

**Cat. no. 305, fig. a**
Karl Bodmer, Swiss (1809–93),
*Péhriska-Rúhpa, Hidatsa
Man,* 1834, watercolor on
paper, 15⅞ x 11½ in, Joslyn
Art Museum, Omaha,
Nebraska, gift of the Enron
Art Foundation, NA23

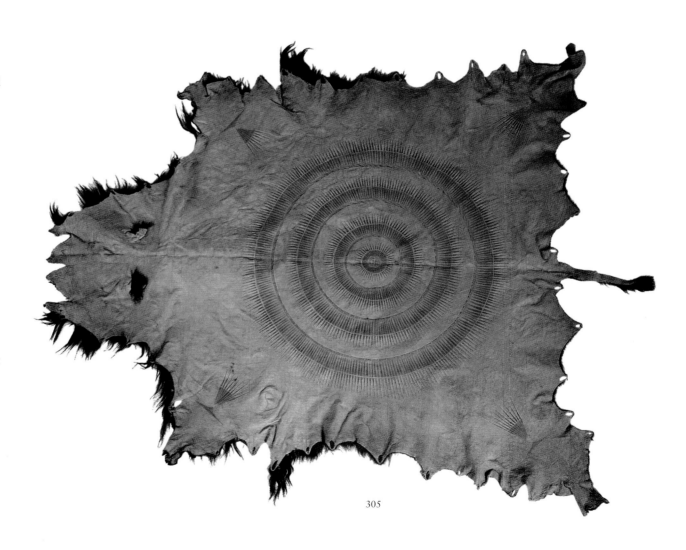

305

**Robe with box and border design**
Lakota, ca. 1870
Native-tanned buffalo hide; red, yellow, blue, and brown pigments
72 x 96½ in
The University Museum, University of Pennsylvania, Philadelphia, NA 3989
Provenance: Collected by James H. McLaughlin, 1911

This type of robe was the most common woman's robe of the Lakota and many other tribes of the central and northern Plains. Robes were painted by women using designs that also appeared on their parfleche cases of rawhide. The border design follows the outline of the untrimmed hide to accentuate the shape of the buffalo, including the legs and the head (which is always worn over the left shoulder). The central design element, the "box," is an abstract reference to the internal organs of the animal. Thus the painting refers to both the exterior and the interior of the buf-

falo. The designs with four points represent eagle feathers, which honor the sacredness of the animal who sustains the people.

Bodmer's 1833 painting of a Lakota woman (fig. a) shows how this type of robe would look when worn. The robe not only provides warmth and protection from weather, it also functions as a symbolic image that is enfolded around the individual and embraces her with its power and presence.
EMM

Cat. no. 306, fig. a
Karl Bodmer, Swiss (1809–93), *Chan-Chä-Uiá-Teüin, Teton Sioux Woman*, 1833, watercolor and pencil on paper, 17 x 11⅞ in, Joslyn Art Museum, Omaha, Nebraska, gift of the Enron Art Foundation, NA102

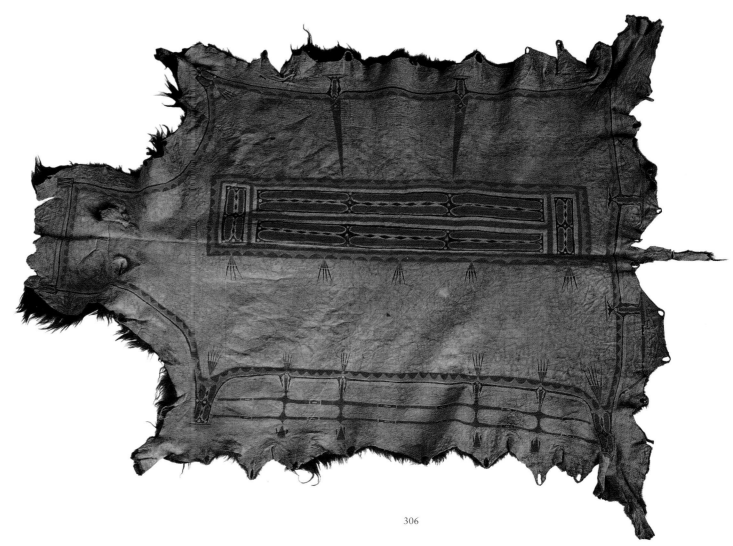

306

**Moccasins**
Arapaho (Inuna-ina)?
ca. 1880
Rawhide, native-tanned
leather, glass beads
10½ x 4 in
State Historical Society of
North Dakota, 15685
Provenance: Collected by
Lyman N. Cary, Mandan,
North Dakota

These moccasins carry the
conventional feather headdress design that was so
popular on painted hide
robes. The circle of blue-
tipped white eagle feathers
is set against a background
of dark green beads, giving
the symbolic image a
strong emphasis.
Important iconographic
motifs were executed in a
variety of media and
object types to emphasize
their significance as vital
cultural symbols.
EMM

Linda Around Him
(b. 1952)
**Star quilt**
Oglala Lakota, 1991
Cotton with polyester fill
77 x 77 in
The Minneapolis Institute
of Arts, the Ethel Morrison
Van Derlip Fund, 91.91
Provenance: Linda Around
Him, Kyle, South Dakota

Carla Running Horse
**Star quilt**
Sicangu Lakota, 1991
Silk satin and cotton with
polyester fill
89½ x 79½ in
The Minneapolis Institute
of Arts, the Ethel Morrison
Van Derlip Fund, 91.90
Provenance: Tipi Shop,
Rapid City, South Dakota;
Rosebud Reservation

Star quilts represent a particularly serendipitous
example of the transformation of an adopted form.
Plains women's quilting is
said to derive from girls'
sewing classes at the
Carlisle Indian School in
Pennsylvania at the end of
the nineteenth century
(M. Powers 1986, p. 138).
The economical recycling of
cloth was as important to
Indian people as it was to
early European Americans,
particularly after the supply
of buffalo robes dimin-
ished. Within Plains society,

308

307

309

however, quilts and quilting became thoroughly integrated into existing social structures and religious ideas.

Photographic and other evidence seems to suggest that in earlier times the quilts were predominantly based on square fragments pieced together in rectilinear patterns. The octagonal star patterns based on diamond-shaped units seem to have come into ubiquitous use only in the mid-twentieth century (M. Powers 1986, p. 139). Among Plains people they are frequently honor gifts, presented at giveaways and other formal occasions. In a domestic context star quilts are used as bed coverings and wall hangings; in more formal use they are worn as robes by vision questers and Sun Dancers, and sometimes function as shrouds or palls. They often play an important role at Lakota *yuwipi* ceremonies (Albers and Medicine 1983, pp. 129–30).

Star quilts quickly came to be associated with the morning star and with a cluster of honorific iconography: eagle feathers, feather bonnets, and the related sunburst patterns on painted robes (see George Horse Capture's essay in this book). Variants of the pattern include the depiction of an eagle within the star and the incorporation of the pipe image, another honor symbol. These two examples elaborate the form by different means: number 309 through the use of luxurious fabric and an unusual palette, and number 308 by the addition of a second ring of "feather" motifs— the so-called broken-star pattern.

LL

# Bibliography

Albers, Patricia, and Beatrice Medicine. 1983. *The Hidden Half: Studies of Plains Indian Women*. Washington, D.C.: University Press of America.

Alexander, Hartley Burr. 1916. *North American Mythology*. Vol. 10. Boston: Marshall Jones Company.

——. 1938. *Sioux Indian Painting*. Nice: C. Szwedzicki.

Barsness, Larry. 1977. *The Bison in Art: A Graphic Chronicle of the American Bison*. Fort Worth, Tex.: North and Press and The Amon Carter Museum of Western Art.

——. 1985. *Heads, Hides, and Horns: The Complete Buffalo Book*. Fort Worth: Texas Christian University Press.

Berlo, Janet Catherine. 1982. "Wo-Haw's Notebooks: Nineteenth Century Kiowa Indian Drawings in the Collections of the Missouri Historical Society." *Gateway Heritage* 3, no. 2 (Fall): 2–13.

——. 1990. "Portraits of Dispossession in Plains Indian and Inuit Graphic Arts." *Art Journal* 49, no. 2 (Summer): 133–40.

Blish, Helen H. 1967. *A Pictographic History of the Oglala Sioux*. Lincoln: University of Nebraska Press.

Boyle, David. 1904. *Ontario Archaeological Report*.

Brasser, Theodore J. 1984. "Backrests among the Plains Cree and Plains Ojibwa." *American Indian Art Magazine* 10, no. 1 (Summer): 56–63.

——. 1987, 1988. "By the Power of Their Dreams: Artistic Traditions of the Northern Plains." In *The Spirit Sings: Artistic Traditions of Canada's First Peoples*. Calgary, Alberta: Glenbow Museum and McClelland & Stewart.

Brown, James A. 1976. *Spiro Studies*. Vol. 4, *The Artifacts*. Norman: University of Oklahoma Research Institute.

Catlin, George. [1844] 1973. *Letters and Notes on the Manners, Customs, and Conditions of North American Indians*. 2 vols. Reprint. New York: Dover Publications.

——. 1857. *Illustrations of the Manners, Customs, and Condition of the American Indians*. 2 vols. London: Chatto and Windus.

Coe, Ralph T. 1977. *Sacred Circles: Two Thousand Years of North American Indian Art*. Kansas City: Nelson-Atkins Museum of Art.

Conn, Richard. 1982. *Circles of the World: Traditional Art of the Plains Indians*. Denver: Denver Art Museum.

——. 1986. *A Persistent Vision: Art of the Reservation Days*. Denver: Denver Art Museum.

Cooper, John M. 1957. *The Gros Ventres of Montana*. Pt. 2, *Religion and Ritual*. Edited by Regina Flannery. Washington, D.C.: Catholic University of America Press.

Cowles, David C. 1982. "White Swan: Crow Artist at the Little Big Horn." *American Indian Art Magazine* 7, no. 4 (Autumn): 52–61.

Deloria, Ella C., and Jay Brandon. 1961. "The Origin of the Courting Flute: A Legend in the Santee Dialect." *University of South Dakota Museum News* 22, no. 6:1–7.

Densmore, Frances. 1918. *Teton Sioux Music*. Smithsonian Institution, Bureau of American Ethnology Bulletin 61. Washington, D.C.

Dockstader, Frederick J. 1966. *Indian Art in America*. Greenwich: New York Graphic Society.

——, ed. 1982. *Oscar Howe: A Retrospective Exhibition*. Tulsa, Okla.: Thomas Gilcrease Museum Association.

Dyck, Paul. 1975. "The Plains Indian Shield." *American Indian Art Magazine* 1, no. 1 (Autumn): 34–41.

Eiteljorg, Harrison. 1981. *Treasures of the American West: Selections from the Collection of Harrison Eiteljorg*. New York: Balance House.

Ewers, John C. 1939. *Plains Indian Painting: A Description of Aboriginal Art*. Palo Alto, Calif.: Stanford University Press.

——. 1958. *The Blackfeet Raiders of the North Western Plains*. Norman: University of Oklahoma Press.

——. 1967. *Indian Life on the Upper Missouri*. Norman: University of Oklahoma Press.

——. 1978a. *Murals in the Round: Painted Tipis of the Kiowa and Kiowa Apache Indians*. Washington, D.C.: Smithsonian Institution Press.

——. 1978b. "Three Effigy Pipes by an Eastern Dakota Master Carver." *American Indian Art Magazine* 3, no. 4 (Autumn): 51–55.

——. 1981a. "The Emergence of the Named Indian Artist in the American West." *American Indian Art Magazine* 6, no. 2 (Spring): 52–77.

——. 1981b. "Water Monsters in Plains Indian Art." *American Indian Art Magazine* 6, no. 4 (Autumn): 38–45.

——. 1982. "The Awesome Bear in Plains Indian Art." *American Indian Art Magazine* 7, no. 3 (Summer): 36–45.

——. 1983. "A Century and a Half of Blackfeet Picture Writing." *American Indian Art Magazine* 8, no. 3 (Summer): 52–61.

——. 1986. *Plains Indians Sculpture*. Washington, D.C.: Smithsonian Institution Press.

Feder, Norman. 1971a. *American Indian Art*. New York: Harry N. Abrams.

———. 1971b. *Two Hundred Years of North American Indian Art*. New York: Praeger Publishers in association with The Whitney Museum of American Art.

Flint Institute of Arts. 1975. *The American Indian, The American Flag*. Michigan: Flint Institute of Arts.

Fundaburk, Emma L., and Mary D. Foreman, eds. 1957. *Sun Circles and Human Hands*. Luverne, Ala.

Grinnell, George B. 1907. *Blackfeet Tales*. New York: Charles Scribner's Sons.

———. 1923. *The Cheyenne Indians: Their History and Ways of Life*. 2 vols. New Haven: Yale University Press.

———. 1955. *The Fighting Cheyenne*. Norman: University of Oklahoma Press.

———. 1962. *The Cheyenne Indians*. 2 vols. New York: Cooper Square Publishers.

Hail, Barbara A. 1980, 1983. *Hau, Kóla! The Plains Indian Collection of the Haffenreffer Museum of Anthropology*. Studies in Anthropology and Material Culture, vol. 3. Providence: Haffenreffer Museum of Anthropology, Brown University.

———. 1988. "Beaded Bibles and Victory Pouches: Twentieth Century Lakota Honoring Gifts; The Thorburn Collection of the South Dakota Art Museum." *American Indian Art Magazine* 13, no. 3 (Summer): 40–47.

Hamilton, Henry W. 1952. "The Spiro Mound." *The Missouri Archaeologist* 14:17–88.

Hamilton, T. M. 1972. *Native American Bows*. York, Pa.: George Shumway Publishers.

Harris, Moira F. 1989. *Between Two Cultures: Kiowa Art from Fort Marion*. St. Paul: Pogo Press.

Harrod, Howard L. 1987. *Renewing the World: Northern Plains Indian Religion and Morality*. Tucson: University of Arizona Press.

Hartmann, Horst. 1973. *Die Plains-und Prärieindianee Nordamerikas*. 2nd ed. 1979. Berlin: Staatliche Museen Preussischer Kultur Besitz, Museum für Völkerkunde.

Heidenreich, C. Adrian, et al. 1985. *Ledger Art of the Crow and Gros Ventre Indians: 1879–1897*. Billings, Mont.: Yellowstone Art Center.

Hodge, Frederick Webb. 1912. *Handbook of American Indians North of Mexico*. 2 pts. Smithsonian Institution, Bureau of American Ethnology Bulletin 30. Washington, D.C.

Honour, Hugh. 1975a. *The European Vision of America*. Cleveland: Cleveland Museum of Art.

———. 1975b. *The New Golden Land: European Images of America from the Discoveries to the Present Time*. New York: Pantheon Books.

Howard, James H. 1960. "Dakota Winter Counts as a Source of Plains Indian History." *Anthropology Papers Numbers 57–62*. Smithsonian Institution, Bureau of American Ethnology Bulletin 173. Washington, D.C.

———. 1976. "Yanktonai Ethnohistory and the John K. Bear Winter Count." *The Plains Anthropologist* 21, no. 73, pt. 2.

Hultgren, Mary Lou. 1987. "American Indian Collection of the Hampton University Museum." *American Indian Art Magazine* 13, no. 1 (Winter): 32–39.

Hunt, David C. 1982. *Legacy of the West*. Center for Western Studies, Joslyn Art Museum. Lincoln: University of Nebraska Press.

Jablow, J. 1951. *The Cheyenne in Plains Indian Trade Relations, 1795–1840*. New York: J. J. Augustin.

Josephy, Alvin M., Jr., Trudy Thomas, and Jeanne Eder. 1990. *Wounded Knee: Lest We Forget*. Cody, Wyo.: Buffalo Bill Historical Center.

Kan, Michael, and William Wierzbowski. 1979. "Notes on an Important Cheyenne Shield." *Bulletin of the Detriot Institute of Arts* 57, no. 3:124–33.

Keyser, James D. 1991. "A Thing to Tie on the Halter: An Addition to the Plains Rock Lexicon." *Plains Anthropologist* 36:261–67.

Kroeber, Alfred L. 1900. "Symbolism of the Arapaho Indians." *Bulletin of the American Museum of Natural History* 13:69–86.

———. 1907. "The Arapaho." *Bulletin of the American Museum of Natural History* 18 (1902–7).

———. 1983. *The Arapaho*. Lincoln: University of Nebraska Press. First published in three parts in the *Bulletin of the American Museum of Natural History* in 1902, 1904, and 1907.

Lame Deer, John (Fire), and Richard Erdoes. 1972. *Lame Deer: Seeker of Visions*. New York: Simon and Schuster.

Lessard, F. Dennis. 1990. "Pictographic Art in Beadwork from the Cheyenne River Sioux." *American Indian Art Magazine* 16, no. 1 (Winter): 54–63.

Lesser, Alexander. 1933. *The Pawnee Ghost Dance Hand Game: A Study of Cultural Change*. Columbia University Contributions to Anthropology, vol. 16. New York: Columbia University Press.

Lowie, Robert H. 1909. "The Assiniboine." *Anthropological Papers of the American Museum of Natural History* 4, pt. 1.

———. 1915. "Dances and Societies of the Plains Shoshone." *Anthropological Papers of the American Museum of Natural History* 11 (1916): 803–35.

———. 1922. "Religion of the Crow Indians." *Anthropological Papers of the American Museum of Natural History* 25, pt. 1.

———. 1935. *The Crow Indians*. New York: Holt, Rinehart, and Winston.

Mallery, Garrick. [1893] 1972. *Picture-Writing of the American Indians*. Smithsonian Institution, Tenth Annual Report of the Bureau of American Ethnology, 1888–89. Reprint. 2 vols. New York: Dover Publications.

Marriott, Alice. 1956. "Trade Guild of the Southern Cheyenne Women." *Bulletin of the Oklahoma Anthropological Society* 4:19–27.

Marriott, Alice, and Linda Poolaw. 1990. *War Bonnets, Tin Lizzies, and Patent Leather Pumps: Kiowa Culture in Transition, 1925–1955*. Palo Alto, Calif.: Stanford University Press.

Maurer, Evan M. 1977. *The Native American Heritage: A Survey of North American Indian Art*. Chicago: Art Institute of Chicago.

———. 1986. "Representational and Symbolic Forms in Great Lakes–Area Wooden Sculpture." In *Great Lakes Indian Art*. Edited by David Penney. Detroit: Wayne State University Press and the Detroit Institute of Arts.

Medicine. 1983. *See* Albers and Medicine.

Minneapolis Institute of Arts. 1976. *I Wear the Morning Star: An Exhibition of American Indian Ghost Dance Objects*. Minneapolis: Minneapolis Institute of Arts.

Minneapolis Institute of Arts and Walker Art Center. 1972. *American Indian Art: Form and Tradition*. New York: Dutton.

Montana Historical Society. 1976. *Not in Precious Metals Alone: A Manuscript History of Montana*. Helena: Montana State Historical Society.

Mooney, James. 1894. "Outline Plan for Ethnologic Museum Collection." Manuscript 4788, National Anthropological Archives. Smithsonian Institution, Washington, D.C.

———. [1896] 1965. *The Ghost-Dance Religion and the Sioux Outbreak of 1890*. Smithsonian Institution, 14th Annual Report of the Bureau of American Ethnology, 1892–93, pt. 2. Washington, D.C. Reprint. Chicago: University of Chicago Press.

———. 1902. Letter to (presumably) W. J. McGee, 2/25/02. Bureau of American Ethnology, Letters Received, 1888–1906, James Mooney. National Anthropological Archives. Smithsonian Institution, Washington, D.C.

———. 1903–6. "Cheyenne Notebook (Oklahoma) 1903–1906." National Anthropological Archives, Bureau of American Ethnology, Manuscript 2531, vol. 5, Cheyenne. Smithsonian Institution, Washington, D.C.

Morse, Dan F. 1960. Introduction to "The Southern Cult in the Central States." *Central States Archaeological Journal* 7, no. 3 (July).

National Geographic Society. 1974. *The World of the American Indian*. Washington, D.C.: National Geographic Society.

Petersen, Karen Daniels. 1971. *Plains Indian Art from Fort Marion*. Norman: University of Oklahoma Press.

Philips, Philip, and James A. Brown. 1979. *Pre-Columbian Shell Engravings from the Craig Mound at Spiro Oklahoma*. Salem, Mass.: Peabody Museum Press.

Pohrt, Richard A. 1975. *The American Indian, The American Flag*. Michigan: Flint Institute of Arts.

Porsche, Audrey. 1987. *Yuto'keca: Transitions, The Burdick Collection*. Bismarck: State Historical Society of North Dakota.

Powell, Peter J. 1970. "Warrior Artists: An Introduction to Northern Cheyenne Ledger Book Art." *Manuscripts* 22, no. 3 (Summer): 155–71.

———. 1981. *People of the Sacred Mountain: A History of the Northern Cheyenne Chiefs and Warrior Societies, 1830–1879, with an Epilogue, 1969–1974*. New York and San Francisco: Harper and Row.

Powers, Marla N. 1986. *Oglala Women: Myth, Ritual, and Reality*. Chicago: University of Chicago Press.

Powers, William K. 1977. *Oglala Religion*. Lincoln: University of Nebraska Press.

———. 1980. "The Art of Courtship among the Oglala." *American Indian Art Magazine* 5, no. 2 (Spring): 40–47.

Raczka, Paul M. 1992. "Sacred Robes of the Blackfoot and Other Northern Plains Tribes." *American Indian Art Magazine* 17, no. 3 (Summer): 66–73.

Rockwell, D. 1991. *Giving Voice to Bear*. Colorado: Roberts Rinehart Publications.

Roe, Frank Gilbert. 1955. *The Indian and the Horse*. Norman: University of Oklahoma Press.

Seton, Ernest T. 1897. Seton Journals, vol. 6, "Yellowstone Bears/Crow Indians." Seton Memorial Museum and Library, Cimarron, N. Mex.

Smith, Jaune Quick-to-See. 1987. "Women of Sweetgrass, Cedar, and Sage." *Women's Studies Quarterly* 15, nos. 1 and 2 (Spring/Summer): 35–41.

Snodgrass, Jeanne O. 1968. *American Indian Painters: A Biographical Directory*. Contributions from the Museum of the American Indian, Heye Foundation, vol. 21, pt. 1. New York: Museum of the American Indian, Heye Foundation.

Sotheby's, New York. 1992. *The Roy G. Cole Collection: Fine American Indian Art*. June 12. (Auction catalogue)

Southern Plains Indian Museum. 1986. *Pictorial Beadwork*. January/February. (Exhibition brochure)

Speck, F. G. 1925. *The Penn Wampum Belts*. New York: Museum of the American Indian, Heye Foundation.

Standing Bear, Luther. 1928. *My People the Sioux*. Boston and New York: Houghton and Mifflin Company.

State Historical Society of North Dakota. 1984. *The Last Years of Sitting Bull*. Bismarck: North Dakota Heritage Center.

———. 1985. *No Two Horns*. Bismarck: North Dakota Heritage Center.

Stewart, James J. 1991. "Historic Shoshone Elk Hides Depicting Chief Washakie's Exploits." Unpublished paper. Lander, Wyo.

Stirling, M. W. 1938. *Three Pictographic Autobiographies of Sitting Bull*. Smithsonian Miscellaneous Collections, vol. 97, no. 5. Washington, D.C.

Storm, Hyemeyohsts. 1972. *Seven Arrows*. New York: Harper and Row.

Sully, Langdon. 1974. *No Tears for the General: The Life of Alfred Sully, 1821–1879*. Palo Alto, Calif.: American West Publishing Company.

Thompson, Judy. 1977. *The North American Indian Collection: A Catalogue*. Bern: Bern Historical Museum.

Thwaites, Reuben Gold, ed. 1906. *Early Western Travels, 1748–1846*. Vols. 22–24. Cleveland: Clark.

Wade, Edwin L. 1986. *The Arts of the North American Indian: Native Tradition in Evolution*. New York: Hudson Hills Press.

Walker, James R. 1982. *Lakota Society*. Edited by Raymond J. DeMallie. Lincoln: University of Nebraska Press.

Walker Art Center and The Minneapolis Institute of Arts. 1972. *American Indian Art: Form and Tradition*. New York: Dutton.

Weitzner, Bella. 1979. "Notes on the Hidatsa Indians Based on Data Recorded by the Late Gilbert L. Wilson." *Anthropological Papers of the American Museum of Natural History* 56, pt. 2.

Wiedman, Dennis. 1985. "Staff, Fan, Rattle, and Drum: Spiritual and Artistic Expressions of Oklahoma Peyotists." *American Indian Art Magazine* 10, no. 3 (Summer): 38–45.

Wiedman, Dennis, and Candace Greene. 1988. "Early Kiowa Peyote Ritual and Symbolism: The Drawing Books of Silverhorn (Haungooah)." *American Indian Art Magazine* 13, no. 4 (Autumn): 32–41.

Wildschut, William. 1975. *Crow Indian Medicine Bundles*. Edited by John C. Ewers. Contributions from the Museum of the American Indian, Heye Foundation, vol. 17. 2nd ed. New York: Museum of the American Indian, Heye Foundation.

Willoughby, C. 1905. "A Few Specimens Collected by Lewis and Clark." *American Anthropologist* 7, no. 190:634.

Wilson, Gilbert. 1905–12. *Diaries, Notebooks, and Reports*. St. Paul: Minnesota Historical Society.

Wissler, Clark. 1907. "Some Protective Designs of the Dakota." *Anthropological Papers of the American Museum of Natural History* 1 (1908), pt. 2:19–54.

———. 1912a. "Ceremonial Bundles of the Blackfoot Indians." *Anthropological Papers of the American Museum of Natural History* 7, pt. 2:65–290.

———. 1912b. "Societies and Ceremonial Associations in the Oglala Division of the Teton-Dakota." *Anthropological Papers of the American Museum of Natural History* 11 (1916), pt. 1:1–99.

———. 1916. *Oglala Societies*. New York: American Museum of Natural History.

Wissler, Clark, and D. C. Duvall. 1908. "Mythology of the Blackfoot Indians." *Anthropological Papers of the American Museum of Natural History* 2.

# Photographic Credits

Cover: Gary Mortensen and Bob Fogt

**1** photo by Gary Mortensen and Robert Fogt; **3** courtesy of FMNH, photo by Diane Alexander White, 111796; **4** photo by Gary Mortensen and Robert Fogt; **6 & 9** PM/HU, photos by Hillel Burger, 1992. Copyright President and Fellows of Harvard College. All rights reserved; **10** photo by Gary Mortensen and Robert Fogt; **12** photo by Dietrich Graf; **13** AMNH, photo by J. Beckett, 2A19087; **14** PM/HU, photo by Hillel Burger, 1977. Copyright President and Fellows of Harvard College. All rights reserved; **15** AMNH, photo by D. Finnin, 4640(1); **17** photo by Gary Mortensen and Robert Fogt; **18** NMAI/SI, photo by Karen Furth; **19** AMNH, photo by D. Finnin, 2A19081; **20** photo by Gary Mortensen and Robert Fogt; **21** PM/HU, photo by Hillel Burger, 1992. Copyright President and Fellows of Harvard College. All rights reserved; **22** photo by Gary Mortensen and Robert Fogt; **23** courtesy of FMNH, photo by Diane Alexander White, A111801c; **24** courtesy of FMNH, photo by Diane Alexander White, 111799; **25** NMNH/SI, 78-15906; **26** PM/HU, photo by Hillel Burger, 1992. Copyright President and Fellows of Harvard College. All rights reserved; **28** UM/UP, All rights reserved, S4-140691; **29** AMNH, photo by D. Finnin, 2A19079; **30, 33 & 35** photos by Gary Mortensen and Robert Fogt; **36** PM/HU, photo by Hillel Burger, 1992. Copyright President and Fellows of Harvard College. All rights reserved; **37** courtesy of FMNH, photo by Diane Alexander White, 111798; **39** NMAI/SI, photo by Carmelo Guadagno; **40** NMAI/SI, photo by Karen Furth; **42** AMNH, photo by D. Finnin, 4648(1); **43** photo by Gary Mortensen and Robert Fogt; **44** photo by Lorran Meares; **48** UM/UP, All rights reserved, S4-140541; **49** photo by Gary Mortensen and Robert Fogt; **50** PM/HU, photo by Hillel Burger, 1992. Copyright President and Fellows of Harvard College. All rights reserved; **51** photo by Blair Clark; **53** photo by Rick Wicker; **54** courtesy of FMNH, photo by Diane Alexander White, 111794; **55** courtesy of FMNH, photo by Diane Alexander White, A111829c; **56** PM/HU, photo by Hillel Burger, 1991. Copyright President and Fellows of Harvard College. All rights reserved; **60** PM/HU, photo by Hillel Burger, 1992. Copyright President and Fellows of Harvard College. All rights reserved; **61 & 62** NMAI/SI, photos by Karen Furth; **63** UM/UP, All rights reserved, S4-140489; **66** AMNH, photo by J. Beckett and A. Michel, 2A19084; **67** AMNH, photo by J. Beckett, 4633(1); **68** AMNH, photo by J. Beckett, 4634(1); **69** NMNH/SI, 77-7721; **70** NMAI/SI, photo by Karen Furth; **71** courtesy of FMNH, photo by Diane Alexander White, A111804c; **74** photo by Bo Gabrielsson; **75** NMAI/SI, photo by Carmelo Guadagno; **77** AMNH, photo by D. Finnin, 2A19083; **79** NMAI/SI, photo by Carmelo Guadagno; **80** photo by Gary Mortensen and Robert Fogt; **81** UM/UP, All rights reserved, S4-133603; **82** NMAI/SI, photo by Karen Furth; **84** AMNH, photo by D. Finnin and C. Chesek, 4632(1); **85** photo by Gary Mortensen and Robert Fogt; **86** AMNH, photo by D. Finnin, 4635(1); **89** photo by Mary McGimsey; **90 & 91** photos by Gary Mortensen and Robert Fogt; **93** UM/UP, All rights reserved, 140483; **95** AMNH, photo by J. Beckett, 2A19086-B; **96** courtesy of FMNH, photo by Diane Alexander White, A111826; **97** NMNH/SI, 92-6887; **99** NMAI/SI, photo by Carmelo Guadagno; **100 & 101** NMAI/SI, photos by Karen Furth; **102** CMC, S84-5883; **103** AIC, copyright 1992. All rights reserved; **104** NAA/SI, photo by Joe A. Goulait; **108** UM/UP, All rights reserved, S4-140654; **109** photo by Gary Mortensen and Robert Fogt; **111** NMAI/SI, photo by Karen Furth; **112** UM/UP, All rights reserved, T4-366c2 and T4-365c2; **115** NMNH/SI, 20581-A; **116** NMNH/SI, 79-4197; **117** NMNH/SI, 92-3699; **118** NMNH/SI, 20851-B; **119** NMNH/SI, 31155-D; **121** NAA/SI, photo by Joe A. Goulait; **122** MHS, photo by Mark McIntyre, Allied Photocolor, MTX Indians 51/Wohaw 46; **123** courtesy of FMNH, photo by Diane Alexander White, A111810c; **125** NMNH/SI, 76-4941; **128** courtesy of FMNH, photo by James Balodimas, A111821c; **129** AMNH, photo by D. Finnin, J. Beckett, and R. Raeihle, 4641(2) and 4642(1); **130** UM/UP, All rights reserved, S4-140544 and S4-140545; **131** photo by Gary Mortensen and Robert Fogt; **132 & 133** NMAI/SI, photos by Karen Furth; **134** courtesy of FMNH, photo by Ron Testa, A120T; **135** photo by Ann Cristine Eek; **136** AMNH, photo by D. Finnin, J.